Developing Reading *Versatility*

First Canadian Edition

Developing Reading Versatility

W. Royce Adams
Santa Barbara City College, Emeritus

Becky Patterson
University of Alaska, Anchorage, Emerita

Ilona Ryder
Grant MacEwan Community College

THOMSON

NELSON

Australia   Canada   Mexico   Singapore   Spain   United Kingdom   United States

THOMSON

NELSON

Developing Reading Versatility
First Canadian Edition

by W. Royce Adams, Becky Patterson, and Ilona Ryder

Editorial Director and Publisher:
Evelyn Veitch

Acquisitions Editor:
Anne Williams

Marketing Manager:
Cara Yarzab

Developmental Editor:
Camille Isaacs

Senior Developmental Editor:
Mike Thompson

Production Editor:
Wendy Yano

Senior Production Coordinator:
Hedy Sellers

Copy Editor/Proofreader:
Susan James

Creative Director:
Angela Cluer

Cover Design:
Ken Phipps

Cover Image:
© Darren Robb/Photonica

Compositor:
Computer Composition

Indexers:
Lazaros and Juanita Simeon

Printer:
Webcom

**National Library of Canada
Cataloguing in Publication**

Adams, W. Royce
Developing reading versatility/
W. Royce Adams, Becky Patterson, Ilona Ryder.—1st Canadian ed.

Includes index.

ISBN 0-17-622508-0

1. Reading (Higher education).
2. Reading comprehension.
I. Patterson, Becky II. Ryder, Ilona, 1947– III. Title.

LB2395.3.R93 2003   428'4'071'1
C2002-905066-9

Brief Contents

Detailed Contents

Chapter Six   Recognizing Inferences and Drawing Conclusions **238**

UNIT THREE   Affecitve Comprehension   277

Preface to the First Canadian Edition

When I was asked to edit this first Canadian edition of a successful American text-book, portions of which I had used in my Canadian classroom in the past, the first question that came to my mind was, "What does it mean to be Canadian?" I belong to the immigrant generation. As a child I had first-hand experience learning to read and write with English as my second language. I have a vested interest in "my new country," but can never forget that other culture I started in. Many Canadians share this experience.

The challenges of "Canadianizing" a text, then, have to do to some extent with what we think is our Canadian identity. To be sure, we cannot totally separate ourselves from our neighbours: American and Canadian cultures are both part of a larger entity, especially when it comes to the way we two peoples express our ideas in writing. Both fiction and non-fiction writing and writers freely cross the longest peaceful border between two nations.

To render an already excellent textbook "Canadian" largely means including more Canadian authors and Canadian sources. When it comes right down to it, though, it's the specific details—people and place names, organizations and social structure—that may differ between our two nations. Oh, and let's not forget the spelling, but even that often demonstrates the mix that is naturally accepted by both Canadians and Americans in the world of the word processor!

The process of Canadianizing *Developing Reading Versatility* has gone ahead without affecting the inherent strengths in methodology found in the eighth American edition. In keeping with the improvements made in that edition, this text continues the pedagogical strategies of building reading skills from *literal comprehension*, through *critical comprehension* to *affective comprehension*.

Here are some things that have been changed:

- The Canadian edition showcases the literary achievements of Canadian authors such as Neil Bissoondath, Hugh MacLennan, Joy Kogawa, and David Suzuki, at the same time keeping such important American authors as James Thurber and Kate Chopin. In addition, the educational writers whose methods create the basic tenets of the text remain intact.

- The text is shorter by some 40 pages, making it easier to use in the common single-semester format that a Canadian reading course usually covers. Most cuts involve duplicated material or exercises that are equally effective with fewer questions or sample passages. These cuts do not affect the theoretic base and layout of the eighth American edition.

- The first Canadian edition moves toward more graphic highlighting, such as bullets and definition boxes, in response to an increasingly visual reading audience and the requests of Canadian instructors. However, the importance of the full paragraph in developing strong reading skills is still recognized. If too much is presented in icons, symbols, and pictures, important skills such as figuring out a paragraph's topic sentence or transitional devices can be lost.

This first Canadian edition presents a useful and challenging text for post-secondary students who need to sharpen their reading skills. The diverse readings and varied exercises give instructors plenty of room to tailor the text to the requirements of their courses and the needs of their students. Students will benefit from all the exercises and especially from the reviews (Putting it All Together) at the end of each chapter. Students can visually track their own progress using the charts provided in the Appendix. Answers to the practice tests included in the text are available to instructors in a separate Answer Key.

Creating this first Canadian edition would not have been possible without the help of many people. I would like, first, to thank my colleagues across Canada who provided direction and advice in the development of this Canadian edition: Denise Blay, Fanshawe College; John Carroll, University College of the Fraser Valley; Brian L. Flack, Seneca College; Barbara Glass, Canadore College; Betty Lucas, Grant MacEwan College; and Diane Shibata, Centennial College. I would also like to thank the editors at Nelson, Anne Williams (Acquisitions Editor), Camille Isaacs (Developmental Editor), and Wendy Yano (Production Editor), and Lazaros and Juanita Simeon for their contributions to the text.

Ilona Ryder, M.A. (Engl.)
Grant MacEwan College
Edmonton, Alberta

To The Student

What is Reading Versatility?

To be versatile means to have aptitude or ability in many different areas. Being a versatile reader means that you are capable of reading many different kinds of writing, moving freely between styles and levels of difficulty in the things you read. This is an important skill in your studies, in your workplace, and in your life generally.

This book contains plenty of strategies, exercises and practice so you can develop your reading versatility, but there are no guarantees. It is quite possible that you could do well on every exercise in this book but still lack the confidence to read a wide range of texts. Ultimately it's up to you to *use* the information and strategies you learn here when you read other material.

To gain confidence, you need to feel that you understand everything you read. The act of understanding is called comprehension.

Levels of Comprehension

To help you develop your ability to better comprehend what you read, we have divided this book into three levels of comprehension: literal, critical, and affective. These levels do not actually operate as separate entities. Rather, each level depends on the other two, something like the three sides of a triangle.

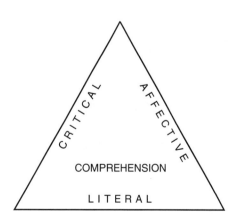

In this book you will work separately with each of these three levels of comprehension as well as with each level broken down into easily managed chunks.

- Unit One covers **literal comprehension**, shown in the diagram as the bottom, or foundation, of the triangle. Literal comprehension is the foundation of understanding and versatility. It makes use of skills such as vocabulary knowledge, understanding and distinguishing main ideas and supporting details, study-reading strategies, graphic aids scanning, and rate flexibility.

- In Unit Two you will be working with the second side of the triangle, **critical comprehension**, which includes separating fact from opinion; recognizing an author's intent, attitude, tone, and bias; being able to draw inferences; and drawing conclusions.

- The third side of the triangle, **affective comprehension**, is found in Unit Three. It involves an understanding of figurative language, use of the imagination and feelings, and an awareness of the aesthetics of imaginative and expository writing.

Each level of comprehension builds on the previous one; each unit in this book builds on the skills learned in the previous one.

Getting the Most Out of This Book

Knowing your way around a textbook, like knowing your way around your neighbourhood, is a good way to start building confidence. Here are some suggestions to help you get the most out of working through this book.

1. *Turn to the Table of Contents.* The Brief Contents lists the subtopics covered in each of the three units. The Detailed Contents acts as a kind of road map to help you find your way to all the topics, readings, and exercises. Notice that the book is further divided into eight chapters, each presenting several topics, exercises, and self-tests. There is also an Appendix, where you can keep records of your progress. Finally, to look up topics you can't easily find in the table of contents, use the index at the back of the book.

2. *Flip through the pages of the book.* Notice that you can do many of the exercises right in the book; other activities are take-home assignments and starting points for class discussion.

3. *Become conscious of your reading rate.* In each chapter, some of the practice readings are timed for reading rate. The pressure of speed is used to prod you from your normal reading habits and get you used to faster rates. Don't make speed your entire goal, however; your speed will naturally increase as a result of good reading habits. Remember that reading speeds will vary depending on purpose, material, and vocabulary level.

4. *Don't expect overnight miracles.* Lifetime results can be obtained from the practices you follow here *if* you learn from your mistakes as well as your successes. It takes time, effort, and patience to improve your reading habits.

5. *Develop your discussion skills.* Some of the practice questions can't be answered by a key. In these cases, class discussion will help develop your comprehension skills and confidence. You will get more out of class discussions if you come prepared with answers or materials and then engage in discussion.

6. *Keep records.* The Student Record Chart for each unit allows you track your progress in comprehension and vocabulary scores as well as reading rate. Don't be

worried about ups and downs in rate and comprehension scores; it's normal to fluctuate. Keep an eye on your overall progress as you work through this book, and check your level of confidence. Only *you* can actually know how much success you are feeling.

Now that these things have been said, you are ready to get down to work. Just remember: the responsibility for learning and transfer of learning to life-long skills is ultimately yours. Plan now to become a versatile reader.

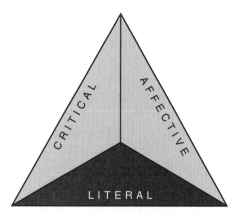

LITERAL COMPREHENSION

What Is Literal Comprehension?

This first unit deals with just one of three complex levels of total comprehension, the literal level.

> Literal comprehension is that basic level of understanding that entails the ability to recognize words accurately, to identify main ideas and supporting details, to understand a sequence of events, to recognize cause-and-effect relationships, to interpret directions, and to understand organizational patterns used in various types of reading matter.

This is the level of comprehension you use when you follow a cooking recipe or the directions for putting a swing set together. It is also the level of comprehension necessary for understanding the main ideas in a news story, a magazine article, or a chapter from a textbook.

Of the three levels of comprehension, literal comprehension is probably the most used. That is because everyday reading skills, such as skimming and scanning telephone directories, catalogues, movie and television listings, and even reading the newspaper or a favourite magazine, seldom require anything beyond literal comprehension. In addition, most training in reading courses—from the early grades through postsecondary classes—places greater emphasis on literal recall than on critical or affective comprehension. This is not to say that there is no training in

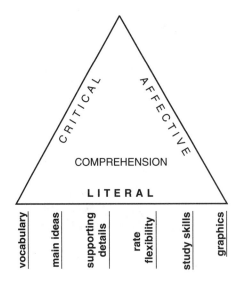

these areas, but an examination of materials and tests used in reading courses, as well as in other subjects, reveals a strong reliance on literal comprehension, with more stress on recall than on forming judgments, evaluations, or personal reactions at the critical and affective levels. In spite of all this practice, however, most people do not read as well as they could at the literal level.

Reading is much more than just recognizing words on a page. Knowing the meaning and function of the words you are reading is basic, of course, but you must also understand those words *in their context*. Then it becomes important to understand the author's main points, the details and how they are being used, and the organization of the material. When these basics have been mastered, speed of comprehension increases and the basis is laid for developing your critical and affective levels of awareness.

What Does This Unit Cover?

In this unit, the practices deal with the development of all facets of *literal comprehension*. Practices are as basic as learning a new vocabulary word and as complex as separating main ideas from supporting details and recognizing writing patterns. A variety of reading experiences will help you feel comfortable with each skill.

There are three chapters in this unit.

- Chapter One offers methods for vocabulary development, an important area for the improvement of reading at any level.
- Chapter Two deals with the development of literal recall, stressing reading for main ideas and supporting details, understanding paragraph patterns, and recognizing an author's thesis.
- Chapter Three gives you practice in developing study-reading skills, including the SQ3R method, surveying strategies, reading note-taking methods (marking, underlining, and mapping techniques), interpreting graphics and how to scan them, test-taking strategies, and flexible reading-rate techniques.

All chapters contain reading practices of varying styles and subject matter with vocabulary, comprehension, and rate practice. "Putting It All Together" sections at the end of each chapter help you tie together all the skills you have learned in that chapter.

There are two points about the reading practices that can't be overstated.

- One is that you should not worry about mistakes you make. Turn your mistakes into "learning experiences." When you miss a question, learn from it. Try to understand what caused you to make an error. If you can't figure it out on your own, get help from your instructor.
- The second point is to take what you learn here and apply it to your reading outside this text. Whether or not this text helps you to read any better is really up to you.

Many students who do well as they proceed through the work required of them in this book still fail to apply the techniques to other required or pleasure readings. This book is designed to develop your awareness of what is required of an intelligent person when reading certain types of materials.

What Should You Know after Completing This Unit?

Here are some goals and objectives you should keep in mind as you work through this unit. You may want to add some of your own. When you have finished this unit, you should be able to:

1. Write a thorough definition of literal comprehension.
2. Select a method that aids you in the continuing development of your vocabulary, and use it regularly.
3. Find main ideas and supporting details in a variety of material.
4. Identify the following writing patterns as an aid to comprehension: definition, illustration/example, cause/effect, comparison/contrast, description, and sequence of events.
5. Incorporate study-reading strategies for reading textbooks and graphic aids.
6. Understand test-taking strategies.
7. Apply flexible reading rates and read expository reading matter at least 100 words per minute faster with no loss in comprehension.

These are not unrealistic objectives to keep in mind as you work through this unit. With proper practice, you will achieve them all. If you have any additional objectives of your own, write them down below and share them with your instructor.

Personal reading objectives for Unit One:

_____

_____

_____

_____

_____

_____

CHAPTER ONE

Developing Vocabulary Skills

INTRODUCTION TO VOCABULARY DEVELOPMENT

INTRODUCING ALBERTO MANGUEL AND "A HISTORY OF READING"

Introduction to Vocabulary Development

One of the first places to begin developing reading versatility is with vocabulary. Without a good vocabulary, reading is slow and comprehension is poor. In order to understand what you read, you need to recognize not only the definitions of the words being read but, more important, the way words are used in context.

Think of strategies you have tried in the past for increasing vocabulary. What do you do when you run across unfamiliar words? In the selection that follows, "A History of Reading," one famous figure, Alberto Manguel, describes his strategy for increasing his vocabulary and learning new words. Throughout this book, we have included brief biographies and quotes from authors or public figures to inspire you by their examples as well as their words. Start by reading about Alberto Manguel.

A way to find more information, quotations, or pictures of Alberto Manguel is to use the World Wide Web. Using a search engine such as go2net.com or AltaVista or Google, type his name under Search.

INTRODUCING ALBERTO MANGUEL

Alberto Manguel, writer, editor and critic, is largely self-taught, having left school early and never having obtained a university degree. He was born in Buenos Aires, Argentina, in 1948 and travelled extensively throughout the world with his parents, who were diplomats. He settled in Canada in 1980 and since then he has developed an international reputation as a translator, anthologist, editor, and novelist. Manguel became a Canadian citizen in 1985. He has edited *The Oxford Book of Canadian Ghost Stories*, two volumes of fantasy literature, *Black Water I* and *II*, and written a novel, *News From a Foreign Country Came*. His latest work is *A History of Reading*, a collection of essays documenting how reading has evolved over time. It provides a historical look at the act of reading, and originates from an intensely personal account of Manguel's own experiences with reading. In an interview with Paula E. Kirman in the *Connecticut Review* (Vol. 20, No. 2, Fall 1998), Manguel describes why the act of reading is so important to him and is something that should be seen apart from writing:

I very much wanted to separate the history of reading from the history of writing because up to a certain point the history of writing seems to me

. . . an artificial history. First of all, it is organized according to the birth date and nationalities of writers, which by and large do not hold great bearing upon where readers place them . . .

. . . The geographical and chronological aspects of literature according to the writers seem to me arbitrary, and even more arbitrary is the literature that is based on the suppositions of what the writers intended—a history of literature that divides literature into social satire, novels for women, and so on. Those are things that a writer has decided, and in our time has been taken over by publicists who label a book in a certain way so that the book-seller knows where to put it on a shelf. That has nothing to do with how readers receive it. Readers decide otherwise, and there are very many books that are remembered as something else simply because the readers have decided that they would be something else . . .

A HISTORY OF READING

ALBERTO MANGUEL

1   I first discovered that I could read at the age of four. I had seen, over and over again, the letters that I knew (because I had been told) were the names of pictures under which they sat. The boy drawn in thick black lines, dressed in red shorts and a green shirt . . . was also somehow, I realized, the stern black shapes beneath him, as if the boy's body had been dismembered into three clean-cut figures: one arm and the torso, **b**; the severed head so perfectly round, **o**; and the limp, low-hanging legs, **y**. I drew eyes in the round face, and a smile, and a filled in the hollow circle of the torso. But there was more: I knew that not only did these shapes mirror the boy above them, but they also could tell me precisely what the boy was doing, arms stretched out and legs apart. **The boy runs**, said the shapes. He wasn't jumping, as I might have thought, or pretending to be frozen into place, or playing a game whose rules and purpose were unknown to me. **The boy runs**. . . .

2   Then one day, from the window of a car, . . . I saw a billboard by the side of the road. The sight could not have lasted very long; . . . large and looming, shapes simi-lar to those in my book, but shapes that I had never seen before. And yet, all of a sud-den, I knew that they were; I heard them in my head, they metamorphosed from black lines and white spaces into a solid, sonorous, meaningful reality. I had done this all by myself. No one had performed the magic for me. I and the shapes were alone together, revealing ourselves in a silently respectful dialogue. Since I could turn bare lines into living reality, I was all-powerful. I could read.

3   What that word was on the long-past billboard I no longer remember . . . , but the impression of suddenly being able to comprehend what before I could only gaze at is as vivid today as it must have been then. It was like acquiring an entirely new sense, so that now certain things no longer consisted merely of what my eyes could seen, my fingers could feel, but of what my whole body could decipher, translate, give voice to, read.

4   The readers of books, into whose family I was unknowingly entering . . . , extend or concentrate a function common to us all. Reading letters on a page is only one of its many guises. The astronomer reading a map of the stars that no longer exist; the

Japanese architect reading the land on which a house is to be built so as to guard it from evil forces; the zoologist reading the spoor of animals in the forest; the card-player reading her partner's gestures before playing the winning card; the dancer reading the choreographer's notations, and the public reading the dancer's movements on stage; the weaver reading the intricate design of a carpet being woven; the organ-player reading various simultaneous strands of music orchestrated on the page; the parent reading the baby's face for signs of joy or fright, or wonder; the Chinese fortune-teller reading the ancient marks on the shell of a tortoise; the lover blindly reading the loved one's body at night, under the sheets; the psychiatrist helping patients read their own bewildering dreams; the Hawaiian fisherman reading the ocean currents by plunging a hand into the water; the farmer reading the weather in the sky—all these share with book-readers the craft of deciphering and translating signs. Some of these readings are coloured by the knowledge that the thing read was created for this specific purpose by other human beings—music notations or road signs, for instance—the tortoise shell, the night sky.

6   And yet, in every case, it is the reader who reads the sense; it is the reader who grants or recognizes in an object, place or event a certain possible readability; it is the reader who must attribute meaning to a system of signs, and then decipher it. We all read ourselves and the world around us in order to glimpse what and where we are. We read to understand, or to begin to understand. We cannot do but read. Reading, almost as much as breathing, is our essential function.

Here is a man whose life was changed for the better by discovering the power of words.

How well you can read and understand begins at the same place it did for Alberto Manguel—with words. As a first step in developing reading versatility, this chapter will provide you with some methods and practice in vocabulary building, understanding words in context, and learning word parts and roots.

Vocabulary development means more than just adding new words to the ones you already know. It also means learning how to change words to different parts of speech, how to add and delete prefixes and suffixes, how to recognize the root elements of a word and its relationship to other words with that root, and how synonyms and antonyms form networks of related words, as well as how to use words correctly in your own speech and writing.

While this book is not a vocabulary textbook, a strong emphasis is placed on vocabulary building because no real reading improvement can take place without it. Several approaches for building your vocabulary are presented in the following pages. Some may seem more helpful to you than others, but give them all a try. Many words will be presented not only in this chapter but throughout the book as part of the reading comprehension and vocabulary practices. Be selective and learn words that you feel you need to learn. You might want to start with those words you "sort of" know but can't really use well. Devote some part of your day to working on your vocabulary. There is no getting around the work part. Building up your vocabulary is like staying in shape. It requires concentrated effort and regular workouts. No one can do it for you.

The first part of this chapter presents three methods for learning words you really want to make your own. Try all three methods before deciding which one you will use during this course.

The second part deals with words in context. For instance, the word *run* can have many different meanings, depending on how it is used in context. Notice these samples:

There was a run on the bank.
She had a run in her stocking.
Run to the store for me.

In each case, and there are many others with the word *run,* the meaning is different, depending on the contextual use of the word. Learning to use contextual clues can also save you many trips to the dictionary.

The third section of this chapter deals with word structure, that is, prefixes, roots, and suffixes. Learning how words are structured and what certain commonly used prefixes, roots, and suffixes mean can help you unlock the meanings of many unfamiliar words. Useful Greek and Latin word roots are presented in practices to help you develop this aspect of vocabulary building.

Vocabulary development is a lifelong process. This chapter is meant only to get you started, not to be a complete course. It will be up to you to continue to use the information provided in this chapter. Select a method that aids you in the continuing development of your vocabulary and use it regularly.

A. Learning New Words: Three Methods

Method 1: A Vocabulary Notebook or Computer Compilation

One way to develop your vocabulary is to keep a notebook of the words you want to learn. If you intend to write the words down on paper, an 8½" × 11" spiral notebook is best. Write in it the words you want to learn, their definitions, and example sentences using the words. For instance, a typical entry might look like this:

perspicacious = having keen insight, judgment, or understanding; shrewd
If he had been more perspicacious, he might not have lost so much money on the stock market.

What type of entries are made is up to you. Some students like to include the sentence where they first encountered the word and then write an example sentence of their own. Some students also write in the phonetic spelling of the word, especially if it is one they have never heard before.

If you use a computer, find a program that allows you to manipulate your new vocabulary. You may want to alphabetize the items, show only the words so that you can supply the definition, or scramble the order.

- *The advantages* to the compilation method are that it is a convenient way to keep all your new words together and a good source for constant review of older entries as new ones are made.
- *The disadvantage* is that the notebook or computer compilation can, if you let them, become nothing more than lists of words unless you make the effort to review your entries constantly.

Method 2: The Column Folds

With this method, you take a regular piece of notebook paper and fold it into three or four columns, three if you do not need to learn the phonetic spelling of the word you want to learn. In the first column, you write the words you wish to learn. In the second column, you write the phonetic spelling. In the third column, you write the definition of the word, and in the fourth column, an example sentence using the word. You leave a blank in the example sentence where the new vocabulary word would go. You can usually get about ten or twelve words on one sheet of paper.

You can then practise learning the words in several ways.

- *One way* is to fold the paper so only the words in the first column show. You then see if you can remember the definitions; if not, you unfold the paper and check the answer.
- *Another way* is to fold the paper so only the definitions show and see if you can identify the word that belongs to that definition.
- *Still another way* is to fold the paper so only the sentences show and try to remember the word that goes in the blank.
- And *still another way* is to fold the paper so that the phonetic spelling shows and try to pronounce the word and give its definition.
- *The advantage* to this method is that it provides you with a means of studying with immediate feedback to the answers.
- *The disadvantage* is that the paper can become rather tattered after awhile if you take very long to learn the words.

Method 3: Vocabulary Cards

You have probably seen boxed sets of vocabulary cards for foreign languages as well as for English. In such sets, each card has a word on one side and its definition on the other. These ready-made cards can be helpful, but chances are you will already know many of the words on the cards.

You can easily personalize the vocabulary card method by making up your own 3" × 5" index file cards. Here's all you need to do:

1. On the front of a card, print the word you want to learn. Use ink, so that after much use it will still be legible. Underneath the word, print the phonetic spelling, unless you already know how to pronounce the word.

2. On the back of the card, put as much information as needed to help you learn the word. Besides the definition, include a synonym (a word that has a similar meaning) and an antonym (a word that has the opposite meaning), if possible. Then add a sentence using the word, either the sentence you found the word in or an example of your own.

3. Be selective and make vocabulary cards only for the words you want to overlearn. It is important to overlearn new words, not just memorize them, because you will gradually forget their meanings if you do not use them. All the words you presently know you have already overlearned and you use them without thinking. The only way to have a truly larger vocabulary is to overlearn new words.

4. Try to learn at least five words a week, more if you can. Practise daily by quickly flashing only the front of the vocabulary card and pronouncing the word to yourself and providing the word's meaning. Try not to refer to the back of the card unless you can't recall the definition.

5. Carry a small stack of cards around so you can refer to them often. At odd times during the day—between classes, while waiting for a friend, on a bus—practise flashing your cards. If you have a friend who is also using this method, practise flashing each other's cards. The more you practise, the sooner you will begin to overlearn the words and recognize them by sight.

mnemonic
(nēmon'ik)

aiding or designed to aid the memory: a device to help remember

Vocabulary cards are <u>mnemonic</u> devices used to remember newly learned words.

6. As you accumulate fifty to a hundred or so cards, set aside the cards for words you feel you know very well and probably will never forget. At a later date, review the cards you have set aside and see if you still remember them. If there are some you don't remember, put them back into your active stack of cards.

- *The advantage* to this method is that it is a convenient way to learn words. If you have your cards with you, you can practise anywhere, anytime. Rather than learning words from a list where association with other words on the list takes place, flash cards can be shuffled and mixed up. Once you have all the information you need on a card, you never have to look up the word again.
- *The disadvantage* is that making up cards does take time, but the advantages far outweigh this one.

All this may seem like too much work. Perhaps it's not the method for you, but it has worked very well for many students. Of the three methods mentioned, the personalized vocabulary card method is the one most recommended.

Application I: Learning New Words

Select one of the three vocabulary development methods and use it on new vocabulary for another class. Have another student test you on your words. Discuss in reading class how your vocabulary development method worked for you.

Check Test

Directions: Answer the following questions in the blanks provided.

   1.   What is meant by vocabulary development? _____

_____

_____

   2.   List the three methods just discussed for developing vocabulary._____

_____

_____

   3.   Describe Method 1. _____

_____

_____

   4.   Describe Method 2. _____

_____

_____

   5.   Describe Method 3. _____

_____

_____

   6.   Which method is most recommended? _____

_____

_____

   7.   Why is this method recommended over the others? _____

_____

_____

   8.   What is meant by overlearning new words? _____

_____

_____

   9.   Why is developing your vocabulary vital to developing reading versatility?

_____

_____

   10.   Which method do you think you will use once you have tried all three?

_____

Why?_____

_____

_____

Name _____ Section _____ Date_____

B.   Learning Words in Context

This section provides practice in figuring out a word's meaning by its use in context. Taking a close look at the context in which a word is used can often, though not always, eliminate the need to use a dictionary.

Contextual Hints

Several different types of context clues will be covered in this section. The first is **contextual hints.** For instance, in the following sentence, notice how the meaning of the word *lucid* is hinted at:

> His lucid lectures, along with his clearly presented explanations, made it easy to take notes.

The phrases "clearly presented explanations" and "easy to take notes" give clues to the meaning of the word *lucid*—easy to understand, clear. Thus, it's generally a good idea not to stop at words you don't know but rather to read on a bit and see if hints or other clues to the word's meaning might be given.

Here's another sentence written with a contextual hint at the meaning of a key word:

> It was imprudent for Lisa to skate on the ice without checking to see how thick it was.

Since we know that skating on ice without making sure it is thick enough is dangerous, we can guess that Lisa was not very wise, perhaps foolish for doing so. Therefore, *imprudent* must mean unwise, rash, or foolish.

PRACTICE B-1: Contextual Hints

Directions: Define the italicized words in the following sentences, and explain the contextual hints.

1. Their *vociferous* arguing made me wish I had earplugs.

   a. *vociferous* means _____

   b. The clue is_____

2. He was so *impudent* to his mother that I would have spanked him if he had talked to me that way.

   a. *impudent* means _____

   b. The clue is_____

3. When asked if she liked her aunt's new hat, she *candidly* gave her frank opinion that it was ugly.

   a. *candidly* means _____

   b. The clue is_____

4. My dad is so *punctilious* that he always corrects my sloppy speech and points out my incorrect use of certain words.

   a. *punctilious* means _____

   b. The clue is_____

5. They think of themselves as the *elite* group on campus, looking down their noses at everyone else.

   a. *elite* means _____

   b. The clue is_____

   Make vocabulary cards for any words that gave you trouble, or use whatever method you have decided to use to develop your word power.

Signal Words

Sometimes there are contextual **signal words** in a sentence that indirectly help to define an unknown word. Signal words are just that: words that signal that a change is about to occur. Just as stoplights and road signs signal that you should slow down, look for curves, and watch out for cross streets while you're driving, signal words are used by writers to help you follow their thoughts. For instance, consider the following sentence:

> While his subjects were grieving for their dead, the king was filled with exultation over his military victory.

Notice how the signal word *while* contrasts the way the subjects feel with the way the king feels. The subjects are grieving (sad) while the king is exulting (happy). So if we didn't know what *exultation* meant, the signal word *while* would alert us that it meant the opposite of grieving.

Here's another example:

> Despite his fear of the snake, Paul managed to subdue his true feelings as it coiled around his arm.

The signal word here is *despite,* meaning in spite of, or even though. Here we have someone who has a fear of snakes, but despite that fear he subdues his feelings; or, as we can guess from the context, Paul manages to control his true feelings.

Here are some signal words that you probably already know but may never have thought of using in this way. In the future, let them help you unlock the meanings of unfamiliar words.

Signal Words

but	while
however	despite
nevertheless	even though
in spite of	in contrast
rather	although
yet	instead

PRACTICE B-2: Signal Words

Directions: Using the signal words, figure out the meaning of the italicized words in the following sentences.

1. Although the patient is usually *morose,* she seems happy today.

    a. *morose* means _____

    b. signal word _____

2. He is usually *loquacious,* but tonight he's rather silent.

    a. *loquacious* means _____

    b. signal word _____

3. The boxer *feigned* a punch with his left rather than actually jabbing.

    a. *feigned* means _____

    b. signal word _____

4. She is usually a *laggard;* however, today she was energetic and did her share.

    a. *laggard* means_____

    b. signal word _____

5. Although his parents were *indigent,* they somehow managed to provide Tommy with proper food and clothing.

    a. *indigent* means _____

    b. signal word _____

Make vocabulary cards or use some other method to learn any words that gave you trouble.

Contextual Examples

Another way you can often figure out the meaning of an unknown word is through **contextual examples.** Writers often provide examples of things or ideas that help define a word. For instance, look at these sentences:

> Luis must be very affluent. He wears expensive clothes and jewellery, drives a Rolls-Royce convertible, and owns a million-dollar house in The Glebe.

Notice all the examples that help define the word *affluent:* expensive clothes, jewellery, car, house in The Glebe. All of these are items that require money or wealth. So it doesn't take much work to figure out that *affluent* means wealthy or well-to-do.

Let's look at another instance of the use of contextual examples:

> The recruitment officer offered her several inducements to join the company, such as the promise of free housing, the opportunity to travel the world, and the chance to live in Victoria.

If the word *inducements* is unclear to begin with, a look at the examples of what the recruitment officer promised gives us a hint that the word must mean reasons or motives to join the company.

Now try using this technique on the following sentences.

PRACTICE B-3: Contextual Examples

Directions: Define the italicized words in the following sentences and give the example clues.

1. In order to show *clemency,* the judge reduced the fine to one dollar and merely gave the man a warning.

   a. *clemency* means _____

   b. example clues _____

2. By burning the village to the ground, shooting all the villagers, and plundering the area for valuables, the rebels committed one of the most *heinous* acts of the war.

   a. *heinous* means _____

   b. example clues _____

3. Jerry is so *indolent!* He sleeps late, never does chores unless yelled at, and would rather lounge around the house than look for a job.

   a. *indolent* means _____

   b. example clues _____

4. Carnegie was very *frugal.* Even though he did not earn a lot, he saved most of his money and lived on very little until he saved $10,000 for the investment that was to make him rich.

   a. *frugal* means _____

   b. example clues _____

5. They *enhanced* the property by pulling weeds, mowing the lawn, and planting trees around the house.

   a. *enhanced* means _____

   b. example clues _____

Make vocabulary cards or use some other method to learn the words that gave you trouble.

Definition Clues

The easiest of context clues to recognize is the **definition clue.** Some sentences actually define the unknown word right in the sentence itself. Notice how that is done in the following example:

> Sue, serving as the chairperson, presided at the meeting.

The phrase "serving as the chairperson" actually defines the word *preside,* which means to hold the position of authority, to be in charge.

Here's another example of a definition clue in a sentence:

> Luke's pretentious manner, standing up and shouting at Sue that he should be running the meeting just to give her a bad time, didn't win him any friends.

Based on Luke's bad manners, we can guess that *pretentious* has something to do with claiming or demanding something when it's unjustified.

While context clues are not always there to help you with unfamiliar words, they do appear frequently. Take the time in your future readings to look for the various types of clues covered in this section.

PRACTICE B-4: Definition Clues

Directions: Define the italicized words in the following sentences.

1. I always felt that the *rapport* between us was good, based on a relationship of trust.

    rapport means _____

2. The most *salient* feature on his face is his chin; it's quite prominent.

    salient means _____

3. Sherry's ill will or, more accurately, *malevolence* toward her brother became obvious when she tried to push him down the stairs.

    malevolence means _____

4. Bret's *jocose* manner soon had all of us laughing and joking.

    jocose means _____

5. Hans Zinsser said, "The rat, like men, has become practically *omnivorous*—it eats anything that lets it."

    omnivorous means _____

    Make vocabulary cards or use some other method to learn the words that gave you trouble.

PRACTICE B-5: Contextual Clues in Paragraphs

Directions: Read the following paragraphs. Then choose the correct definitions for each of the bold print words as they are used in context.

Paragraph 1

I wrote in almost every form I have since written in and then I **laboriously** typed these pieces out, using all four of the fingers I have continued to **employ** until this day. In the college reading room I was able to **obsess** over the few thin literary magazines then published in the country in English, and wondered why the poems in them might be judged by some white-bearded Godlike editor to be better than mine. (From Margaret Atwood, *The Writer's Apprenticeship.*)

Circle the correct response.

1. laboriously
    a. with great knowledge
    b. with suspicion
    c. with great effort

2. employ
    a. develop
    b. use
    c. produce

3. obsess
    a. deliver quickly
    b. fulfill
    c. become preoccupied with

Paragraph 2

This anti-literature attitude includes the idea that reading of literature is impractical, unproductive and perhaps slightly **immoral** or at least **effeminate,** because it is basically a pleasure-centered, leisure-time activity. Many people think that literary interests are undemocratic, **pseudo-aristocratic** and **pretentious** because of "upper-class" and "**elite**" connotations, and because some people have attempted to use "culture" and literary knowledge in a snobbish way for social-climbing and as a status symbol. (From Hugo Hortig, "Why Do They Hate Literature?" *Reading Improvement,* Vol. 2, No. 2, Winter 1965, p. 39.)

Circle the correct response.

1. immoral
   a. sexually attractive
   b. long-lasting
   c. wicked

2. effeminate
   a. tiresome
   b. womanly
   c. sinful

3. pseudo-aristocratic
   a. falsely proud or pretending "upper-classness"
   b. not genuine
   c. abnormal, according to accepted standards

4. pretentious
   a. false
   b. showy
   c. taken for granted

5. elite
   a. a type size
   b. choicest part
   c. enlightened

Paragraph 3

Weekdays my father awakened every morning at six, put on his **phylacteries,** said his morning prayers, and drove his truck through the wintry dark to the family scrapyard near the waterfront. He worked there for my fierce, hot-tempered grandfather and a **pompous** younger brother. Uncle Solly, who had been to high school, had been made a partner in the yard, but not my father, the firstborn. He was a mere employee, working for a salary, which fed my mother's **wrath**. Younger brothers, determined to escape an **overbearing** father, had slipped free to form their own business, but my father was too **timid** to join them. "When times are bad they'll be back. Remember the Depression. Oh, boy!"(From *Home Sweet Home* by Mordecai Richler. Copyright © 1984 by Mordecai Richler.)

Define the following words as they are used in context in the passage.

1. phylacteries _____

2. pompous _____

3. wrath _____

4. overbearing _____

5. timid _____

Paragraph 4

More than this, we have spontaneously arranged ourselves in **dense** clusters, cities, for all the world like **ganglia,** all over the surface of the earth. We are becoming a live network of thought, a meshwork of messages, measuring things, turning things over, talking forever to each other, **gabbling** sometimes, but thinking all the way. Maybe, with luck and long enough survival, we could turn out to be a kind of consciousness for the whole System. Maybe everything you say, perhaps even everything you think, is zipping around out there in the network. . . . I view this as a practical, down-to-earth, nonmystical notion. Nature is **profligate** in many ways, with seeds for instance, but **parsimonious** with mechanisms that require a great deal of energy. I cannot imagine anything more specialized and harder to make than a thought. (From Lewis Thomas, "The Strangeness of Nature," *The New England Journal of Medicine,* vol. 298, no. 26, June 29, 1978.)

Define the following words from the paragraph:

1. dense _____

2. ganglia _____

3. gabbling _____

4. profligate _____

5. parsimonious _____

Paragraph 5

One teaching of Aboriginal peoples that is having an **impact** on the world is the Seventh Generation philosophy/prediction. Simply put, it refers to how **indigenous** peoples make decisions with the Seventh Generation in mind. The present generation is responsible for leaving future generations with a **continuous** cycle of resources and a **habitable** and safe environment. This contrasts with Western planners, who once thought they were **morally** responsible only for a planning period, usually five years. . . . The Seventh Generation teaching is also a prophecy that **predicts** that one day the world will come to indigenous peoples to relearn how to live in **harmony** with the Earth. (From S. Brascoupe, "Aboriginal Peoples' Vision of the Future: Interweaving Traditional Knowledge and New Technologies," *Vision of the Heart: Canadian Aboriginal Issues,* 2nd Edition, D. Long and O. Dickason, Harcourt Canada, 2000, pp. 413–4.)

Define the following words as they are used in the paragraph:

1. impact _____

2. indigenous _____

3. continuous _____

4. habitable _____

5. morally _____

6. predicts _____

7. harmony _____

After your answers have been checked, make vocabulary cards or use some other method to learn the words that gave you trouble.

PRACTICE B-6: Quick Quiz

Directions: The following words are taken from the practices you've been doing on context clues. Define each word and then write a sentence using it correctly in context.

1. *vociferous* (B-1, #1)

   a. definition _____

   b. sentence _____

   _____

2. *loquacious* (B-2, #2)

   a. definition _____

   b. sentence _____

   _____

3. *frugal* (B-3, #4)

   a. definition _____

   b. sentence _____

   _____

4. *rapport* (B-4, #1)

   a. definition _____

   b. sentence _____

   _____

5. *obsess* (B-5, paragraph 1, #3)

   a. definition _____

   b. sentence _____

   _____

6. *dense* (B-5, paragraph 4, #1)

   a. definition _____

   b. sentence _____

   _____

Hand in the quiz to your instructor.

Name _____ Section _____ Date_____

C. Learning Word Parts and Structure

Another good way to develop your vocabulary is to learn some of the basic word parts that make up the English language. Many of our words are derived from other languages, and many prefixes, suffixes, and root word parts come from Latin and Greek. You probably already know many of them but have never taken the time to see how frequently they appear in our language or why certain words mean what they do. In this section, you will review and learn some of the commonly used word parts in English.

Take the word *phonograph*. This common word in English is actually made up of two Greek word roots—*phon*, meaning sound, and *graph*, meaning write or record. Technically, the grooves in a recording are a record of sound, or, if you will, sound written on a record. The advantage of knowing the meanings to word parts is that you can often figure out what an unknown word means by looking at its parts. Look at some of the words that contain the word part *phon*:

phone = informal verb meaning to telephone someone, as well as the informal word for a telephone

phonetic = representing the sounds of speech with distinct symbols

phonetician = an expert in phonetics

phonic = having sound

phonics = the study or science of sound

phonogram = a character or symbol representing a word or distinct sound

phonology = the science of studying speech sounds

phonotype = text printed in phonetic symbols

symphony = a long sonata for orchestra (*sym* means together or in harmony)

euphony = good, pleasant sounds (*eu* means good)

cacophony = harsh, unpleasant sound (*caco* means bad)

Even though some of these words are specialized words, you are one step ahead when you know that all the words have something to do with sound.

Many words in English are made up of *prefixes* (small but meaningful letter groups added before a root or base word that change the meaning) and *suffixes* (letter groups that are added to the end of a root or base word to alter the meaning). Learning the meanings of these word parts, along with the meanings of common base words and Greek and Latin roots, will give you the key to unlock the meanings of hundreds of words.

Following are several practices dealing with word parts and structure. Some you will know; some will be new to you. Make vocabulary cards for those you want to overlearn, or use whatever method you have decided upon for enlarging your vocabulary.

PRACTICE C-1: Prefixes that Express Negativity and Reversal

Directions: There are several prefixes that have to do with negation or reversal. For instance, placing the prefix *dis* in front of the root word *approve* creates the word *disapprove,* changing the word to a negative one. Placing the prefix *dis* on the root word *arm* creates the word *disarm,* reversing the root's meaning.

Below there are three columns. Column 1 contains some prefixes that express negative or reverse meanings. Column 2 contains words you should know. In column 3, you should write in the words from column 2, adding to each what you think is the correct prefix from column 1 to reverse the root word's meaning. The first one has been done for you. Here are clues for using *il, im,* and *ir:*

use *il* with words beginning with *l*

use *im* with words beginning with *b, m,* and *p*

use *ir* with words beginning with *r*

Column 1	Column 2	Column 3
a	active	1. *inactive*
	comfortable	2.
	expensive	3.
c s	logical	4.
r	violent	5.
il	fair	6.
im	regulate	7.
in	typical	8.
ir	pleasant	9.
un	settle	10.
	proper	11.
	legal	12.
	regular	13.
	polite	14.
	decisive	15.
	easy	16.
	movable	17.
	possible	18.
	rational	19.
	legitimate	20.

PRACTICE C-2: Prefixes that Express Time and Place

Directions: Below are some commonly used prefixes that express time and place. Study them carefully. Then fill in the blanks in the numbered exercises. The first one has been done for you.

Prefix	Meaning	Prefix	Meaning
intro, intra	inside, within	re	back, again
inter	between, among	super	above
pre	before	trans	across
de	away, undo	sub	under
ex	out, not any longer	retro	back, backward
post	after	circum	around

1. What is the opposite of *inflate* (to fill)? _____ *deflate* _____

2. If a patriot is a loyal countryman, what is an *expatriate?* _____

3. What is the opposite of *activate?* _____

4. If import means to bring in, *export* means _____

5. If urban refers to the city, what is an *intraurban* truck line? _____
    _____

6. Is *postgraduate* work done before or after you graduate from university? _____

7. A *prefix* is called what it is because it is fixed _____ the root word.

8. If the root word *vive* refers to life, what does *revive* mean? _____

9. A *transatlantic* voyage would take you _____

10. If you *intercede* during an argument, what are you doing? _____

11. *Intercollegiate* sports are activities that take place _____
    different colleges.

12. *Intracollegiate* sports are activities that take place _____

13. Is the *pre*-Victorian period before or after the Victorian period? _____

14. *Mortem* refers to death; what is a *postmortem?* _____

15. Who is higher in rank, a *subprincipal* or a principal? _____

16. What is meant by a *superhuman* effort? _____

17. What would it mean if your boss said you had some *retroactive* pay coming to you? _____

18. What's the difference between *circumference* and diameter measurements?
    _____

19. Why are *subways* called what they are? _____

20. What is the difference between *interisland* ships and those that *circumnavigate?*
    _____

PRACTICE C-3: Miscellaneous Prefixes

Directions: Study the following miscellaneous prefixes and their meanings. Then answer the questions that follow. The first one has been done for you.

Prefix	Meaning	Prefix	Meaning
anti	against	hetero	different
auto	self	mis, miso	wrong; hatred
bene	good, well	mal	bad, wrong
bi	two	poly	many
eu	good, nice		

1. If a newspaper is printed *bimonthly,* it is printed _____ *twice a month* _____

2. If *phon* means sound, what does *euphonious* mean? _____

3. If *toxin* means poison, what does *antitoxin* mean? _____

4. If *gen* refers to types or kinds, what does *heterogeneous* mean? _____

5. If *homogeneous* is the opposite of *heterogeneous,* what does it mean?_____

6. If *sect* means to cut or divide, what does *bisect* mean? _____

7. If *caco* means bad, or unpleasant, how would you form a word that means the opposite of *euphony?* _____

8. Since *gam* refers to marriage, *misogamy* means_____

9. Since *gyn* refers to women, a *misogynist* is _____

10. What is a *polygamist?*_____

11. Why is an *automatic* transmission called what it is? _____

12. Which is better: a tumour that is *malignant* or *benign?* _____

13. What is *malpractice?*_____

14. Why are fund-raisers often called *benefits?* _____

15. Why is someone who donates money called a *benefactor?* _____

PRACTICE C-4: Quick Quiz

Directions: Define the following prefixes and write a word that contains each prefix.

Prefix	Definition	Word Using Prefix
1. auto	_____	_____
2. il	_____	_____
3. intra	_____	_____
4. in	_____	_____
5. un	_____	_____
6. ir	_____	_____
7. anti	_____	_____
8. a/an	_____	_____
9. bi	_____	_____
10. de	_____	_____
11. dis	_____	_____
12. hetero	_____	_____
13. bene	_____	_____
14. eu	_____	_____
15. sub	_____	_____
16. im	_____	_____
17. mis	_____	_____
18. post	_____	_____
19. trans	_____	_____
20. re	_____	_____

Hand in the quiz to your instructor.

Name _____ Section _____ Date _____

PRACTICE C-5: Noun Suffixes

Directions: A noun, as you may remember, is frequently defined as a person, place, or thing: woman, Fred, city, farm, hammer, car—all are nouns. There are some suffixes (letters at the end of a word) that change root words into nouns. For instance, *er* on the end of the word *teach* (a verb) forms the word *teacher,* a noun. The suffix *dom* on the end of *free* (an adjective) creates the noun *freedom.*

Study the following list of suffixes. They all mean "a person who is or does something." Then fill in the blanks that follow. The first one has been done for you.

ent	ant	ist
er	ar	ee
or	ess	ard

1. Someone who acts is an _____ *actor, actress* _____

2. A person paid to serve in a household used to be called a _____

3. Someone who is drunk much of the time is a _____

4. A person who practices science is _____

5. A woman who waits on tables in a restaurant is a _____

6. One who begs is a _____

7. A person who rents an apartment to live in is called a _____

8. One who is elected to preside over an organization is called the _____

    _____

9. A payer _____ while a payee _____

10. Someone who encourages or promotes anarchy is an _____

11. A friend who keeps your confidences is called a _____

12. One who sails is a _____

13. Someone who practices biology is a _____

14. A person who narrates a story is a _____

15. One who studies is a _____

PRACTICE C-6: More Noun Suffixes

Directions: Column 1 contains a list of suffixes that mean "a state or quality of being." For instance, *violence* is the state of being *violent; loyalty* is the state of being *loyal.* Column 2 contains some words that can be changed to nouns by adding the suffixes from column 1. Using the suffixes in column 1, write in the correct noun form in column 3. The first one has been done for you.

Column 1	Column 2	Column 3
ance	fail	1. _____ *failure* _____
ation	hero	2. _____
dom	amuse	3. _____

Column 1	Column 2	Column 3
hood	friend	4. _____
ion	free	5. _____
ism	tense	6. _____
ity	necessary	7. _____
ment	repent	8. _____
ness	starve	9. _____
ty	royal	10. _____
ship	happy	11. _____
ure	seize	12. _____
	lively	13. _____
	content	14. _____
	moderate	15. _____

PRACTICE C-7: Miscellaneous Suffixes

Directions: Study the following list of suffixes and their definitions. Then, using the list, add suffixes to the words that follow. Some words may take more than one suffix. The first one has been done for you.

Suffix	Definition	Suffix	Definition
able, ible	able to	less	without
cy	state or condition	ize	to make
full, ous	full of	ly	a characteristic or in
ic, al	related to		a certain manner
ish, ive	inclined to, similar		

1. care _____ *careful, careless, carefully, carelessly* _____

2. depend _____

3. instruct _____

4. infant _____

5. vocal _____

6. expend _____

7. form _____

8. permanent _____

9. tropic _____

10. active _____

11. popular_____

12. combat _____

13. compete _____

14. caution _____

15. history _____

PRACTICE C-8: Roots

Directions: Using the list below of word roots and their definitions, answer the questions that follow.

Root	Definition	Root	Definition
aud	hear	graph	write, record
chron	time	man, manu	hand
cred	belief	mort	death
dent	tooth	phil	love
dict	tell, say	phon	sound

1. If *meter* means measure, a *chronometer*_____

_____

2. If something is *audible*, you can _____it.

3. *Incredulous* means _____

_____

4. The suffix *ist* refers to a person; that's why someone who works on your teeth is called a _____

5. If *contra* means against or opposite, *contradict* means _____

_____

6. A *chronograph* is_____

_____

7. The opposite of *automatic* is _____

_____

8. Does a *postmortem* occur before or after death? _____

9. If *anthrop* refers to man or mankind, what is a *philanthropist*? _____

_____

10. If you talk into a *dictaphone,* you are recording the_____ of your voice.

PRACTICE C-9: More Roots

Directions: Define the following words. Don't look back at any previous exercises. You should be able to define all of these words if you have learned well from the previous drills.

Root	Definition	Root	Definition
biblio	book	phobia	fear
bio	life	poly	many
gam	marriage	port	carry
gen	kinds, types	tele	far, distance
log(y)	study of	theo	god
mono	one	vis	see

1. bibliography _____

2. biology _____

3. biography _____

4. monogamy _____

5. polyphonous _____

6. heterogeneous _____

7. bibliophobia _____

8. portable _____

9. televise _____

10. theology _____

Application 2: Finding Word Parts in Other Readings

In your textbooks or other reading material, find at least ten words that use the roots you have learned. Write out the words and their definitions so that you can discuss them in reading class.

PRACTICE C-10: Quick Quiz

Directions: Define the following words. You should be able to define all of these words using what you have learned from previous drills.

1. dictation (C-8) _____
2. credible (C-8) _____
3. bibliography (C-9) _____
4. philanthropist (C-8) _____
5. bibliophile (C-9) _____
6. incredulous (C-8) _____
7. audiometer (C-8) _____
8. submariner (C-2) _____
9. monogamy (C-9) _____
10. autograph (C-3) _____
11. misanthropist (C-3) _____
12. intraoffice (C-2) _____
13. deflate (C-2) _____
14. heterogeneous (C-9) _____
15. antitheological (C-3) _____
16. euphonious (C-3) _____
17. bimotored (C-3) _____
18. atypical (C-1) _____
19. irrational (C-1) _____
20. illogical (C-1) _____

Hand in the quiz to your instructor. Make vocabulary cards for any words you missed or need to learn better.

Name _____ Section _____ Date _____

D. Learning Dictionary Skills

There comes a time when context clues and knowledge of word parts are not enough to enable you to understand the meaning of an unknown word. That usually means a trip to the dictionary. The dictionary is more than a recorder of a word's meaning. It gives information on the word's origin, its various meanings, pronunciation, parts of speech, spellings, synonyms and antonyms, and its formal and informal usage. If you don't have a good, up-to-date dictionary, you should get one. (In a later practice, you will read an essay entitled "What You Should Look for in a Dictionary," by Robert M. Pierson, which will help you choose one that is appropriate for you.)

Here is a typical dictionary word entry:

com•pound[1] (kŏm-pound′, kəm-, kŏm′pound′) v. **-pound•ed, -pound•ing, -pounds.** —tr. **1.** To combine so as to form a whole; mix. **2.** To produce or create by combining two or more ingredients or parts. **3.** To settle (a debt, for example) by agreeing on an amount less than the claim; adjust. **4.** To compute (interest) on the principal and accrued interest. **5.** To add to; increase. —intr. **1.** To form a compound. **2.** To come to terms; agree. —adj. (kŏm′pound′, kŏm-pound′, kəm-). **1.** Consisting of two or more substances, ingredients, elements, or parts. **2.** Bot. Composed of more than one part. —n. (kŏm′pound′). **1.** A combination of two or more elements or parts. See Syns at **mixture. 2.** Ling. A word that consists either of two or more elements that are independent words, such as loudspeaker, or of specially modified combining forms of words, such as Greek philosophia, from philo-, "loving," and sophia, "wisdom." **3.** Chem. A substance consisting of atoms or ions of two or more different elements in definite proportions that cannot be separated by physical means. **4.** Bot. **a.** A leaf whose blade is divided into two or more distinct leaflets. **b.** A pistil composed of two or more united carpels. [Alteration of ME compounen < OFr. compondre, to put together < Lat. compōnere. See COMPONENT.] —com•pound′a•ble adj. —com•pound′er n.
com•pound[2] (kŏm′pound′) n. **1.** A building or buildings set off and enclosed by a barrier. **2.** An enclosed area used for prisoners of war. [Alteration of Malay kampong, village.]

From the *Nelson Canadian Dictionary of the English Language*.

In almost all dictionaries, the main word appears in bold type and is divided into syllables by dots. In the *Nelson Canadian Dictionary* used in these exercises, different definitions of the same word are given separate entries and are distinguished by superscript numerals preceding each word. The word *compound* in this entry thus has two quite different meanings. The first *compound* has 13 meanings; the second has two meanings.

Following in parentheses are the pronunciation symbols. If you are unfamiliar with the symbols, a pronunciation key usually appears on the inside front or rear cover of the dictionary. The first exercise in this section will help you learn how to use pronunciation keys. Notice that the first entry of *compound* has a different pronunciation than the other entry.

Immediately after the head word is its part of speech. The abbreviation *v* means verb, *adj* means adjective, and *n* means noun. The word can thus be used as a verb, adjective, or noun. It's important to understand what part of speech a word is so that you can use it correctly.

The bracketed section that appears near the end of an entry provides the word's etymology, or historical origin. In this case, the first entry originally came from Middle English and Middle French. The second entry shows that it came from a Malay word, *kampung*: group of buildings, village.

Notice that there are five definitions of the word *compound* as a transitive verb and two as an intransitive verb. (Transitive verbs require objects to complete the predicate: They *compounded the three metals* to make the alloy. Intransitive verbs do not require objects: After the match, the winners completely *compounded with the losers.*) There are two definitions of the word as an adjective and four as a noun. In this dictionary, the word meanings are arranged from the oldest to the most recent, so the most common present-day definition of *compound* as a verb is "to add; increase."

Sometimes the definitions given for words in some dictionaries are not easy to understand. Frequently, a word that is being used in a definition must also be looked up in the dictionary! All dictionaries are not the same, so be selective in your choice.

The following practices should help you become more familiar with how to get the most from whatever dictionary you buy.

PRACTICE D-1: Pronunciation Keys

Directions: Using the pronunciation key below, answer the following questions. Answers with explanations follow each question.

Symbols	Examples	Symbols	Examples	Symbols	Examples	Symbols	Examples
ă	pat	j	judge	r	roar	ə	about, item, edible gallop, circus
ā	pay	k	kick, cat, pique	s	sauce	ər	butter
âr	care	l	lid, needle* (nĕd′l)	sh	ship, dish		
b	bib	m	mum	t	tight, stopped	**Foreign**	
ch	church	n	no, sudden* (sŭd′n)	th	thin		
d	deed, milled	ng	thing	*th*	this	A	*French* voilà
ĕ	pet	ŏ	pot, bother, father	ŭ	cut	ø	*French* deux
ē	bee	ō	toe	ûr	urge, term, firm, word, heard	œ	*French* oeuf *German* schön
f	fife, phase, rough	ô	caught, paw			ü	*French* tu *German* über
g	gag	oi	noise	v	valve	KH	*German* ich *Scottish* loch
h	hat	ŏŏ	took	w	with	N	*French* bon
hw	which	ōō	boot	y	yes	ny	*French* gagner
ĭ	pit	ôr	pour	z	zebra, xylem	R	*French* rouge
ī	pie, by	ou	cow, out, loud	zh	vision, pleasure garage		
îr	pier	p	pop				

*In English the consonants *l* and *n* often constitute complete syllables by themselves.

From the *Nelson Canadian Dictionary of the English Language.*

1. The first *o* in *loquacious* (lō-kwā′-shəs) is pronounced like the o in the key word _____.

   The key word is *toe*. Since the first *o* in loquacious is marked, ō, it is necessary to scan the dictionary symbol column and find an ō listed. Such a symbol appears in the second column, in the middle. This sound is called the "long o" sound. The symbols appearing over the vowel letters are called diacritical marks.

2. The *a* in the word *loquacious* (lō-kwā′-shəs) is pronounced like the *a* in the key word _____.

   The key word is *pay*. The answer is found in the first column, second listing of the vowel pronunciation symbols. This sound is called the "long a" sound.

3. The ə symbol used in the pronunciation clues (lō-kwā′-shəs) symbolizes the sound of the letter _____ in the word *about*.

   The symbol is called the "schwa."

4. The *a* in the word *chartreuse* (shŏr trooz') is pronounced like the _____ in the words _____ and like the _____ in the word _____.

The "cup" over the *o* gives the *a* a completely different sound, which is sometimes called the "short vowel" sound. The vowel sound is in the middle of the second column.

5. The *u* sound in *chartreuse* (shŏr trooz') is pronounced like the *oo* sound in the word _____.

This sound, which is found in the word *boot,* is located fourth from the bottom in the second column.

6. The first *e* in the word *egocentric* (ē'-gō-sen'-trik)—meaning self-centred—is pronounced like the *ee* in the word _____.

The *e* is the "long e" sound, and the correct answer is *bee.*

7. The *dg* sound in *judge* appears as _____ in the pronunciation clue.

Unless you already knew the answer, you needed to scan the key words column and look for the letter *j.*

8. Sometimes the letter *x* is pronounced like the letter *z.* What is one word that has an *x* that sounds like *z*? _____.

In the pronunciation key, go to the letter *z.* Notice that the second key word is *xylem,* which is the answer you should have written.

9. What letters besides *ur* are often pronounced as *ur*?

_____

Your answer should be *er* as in *term, ir* as in *firm, or* as in *word,* and *ear* as in *heard.*

10. The *s* in *pleasure* is pronounced like the letters _____. Find the key word *pleasure* at the bottom of the third column. Your answer should be *zh.*

PRACTICE D-2: Word Entry Knowledge

Directions: Using the following dictionary word entry, answer the questions that follow.

out•side (out-sīd', out'sīd') *n.* **1.** The part or parts that face out; the outer surface. **2.a.** The part or side of an object that is presented to the viewer; the external aspect. **b.** Outward aspect or appearance. **3.** The space beyond a boundary or limit. **4.** *Sports.* A position at a distance from the inside or centre, as of a playing field or racetrack. **5.** The utmost limit; the maximum: *in ten days at the outside.* **6.** *Northern Canada.* The more heavily settled parts of Canada. —*adj.* **1.a.** Of, relating to, or being on or near the outer side; outer: *the outside margin.* **b.** Of, restricted to, or situated on the outer side of an enclosure or a boundary; external: *an outside door lock.* **2.** Located away from the inside or centre: *the outside traffic lane.* **3.a.** Acting, occurring, originating, or being at a place beyond certain limits: *the outside world.* **b.** Gaining or providing access to the external side: *an outside telephone line.* **4.a.** Not belonging to or originating in a certain group or association: *outside assistance.* **b.** Being beyond the limits of one's usual work or responsibilities. **5.** Extreme, uttermost: *our outside estimates.* **6.** Very unlikely; remote. **7.** *Baseball.* Passing on the side of home plate away from the batter. Used of a pitch. —*adv.* **1.** On or to the outer or external side. **2.** Outdoors. —*prep.* **1.** On or to the outer or external side of. **2.** Beyond the limits of: *outside the city.* **3.** With the exception of; except.

From the *Nelson Canadian Dictionary of the English Language.*

1. How many definitions are given for the word *outside* as a noun? _____

    _____

2. For how many parts of speech can *outside* be used? _____

    _____

3. Two ways to pronounce *outside* are given. What is the difference between the two?

    _____

    _____

4. What does it mean to say there is an *outside chance* you might win?

    _____

    _____

5. Locate the definition of the word *outside* that is peculiar to the Canadian North.
    What does it mean to someone living in the North?_____

    _____

    _____

6. What is one meaning of saying you're working *at the outside* of your ability? Hint:
    outside is used as a noun in this phrase, so look under the noun definitions.

    _____

    _____

7. Use *outside* as a noun in a sentence. _____

    _____

8. Use *outside* as an adjective in a sentence. _____

    _____

9. Use *outside* as an adverb in a sentence. _____

    _____

10. Use *outside* as a preposition in a sentence. _____

    _____

PRACTICE D-3: Finding Information

Directions: Using the dictionary excerpt of "b" entries on page 34, look for the answers to the following questions. Write your answers in the blanks.

1. What is one slang meaning of *babe?* _____

    _____

2. *Babel* is the name of a city, but it also refers to a place of what? _____

    _____

3. Which definition of *baby* is used in this example: "A woman in my book club
    babies her husband." _____

    _____

1700?–60. Polish-born Jewish leader who founded Hasidism.

Bab (bŏb, bäb), **the.** Ali Mohammad of Shiraz. 1819?–50. Persian founder of Babism.

ba•ba (bŏb′ə) *n.* A leavened rum cake, usu. made with raisins. |Fr. < Pol., old woman.|

Ba•bar (bŏb′ər). See **Baber.**

ba•bas•su (bŏb′ə-sōō′) *n.* A Brazilian feather-leaved palm (*Orbignya barbosiana*) bearing seeds that yield an edible vegetable oil. |Port. *babaçu* < Tupi *babassú, oauauassu.*|

Bab•bage (băb′ij), **Charles.** 1792–1871. British mathematician and inventor of a forerunner to the digital computer.

Bab•bitt (băb′it) *n.* A self-satisfied person concerned chiefly with business and middle-class ideals like material success. |After George F. *Babbitt*, the main character in the novel *Babbitt* by Sinclair Lewis.| **—Bab′bitt•ry** *n.*

Bab•bitt (băb′it), **Irving.** 1865–1933. U.S. humanist and scholar who founded the New Humanism movement.

bab•bitt metal (băb′it) *n.* Any of several soft, silvery antifriction alloys composed of tin usu. with small amounts of copper and antimony. |After Isaac *Babbitt* (1799–1862), U.S. inventor.|

bab•ble (băb′əl) *v.* **-bled, -bling, -bles.** *—intr.* **1.** To utter a meaningless confusion of words or sounds. **2.** To talk foolishly or idly; chatter. **3.** To make a low, murmuring sound, as flowing water. *—tr.* **1.** To utter rapidly and indistinctly. **2.** To utter carelessly; blurt out. *—n.* **1.** Inarticulate or meaningless talk or sounds. **2.** Idle talk; prattle. **3.** A low, murmuring sound. [ME *babelen.*] **—bab′bler** *n.*

babe (bāb) *n.* **1.** A baby; an infant. **2.** An innocent or naive person. **3.** *Slang.* A young woman. [ME.]

ba•bel also **Ba•bel** (băb′əl, bā′bal) *n.* **1.** A confusion of sounds or voices. See Syns at **noise. 2.** A scene of noise and confusion. [After BABEL.]

Ba•bel (bā′bal, băb′əl). In the Bible, a city (now thought to be Babylon) in Shinar where construction of a tower intended to reach heaven was ended when the builders became unable to understand each other's language.

Bab el Man•deb (bŏb′ ĕl mŏn′dĕb). A strait, c. 27 km wide, between the Arabian Peninsula and E Africa linking the Red Sea with the Gulf of Aden.

Ba•ber also **Ba•bur** (bŏb′ər). Orig. Zahir ud-Din Mohammed. 1483–1530. Mongol conqueror of India who founded the Mogul dynasty.

ba•be•sia (bə-bē′zhə) *n.* A genus of parasitic sporozoans of the family Babesiidae that infect mammalian red blood cells. [NLat. *Babesia*, genus name, after Victor *Babeş* (1854–1926), Romanian bacteriologist.]

ba•be•si•o•sis (bə-bē′zē-ō′sĭs) also **bab•e•si•a•sis** (băb′ĭ-zī′ə-sĭs) *n.* **1.** A tick-borne infection of animals that is caused by species of *Babesia.* **2.** A disease of human red blood cells caused by *Babesia* species.

Ba•bian Jiang (bŏ′byĕn′ jyŏng′). See **Black River** 1.

ba•biche (bə-bēsh′, bă-, băb′ish) *n. Canadian.* Animal hide fashioned into strips and used as thread or lacing. [Cdn.Fr. < Micmac *âpapīc*, string.]

Ba•bine (bă-bēn′) *n., pl.* **Babine** or **-bines. 1.** A member of an Aboriginal people, a subdivision of the Carrier, inhabiting the Babine River valley of central British Columbia. **2.** The Babine dialect of the Carrier language. [Cdn.Fr. *babine*, labret (from the Babine women's custom of wearing wooden labrets).]

bab•i•ru•sa also **bab•i•rus•sa** or **bab•i•rous•sa** (băb′ə-rōō′sə, bŏb′ə-) *n.* A wild pig (*Babyrousa babyrussa*) of the East Indies, having upward-curving tusks in the male. [Malay *bābīrūsa : bābī*, hog + *rūsa*, deer.]

Bab•ism (bŏb′ĭz-əm, băb′-) *n.* A Persian religious sect founded in 1844, whose doctrines include elements from Islam, Judaism, Christianity, and Zoroastrianism. |Short for Ar. *bāb al-dīn*, gateway of the faith + -ISM.|

Ba•bi Yar (bŏb′ē yör′). A ravine outside Kiev in N-central Ukraine where the Jews of the city were killed by German troops (1941).

bab•ka (bŏb′kə) *n.* A coffee cake flavoured with orange rind, rum, almonds, and raisins. |Pol., dim. of *baba*, old woman.|

ba•boon (bă-bōōn′) *n.* **1.** Any of several large, terrestrial African and Asian monkeys of the family Cercopithecidae, esp. of the genus *Papio* and related genera, characterized by a doglike muzzle and a short tail. **2.** *Slang.* A brutish person; a boor. [ME *babewin* < OFr. *babuin*, gaping figure, gargoyle, baboon, perh. blend of OFr. *babine*, muzzle, and *babau*, grimace.] **—ba•boon′er•y** *n.* **—ba•boon′ish** *adj.*

ba•bu also **Ba•boo** (bŏb′ōō) *n.* **1.** Used as a Hindu courtesy title for a man, equivalent to Mr. **2.a.** A Hindu clerk who is literate in English. **b.** *Offensive.* A native of India who has acquired some education in English. |Hindi *bābū*, father.|

ba•bul (bə-bōōl′) *n.* A tropical African tree (*Acacia nilotica*) that yields a gum similar to gum arabic and has a bark used in tanning. |Pers. *babul.*|

Ba•bur (băb′ər). See **Baber.**

ba•bush•ka (bə-bōōsh′kə) *n.* A woman's head scarf, folded triangularly and worn tied under the chin. |Russ., grandmother, dim. of *baba*, woman.|

Ba•bu•yan Islands (bŏb′ōō-yŏn′). An island group of the Philippines separated from the N coast of Luzon by the **Babuyan Channel.**

ba•by (bā′bē) *n., pl.* **-bies. 1.a.** A very young child; an infant. **b.** The youngest member of a family or group. **c.** A very young animal. **2.** An adult or a young person who behaves in an infantile way. **3.** *Slang.* A girl or young woman. **4.** *Slang.* An object of personal concern: *That boat is your baby.* *—adj.* **-i•er, -iest. 1.** Of or having to do with a baby. **2.** Infantile or childish. **3.** Smaller than others of the same kind: *baby vegetables. —tr.v.* **-bied, -by•ing, -bies.** To treat with indulgence and solicitude. [ME.] **—ba′by•hood′** *n.* **—ba′by•ish** *adj.*

baby beef *n.* **1.** A yearling calf fattened for market. **2.** Meat from the calf.

baby blue *n. Colour.* A very light to very pale greenish or purplish blue.

ba•by-blue-eyes (bā′bē-blōō′īz′) *pl.n.* (*used with a sing. or pl. v.*) An annual plant (*Nemophila menziesii*) native to California and having blue flowers with white centres.

baby bonus *n. Canadian.* See **family allowance.**

baby boom *n.* A large increase in the birthrate, esp. the one in Canada and the United States from 1947 through 1961. **—ba′by-boom′** (bā′bē-bōōm′) *adj.*

ba•by boom•er also **ba•by-boom•er** (bā′bē-bōō′mər) *n.* A member of a baby-boom generation.

baby bust *n.* A sudden decline in the birthrate.

baby carriage *n.* A four-wheeled carriage, often with a hood that folds back, used for wheeling an infant about.

baby grand *n. Mus.* A small grand piano about 1.5 m long.

Bab•y•lon¹ (băb′ə-lŏn′, -lən). The cap. of ancient Babylonia, in Mesopotamia on the Euphrates R.; estab. as cap. c. 1750 B.C. and site of the Hanging Gardens, one of the Seven Wonders of the World.

Bab•y•lon² (băb′ə-lŏn, -lən) *n.* **1.** A city or place of great luxury, sensuality, and often vice and corruption. **2.** A place of captivity or exile.

Bab•y•lo•ni•a (băb′ə-lō′nē-ə). An ancient empire of Mesopotamia in the Euphrates R. valley; fell to the Persians in 539 B.C.

Bab•y•lo•ni•an (băb′ə-lō′nē-ən) *adj.* **1.** Of or relating to Babylonia or Babylon or their people, culture, or language. **2.** Marked by a luxurious, pleasure-seeking, and often immoral way of life. *—n.* **1.** A native or inhabitant of Babylon or Babylonia. **2.** The form of Akkadian used in Babylonia.

ba•by's breath (bā′bēz) *n.* Any of several Eurasian plants of the genus *Gypsophila*, such as *G. paniculata*, having numerous small white flowers in profusely branched panicles.

ba•by-sit (bā′bē-sĭt′) *v.* **-sat** (-săt′), **-sit•ting, -sits.** *—intr.* To act as a baby sitter. *—tr.* To take care of.

Word History: One normally would expect the agent noun *baby sitter* with its *-er* suffix to come from the verb *baby-sit*, as *diver* comes from *dive*, but in fact *baby sitter* is first recorded in 1937, ten years earlier than the first appearance of *baby sit*. Thus, the verb was shortened from the agent noun and presents a good example of back-formation.

baby sitter *n.* **1.** A person engaged to care for one or more children when the parents or guardians are not at home. **2.** A person who watches over someone or something.

baby tooth *n.* See **milk tooth.**

ba•ca•la•o (bŏk′ə-lä′ō) *n., pl.* **-os. 1.** Dried, salted cod. **2.** Any dish prepared with such cod. [Sp. *bacallao* prob. < Basque *bakailao* < Gascon < MDu. *cab(b)eliau*, codfish.]

Bac•ca•la•os or **Bac•col•la•os** (bŏk′ə-lä′ōs). In the 16th cent., the cod-fishing areas of present-day Atlantic Canada. [Sp. (land of) codfish. See BACALAO.]

bac•ca•lau•re•ate (băk′ə-lôr′ē-ĭt) *n.* **1.** See **bachelor's degree. 2.** A farewell address delivered to a graduating class. [Med.Lat. *baccalaureātus* (influenced by *bacca*, berry + *laureātus*, crowned with laurel) < *baccalārius*, bachelor. See BACHELOR.]

bac•ca•rat (bŏk′ə-rö′, băk′-) *n. Games.* A card game in which the winner is the player who holds two or three cards totalling closest to nine. |Fr. *baccara* < Prov.|

bac•cate (băk′āt′) *adj.* **1.** Resembling a berry in texture or form; berrylike. **2.** Bearing berries. |< Lat. *bacca*, berry.|

Bac•chae (băk′ē) *pl.n. Gk. & Rom. Myth.* The priestesses and women followers of Bacchus. |Lat. < Gk. *Bakkhai*, pl. of *Bakkhē*, female worshipper of Bacchus < *Bakkhos*, Bacchus.|

bac•cha•nal (băk′ə-nŏl′, -nöl′, băk′ə-nəl) *n.* **1.** A participant in the Bacchanalia. **2.** The Bacchanalia. Often used in the plural. **3.** A drunken or riotous celebration. **4.** A reveller. *—adj.* Of or relating to the worship of Bacchus. |< Lat. *bacchānālis*, of Bacchus, prob. < *Bacchānālia*, Bacchanalia < *Bacchus*, Bacchus < Gk. *Bakkhos.*|

Bac•cha•na•lia (băk′ə-nā′lē-ə, -nāl′yə) *n., pl.* **Bacchanalia. 1.** The ancient Roman festival in honour of Bacchus. **2. bacchanalia.** A riotous drunken festivity; a revel. |Lat. < *Baccha-nalia* < *Bacchus* < Gk. *Bakkhos.*| **—Bac′cha•na′lian** *adj. & n.*

bac•chant (bə-kănt′, -könt′, băk′ənt) *n., pl.* **bac•chants** or **bac•chan•tes** (bə-kăn′tēz, -kön′-, -kănts′, -könts′). **1.** *Gk. & Rom. Myth.* A priest or votary of Bacchus. **2.** A boisterous reveller. |Lat. *bacchāns, bacchant-*, pr.part. of *bacchārī*, to

From the *Nelson Canadian Dictionary of the English Language.*

4. Where is *baccarat* usually played? _____

5. What is the more common term for a *baccalaureate*? _____

_____

6. On the sample dictionary page, which phrase is the opposite of the term *baby boom*, also on this page? _____

7. Why is the word *baby sit* a good example of "back-formation" according to the word history of *baby sit.* _____

_____

8. The words *baba* and *babka* are the names of two desserts that are derived from the word *old lady* in what language? _____

9. What is the slang meaning of *baboon*? _____

_____

10. Of the two Babbitts that appear on this page, which is based on a fictional character?

_____

E.   Putting It All Together

Below are two reading selections. Both are followed by comprehension and vocabulary checks; the second one is a timed reading. Increasing your ability to read well involves these three components: vocabulary, comprehension, and rate. In this chapter, you have worked primarily on the first component—vocabulary. If you don't recognize the words when you are reading, you will have a hard time understanding what you read. You will now be asked to answer comprehension questions, too, showing that you understand the selections you are reading. Much of this book will be devoted to increasing your comprehension of what you read. The second reading is a timed reading because if you read too slowly (under 180 words per minute [wpm]), your mind may wander and comprehension may fall. The comprehension questions and timed reading in this section are intended primarily to help you see what your understanding and reading rate are at the beginning of the book. Your scores at this point are less important than understanding why you may have missed a question. Always make sure you understand why you may have missed any questions. Learn from your mistakes.

PRACTICE E-1

Directions: Before reading the selection, look at the introductory paragraph and the title and answer the following questions:

1. What is your method for selecting a new dictionary now? _____

_____

2. What do you think is one characteristic of a good dictionary? _____

_____

3. Do dictionaries tell you how words are now used or how they should be used?

_____

Dictionaries are an important tool for increasing your vocabulary and should be chosen carefully. In the following article, Pierson not only gives you interesting information about what dictionaries do and don't do (some of which may surprise you) but he also helps you evaluate dictionaries by looking at twelve different parts of them.

WHAT YOU SHOULD LOOK FOR IN A DICTIONARY

ROBERT M. PIERSON

1   First, does it describe or prescribe? Does it tell you how words *are* used or does it tell you how its compiler thinks words *should* be used? Most modern dictionaries do the former—most of the time. They are—or strive to be—objective reports of the state of the language. (The big exceptions are usage manuals and stylebooks—on which more below.) Editors of today's dictionaries may privately shudder at *presently* for *now*, at *hose* for *stockings*, at *cremains* for *ashes of people who have been cremated*, at *home* for *house*. But . . . [t]he day is . . . past when you can defend the artistic effect of your use of a word by saying, "But I found it in the dictionary."

2   It was not always so. In centuries past, dictionaries existed primarily to establish and maintain good French—or whatever. Sometimes the motive was to replace Latin (a nearly frozen language) with something just as stable and "classic"; sometimes, to make one dialect (that of the capital?) supreme; sometimes, to encourage the use of a national language (as opposed to that of a foreign oppressor). Times have indeed changed.

3   Not that today's dictionaries are completely value-free. They identify some uses as slang, some as obsolete, some as dialectal, some as illiterate—and some words as taboo, even offensive. But even here they strive to explain how society in general views words, not how *the dictionaries* view them. They are not saying that it is "bad" to use *smashed* for *drunk*—only that most people will regard *smashed* as an informal way of putting it. Only you and your editor can decide whether, in a particular situation, you should write *smashed* or *drunk*—or *blotto* or *feeling no pain* or *intoxicated* or *inebriated* or *under the influence* (without, perhaps, saying of what!).

4   Some other points to note in dictionaries:

1. **Their scope.** Are they *general* or are they in some way *specialized*? Do they cover the language as a whole or are they in some way limited? Do they, for example, cover new words only? or slang only? or only the special vocabulary of science—or of one particular science? As a writer, you will surely want a general dictionary—plus one or more specialized ones, depending on your interests.

2. **Their scale** (a result of their *degree of selectivity*). Are they more or less complete—unabridged—or are they selective—*abridged*? If the latter, is abridgement a matter of less information about the same number of words or a matter of the same amount of information about fewer words—or, as is usually the case, mostly the latter but with some of the former? As a writer you may, deep in your heart, want an unabridged dictionary, plus a revolving stand to mount it on. You will probably find that an abridged dictionary designated, in its title, as "college" or "collegiate" will meet your needs well enough—and with less pain to your wallet and your arm muscles. If you can afford to do so, get two such dictionaries and, when a problem arises, compare what they have to say.

3. **Their intended readership.** Are they for children or for adults? If for adults, for adults of what level of sophistication? Again, the "collegiate" dictionaries will probably best suit you as a writer: they will give you not only *the* meaning of

Excerpted from "A Writer's Guide to Dictionaries" by Robert M. Pierson. Originally published in *Writer's Digest*, November 1983, pp. 34–38.

each word they list but also other meanings, with labels to alert you to how words are likely to be received. They will also tell you a little about the origins and histories of the words they list.

4. **Their overall arrangement.** Basically, are they in one alphabetical sequence or in several? Opinions differ as to which way is best. Should place-names be in a separate list? What about personal names? foreign words widely used in English? abbreviations? How about new words and new uses of old words? Some dictionaries merge all categories into (as information scientists say) one file. Others lift out one or more categories and file them separately. The best solution, so far as users of dictionaries are concerned, is to look, first of all, at each dictionary's table of contents. And once you are within an alphabetical sequence, remember what I said before about word-by-word, letter-by-letter, and keyword-by-keyword alphabetizing. Remember, too, that *Mc* and *Mac* names may be filed as spelled, filed separately, or all filed as if spelled *Mac* (which is how most library catalogs do it, by the way). Again, don't struggle to remember which system is used: just be ready to shift gears.

5. **The order in which they list multiple definitions.** There are two main sequences: "historical" sequence, with oldest extant uses defined first, newest last; and "frequence" sequence, with most common first, least common last. . . . As a writer, you must be aware of all the ways in which the words you use *may* be understood, so always read the whole entry. Just bear in mind that the first meaning listed may or may not be the one most likely to come to mind.

6. **The readability of their definitions.** . . . Occasionally, if the editors of dictionaries are not watchful, circular definitions, which leave you where you were, creep in—e.g., calling a *prosthesis* a *prosthetic appliance.* Sometimes definitions will seem duskier than the words they are said to illumine. On the other hand, dictionaries tend to be brief—and who said brevity always leads to clarity? If dictionary editors spun out their definitions to make them more readable, their products would weigh and cost much more. Still and all, try looking up some words in fields you know a *little* about and see how they read: if you look up words you already know a lot about, you may "read in" meaning not provided by their definitions; and if you look up totally unfamiliar words, you will be in no position to judge. Either way, try not to mistake oversimplification for genuine clarity: sure, it's "readable" to call an apricot "a delicious fruit of a pale creamy pinky yellow," but would not that definition apply equally well to nectarines and some grapefruits?

7. **Their labelling of meanings and uses.** As suggested earlier, it is helpful to know that *braces* in the sense of *suspenders* is British, as is *suspender* in the sense of *garter*— that in botanical usage, the Irish potato is a *stem*, strawberry not essentially a *fruit*, and a tomato only a *berry!* The constant reminder as to what is *standard* (unlabelled) and what is not, really keeps us on our toes—as writers. Not that labelling is always perfect: one dictionary I reviewed several years ago carefully labelled racial and religious slurs as offensive, e.g., *nigger* and *kike*, but did not so label *broad* ("woman") and *queer* ("homosexual")—surely just as offensive to those to whom the words are applied—although just possibly, I grant, those particular words are not always *intended* to be offensive. But surely that is just the point. As writers, we need to express ourselves, yes, choosing the words that most exactly say—to us—what we mean; but if we are to communicate successfully, we must also think of how our words are likely to be received, regardless of our intentions. Hence the usefulness of labels . . .

8. **What they may tell [you about] words besides their meanings.** Pronunciation, syllabification, grammatical inflections (plurals, past tense forms, etc.), origins

and histories—and, of course, spelling!: all these are likely to be indicated in "collegiate" dictionaries. Often the presentation of this material is extremely condensed and literally hard to read: I know one dictionary whose print is so small and so dull that it is hard to tell whether the little marks between syllables are only raised periods (meaning, in that dictionary, syllabic division) or actual hyphens (meaning to spell with hyphens). In an age when we are encouraged to read faster and faster, you may need to slow down, as if reading the thorniest Rossetti or Hopkins sonnet! And to be sure to study the system of symbols used—e.g., > for "derived from" and the "schwa" (ə) for the "uh" sound—and abbreviations too, like *O.F.* for "Old French." There may well be a key at the bottom of the page. Just don't assume that every new dictionary—or dictionary new to you—is, in this respect, like one you are used to.

9. **Their references to related words.** Often defining a word precisely is very difficult. One solution to that problem is to refer to words of more or less similar meaning (from *awkward* to *clumsy*, from *rude* to *boorish*, from *immaculate* to *clean*) or to words of opposite meaning (from *calm* to *agitated*, from *mellifluous* to *harsh*). The more a dictionary does this—and the more it explains subtle differences—the better for you as a writer. Sensitivity to such matters will give your writing precision.

10. **Their use of examples—including quotations—to clarify meaning.** These may be "made-up" illustrations of their usage or they may be quotations from published material. If the latter, observe their age. As a reader of old and new material, you may be helped by a quotation from the Bible or from Shakespeare. As a writer, you may be helped more by a quotation from *Time* or *Natural History* or *Organic Gardening*. In any case, quotations—giving words in context—may hint at shades of meaning exceedingly difficult to convey otherwise.

11. **Their use of graphics, especially line drawings.** Again, the more the better—to label the parts of a Greek column, for instance, or the components of a threshing machine. I do not share the view that a picture is always worth a thousand words, but sometimes a picture can do what dozens of words fail to do—at least as you and I use them.

12. **The presence of encyclopedic information.** In theory, a dictionary is a word book; an encyclopedia, a subject-matter book. When you define *grizzly bear* so as to make it clear how grizzlies differ, basically, from American black bears, you are doing only what dictionaries traditionally do; when you tell what they feed on (cow parsnips, I am told) and how many are left—and go on to mention a good book on the subject—you are doing, in addition, what encyclopedias do. Some dictionaries go very far along this line, even to the point of giving lists of chemical elements, evolutionary trees for animals and plants and languages, maps of continents, rules of grammar and punctuation, . . . —you name it; some dictionary—some "word book"—will provide it. And when you get into specialized subject dictionaries, the tendency is even more marked—with *dictionary* used to designate just about any book featuring alphabetical sequence. When it comes to selecting a general English-language dictionary of "desk size," my advice is this: don't buy a book on the basis of bonus features unless you really need the bonus features. How much space do you have for other books? Do you already own an encyclopedia? How far do you live from the public library?

5   My advice, then, is this: Get to know your dictionaries. Look at *all* their parts—including those little appendices and supplements at the back. Imagine how you might use what you find. Keep your dictionaries at hand, and form the habit of consulting them often. And read them for pleasure. Though not set up for consecutive reading, as are novels and treatises, they can be read in much the same way. Read

them again and again—and note your findings, whether in your "writer's journal," on note cards for orderly filing, or in that secret file at the back of your mind. Save all these bits and pieces. You never know when they will rise to the surface for you to hook them. They will be "there for you," like old friends, to enrich your creative output; to help you say what you mean, not just something close; to help you convey a sense of truth-telling, not of weary echoing of the thoughts and feelings of others; to help give your writing the sheen, the glow, the magic that we, all of us, strive for but so seldom achieve, let alone sustain.

Comprehension Check

Directions: In the spaces provided, answer the following questions about the selection you just read.

1. Some of the examples Pierson uses are words that have changed common meanings since he wrote this article. He says *stockings* would be preferred over *hose*, yet *hose* sounds more current to us. What is one other current term for this piece of clothing? _____

    _____

    _____

    The following are some of the points the author says to note when looking for a good dictionary. Explain briefly what he means by each:

2. scope _____

3. scale _____

4. intended readership _____

5. overall arrangement _____

6. What is one of the two ways some dictionaries list multiple definitions?

    _____

7. Explain what the author means by circular definitions. _____

    _____

8. T/F Good dictionaries have more graphics or pictures.

9. T/F The author believes all dictionaries are basically the same.

10. Briefly list the three methods suggested for remembering your findings from reading the dictionary. _____

    _____

    _____

Vocabulary Check

Directions: Define the following underlined words from the article.

1. First, does it describe or <u>prescribe</u>? Does it tell you how words *are* used or does it tell you how its compiler thinks words *should* be used? (paragraph 1)

    _____

2. Not that today's dictionaries are completely value-free. They identify some uses as slang, some as <u>obsolete</u> . . . (paragraph 3) _____

_____

3. Only you and your editor can decide whether, in a particular situation, you should write *smashed* for *drunk*—or *blotto* or *feeling no pain* or . . . <u>inebriated</u> (paragraph 3) _____

_____

4. Are they more or less complete—<u>unabridged</u>—or are they selective—*abridged?* (point #2) _____

_____

5. Try not to mistake oversimplification for genuine <u>clarity</u>. (point #6)_____

_____

6. One dictionary I reviewed several years ago carefully labelled racial and religious slurs as <u>offensive</u> . . . (point #7) _____

_____

7. Pronunciation, syllabification, <u>grammatical inflections</u> (plurals, past tense forms, etc.) are all likely to be indicated in collegiate dictionaries. (point #8)_____

_____

8. Often the presentation of this material is extremely <u>condensed</u> and literally hard to read. (point #8) _____

_____

9. One solution to that problem is to refer to words of more or less similar meaning (from *awkward* to *clumsy,* from *rude* to <u>boorish</u> . . . (point #9) _____

_____

10. Look at *all* their parts—including those little <u>appendices</u> and supplements at the back. (final paragraph) _____

_____

After the results of the comprehension check and vocabulary check have been scored, record them on the Student Record Chart in the Appendix. Divide the number of correct answers by the number of questions in each check to determine your scores.

Remember to make vocabulary cards for any words that gave you trouble.

Application 3: Evaluating Your Own Dictionary

Evaluate the dictionary you currently use according to any six of the twelve criteria for evaluating dictionaries in Robert Pierson's article. Briefly explain what this shows you about your personal dictionary that you didn't know before. Bring your evaluation and explanation for class discussion.

PRACTICE E-2: Timed Reading

Directions: This is your first chance to see what your current reading rate is. Remember that your current rate is not as important as understanding why you are reading at that rate and how it helps or hinders you. If you read too slowly (below approximately 180 wpm), keeping your concentration on the reading will be difficult. If you read too quickly and can't answer the questions, you are reading fast but with too little comprehension. You want to read this first timed reading at a rate that is fast enough to feel slightly forced but slow enough to understand what you read. This article has 900 words.

Begin timing: _____

AWFUL AND WONDERFUL

WENDELL S. JOHNSON

When we say that language itself is alive, we suggest that it is the expression of the ideas and emotions of live people. But the idea of living language implies something else too. The first sign of life is growth and change. And, like living people, animals, and plants, a living language is always changing.

HOW MEANINGS CHANGE

1   We see one example of how words change in the art expert's phrase "awful majesty." The dictionary tells us that *awful* can mean "awe-inspiring" or "impressive," but this is not at all what most of us mean by the word most of the time. If a friend asks, "How did you like the way I read that story?" you might be tempted to reply, "It was awful." But if you want to go on being friends, you had better add, "By which I mean, it was scary and impressive."

2   If two people give reports on a book they both have read, and one says that it was "awful" while the other says that it was "wonderful," it is clear that they disagree completely. Today these two words are generally used as *antonyms*, words that mean exactly the opposite of each other. (Some pairs of antonyms are *good* and *bad*, *high* and *low*, *joy* and *grief*, *sweet* and *sour*, *fast* and *slow*.) Yet, less than two hundred years ago, the words *awful* and *wonderful* did not have exactly opposite meanings; in fact, they meant the very same thing. They were *synonyms*, words that have the same meanings, like *big* and *large*, *joy* and *happiness*, *small* and *little*. One synonym the dictionary still gives for *wonder* is "awe."

3   How did these two words that once had the same meaning come to have opposite meanings? Probably because the feeling of awe, or of wonder, is a complicated, mixed-up feeling. When you are awed, or filled with wonder, by a wild thunderstorm, you are partly frightened, but also partly fascinated and overwhelmed. Maybe, then, the "bad" reaction of frightened awe gradually dominated the word *awful*, while the "good" reaction of fascination and even delight took over the word *wonderful*.

4   There are other examples of how the attitudes or emotions associated with a word gradually change the basic meaning of that word. Many words that we use in everyday speech have overtones that may not be included in their strict dictionary definitions—or at least not yet. These overtones, or suggestions of meaning, are called "connotations," while the limited definitions, or strict meanings, are called

"denotations." The connotation of the word *operator* as we use it now may be of someone who takes advantage of people and situations for his own benefit, as in the phrase "big-time operator," and the word may even suggest a hard-hearted cynic. But the denotation, the dictionary definition, for the word is simply "one who operates"—that is, anybody who operates any kind of machine. Perhaps, in another fifty or hundred years, the connotation will have become the principal denotation, the basic meaning, so that the dictionary definition of operator will be "one who selfishly exploits others."

5   This process of change, with some words slowly taking on new significance, has gone on with much of our familiar vocabulary, and, as we see, it is still going on. The word *villain* once referred to country man or farmer. Gradually it came to mean a person of low standing and rough manners, and now it is used to refer to a "bad guy" in a play or film. On the other hand, the word *guy* originally referred to the strange-looking dummy representing the English traitor Guy Fawkes. For years the word was used to mean any odd-looking or ragged man, something like a tramp or clown. But now, in ordinary . . . speech, *guy* is simply a slang word for "man."

6   The tendency of words to change meanings over the years is not limited to words that have always been part of the English language. Words that enter English from other languages often change their meanings. For example, *left-handed, sinister,* and *gauche* seem to be unrelated terms. *Left-handed* is a familiar English word; *sinister,* a fairly well-known word, was originally Latin; and *gauche,* a word used less often, was originally French. But, to begin with, they all meant the same thing: to be *sinister* or *gauche* was literally to be left-handed. The left side used to be considered unlucky or just plain bad, and so *sinister* came to mean "evil" or "harmful." And because left-handed people were once thought to be clumsy, *gauche* now means in English (but not always in French) "awkward" or "tactless." (Still, if you happen to be left-handed, you are not necesarily *sinister* or *gauche.*)

7   In fact, then, all languages still being spoken—what we call "living" instead of "dead" languages—are constantly changing. Words change their meanings slowly, as overtones and hints of meaning very gradually take over, and as slang and fanciful new words become part of ordinary everyday speech. But they do inevitably change. And so we sometimes have to know not only who is using words and in what time and place, but also whether these words were first written or spoken this morning or two hundred years ago.

Finish timing. Record time here:_____ and use the Timed Readings Conversion Chart in the Appendix to figure your rate: _____ wpm. Remember to record this rate on the Student Record Sheet in the Appendix. This is your initial reading rate and will give you an idea of whether you need to work on the other timed readings in this textbook.

Comprehension Check

Directions: In the spaces provided, answer the following questions about the selection you have just read.

   1. What does the title of this reading selection mean? _____

   _____

   _____

   2. What does the author mean when he says language is alive? _____

   _____

   _____

3. How does the author think *awful* and *wonderful,* which had the same meaning at one time, came to have opposite meanings? _____

_____

4. What are two meanings of *operator* the author discusses? _____

_____

5. According to this author, are words still changing their meanings today? Briefly explain. _____

_____

6. Give an example of a word that has entered English from another language and then changed its meaning in English. _____

_____

7. Words change their meaning
   a. quickly
   b. rarely
   c. slowly
   d. at varying paces

8. Do slang words ever become the common usage of the English language? _____

_____

9. What is the difference between dead and living languages? _____

_____

10. Briefly explain how the word *villain* has changed its meaning. _____

_____

Vocabulary Check

Directions: Define the following underlined words as they are used in the reading selection. You may look back at the selection to see the entire context if you need to.

1. Today these two words (*awful* and *wonderful*) are generally used as <u>antonyms</u>. (paragraph 2) _____

_____

2. These same two words used to mean the same thing and were <u>synonyms</u>. (paragraph 2) _____

_____

3. What is one current definition of <u>awful</u>? (paragraph 3) _____

_____

4. What is one current definition of <u>wonderful</u>? (paragraph 3) _____

_____

5. the <u>connotations</u> of words (paragraph 4) _____

_____

6. the <u>denotations</u> of words (paragraph 4) _____

_____

7. What is one current definition of <u>operator</u>? (paragraph 4) _____

_____

8. What is one current definition of <u>guy</u>? (paragraph 5) _____

_____

9. What is one current definition of <u>gauche</u>? (paragraph 6)_____

_____

10. What is one current definition of <u>sinister</u>? (paragraph 6)_____

_____

Record your comprehension check and vocabulary check scores in the Student Record Chart in the Appendix. Divide the number of correct answers by the number of questions in each check to determine your scores. Continue to add any problematic vocabulary words to your vocabulary list.

Questions for Group Discussion

1. Now that you have finished the chapter on vocabulary, discuss the power of new vocabulary in your life. As a group, be specific about where you notice the effects of new vocabulary.

2. The two selections you have just read deal with using the dictionary for vocabulary development, the importance of reading books and writing, and how words change all the time. As a group, discuss the similarities you find in these two articles.

3. We have different vocabularies for listening, reading, writing, and speaking. Decide which is your largest vocabulary and arrange the others in descending order.

4. As a group, decide which method of vocabulary development helps the most for class terminology you are learning right now.

◇   ◇   ◇

CHAPTER TWO

Developing Literal Recall

A.   Finding the Topic, Main Idea, and Supporting Details

One of the keys to good comprehension is the ability to find the topic and separate main ideas from supporting details. Finding the main idea gets easier with practice.

Topic

First, identify the **topic** of the paragraph or passage. Read the entire passage and identify which word or phrase is used most often or dominates the idea of the passage. The topic is usually a word *(leadership, food, Turkey)* but may also be a phrase *(leadership in corporations, foods and popular trends, Turkish history and culture)*.

Main Idea

Then, find the **main idea** by looking for the most general statement that explains that topic. In the following three series, pick the *most general word or phrase* and mark it.

_____ cars	_____ retriever	_____ set aside a worry period
_____ Chevrolet	_____ dog	_____ how to stop worrying
_____ Mercedes	_____ pets	_____ breathe deeply

Did you select "car," "pets," and "how to stop worrying"? In the first example, the other two words are specific auto makers. Your pet could be a dog or a retriever. Two specific techniques that will help you stop worrying are setting aside a worry period and practicing deep-breathing techniques. Once you get so you can quickly pick out the most general statement, you are well on your way to identifying main ideas in paragraphs and passages.

Try one more practice on the following sentences. Which of the three sentences is the most general?

_____Research the company by looking at internal publications or reports.
_____Practice by role-playing your interview with a friend.
_____Thorough preparation for a job interview helps your chances.

Did you select the last sentence? These sentences are all about job interviews (the topic), and the first two sentences give you two specific strategies that will help you prepare for a successful job interview.

Understanding where in the paragraph main ideas are most often found is another helpful strategy. Usually, though not always, the best place to look first for the main idea is the first sentence in a paragraph.

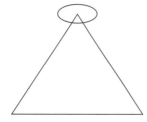

There are several good ways to prepare for a job interview. One is to anticipate questions by reading the job description carefully. Another is to research the company's publications or Web sites.

Main ideas can also come at the end (especially in philosophy or law),

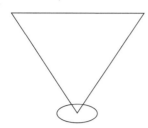

Gerald studied late into the night, every night, and never without his music playing. His friends came and went, and none of them cleaned up after themselves. Mrs. Kroker became more and more nervous as the months went by; she waited for June with a different set of expectations than Gerald had. The natural enmity between landlord and tenant seems to intensify when the renter is a student.

in the middle (especially in technical writing or in math),

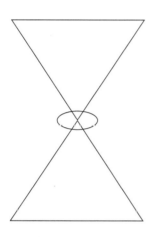

A math symbol such as % has no meaning inherent in it. In math, always memorize the meaning of any symbol or definition. There is nothing about the word "parallel" that describes its meaning.

or not at all.

Managing your time becomes an important skill in college. Learning how to remember and when to memorize are two other college success skills. Reading textbooks well will enhance your college experience.

When the main idea does not appear in the paragraph at all, it is called an implied main idea and is probably the most difficult to identify. In the last example paragraph, the implied main idea is that there are several strategies that will help a college student succeed. Sometimes the main idea in a passage is easy to identify, sometimes not.

Supporting Details

Finally, identify the **supporting details** that explain the main idea by using specifics. If the main idea is the most general statement about the topic, then supporting details are specifics about that idea. If "textbooks are helpful" is a general statement, then "reading versatility textbook" is a supporting detail. If "the flu vaccine is controversial" is the main idea, one supporting detail might be, "Ambulance drivers are sometimes refusing to have the vaccine."

Here is a final example to make the difference between these parts clear. If the *topic* of a passage is DTV, or digital television, the *main idea* might be the benefits you can expect from digital television. The *supporting details* may then include such items as good picture quality, better sound, wider screen, interactivity, and data services.

Topic: DTV
     Main idea: the benefits to expect from DTV
          Supporting details: good picture quality
                           better sound
                           wider screen
                           interactivity
                           data services

Finding these three parts in any paragraph or passage (topic, main idea, supporting details) will help your comprehension a great deal.

Your comprehension can be enhanced if you understand how writers form paragraphs, so let's look at some samples of writers at work. Read the following paragraphs to identify topics and main ideas.

Paragraph A

Some words are loaded with pleasant associations. Such words as *home, happiness, tenderness, contentment, baby,* and *mother* usually bring out favourable feelings or connotations. The word *mother,* for instance, makes most people think of home, safety, love, care, food, security, and the like.

What is the topic of the paragraph? _____

_____

What is the main idea or most general statement about that topic?_____

_____

_____

The topic of this paragraph is *words* because every sentence in the paragraph is about words or examples of words. The main idea is the first sentence in the paragraph because it is the most general statement about the topic. The other sentences are specific details about words.

Paragraph B

Attention Deficit Disorder is a neurological condition that affects learning and behaviour. ADD occurs in approximately 5 to 10 percent of the population, depending on what scientific studies you read. It begins in childhood, and about 50 percent of the people with ADD outgrow it by adolescence. For some, ADD symptoms may not be as bothersome in adulthood, but they are still present to some degree.

What is the topic of the paragraph? _____

_____

What is the main idea or most general statement about that topic?_____

_____

_____

The topic of the paragraph is Attention Deficit Disorder because every sentence in the paragraph is about ADD. The main idea is again the first sentence in the paragraph because it is the most general statement about the topic. The other sentences are all specifics about ADD.

Paragraph C

I'm enjoying the new friends I've made in college. I'm also lucky to have good college instructors. The campus offers many activities for students and I'm participating in many of them. College is an enjoyable experience for me.

What is the topic of the paragraph? _____

_____

What is the main idea or most general statement about that topic?_____

_____

_____

The topic of the paragraph is college, and the main idea is the last sentence in the paragraph. Notice how we tend to think the main idea is in the beginning. Your comprehension would be poor if you thought this entire paragraph was about the friends one makes in college. The details are friends, professors, and college activities.

Once you have identified the topic and main idea of a paragraph or passage, you then need to identify the details or specifics that support the main idea. In Paragraph A, the details are the specific words.

> Topic: words
>> Main idea: Some words are loaded with pleasant associations.
>>> Supporting details: Examples are home, happiness, tenderness, contentment, baby, mother.
>>>> Minor details: mother associated with home, safety, love, care, food, security, and the like.

In Paragraph B:

> Topic: ADD
>> Main idea: ADD is a neurological condition that affects learning and behaviour.
>>> Supporting details: 5 to 10 percent of population, 50 percent outgrow by adolescence, ADD symptoms still present in some adults to some degree.

In Paragraph C:

> Topic: college
>> Main idea: College is an enjoyable experience for me.
>>> Supporting details: friends, instructors, college activities.

Making an Outline

Once you have identified the main idea and supporting details, you can outline the paragraph or passage. In an outline, the main ideas are the first points written at the left margin and usually have Roman numerals I, II, III, and so on. Supporting details are indented about five spaces and numbered 1, 2, 3, and so on. The specifics or minor details are indented ten spaces and labelled with small letters a, b, c, d, and so on. An outline of a paragraph (or passage) looks like this:

I. (main idea)
   1. (first supporting detail)
      a. (specific about the detail or minor detail)
      b. (another specific example)
   2. (second supporting detail)
      a. (specific about the detail or minor detail)
      b. (another specific example)

When you can pick out the main idea and differentiate between supporting and specific details, an outline is one logical way of showing those relationships.

Find the topic, main idea, and supporting details in the following paragraph.

A yoZung college student is constantly discouraged, irritable, and unable to sleep. Frequent crying spells have ended, but she's still very unhappy. A middle-aged man has become increasingly indecisive in business affairs. He has strong feelings of worthlessness and guilt, and has lost interest in sex. An elderly woman complains of fatigue and lack of appetite. Her weight has been dropping steadily. Three different problems? Not really. These people—and millions like them—suffer from the most common mental ailment in the book: depression. (From Maxine Abram, "Rx for Depression," *TWA Ambassador*, January 1987.)

Topic: _____

Main idea: _____

Three supporting details: _____

_____

_____

The topic is depression, and the main idea comes in the last sentence. Everything up to this point is an example or specific about the main idea.

Here's a blank outline of the paragraph for you to practise your outlining skills. Cover up the answer as you try your hand at outlining.

I.
   1.
      a.
      b.
      c.
      d.
      e.

2.

    a.

    b.

    c.

3.

    a.

    b.

    c.

Does your outline look like the following? If not, analyze where you went wrong and figure out how to do it right the next time. If it does look like this, congratulate yourself on your outlining skills.

I. These people—and millions like them—suffer from the most common mental ailment in the books: depression.

    1. young college student's problems

        a. discouraged

        b. irritable

        c. unable to sleep

        d. frequent crying spells

        e. unhappy

    2. middle-aged man's problems

        a. indecisive

        b. feelings of worthlessness and guilt

        c. lost interest in sex

    3. elderly woman's problems

        a. fatigue

        b. lack of appetite

        c. loss of weight

Now analyze the following paragraph.

> Distractibility is one symptom of Attention Deficit Disorder (ADD) in college students. ADD students are easily sidetracked and jump from topic to topic in conversation. Time management problems are another symptom. Both procrastination and being unrealistic about how long a task will take can be ADD issues. Lack of organization is yet another symptom of ADD. ADD students tend to be messy, have trouble keeping up with several simultaneous projects, and have a difficult time prioritizing. Knowing these and other symptoms of ADD may help a college student gain better self-awareness.

Topic: _____

Main idea: _____

Three supporting details:_____

_____

_____

The topic is ADD and the main idea is the last sentence of the paragraph. The three symptoms are specifics about ADD and include distractibility, time management, and lack of organization. Notice that this paragraph also contains quite a few specifics (or minor details) about the three symptoms.

The next paragraph is more complex and has an implied main idea. See if you can take the skills you've learned so far and apply them to this paragraph from a history textbook.

> During the period 1890-1920, [...] the most rapid urban growth occurred in the West, thanks mainly to large-scale immigration. Winnipeg's population increased to seven times its former size; Vancouver's, twelve times (growing at a rate of 1000 new residents per month in the peak year of 1910); and Calgary's, sixteen times. Of all the major western cities, though, Saskatoon eclipsed the rest in rate of growth, rising from several hundred to nearly 10 000 people in the first decade of the new century. From 1901 to 1911, the Canadian urban population increased 63 percent. In 1901, Canada had only 58 urban centres with a population greater than 5000. By 1911, that number had grown to 90. (From R. D. Francis, R. Jones, and D.B. Smith, *Destinies: Canadian History Since Confederation,* 4th Edition, Harcourt Canada, 2000, p. 141.)

Topic: _____

Main idea (in your own words): _____

_____

_____

Three supporting details: _____

_____

_____

_____

The topic is Canadian population in cities. Note once again that a topic may be a phrase rather than a single word. You need to think about all the details and what they are saying in order to come up with a main idea. It isn't stated anywhere in the paragraph. The main idea: At the end of the 19th century and the beginning of the 20th century, cities in western Canada experienced major population growth. The main examples the historians use are the population growth of Winnipeg, Vancouver, Calgary, and Saskatoon.

Because the authors provide us with dates and statistics, we are able to infer the main idea. Notice that all the dates provided fall between 1890 and 1920, the latter part of the 19th century and the early 20th century. All of the cities (Winnipeg, Vancouver, Calgary and Saskatoon) are examples of fast population growth during these dates. Because of these details we see for ourselves, without the authors telling us, that western Canada's urban population grew very rapidly during this time.

As you can see, sometimes it is easy to figure out an author's main idea and separate it from details, but sometimes we have to be more alert to what is being said. As you work through the following practices, try to become more conscious of how writers express their main points and provide details to support them.

PRACTICE A-1: Recognizing Topics, Main Ideas, and Supporting Details

Directions: Read the following paragraphs and in the appropriate blanks write the topic, the main idea, and the supporting details. Use your own words as much as possible. The first one has been done for you.

Paragraph 1

Many of us impose unnecessary limitations on ourselves. We say, or think, we can't do something without checking. We hold ourselves back when we could move ahead. We assume that certain good occupations are closed to us when they're really not closed at all. We think we're not as good as the next person when, really, we are.

Topic: *limitations*

Main idea: *Many of us limit our potential unnecessarily*

Supporting details:

1. *We say we can't without really knowing*
2. *We hold back*
3. *We think we're not good enough for certain jobs*
4. *We think we're not as good as others*

Paragraph 2

Television was born as an advertising medium. Never questioning how television would be financed, the networks assumed that they would attract commercial support. They were right. Even by 1949, in the United States, television advertisers spent $12.3 million. In 1950, the total was $40.8 million and in 1951, $128 million. In Canada, advertising expenditures on television did not reach $50 million until 1960, largely because of public funding and more stringent standards. In areas near the border, Canadian advertisers bought time on U.S. local stations in Detroit, Niagara Falls, and Buffalo, for example. (From S. Biagi and C. McKie, *Media/Impact,* ITP Nelson, 1999, p. 220.)

Topic: _____

Main idea: _____

Supporting details: _____

_____

_____

_____

_____

Paragraph 3

By the time we are five years old, our parents have influenced us to be affectionate, tender, angry, or hateful. We judge our emotions as either good or bad. We tell ourselves it is good to feel grateful but bad to feel angry or jealous. So we suppress emotions we should release. We get into "value conflicts." Boys and men are not supposed to cry or show fear. So some men attempt to bury their true feelings and create a false self-image. Sometimes we bury or hide our true emotions because we have been programmed to do this.

Topic: _____

Main idea: _____

Supporting details: _____

_____

_____

_____

_____

Paragraph 4

The meanings of words change as their uses change. "Stout" at one time meant "valiant." Today it is used to characterize people who are portly. "Courtesan" once meant "lady at court" and "wench" meant any young girl. "Get off," according to Harper Barnes, "started as a drug term, became a sexual term and ending up meaning, more or less, to have a good time." "Sophomore" no longer means "person with the wisdom of a moron," and "professor" no longer means "person who has taken religious vows." Some words have no contemporary meaning at all, and if they are listed in the dictionary are labelled "archaic" or "obsolete." We usually find the word "prithee," but most dictionaries no longer include such splendid terms from the past as "snollygoster," "poop-noddy," "snodderclout," "bedswerver," and "mubblefubbles." (From Gerald Runkle, *Good Thinking: An Introduction to Logic,* 3rd edition, Holt, Rinehart and Winston, 1991, p. 14.)

Topic: _____

Main idea: _____

Supporting details: _____

_____

_____

_____

_____

Paragraph 5

Most of us are unaware that we use probably only a third of our lung capacity. Our breathing is shallow and occurs about fifteen to seventeen times a minute, taking in about a pint of air each time. Yet our lungs can hold eight times as much air. Therefore, shallow breathing provides only a limited amount of fresh oxygen and doesn't fully expel all the burnt gases, such as carbon dioxide. Despite the central role breathing plays in our lives as organisms, few of us have been taught to breathe. (From Richard Stein, "What Is the Best Form of Exercise?" John Gallagher Communications, p. 1.)

Topic: _____

Main idea: _____

Supporting details: _____

_____

_____

_____

_____

Paragraph 6

Unions benefit their members financially. Research by Canadian economists suggests that, on average, unionized workers earn about 10 percent more than non-union workers do. . . . But unions negotiate for more than wages. Consequently, union members are more than twice as likely to have pension plans provided by their employer. And unionized workers receive more paid vacations and holidays, and are more likely to have dental and medical plans and better job security than comparable non-union workers. Unions also contribute to reducing overall wage inequality in a nation's labour market. This is largely because the union impact on wages is greatest for workers in the lower and middle ranges of the income, education, and skill distributions. In other words, without unions income inequality in Canada would most likely rise. Indeed, in the United States and Britain growing income inequality has been linked, in part, to declining union membership. (From *Work, Industry and Canadian Society,* 4th Edition by Krahn/Lowe, © 2003. Reprinted with permission of Nelson, a division of Thomson Learning: www.thomsonrights.com. Fax 800-730-2215.)

Topic: _____

Main idea: _____

Supporting details: _____

_____

_____

_____

_____

PRACTICE A-2: Separating Main Ideas from Supporting Details

Directions: For each of the paragraphs that follow, circle the topic and underline the main idea sentence. Then, in the space provided, write the major supporting details.

1.   An unrealistically poor self-concept can also arise from the inaccurate feed-back of others. Perhaps you are in an environment where you receive an excessive number of downer messages, many of which are undeserved, and a minimum of upper messages. We've known many housewives, for example, who have returned to college after many years spent in homemaking, where they received virtually no recognition for their intellectual strengths. It's amazing that these women have the courage to come to college at all, so low are their self-concepts; but come they do, and most are thrilled to find that they are much brighter and more competent intellectually than they suspected. In the same way, workers with overly critical

supervisors, children with cruel "friends," and students with unsupportive teachers are all prone to low self-concepts owing to excessively negative feedback. (From Ronald B. Adler and Neil Towne, *Looking Out, Looking In,* 6th edition, Holt, Rinehart and Winston, 1990, p. 69.)

Supporting details: _____

_____

_____

2.   With digital television (DTV), benefits will include spectacular picture quality and better sound. The screen will be wider, so televisions will look quite different than they do today. Better reception is another plus; we'll no longer get poor reception when certain weather patterns hang over our area. Even more impressive will be the wider choices of programs and the interactivity. If the news anchor mentions problems in Malaysia, the viewer can click on Malaysia and find out background information about that country. DTV represents a major revolution in broadcasting technology with the potential to significantly change, for the better, the way televisions are used and viewed.

Supporting details: _____

_____

_____

3.   There is not one of us who is always a teacher or always a learner. In fact, the children often teach us to look at something differently—a story or picture, which they see more clearly than we do. The other day I came upon Tonia and a six-year-old friend sitting in her bedroom reading a simple comic book. He was teaching her what he learned in school—pointing out words, reading sentences, explaining the story. He remembered what he picked up in school and being just a first-grader saw nothing wrong with sharing that knowledge. (From Herbert Kohl, *Reading, How To.*)

Supporting details: _____

_____

_____

4.   According to the latest data from the United Nations Population Division, the birth rate in many countries we still think are baby-booming has fallen very near the replacement level of 2.1 children per woman. Because of a strict family planning policy, China's rate has dropped to 1.8 children per woman. Thailand's rate has fallen to 2.0 due to a family planning program sponsored by the government. For reasons no one can fathom, Brazil's fertility rate has also dropped to 2.1. Perhaps the greatest decline in population has been experienced by Japan, which is now at a mere 1.3 children per woman. (From John Ibbitson, "Lonely Planet," *The Globe and Mail,* March 2, 2002.)

Supporting details: _____

_____

_____

5. Comprehension is the act of understanding or the capacity to understand. It can be divided into three levels: literal, critical, and affective. Literal comprehension, the basic level of understanding, entails the ability to identify main ideas and supporting details, to follow the sequence of events, to recognize cause-effect relationships, to interpret directions, and to perceive organizational patterns in various reading matter. Critical comprehension requires distinguishing opinion from fact, recognizing an author's intent, attitude, and bias, and making critical judgments. Affective comprehension is your intellectual and emotional response to what you read.

Supporting details: _____

_____

_____

6. Several factors explain Upper Canada's initial success in the War of 1812. First, the Americans had a faulty strategy: Canada's key strategic points, in order of importance, were Quebec, Montreal, Kingston, Niagara, and the Detroit River, but the Americans chose to attack east of the Detroit River first, and then to strike at Niagara. . . . Second, Major General Isaac Brock, who had fought in the French wars in Europe, . . . built up the province's fortifications, trained the provincial militia, and maintained good relations with the Native peoples. . . . [Finally,] the Amerindians' military contribution also explains Brock's subsequent success. They assisted the British forces in taking key positions from the Americans, most notable of which was Fort Detroit. A force of some 500 Iroquois warriors also helped to defeat the invading American army in Queenston Heights near Niagara Falls. (From Origins 4E + DESTINIES 4E, 4th Edition by Francis © 2000. Reprinted with permission of Nelson, a division of Thomson Learning: www.thomsonrights.com. Fax 800-730-2215.)

Supporting details: _____

_____

_____

PRACTICE A-3: More on Main Ideas

Directions: Read the following article. At the end of each paragraph, write a one-sentence statement in the blank, stating what you think is the main idea of the paragraph.

Interviewing for a Job

1. One of the most important components of successful job hunting is the job interview. There are thousands of people entering new careers and searching for job placement. In order to give yourself an edge over others applying for the job you want, it is important to create a solid impression during the job interview.

Main idea: _____

_____

2. Because what you say during an interview is so important, there are two rules to remember. One is to present yourself in a favourable way and stress your areas of competence. However, don't exaggerate; tell the truth. Second, listen carefully and get involved in what the interviewer is saying. Notice the interviewer's interests and relate your comments to them.

Main idea: _____

_____

3.   The job interview is the time to "sell" yourself by giving examples of experiences you've had related to the job and by revealing your good points. It's a good idea to have handy your job résumé or a list of school courses that prepared you for the job. Don't exaggerate the truth. Be honest, but show confidence in yourself and your ability to do the job.

Main idea: _____

_____

4.   If you are not certain what the job will require of you, ask questions to see whether you do feel qualified. Do more listening than talking. Don't be afraid to ask for a second interview if you need time to gather information that will be more useful in the second interview. Most interviewers will appreciate your questions and your ability to listen and respond.

Main idea: _____

_____

5.   Some people talk themselves out of a job by saying too much or by digressing. Although it's important to talk about your successful experiences, don't come on too strong and sound like a braggart.

Main idea: _____

_____

6.   Each of us has sensitive areas, and you might anticipate your responses in the event that you are asked about your own. Such questions could refer to your lack of an academic degree, a long period of unemployment, or lack of work experience if you are entering a new field. Answer sensitive questions briefly and positively, because even one negative example can create doubt in the interviewer's mind. If you believe that this area presents a real obstacle to a job offer, you could be communicating this doubt to the interviewer. Many times, however, an interviewer will override these sensitive areas if you have a confident, positive attitude.

Main idea: _____

_____

7.   Making a favourable impression is especially important in light of recent estimates, which show that most hiring is done on an emotional rather than a factual basis. An interviewer who accepts you as a person and is emotionally on your side may consider you favourably for the job—even if you don't fit the pre-established qualifications.

Main idea: _____

_____

8.   The job interview is an important part of the job search because the attitude and impression you project can make the interviewer feel "with you" or "against you." Remember that you have the power to create a favourable impression. Interviewers have the intelligence to recognize genuine enthusiasm and interest.

Main idea: _____

_____

> ### Application I: Finding Main Ideas and Supporting Details
>
> In a textbook for another class, select five paragraphs throughout the text and mark the main idea for each paragraph or write out the implied main idea. List the supporting details for each paragraph. Bring your text to class and be prepared to justify your choices of main ideas with a class study partner.

B.   Reading for Main Ideas: Paragraph Patterns

Another way to distinguish between an author's main ideas and supporting points is to pay attention to the writing patterns used frequently by authors. Authors use a variety of writing patterns to develop their ideas: illustration or example, definition of terms, comparison or contrast, sequence of events, cause and effect, description, or a combination of these. These patterns are called **rhetorical modes.** They are useful for better understanding paragraphs and entire reading passages. If you have taken an English composition course, you may already know the terms. They are frequently used to teach students how to write better. As a reader, your awareness of these patterns can help you more readily identify an author's main idea and supporting details. Let's examine each pattern.

Illustration/Example

One of the most widely used writing patterns is *illustration/example.* In this pattern, the author uses examples to illustrate or support the main idea. Notice in the following example how the topic sentence, the first one, is made clearer and supported by examples:

> It would seem the lesson to be gained from famous love stories is that passionate love and marriage do not mix. For instance, witness the ending to the stories of Antony and Cleopatra, Tristan and Isolde, Lancelot and Guinevere, Dante and Beatrice, and poor Cyrano and Roxanne. Even Romeo and Juliet ran into problems.

All of the names listed in the paragraph are given as examples to illustrate and support the main idea: marriage and passionate love don't seem to go together. Even if you don't know who all the characters listed are, you can infer that they were all passionate lovers who never got married, or if they did, presumably the marriages didn't last. Otherwise, the author wouldn't use them as examples to support the main idea.

A clue to the illustration/example pattern is usually given through what are called *signal words*. Signal words or phrases such as *for instance, for example, to illustrate, such as, much like,* and *similar to* all signal or alert you that examples are about to be given. If what follows is an example, then it can't be the main idea. Instead, it supports a main idea that you need to recognize.

Definition

Another frequently used writing pattern is *definition,* or an attempt to explain what is being discussed through elaborate defining of terms. Here is an example:

> A word generally has two meanings: a denotative meaning and a connotative meaning. The denotative meaning of a word is its most direct or literal meaning as found in the dictionary. What the word suggests or implies beyond its literal definition is its connotative meaning.

The author's main point here is to define the terms denotative and connotative.

Frequently, when authors define a word or term, they also use examples. Notice in the following example how a definition of inference is provided, then an example of how we make inferences is given:

> An inference is a statement or conclusion about the unknown made on the basis of the known. In other words, an inference is an educated guess. If a woman smiles when we see a man whisper something in her ear, we can infer or assume that she is pleased or amused. Because smiles generally mean pleasure and frowns generally mean displeasure, we can infer that she is pleased.

In this example, the definition of inference is given, then an example of how we make inferences is given, thus combining both the definition and illustration/example patterns.

Comparison/Contrast

The *comparison/contrast* writing pattern is also used with some frequency. With this pattern, authors attempt to develop the main point by either comparing or contrasting one thing or idea with another, or by using both. Here's an example of the use of comparison/contrast:

> Crime as presented on television is different from what it is in reality. On television, murder, assault, and armed robbery are the most common crimes. However, in reality, quiet burglaries, clever larcenies, unspectacular auto thefts, and drunkenness are the most common. Video detectives solve 90 percent of their cases. But in reality, the figure is much lower. On TV only 7 percent of violence occurs between relatives. In reality, this accounts for 25 to 30 percent of interpersonal violence.

Notice that what is being contrasted is crime as portrayed on television and what it is like in reality. The author's main idea is that television does not portray crime realistically. To prove this, the author contrasts three points: the most common crimes as portrayed on television with real crime, the difference in the number of cases detectives solve on television and in reality, and the percentage of interpersonal violence on television and in reality.

There are some signal words that alert you to the use of comparison/ contrast. Notice in the example paragraph the use of such words as *different from, however,* and *but.* These signal that a change or contrast will be made. Other signal words you may see that contrast are *more than, yet, opposite, though, less, more, in contrast, even though, on the other hand,* and *on the contrary.*

Words that signal comparison or more of the same are *and, too, also, same, like, similar, in comparison,* and *analogous to.* When you see such words being used, you know that you are being provided with supporting details or information, not the main idea. The main idea will be whatever the comparison or contrast details are supporting.

Sequence of Events

A fourth writing pattern is *sequence of events.* This is a pattern used when directions are given, when there is a certain order to events, or when chronology is important. Sometimes certain key words, such as *first, second,* and *third,* or the numbers themselves are used. Words such as *then, later, finally,* and *thus* also serve as guides to a sequence of events. Notice the sequence of events in the following example:

> An algorithm is a step-by-step procedure for solving a problem in a finite amount of time. When you start your car, you go through a step-by-step procedure. First, you insert the key. Second, you make sure the transmission is in neutral or park. Third, you depress the gas pedal. Fourth, you turn the key to the start position. If the engine starts within a few seconds, you then release the key to the ignition position. If the engine doesn't start, you wait ten seconds and repeat steps three through six. Finally, if the car doesn't start, you call the garage. (From Nell Dale, *Programming in Pascal,* D.C. Heath, 1990, pp. 27–28.)

Notice how the author has related the sequence of events necessary in starting a car. Numbers and words such as *first, second, then,* and *finally* aid the reader. An awareness of this use of words provides a pattern for understanding as you read, as well as a way to remember the information.

Cause and Effect

Still another writing pattern is the use of *cause and effect.* With this pattern, the author attempts to show how one action or a series of actions causes something to happen. For instance, tapping a raw egg on a skillet causes it to crack. In a cause/effect paragraph, the author links what causes an event with the effects it brings. Here is an example of cause/effect relationship in a paragraph:

> One contributing factor in the lower birth rate is that women are choosing to have their children later in life.... For women in their 30s, the birth rate has increased considerably in the past decade; whereas for women between 25 and 29, the increase has been marginal; and for women in their early 20s, it has declined. As a result of these changes, families in Canada are becoming smaller, on average, than they have ever been, and the age gap between parents and their children is growing as families put off having children until later in life. (From G. Ondercin-Bourne, "The Myth of the Traditional Family: Diversity in Canadian Families," *Our Society: Human Diversity in Canada,* Ed. P.U. Angelini, ITP Nelson, 1997, pp. 255–256.)

Notice that the point of the paragraph is that women in Canada are putting off having children (cause). Families in Canada are becoming smaller (effect) and the age gap between parents and their children is growing (effect). Thus, the author of the preceding paragraph sees the two effects of one cause.

Description

The last writing pattern to be discussed here is the use of *description*. Usually the author is attempting to give you a visual picture or a feeling for something. Generally, but not always, there is no topic sentence. Notice this example:

> Amid the black swells of a murderously cold October sea, Frank McCarthy leans straight into the North Atlantic wind, ball cap pointed toward the sky, hazel eyes searching for sunkers. Standing fast against the oncoming weather, he expertly guides the tiller of the small wooden boat he borrowed from a neighbour. She's cracked and chipped, stripped of both paint and, until Frank was in need of her, usefulness. She's just good enough to be out on the water, nothing more. Despite the forbidding weather we pass several other small boats—local fishermen jigging for cod. They pull their lines with ease, and given the customs of Newfoundland outport life, I assume we'll pull up alongside for a bit of gossip. When we wave a welcome, however, the men look up sharply and speed off in the opposite direction. With a resigned shrug, Frank explains that they don't know me; after all, I could be an undercover fisheries officer. (From *A Passion for Identity: Canadian Studies for the 21st Century*, 4th Edition by Teras/Rasporich, © 2001. Reprinted with permission of Nelson, a division of Thomson Learning: www.thomsonrights.com. Fax 800-730-2215.)

As you can see, there is no topic sentence. The whole paragraph is a description of riding in a small boat off the coast of Newfoundland.

Your ability to understand what you read can be enhanced by an awareness of these writing patterns. The patterns are important because an awareness of how an author presents information can aid comprehension. To help you develop this ability, the next practices provide you with opportunities to work on identifying writing patterns.

As you progress through this section, keep in mind the fourth objective listed in the introduction to this unit. You should be able to identify the following writing patterns: illustration/example, definition, cause and effect, comparison/contrast, description, and sequence of events.

PRACTICE B-1: Finding Main Ideas through Paragraph Patterns

Directions: For each of the following paragraphs, write what you think are the main idea and key supporting details. As organizational patterns get more complex, main ideas are often implied. Then, identify which of the organizational patterns listed below best describes the paragraph.

a. illustration/example   e. cause/effect

b. definition   f. description

c. comparison/contrast   g. combination (include the letters of the patterns)

d. sequence of events

Write the letter of the correct pattern in the blank before the paragraph.

_____ **1.**   Stress is a normal and inevitable part of life. Virtually any change that we experience causes stress. Exercising, going on vacation, and even getting up in the morning are all examples of stressors that require us to respond in some way. Student life is full of stressors. These include writing exams, presenting seminars, doing assignments, and attending classes. Other stressors may include changing schools, deciding on a career, and balancing academic expectations with family, work, and social demands. In itself, stress is neither good nor bad. How we respond to stress, however, determines whether it has a positive or negative effect on our lives. (From J. Fleet and D. Reaume, _Power Over Time: Student Success with Time Management,_ Harcourt Brace Canada, 1994, p. 74.)

Main idea: _____

_____

Supporting details: _____

_____

_____

_____   _____

_____ **2.**   The perfectionist is motivated to do an exceptional job on every academic task. This type of student works very hard and tries to complete all of the assigned work without any short cuts at all. While conscientiousness and diligence can be strengths, perfectionism becomes a weakness when a student is not very strategic or [aware of cues]. The student is inefficient because he or she believes that everything is equally important and requires a lot of work. It is important to prioritize tasks and make time-saving decisions, especially during busy times of the school year. (From J. Fleet and D. Reaume, _Power Over Time: Student Success with Time Management,_ Harcourt Brace Canada, 1994, p. 54.)

Main idea: _____

_____

Supporting details: _____

_____

_____

_____

_____ **3.**   Here is a four-step method to prevent your mind from wandering while reading. First, before you attempt to read anything, look over the length of the material to see whether you have time to read it all; if not, mark a spot where you intend to stop. Second, read the title and the first paragraph, looking for the main idea of the article. Next, read the boldface headings, if there are any, and the first sentence of each paragraph. Finally, read the last paragraph, which probably contains a summary of the material. These steps condition your mind to accept the material you want to read and keep it from wandering.

Main idea: _____

_____

Supporting details: _____

_____

_____

_____

_____

_____ **4.**   Irony is a figure of speech whereby the writer or speaker says the opposite of what is meant; for the irony to be successful, however, the audience must understand the writer's true intent. For example, if you have slopped to school in a rainstorm and your drenched teacher enters the classroom saying, "Ah, nothing like this beautiful sunny weather," you know that your teacher is being ironic. Perhaps one of the most famous cases of irony occurred in 1938, when Sigmund Freud, the famous Viennese psychiatrist, was arrested by the Nazis. After being harassed by the Gestapo, he was released on the condition that he sign a statement swearing he had been treated well by the secret police. Freud signed it, but he added a few words after his signature: "I can heartily recommend the Gestapo to anyone." Looking back, we easily recognize Freud's jab at his captors; the Gestapo, however, apparently overlooked the irony and let him go. (From Jean Wyrick, *Steps to Writing Well*, 3rd edition, Holt, Rinehart and Winston, 1987, p. 112.)

Main idea: _____

_____

Supporting details: _____

_____

_____

_____

_____

_____ **5.**   Physical objects and their positioning within the sphere of communication also influence . . . behaviour patterns. How we react to physical objects in social situations indicates our willingness to communicate with others as well as the level at which we wish to communicate. In an airport lounge or bus terminal, people will rarely choose to sit right next to one another unless all the other seats are taken. Even people arriving early at a meeting will rarely choose the seat next to the one reserved for the Chairperson. On the other hand, those on intimate terms will often choose to sit beside one another. (From A. Lieb, *Speaking for Success*, Harcourt Brace Canada, 1993, p. 27.)

Main idea: _____

_____

Supporting details: _____

_____

_____

_____

_____

_____   **6.**   The forced separation of children from their families and communities, combined with the harsh policies and practices of the residential school, have contributed to disrupting Aboriginal families. Children were socialized in an environment devoid of any of the nurturing that parents provide. Students of different sexes were almost always separated in residential schools, and siblings in the same school often could not even speak to each other for months and years on end. As a result, many former students have reported they lack not only the confidence and ability to parent, but also interpersonal relationship skills. (From J. Hare and J. Barman, "Aboriginal Education: Is There a Way Ahead?" _Visions of the Heart: Canadian Aboriginal Issues,_ Ed. D. Long and O.P. Dickason, Harcourt Canada, 2000, p. 342.)

Main idea: _____

_____

Supporting details: _____

_____

_____

_____

_____

_____   **7.**   The patients wandered aimlessly about, mumbling incoherently. Violent ones were wrapped in wet sheets with their arms pinned, or they wore strait-jackets. Attendants, in danger of assault, peered at their charges through screens. The floor lay bare, because rugs would have quickly been soiled with excrement. The large mental institution of thirty years ago was a madhouse.

Main idea: _____

_____

Supporting details: _____

_____

_____

_____

_____

_____   **8.**   [T]elevision news is by definition highly subjective. Some of the most effective editorializing in that medium is accomplished visually, even when script and structure appear to be even-handed. For example, a report on a local CBC station in Windsor, Ontario, appeared to give equal treatment to both sides of a dispute between municipal officials and a rejected applicant for a job in the fire department. The applicant had failed to meet standards for eyesight that he regarded as unrealistic. Both sides were interviewed on camera, but the municipal official was videotaped looking up at the camera—a technique known to produce an impression of weakness and subservience. An ophthalmologist who supported the applicant was interviewed . . . looking straight at the camera. This produced an unmistakable impression of authority. The reporter was quite clearly on the side of individual underdog fighting the system. . . . The net effect was far more powerful than any newspaper editorial could have been in raising questions about the validity of the fire department's entrance requirements. (From _Guide to Canadian News Media,_ 2nd Edition by Desbarats © 1996. Reprinted with permission of Nelson, a division of Thomson Learning: www.thomsonrights.com. Fax 800-730-2215.)

Main idea: _____

_____

Supporting details: _____

_____

_____

_____

_____

_____ **9.**   There are basically two different types of purchasers who respond to advertising. One type rushes out to buy 50 percent of all the products they see advertised. Such buyers help make advertising a highly successful, multibillion-dollar-a-year industry. People of the second type think they are immune to ads; they think most ads are silly, stupid, and "beneath their dignity." This type of purchaser believes ads are aimed at the "suckers" of the first type. Yet 90 percent of the nation's adults who believe themselves immune are responsible for about 90 percent of all purchases of advertised products.

Main idea: _____

_____

Supporting details: _____

_____

_____

_____

_____

_____ **10.**   Television is addictive. For example, when a set breaks, most families rush to have it repaired, often renting one if the repair process takes longer than a day or two. When "nothing's on TV," people experience boredom with their lives, not knowing what to do with themselves. Perhaps the best example of television addiction was an experiment in Germany where 184 volunteers were paid to go without television for a year. At first, most volunteers did well, reporting that they were spending more time with their children, reading, and visiting friends. Then, within a month, tension, restlessness, and quarrelling increased. Not one volunteer lasted more than five months without a television set. Once the sets were on again, people lost their anxieties and returned to normal.

Main idea: _____

_____

Supporting details: _____

_____

_____

_____

_____

> ### Application 2: Finding Paragraph Patterns
>
> In a textbook for another class, find an example of at least five different paragraph patterns. Label each one, put a line in the margin by the main idea sentence or sentences, and number the supporting details. Bring your paragraphs to class and be prepared to explain your paragraph patterns to a class study partner.

PRACTICE B-2: Main Ideas in Longer Passages

Directions: The following reading passages are longer than the ones in the previous drills. Read them and answer the questions that follow. Use what you have learned about main ideas, supporting details, and paragraph patterns.

Passage A

The two most popular aerobic exercises are jogging and swimming. The latter is more enthusiastically recommended because it avoids the trauma to the legs and spine of jogging and utilizes the arms and chest muscles as well as the legs. It is done with the help, or buoyancy, of water. The gravitational force on your joints is not nearly so great as when standing out of water. Your weight in the water (with only your head and neck exposed) is only one-tenth what it is out of water.

Since the water, and not your body, bears much of your weight, swimming is an excellent exercise for those suffering with arthritis. At the same time the buoyancy also spares your knees, ankles, and lower back from the constant pounding associated with jogging. In fact, swimming is often prescribed for people who have suffered joint injuries from other sports or exercise activities. It strengthens the muscles of your abdomen and has been prescribed as the one exercise program for those with chronic back problems. (From Richard Stein, "What Is the Best Form of Exercise?" John Gallagher Communications.)

1. Which statement best describes the main idea of the passage?

   a. The two most popular aerobic exercises are jogging and swimming.

   b. Jogging is better than swimming.

   c. Swimming is more popular than jogging.

   d. Swimming is recommended over jogging.

2. The writing pattern most used in this passage is

   a. definition   c. cause/effect

   b. comparison/contrast   d. both b and c

3. In the space provided, list some of the details given to support your answer to question 1. _____

   _____

   _____

   _____

   _____

Passage B

A number of factors affected the socialization of the baby-boom generation. First, the country was in boom times, and the general affluence led people to expect that life would be easy. Second, there was a mushrooming of technology. Third, institutions were weakened, and a loss of respect for authority resulted. Fourth, parents made Dr. Spock's *Baby and Child Care* a bestseller. His advice was for a much more permissive kind of care than that recommended in earlier years. . . . Some parents, however, took his advice to the extreme, and provided very little structure for their children. Fifth, the effect of being born into a large family meant that more of the process of socialization was carried on by children, and that teamwork and social skills were emphasized. These children also experienced more family instability because of an increasing number of broken marriages. Sixth, this is the first generation that never knew what it was like to live without television. Seventh, the period after the Second World War saw a swift migration from farm to town, and from town to city. Small towns tend to set and enforce standards more than cities do, but are also much more supportive to families. Finally, advances in medicine meant a rapid drop in infant and child mortality and a reduction of physical suffering. (From *The Family Dynamic: A Canadian Perspective*, 3rd Edition by Ward, © 2002. Reprinted with permission of Nelson, a division of Thomson Learning: www.thomsonrights.com. Fax 800-730-2215.)

1. Which is the basic pattern used in the above passage?

   a. illustration/example   **c.** cause/effect

   b. definition   **d.** comparison/contrast

2. Explain why you selected the writing pattern you circled.

   _____

   _____

3. The family was an institution undergoing change during the era of the baby-boomers' childhood. What were the two conditions mentioned in the passage relating to the family structure of the typical baby-boomer?

   _____

   _____

   _____

4. Which sentence best reflects the main idea of this passage?

   _____

   _____

   _____

Passage C

I am of the opinion that true Elders are superb embodiments of highly developed human potential. They exemplify the kind of person that a traditional, culturally based learning environment can and does form and mould. Elders also are evidence that Natives know a way to high human development, to a degree greater than generally suspected. Their qualities of mind (intuition, intellect, memory, imagination) and emotion, their profound and refined moral sense manifest in an exquisite sense of humour, in a sense of caring and communication finesse in teaching and counselling, together with a high level of spiritual and psychic attainment, are perceived as clear behavioural indicators deserving careful attention, if not compelling emulation. (From J.E. Couture, "The Role of Native Elders: Emergent Issues," in *Visions of the Heart: Canadian Aboriginal Issues,* Harcourt Canada, 2000, p. 38.)

1. What writing pattern is used in this passage?

a. comparison/contrast   **c.** description

b. definition   **d.** sequence of events

2. Which sentence in this passage displays a cause and effect relationship?

_____

_____

3. State in your own words what the main idea of this paragraph is.

_____

_____

Passage D

1   [N]onverbal communication is similar to verbal communication in expressing cultural values. Like verbal communication, nonverbal patterns reflect the values, perspectives, and heritage of specific cultures. This implies that the majority of nonverbal actions are not instinctive but are learned as we are socialized in particular cultures. . . . In addition to diversity among groups within our country, nonverbal behaviours vary from one country to another. As you might expect, dissimilarities reflect cultural values.

2   Have you ever seen the bumper sticker "If you can read this, you're too close"? That slogan proclaims North Americans' fierce territoriality. We prize private space, and we resent, and sometimes fight, anyone who trespasses on what we consider our turf. . . . The German culture also emphasizes private space. Germans routinely build walls and hedges to insulate themselves from neighbours. In cultures where individuality is not such a pronounced value, people are less territorial. For instance, Brazilians tend to stand close in shops, buses, and elevators, and when they bump into one another they don't apologize or draw back. In many middle Eastern countries, men often walk with their arms around other men, but in Canada touch between male friends is less common.

3   Norms for touching also reflect cultural values. In one study, North Americans, who are relatively reserved, were observed engaging in an average of only two touches an hour. The emotionally restrained British averaged zero touches per hour. Parisians, long known for their emotional expressiveness, touched 110 times per hour. Puerto Ricans touched the most, averaging 180 touches an hour.

4   Patterns of eye contact also reflect cultural values. In North America, frankness and assertion are valued, so meeting another's eyes is considered appropriate and a demonstration of personal honesty. Yet in many Asian and northern European countries, direct eye contact is considered abrasive and disrespectful. In Brazil, eye contact

is often so intense that people from North America consider it rude. Imagine the confusion this causes in intercultural business negotiations.

5   Cultural training also influences how we express emotions and which emotions we express. In some ethnic groups dramatic emotional displays are typical. For example, many people raised in Italian and Jewish communities are more emotionally expressive than people raised in English or German communities. In Japan and many other Asian cultures it is considered rude to express negative feelings toward others. Thus, the Japanese may not show dislike, disrespect, or irritation, even if they feel those emotions. In most of Canada, there is less constraint on displaying negative emotions.

6   Cultures also differ in their orientations toward time. [One anthropologist] distinguished between cultures that have monochronic and polychronic orientations. Monochronic (one time) cultures, such as non-aboriginal Canada, view time as a valuable commodity to be saved, scheduled, and carefully guarded. Within monochromic cultures, punctuality and efficiency are valued. Thus, people are expected to be on time for appointments, and classes, and they are expected to complete work quickly. In contrast, polychronic (many times) cultures take a more holistic systemic view of time. Members of these cultures assume that many things are happening simultaneously. Thus, punctuality is seldom stressed. Meetings may start late, with people joining in after discussions begin. Tangential discussions and social conversations are part of normal meetings in polychronic cultures. People may even cancel meetings without the dramatic reasons required for politeness in monochronic cultures. The belief that time is holistic leads members of polychronic cultures to assume that the rhythms of life—working, socializing, attending to personal matters—are interrelated. This becomes especially important for teachers to remember when First Nations children do not conform to time constraints.

1. What is the main idea of paragraph 2?

_____

2. What pattern is used in paragraph 5 and for what purpose?

_____

_____

3. What is being contrasted in paragraph 6?

_____

_____

4. The topic of this passage is nonverbal communication. What is the main point being made?

_____

_____

C.   Finding an Author's Thesis

Now is the time to put together all the skills you have learned and practiced in paragraphs. When you are reading essays or articles, you will need to follow many of the same steps used in reading individual paragraphs to increase your comprehension, but note that they often have slightly different terminology.

- *The thesis is different from the subject.* Every article or essay has a topic, or subject. The topic or subject is what the author is writing about, such as computers, good manners, horse racing, war, a country, and the like. A thesis is not the same as the topic or subject. A thesis is what the author wants to say about the subject or it is the author's feelings about the subject.

- *The thesis is the author's main point about the subject.* It is what the author wants the reader to accept or think about. In an essay about grades and their value (the subject), the author may be in favour of grades or against them. The author may be presenting a new concept about grading that he or she wants the reader to accept.

- *The thesis may be placed near the beginning or near the end.* If an author wants to announce her main idea about the subject, she will place the thesis near the beginning. If an author wants to lead up to his main idea, he will present details first and state the main point near the end of the essay or article.

Find the thesis in the same way you look for topics and main ideas in paragraphs. First, read through the article quickly to discover the subject or topic. Then, use headings or subheadings to get the big picture about what the author is saying about this subject. Now, look through the article for the most general statement about that topic. Don't forget that main ideas may be implied.

Finding the subject and thesis of an article is central to understanding the article. Poor readers often get bogged down in details and then have no idea what the article is about. Make this search for the author's subject and thesis the first priority of your reading.

The next two practices will help you recognize an author's thesis.

PRACTICE C-1

Directions: In the following essay, the subject is record companies. As you read the essay, look for the authors' thesis and the major details used to develop the thesis.

WORKING IN THE RECORDING INDUSTRY

SHIRLEY BIAGI AND CRAIG MCKIE

1   Recordings, like books, are supported primarily by direct purchases. But a recording company involves five separate levels of responsibility before the public hears a sound: artists and repertoire, operations, marketing and promotion, distribution, and administration.

2   *Artists and repertoire*, or A&R, functions like an editorial department in book publishing to develop and co-ordinate talent. Employees of this division are the true talent scouts.

3   *Operations* manages the technical aspects of the recording, overseeing the sound technicians, musicians, even the people who copy the discs. This work centres on creating the master recording, from which all other recordings are made. Before stereophonic recording was developed in 1956, a recording session meant gathering

From Shirley Biagi and Craig McKie, *Media/Impact: An Introduction to Mass Media*, First Canadian Edition, © 1999. Reprinted with permission of Nelson, a division of Thomson Learning: www.thomsonrights.com. Fax 800-730-2215.

4   all the musicians in one room, setting up a group of microphones, and recording a song in one take. Today, artists on the same song-vocals, drums, bass, horns, guitars-are recorded individually, and then the separate performances are mixed for the best sound.

4   The *producer*, who works within the operations group, can be on the staff of a recording company or may be an independent freelancer. Producers co-ordinate the artist with the music, the arrangement, and the engineers.

5   *Marketing and promotion* decides the best way to sell the record. These employees oversee the cover design and the copy on the cover (jacket or sleeve). They also organize giveaways to retailers and to reviewers to find an audience for their product. Marketing and promotion might decide that the artist should tour or that the record needs a music video to succeed. Recording companies often use promoters to help guarantee radio play for their artists.

6   *Distribution* gets the record into the stores. There are two kinds of distributors: independents and branches. Independents contract separately with different companies to deliver their recordings. But independents, usually responsible for discovering a record that is outside of the mainstream, are disappearing as the big studios handle distribution through their own companies, called *branches*. Because branches are connected with the major companies, they typically can offer the retailer better discounts.

7   *Administration*, as in all industries, handles the bills. Accounting tracks sales and royalties. Legal departments handle wrangles over contracts.

8   All of these steps are important in the creation of a recording, but if no one hears the recording, no one will buy it. This makes record promotion particularly important.

9   A new type of promotional partnership between a recording company and a television show was introduced in 1992. Giant Records, which produced the soundtrack for the television program *Beverly Hills, 90210*, ran videoclips from the album during the closing credits of the 1992–1993 season of the television show. After the first video—"Saving Forever for You," featuring 90210 star Brian Austin Green—played during the closing credits of a November episode, the song reached number 8 on the Billboard Hot 100 Singles Chart in two weeks.

Directions: Answer the following questions. To answer some questions, you will need to reread portions of the article.

1. The main idea of this selection is

    a. a recording company is interested in developing new talent

    b. a record company is dominated by a small group of executives

    c. a record company is comprised of one or two divisions the operate independently of each other

    d. a record company involves no fewer than five separate levels of responsibility before the public hears a sound.

    e. none of the above

2. Paragraph 3 contains many details about what is involved in the operations level of a record company. What two things are contrasted in this paragraph?

    _____

    _____

3. List at least three other departments in a record company.

_____

_____

_____

4. The final two paragraphs in the selection develop the idea that the following department in a record company is particularly important:

   a. operations   **d.** administration

   b. distribution   **e.** all of the above

   c. marketing and promotions

5. T/F According to the authors, the A&R department functions like "an editorial department in book publishing to develop and co-ordinate talent."

6. What three departments in a record company are not dealt with at any great length? Why do you think the authors have spent so little time on them?

_____

_____

_____

7. T/F The distribution department decides whether an artist should tour or that the record needs a music video to succeed.

Let's look at the questions and your answers to make certain you have put to use what you learned in previous practices. Finding the thesis in a reading selection, such as the one you just read, is similar to finding the main idea in paragraphs. The difference is that in a longer selection paragraphs are used to support the thesis, just as sentences are used in paragraphs to support the topic sentence.

The best answer for the first question is d. Italicized words in the paragraphs support this answer.

To answer the second question, you should have noticed that the paragraph contrasts the way recordings were done prior to 1956 with the way they are done today.

To answer the third question you have to look at the italicized words at the beginning of each paragraph again and say something like this: Three other departments in a record company include artists and repertoire, marketing and promotions, and distribution.

The best answer to question 4 is c; the final two paragraphs support the idea that the marketing and promotions department is the most important.

The answer to question 5 is True. The answer is found in paragraph 2 of the selection.

For question 6, the answer is administration, accounting, and legal. The authors probably did not discuss the role of these departments because they are not unique to the recording industry. Most large companies have administration, accounting, and legal departments, and therefore they do not need to be discussed at great length. Remember, the point of this selection is to highlight the unique characteristics of a record company.

If you answered False to question 7, you are correct. It is the role of the marketing and promotions department to decide whether or not an artist goes on tour or a record needs a music video to succeed.

PRACTICE C-2

Directions: Follow the same directions as for the last practice: read carefully, looking for the subject, the thesis, and the supporting details in the essay. If you had any problems with the last practice, make certain you understand your mistakes before going on.

ANCESTORS—THE GENETIC SOURCE

DAVID SUZUKI

1   My genes can be traced in a direct line to Japan. I am a pure-blooded member of the Japanese race. And whenever I go there, I am always astonished to see the power of that biological connection. In subways in Tokyo, I catch familiar glimpses of the eyes, hairline or smile of my Japanese relatives. Yet when those same people open their mouths to communicate, the vast cultural gulf that separates them from me becomes obvious: English is my language, Shakespeare is my literature, British history is what I learned and Beethoven is my music.

2   For those who believe that in people, just as in animals, genes are the primary determinant of behaviour, a look at second- and third-generation immigrants to Canada gives powerful evidence to the contrary. The overriding influence is environmental. We make a great mistake by associating the inheritance of physical characteristics with far more complex traits of human personality and behaviour.

3   Each time I visit Japan, I am reminded of how Canadian I am and how little the racial connection matters. I first visited Japan in 1968 to attend the International Congress of Genetics in Tokyo. For the first time in my life, I was surrounded by people who all looked like me. While sitting in a train and looking at the reflections in the window, I found that it was hard to pick out my own image in the crowd. I had grown up in a Caucasian society in which I was a minority member. My whole sense of self had developed with that perspective of looking different. All my life I had wanted large eyes and brown hair so I could be like everyone else. Yet on that train, where I did fit in, I didn't like it.

4   On this first visit to Japan I had asked my grandparents to contact relatives and let them know I was coming. I was the first in the Suzuki clan in Canada to visit them. The closest relative on my father's side was my grandmother's younger brother, and we arranged to meet in a seaside resort near his home. He came to my hotel room with two of his daughters. None of them spoke any English, while my Japanese was so primitive as to be useless. In typical Japanese fashion, they showered me with gifts, the most important being a package of what looked like wood carved in the shape of bananas! I had no idea what it was. (Later I learned the package contained dried tuna fish from which slivers are shaved off to flavour soup. This is considered a highly prized gift.) We sat in stiff silence and embarrassment, each of us struggling to dredge up a common word or two to break the quiet. It was excruciating! My great uncle later wrote my grandmother to tell her how painful it had been to sit with her grandson and yet be unable to communicate a word.

5   To people in Japan, all non-Japanese—black, white, or yellow—are *gaijin* or foreigners. While *gaijin* is not derogatory, I find that its use is harsh because I sense doors clanging shut on me when I'm called one. The Japanese do have a hell of a time with

me because I look like them and can say in perfect Japanese, "I'm a foreigner and I can't speak Japanese." Their reactions are usually complete incomprehension followed by a sputtering, "What do you mean? You're speaking Japanese." And finally a pejorative, "Oh, a *gaijin!*"

6   Once when my wife, Tara, who is English, and I went to Japan we asked a man at the travel bureau at the airport to book a *ryokan*-a traditional Japanese inn-for us in Tokyo. He found one and booked it for "*Suzuki-san*" and off we went. When we arrived at the inn and I entered the foyer, the owner was confused by my terrible Japanese. When Tara entered, the shock was obvious in his face. Because of my name, they had expected a "real" Japanese. Instead, I was a *gaijin* and the owner told us he wouldn't take us. I was furious and we stomped off to a phone booth where I called the agent at the airport. He was astonished and came all the way into town to plead our case with the innkeeper. But the innkeeper stood firm and denied us a room. Apparently he had accepted *gaijin* in the past with terrible consequences.

7   As an example of the problem, Japanese always take their shoes off when entering a *ryokan* because the straw mats (*tatami*) are quickly frayed. To a Japanese, clomping into a room with shoes on would be comparable to someone entering our homes and spitting on the floor. Similarly, the *ofuro*, or traditional tub, has hot clean water that all bathers use. So one must first enter the bathroom, wash carefully and rinse off *before* entering the tub. Time in the *ofuro* is for relaxing and soaking. Again, Westerners who lather up in the tub are committing a terrible desecration.

8   To many Canadians today, the word "Jap" seems like a natural abbreviation for Japanese. Certainly for newspaper headlines it would seem to make sense. So people are often shocked to see me bristle when they have used the word Jap innocently. To Japanese-Canadians, Jap or Nip (from "*Nippon*") were epithets used generously during the pre-war and war years. They conjure up all of the hatred and bigotry of those times. While a person using the term today may be unaware of its past use, every Japanese-Canadian remembers.

9   The thin thread of Japanese culture that does link me to Japan was spun out of the poverty and desperation of my ancestors. My grandparents came to a Canadian province openly hostile to their strange appearance and different ways. There were severe restrictions on how much and where they could buy property. Their children, who were born and raised in Canada, couldn't vote until 1948 and encountered many barriers to professional training and property ownership. Asians, regardless of birthplace, were third-class citizens. That is the reality of the Japanese-Canadian experience and the historical cultural legacy that came down to the third and fourth generations—to me and my children.

10   The first Japanese immigrants came to Canada to make their fortunes so they could return to Japan as people of wealth. The vast majority was uneducated and impoverished. But in the century spanning my grandparents' births and the present, Japan has leapt from an agrarian society to a technological and economic giant.

11   Now, the Japanese I meet in Japan or as recent immigrants to Canada come with far different cultural roots. Present-day Japanese are highly educated, upper-middle class and proud of their heritage. In Canada they encounter respect, envy and curiosity in sharp contrast to the hostility and bigotry met by my grandparents.

12   Japanese immigrants to North America have names that signify the number of generations in the new land (or just as significantly, that count the generational distance *away* from Japan). My grandparents are *Issei*, meaning the first generation in Canada. Most Issei never learned more than a rudimentary knowledge of English. *Nisei*, like my parents, are the second generation here and the first native-born group. While growing up they first spoke Japanese in the home and then learned English

from playmates and teachers. Before the Second World War, many *Issei* sent their children to be educated in Japan. When they returned to Canada, they were called *Kika-nisei* (or *Kibei* in the United States). Most have remained bilingual, but many of the younger *Nisei* now speak Japanese with difficulty because English is their native tongue. My sisters and I are Sansei (third generation); our children are Yonsei. These generations, and especially Yonsei, are growing up in homes where English is the only spoken language, so they are far more likely to speak school-taught French as their second language than Japanese.

13   Most *Sansei*, like me, do not speak Japanese. To us, the Issei are mysteries. They came from a cultural tradition that is a hundred years old. Unlike people in present-day Japan, the Issei clung tightly to the culture they remembered and froze that culture into a static museum piece like a relic of the past. Not being able to speak each other's language, Issei and Sansei were cut off from each other. My parents dutifully visited my grandparents and we children would be trotted out to be lectured at or displayed. These visits were excruciating, because we children didn't understand the old culture, and didn't have the slightest interest—we were Canadians.

14   My father's mother died in 1978 at the age of ninety-one. She was the last of the Issei in our family. The final months of her life, after a left-hemisphere stroke, were spent in that terrible twilight—crippled, still aware, but unable to communicate. She lived the terminal months of her life, comprehending but mute, in a ward with Caucasian strangers. For over thirty years I had listened to her psychologically blackmailing my father by warning him of her imminent death. Yet in the end, she hung on long after there was reason to. When she died, I was astonished at my own reaction, a great sense of sadness and regret at the cleavage of my last link with the source of my genes. I had never been able to ask what made her and others of her generation come to Canada, what they felt when they arrived, what their hopes and dreams had been, and whether it was worth it. And I wanted to thank her, to show her that I was grateful that, through them, I was born a Canadian.

Directions: Now answer the following questions. You may need to reread portions of the essay, especially when certain paragraphs are referred to.

1. Which of the following best states the main idea of the essay?

    a. People born in Canada need to retrace their ancestral roots.

    b. Japanese immigrants have suffered in Canada because of their race.

    c. People should stay in touch with relatives.

    d. Genes do not necessarily ensure that generations will behave alike.

    e. None of the above.

2. In paragraph 3, what does the author say about his visits to Japan?

    _____

    _____

3. T/F We can infer from this essay that David Suzuki regrets that his family emigrated to Canada.

4. List the ways in which Japanese-Canadians have been discriminated against.

    _____

    _____

5. According to Suzuki, how are the following terms defined: *gaijin, ofuro, Sansei.*

_____

_____

6. Give an example of how people in Japan have discriminated against Suzuki.

_____

_____

D.   Summarizing as a Way to Test Your Understanding

Now that you have some practice identifying main ideas and supporting details, recognizing basic patterns, and finding the thesis of longer articles, you have the skills to put all these together by learning how to summarize. You will need to use all the skills you've learned in this chapter in order to write a summary.

Frequently, instructors in your college classes will ask you to write summaries of reading assignments. In addition, many essay exams you will be required to take are really nothing more than a test of your ability to write summaries in answer to questions based on sections from your textbooks. What, then, *is* a summary, and how do you write one?

A summary is a brief statement in your own words of the main ideas and support used in a reading selection. Writing summaries requires that you include only the most vital information presented in a piece of writing. The practices you have been doing that require you to separate the main ideas from details provide the basis for writing summaries.

There are three basic things to keep in mind when you write a summary: be brief, be complete, and be objective. This may sound easier than it is. If you are too brief, you may not be complete; if you try to be too complete, you may write too much; if you're not careful, you may slip into subjectivity, allowing your own feelings and opinions to creep in. A summary has no place for your views. As a guideline, a good rule of thumb in writing summaries is to make them no longer than one quarter of the length of the passage you are summarizing. But this may vary depending on the instructor's summary assignment.

Let's say you are asked to summarize the essay you just read in Practice C-2, "Ancestors—The Genetic Source." The best way to get started is to begin with the author's thesis, which is reflected in his title. Suzuki believes that although ancestors pass on many physical characteristics to their progeny, they do not pass on behaviour. Why does Suzuki believe this? What does he want us to do with this information?

As we look over the essay paragraph by paragraph, we see that the first paragraph sets up his discussion. The second paragraph contains his thesis.

The next four paragraphs discuss Suzuki's encounters with Japanese people while visiting Japan. Paragraph 8 recounts the derogatory phrases that have been applied to Japanese-Canadians.

Paragraphs 9 to 13 trace, albeit briefly, the various immigrant experiences of the Japanese-Canadians.

The last paragraph ends with the death of Suzuki's grandmother, and his regret at not being able to communicate to her his gratitude that she came to Canada.

As we move through the paragraphs, we can list how the author proves his thesis.

1. Although Suzuki shares many genes with the Japanese race, a cultural gap separates him from those who live in Japan.

2. Environmental influence plays a stronger role than genes in determining behaviour.

3. When Suzuki visits Japan, even though he looks Japanese, he realizes he has little in common with those who live there.

4. Many Japanese cannot comprehend Suzuki's inability to communicate with them: they assume that because he looks Japanese he should be able to speak Japanese.

5. In fact, Suzuki and his wife have even been discriminated against in Japan. When Suzuki asked a man at the travel bureau to book a room at an inn, the innkeeper assumed that Suzuki was from Japan because of his last name. When Suzuki and his wife arrived at the inn, he wouldn't let Suzuki and his wife stay there because he realized that they were *gaijin* (or foreigners).

6. There are many cultural traditions that Canadians of Japanese descent do not share with those who still live in Japan.

7. The legacy of racism in Canada is still felt by Suzuki and others of his generation.

8. There are still some ties that link Suzuki to Japan; in particular, the history of poverty and desperation that his ancestors experienced.

9. There is a big difference between those first uneducated and impoverished immigrants who came to Canada looking to make a fortune and those who come now, who are already educated and better off financially.

10. Each generation born since the ancestors left Japan is given a different name to symbolize the generational distance from Japan. These generations are all very different from each other in the way that they adapted to their new country.

11. When Suzuki's grandmother died, he regretted not closing the cultural gap that existed between them. He wished that he could thank her for enabling him to be a Canadian.

Now, if we put all this together, we might have a summary that reads something like this:

> In his essay, "Ancestors—The Genetic Source," David Suzuki asserts that although he shares many genes with the Japanese race, there is a cultural gap that exists between him and those who live in Japan. He believes that environmental influence plays a stronger role than genes in determining behaviour.
>
> He uses his experiences in Japan to prove his point. When Suzuki visits Japan, even though he looks Japanese, he realizes he has little in common with those who live there. For example, many Japanese cannot comprehend Suzuki's inability to communicate with them: they assume that because he looks Japanese, he should be able to speak Japanese. In fact, Suzuki and his wife were even discriminated against while in Japan. Suzuki points out that there are many cultural traditions that Canadians of Japanese descent do not share with those who still live in Japan. He contends, though, that there are still some ties that link him to Japan; in particular, the history of poverty and desperation that his ancestors experienced when they immigrated to Canada. Each

generation born since the ancestors left Japan is given a different name to symbolize the generational distance from Japan. These generations are all very dissimilar in the way that they adapted to their new country. Suzuki notes that there is a big difference between those first uneducated and impoverished immigrants who came to Canada looking to make a fortune and those who come now, who are already educated and better off financially. Suzuki concludes on a note of regret that he had not better understood the immigrant generation, and says he is thankful to be Canadian.

As you can see by the summary, some of the details have been left out. Be sure to include only those main points in the essay that support the thesis. Note that the summary starts by identifying the article and the author, followed by Suzuki's subject and thesis. When writing a summary, you should write as much as possible in your own words (quote where you have to), and you should refer to the author periodically to make it clear these are his or her ideas and not your own. Doing these things will prevent unintentional plagiarism.

In order to write this summary, it was necessary to go over Suzuki's essay very carefully. Summary writing requires separating main ideas from details and identifying the author's thesis, both skills that you learned in this unit. The practice you get from writing summaries of what you read can be of great benefit to your literal comprehension development.

PRACTICE D-1: Practice in Summarizing

Directions: In the space provided, write a summary of passage B on page 68 that you have already read. You may want to use the answers to your questions as a guide.

_____

_____

_____

_____

_____

_____

_____

_____

_____

_____

_____

_____

_____

PRACTICE D-2: More Summarizing

Directions: On another sheet of paper, write a summary of the essay "Working in the Recording Industry" (page 71) and hand it in to your instructor.

> ### Application 3: Summarizing Materials of Your Own Choice
>
> Find a 750–1000 word article in a current magazine or a textbook and summarize it. Bring it to class for discussion.

E.   Putting It All Together

The next two practices give you the opportunity to use what you have learned about reading to find an author's thesis and use of main ideas and supporting details. Before you begin, it is recommended that you refer to the Student Record Chart and review your scores for the reading selections in Chapter One. Note your comprehension and vocabulary scores. Try to either match your scores or do better this time. As you progress through this book, use these scores as a motivation and challenge to do better each time. Your only competition is yourself.

PRACTICE E-1

Directions: As you read the following essay, distinguish between the subject and the thesis and note what main ideas and supporting details are used to back up the authors' thesis.

"WE CAN HEAL": ABORIGINAL CHILDREN TODAY

SUZANNE FOURNIER AND ERNIE CREY

1   First Nations people in Canada agree that the next two decades will belong to Aboriginal youth. Today a strong young generation is struggling to emerge from the dark colonial days into the bright hope of autonomy and self-determination. All across the country, Aboriginal young people are making themselves heard: in schools and universities, in Native politics, at protests over education cutbacks, at community marches to combat child abuse, and in healing circles and sobriety treatment centres.

2   Young First Nations athletes are cheerfully clashing at basketball games, hockey playoffs, lacrosse tournaments, and canoe races; there are rowers, runners, and hockey players of national renown. Angela Chalmers of Manitoba's Birdtail Sioux First Nation, the first woman in the history of the Commonwealth Games to win both the 1500-metre and the 3000-metre races, in 1990, credits her Aboriginal roots for teaching her patience and perseverance. "Look at my grandmothers, how tough they had to be, and my mother, the discrimination I saw her deal with," says Chalmers today. "I've faced racism too, and I tell the Aboriginal kids I speak to as part

of the Native role model program [sponsored by the federal Indian Affairs department] that you can put that anger to good use: in physical exertion, in confidence and passion. Find out what you care about and prove you can excel as well or better than anyone; for the community, your family, but above all for yourself. Don't forget, I say when I talk to young Aboriginal kids, because we've been through a lot, we're strong people and we have a deep, deep well of strength to draw on."

3   At the Splat'sin day-care in Spallumcheen; at Xitolacw school in Mount Currie; inside a kukeli hut or traditional pit-house in Alkali Lake's elementary school; in the Nisga'a school board districts from kindergarten to Grade 12, First Nations children are learning their language and culture along with their math and science. At Keremeos Senior Secondary School, in B.C.'s southern interior, almost all the teens from the Lower and Upper Similkameen bands who enroll also graduate, and some rank among the school's top achievers. An ever-increasing number of Aboriginal youth are going on to university and college and actively seeking careers. They are speaking out in Aboriginal and mainstream media. They are connecting with indigenous people all over the world via the Internet through hundreds of websites, such as the popular Canadian-based Aboriginal Youth Network. And they are flocking by the thousands to the youth conferences held over the past few years everywhere from Inuvik to Regina, Ottawa, Montreal, Halifax, Edmonton, and Vancouver. A young Aboriginal man named Randy Nepoose spoke for all when he declared at a northern youth conference in 1992: "Now is our time."

4   There have never been, in recorded history, more Aboriginal young people than there are now in Canada. Today, more than 36 percent of the Aboriginal population is under the age of 14, compared to 21 percent of the non-Native population. Another 20 percent of Aboriginal youth is aged 15 to 24. The population of young Aboriginal people will continue to grow until there are almost 200 000 First Nations youths in the 15- to 24-year-old age bracket by the year 2011.

5   The traditional values that sustained First Nations for thousands of years before contact are emerging as the foundation that will carry Aboriginal nations to recovery and renewal. After five centuries of a cultural and economic war waged primarily against their children, First Nations still believe it is the young who will prove to be the mainstay of the renaissance now under way. The Aboriginal birth rate, in itself a sign of hope, is almost twice that of the rest of Canada. More and more Aboriginal children are being raised by sober parents connected to their culture. Children who require substitute care while their families are in recovery are increasingly cared for by Aboriginal child welfare agencies in all parts of the country. Although Aboriginal children still face immense challenges, there are generations of young people ready to become politically astute future leaders and contributing members of autonomous nations.

Comprehension Check

Directions: Answer the following questions without looking back.

1. What is the *subject* of the essay you just read?_____
_____

2. What is the *thesis* of this essay? _____
_____

3. According to the authors, the Aboriginal birthrate is _____

   a. half that of the rest of Canada

   b. decreasing steadily year-over-year

   c. twice that of the rest of Canada

   d. two-thirds higher than the rest of Canada

4. State two reasons the authors give for the next two decades belonging to Aboriginal youth. _____

   _____

5. According to the authors, traditional values are the foundation of

   a. recovery and renewal   b. education

   c. life   d. experience

6. In paragraph 4, the authors use statistics to support some of her ideas. What point are they making? _____

   _____

7. What is the significance of more Aboriginal youth going to college and university?

   _____

8. What strategies do the authors suggest will heal aboriginal communities?

   _____

9. What is meant by the phrase, "Now is our time"? (See paragraph 3). _____

   _____

10. T/F According to the authors, there is little hope for Aboriginal youth.

Vocabulary Check

Directions: Define the following underlined words used in the essay.

1. Aboriginal youth (paragraph 1)_____

   _____

2. dark colonial days (paragraph 1)_____

   _____

3. sobriety treatment centres (paragraph 1) _____

   _____

4. her patience and perseverance (paragraph 2) _____

   _____

5. physical exertion (paragraph 2)_____

   _____

6. mainstream media (paragraph 3) _____

   _____

7. flocking by the thousands (paragraph 3)_____

   _____

8. <u>mainstay</u> of the renaissance (paragraph 5) _____

_____

9. <u>immense</u> challenges (paragraph 5) _____

_____

10. politically <u>astute</u> future leaders (paragraph 5)_____

_____

Record the results of the comprehension and vocabulary checks on the Student Record Chart. Make certain you understand any mistakes you may have made before going on. Use whatever method you are using to learn any words you missed.

PRACTICE E-2: Timed Reading

Directions: You have a lot of information about vocabulary and literal comprehension strategies now. The third—and most often overlooked—strategy to improve your reading is reading rate. The purpose is not to make you read faster and lose your comprehension but rather to read faster and increase your comprehension. Very slow readers (under 180 wpm) will often lose concentration and focus only on details or isolated words rather than understanding what the article or essay is saying. If you read too slowly, you also can't get through all your college assignments (unless you give up sleep!).

The first step to reading faster is to decide what rate you want to set, based on three factors. The first factor is how familiar you are with the topic in the first place. In this article, you can look at the title, and realize that it is about reading and what importance we give to it. This topic is familiar to all of us, even if we haven't actually thought about it before. If the topic is particle physics, on the other hand, you would probably not know much about it and would need to set a slower rate.

The second factor to help you set your rate is the difficulty of the material. Glance at any paragraph and see if you understand the vocabulary. If there are more than three unfamiliar words on a page, you will find the material more difficult and will need to set a slower rate. Can you figure out the unfamiliar words from context, or will it affect your comprehension if you don't know the words? If English is not your primary language, you may find that unfamiliar words are hampering your comprehension. If that is the case, practice the rate exercises and learn the skills, but make comprehension your primary goal.

The third factor is your purpose for reading the material. In this text, the purpose is to answer the comprehension questions accurately and well. In order to help you do this, you should look at the questions first—before you even start reading. This will help you decide what you need to get out of the reading. If there are questions at the end of your college textbook chapters, read them first. If the instructor asks questions in class, let those questions guide your reading. Now, look at the ten comprehension questions and read them before you actually start reading the article.

You should have now looked at the title and read the comprehension questions. Now you want to read this 801-word article at a faster rate. Try to read at least 50 wpm faster than you read the article in Chapter One. See if it helps your comprehension to push yourself as you read.

Begin timing:_____

GETTING IDEAS

CLIFFORD WERIER AND M. GARRETT BAUMAN

1. A former editor-in-chief of a major women's magazine once said that she learned to be an idea person when she first started working as a young assistant editor. Each Monday, she and every other staff member had to bring to a meeting a list of 25 great ideas for articles. This brainstorming gave her boss, the editor-in-chief at that time, hundreds of ideas from which to choose for the dozen or so she needed each month. It also gave the young assistant editor a headache.

2. Then the ideas began to come more easily. Some weeks she had 30 or 40 ideas—better ones her boss could use. The important trick she learned was to let her subconscious mind work on the problem during the week and not to sit down at three o'clock on Friday afternoon to create 25 ideas spontaneously. All week long she'd jot down ideas as they came to her, stimulated by all sorts of things—a taxi ride, a meal in a Hungarian restaurant, an unusual garden she saw, a newspaper article. Soon she realized that almost anything could become an idea for a magazine article. "Just knowing I had such an assignment made me remember things I'd otherwise have forgotten," she said. One of the side benefits of becoming an idea-creating person was that she lived at a more intense pace, appreciated life more.

3. This is *incubation*. You plant a seed of an idea, and your subconscious mind—which is far more powerful than your conscious mind—will work on the problem. The solution that finally comes to you has been growing in your subconscious, which thinks about it while you go about your normal life, unaware of its activity except in flashes here and there. When the idea has ripened, it rises to the conscious level. The point is, you don't have to wait helplessly for a magic moment to strike in order to write. You can arrange your own inspiration. In fact, working with ideas creates inspirations.

4. There are two things to remember about using your subconscious brain power. The first is that better ideas come if you give your subconscious mind subtle reminders from time to time. The subconscious needs to be tickled once or twice a day if it's to keep going. The second thing to remember about incubation is that ideas often don't come out fully formed like newborn babies. They usually emerge in bits and pieces—the arm or leg of an idea. I'm using this grotesque image to describe ideas because most people don't want to accept such fragments as the offspring of their minds. Have faith. Be prepared to write down the fragments as they're delivered. You don't need index cards or a computer—although they work for many people. Novelist H.G. Wells had an unusual system to keep new ideas organized as they emerged in bits and pieces. He kept a dozen big barrels around his home, one for each book he planned to write. When fragments of an idea or details came to him, he'd jot them on a slip of paper and toss it into the appropriate barrel. When a barrel filled, Wells knew he had enough material to write a book.

5. There's no need to buy barrels. Two pages of notes are plenty to create a two- or three-page paper. "Two pages of notes?" I imagine some students protesting. "Why not just write it out? I thought you were going to save us work in this book." . . .

6. A few comments are in order now. First, notetaking is rarely wasted. Researchers into creativity in many fields have shown that this is how the best idea people oper-

ate. They've proved it's dependable, saves time, produces more interesting ideas, and helps blocked writers to get going again. Why shouldn't it help you? And remember: notetaking is easy writing, because you pay no attention to spelling, word choice, or complete sentences.

7   Suppose your anthropology professor tells you to write on the notion of personal space. Start by observing the way people stand and sit in public places. For example, the way people arrange themselves in elevators—where do they direct their attention, and how much space do they give each other? Perhaps you notice two women of Indian background touching while talking, and you consider that personal space might be culturally determined. Later, you watch how your friends arrange themselves around a table in the cafeteria, or the way lovers stand together talking, face to face.

8   At this point, it is important to find a piece of paper or boot up the computer and start writing; it doesn't matter how you write, but it is crucial that you start keeping lists of all the details you observe and all the ideas you generate. This is the way to "prime the pump," to get your mind engaged in the consideration of the topic and the generation of innovative approaches. These activities will fuel your subconscious, and when you write your paper, deeper, more original ideas are likely to arise. Inspiration results from many good ideas banging into each other.

Finish timing. Record time here: _____ and use the Timed Readings Conversion Chart in the Appendix to figure your rate: _____ wpm.

Comprehension Check

Directions: Answer the following questions without looking back.

1. What is the *subject* of the essay you just read?_____
   _____

2. What is the *thesis* of this essay? _____
   _____

3. According to the authors, incubation is
   a. ripening the seed of an idea.
   b. an intense brainstorming session.
   c. an embryo.
   d. cramming for an essay.

4. T/F The authors believe incubation boosts creativity.

5. According to the authors, your subconscious brain power
   a. does not exist.
   b. is easy to tap into.
   c. is difficult to trick.
   d. helps maintain concentration.

6. What two things do you need to remember about using your subconscious brain power? _____
   _____

7. When did H.G. Wells know that it was time to write a book? _____
   _____

8. Why does the essay begin with a brief story about an editor-in-chief of a women's magazine? _____

_____

9. Besides generating ideas, we need to

    a. rush to get our ideas down on paper.

    b. mull our ideas over for some time.

    c. forget about them—if they're important they'll come back.

    d. record all ideas on the computer.

10. T/F The authors believe that most ideas are fully formed when they are first imagined.

Vocabulary Check

Directions: Define the following underlined words from the essay.

    1. editor-in-chief of a women's magazine (paragraph 1) _____

_____

    2. brainstorming gave her boss (paragraph 1) _____

_____

    3. her subconscious mind (paragraph 2) _____

_____

    4. she'd jot down ideas (paragraph 2) _____

_____

    5. your conscious mind (paragraph 3) _____

_____

    6. the idea has ripened (paragraph 3) _____

_____

    7. give your subconscious mind subtle reminders (paragraph 4) _____

_____

    8. this grotesque image (paragraph 4) _____

_____

    9. offspring of their minds (paragraph 4) _____

_____

    10. the generation of innovative approaches (paragraph B) _____

_____

Record the results of the rate, comprehension, and vocabulary checks on the Student Record Chart.

Before you go on to the next chapter, make certain you understand any mistakes or problems you may have encountered in this one. It is important that you learn from mistakes, so don't despair when you make them. Accept mistakes as normal. Making mistakes is often the best way to discover what you do and don't know.

Questions for Group Discussion

1. As a group, come up with a summary of what this chapter taught you about how to improve your comprehension.

2. Why do you think the first two chapters in this text deal first with vocabulary and second with comprehension? Can you think of other orders or other topics that should be covered first?

3. Have each person in the group come up with at least one thing learned in this chapter that he/she didn't know before.

CHAPTER THREE

Developing Study-Reading Skills and Rate Flexibility

In addition to being able to understand word meanings, recall main ideas and supporting details, and recognize the difference between a subject and a thesis (the content of Chapters One and Two), you need to develop a study-reading strategy.

> A **study-reading strategy** is a method or approach to studying that will offer you the best results for the time and effort you put into studying.

Textbooks and teachers are not all alike, as you well know. Therefore, you usually have to adapt or modify your study-reading approaches for different classes. Obviously, one of the best places to start is to familiarize yourself with each of the textbooks required for the classes you are taking. Most textbooks contain aids for students, but they are often overlooked, ignored, or considered unimportant. The best thing you can do is to take the time to look over your textbooks to see what kinds of aids and information will be helpful when you study-read.

Almost all textbooks contain a table of contents, glossary, index, pictures, charts, and graphic aids. Often these items are designed as aids to studying, but not always. To find out how helpful such aids are, you should spend a few minutes looking over your books for things such as these:

1. *Title page:* It will give you the full title of the book, the edition, the authors and their school affiliation, and the publishing company. The complete title often helps you understand what the book will cover in regard to the subject. For instance, an introductory textbook is going to be more general than one that specifies a particular area. A history text that states "Volume 2" on the title page indicates an entire volume of history should have been studied before that one.

2. *Copyright page:* This tells you when the book was published and the date of any previous editions, so you will have some idea how dated the information in the book is.

3. *Preface:* This explains the author's purpose in writing the book, states what readers the book is intended for, and usually includes an acknowledgment of the people who helped with the book.

4. *Table of contents:* This shows how the book is organized. Some tables of contents are very comprehensive, some not; but at least they show you if the book is divided into units, chapters, sections, whether or not there is a glossary, index, appendix, and so on.

5. *Index:* This is an alphabetical listing of the various topics covered in the book. Names, places, events, definitions of terms, and the like are usually listed. Looking over an index can give you an idea of the book's subject matter, plus call to mind anything you may already have studied in the past in another course.

6. *Glossary:* The glossary is a small dictionary of sorts that usually defines the specialized terms covered in the book. It can save you from using the dictionary, but better yet, it defines the words and terms as they are used in the context of the book.

7. *Appendixes:* Textbooks frequently contain an appendix (sometimes more than one) that provides supplemental information related to the topic of the book.

As you progress through a particular course, these aids can sometimes be very beneficial. It is unlikely that you would buy a car without test-driving it, looking it over carefully to see what features it has, and even comparing it with other cars. But when it comes to textbooks, most students buy them because they are required and never bother to get to know what they offer.

This chapter is divided into seven sections.

- Part A will offer you practice in preparing to read an assignment as well as provide you with a tried-and-true study strategy.

- Part B gives practice in marking and underlining textbooks for better comprehension.

- Part C includes practice in scanning graphic aids.

- Part D provides practice in taking notes while reading, in case you are using a book you shouldn't or don't want to underline. All the reading selections in the practices from the first three sections are taken from actual college textbooks in various content areas.

- Part E deals with clues for taking both objective and subjective tests.

- Part F shows you how to attain flexible reading rates.

- Part G, the last part, as in the first two chapters, provides reading practices that include both comprehension and vocabulary checks and helps you put together everything you have learned in this chapter.

A. Study-Reading Strategies

Research has shown that the typical reader remembers only about half of what he or she reads when given a test right after reading an assignment. Several factors contribute to this, but one of the major ones is lack of preparation before beginning to study-read. In order to get the maximum efficiency from a study-reading session, it has been found that "looking before you leap," that is, surveying or looking over what has been assigned before trying to read it, works best.

To survey an assignment means that you should:

1. *Check the length of the assignment.* Flip through the assigned pages. Can you read it in one sitting or should you divide it up and cover a certain number of pages at a time? Don't try to take in too much at once, especially if it is a subject you don't know well or are having trouble understanding.

2. *Read the title of the chapter and the subheadings carefully.* These serve as clues to what the assignment will cover. If you already know something about the subject, your memory will be triggered by the title and headings. If you know nothing about the content of the assignment, carefully noting the chapter title and headings will help you focus on the subject of the chapter so that your mind will not wander. If something in the title or headings is unclear, make up a question about it that you can use as a guide when you are ready to read. In fact, the more questions you have about what you are going to study-read the better, since reading for the answers will keep your mind from wandering.

3. *Look for any study aids the chapter may have to offer.* See if there are any questions at the beginning or end of the chapter. Look them over closely before reading. Reading for answers will focus your attention on the subject matter. If there is a summary, read it to see what will be covered. Look for pictures and other visual aids. Read the captions under them. These types of aids help prepare you for better reading comprehension.

4. *Find the major idea related to each heading or subheading of the chapter.* Most chapters have three to six main ideas, and you need to identify these in your survey. If there are no subheadings, you need to look through the chapter for changes of subject. If there are too many subheadings, you need to group them together and see if you can find the main ideas.

The next practice provides you with some experience in surveying a chapter from a textbook.

PRACTICE A-1: Look Before You Leap

Directions: The following reading selection is part of a chapter from a textbook entitled *Effective Study* by Francis Robinson. Professor Robinson devised a study strategy known as the SQ3R method. Since then, many others have adapted his technique, but basically they all borrowed from him. In this practice, do not try to read the selection. You'll get to do that in the next practice. For now, just survey it:

a. check the length to judge how long it will take you to read;

b. read the title and subheadings carefully to see what you will be reading about in detail;

c. look for any study aids the chapter may provide; and

d. find the major idea related to each heading or subheading.

Remember, don't read the chapter selection, just survey it. Normally, a survey of material this length should take about two minutes or less. But for now, don't worry about how much time it takes. Just apply the survey steps correctly so that you will see their benefits. When you have finished, return here and answer the following questions to see how well you surveyed the chapter.

1. Based on the length of the reading selection, how long will it take you to read it?

_____

2. What is the title of the chapter?_____

_____

3. How many steps are there in the SQ3R method? _____

4. Name the three main headings of the selection. Your wording does not have to be exactly the same. _____

_____

_____

5. Are there any study aids in the chapter? _____

6. What do you think the chapter will cover? _____

_____

_____

7. What questions do you have that you can focus on when you study-read the chapter? _____

_____

_____

8. What do you now know about the chapter that you did not know before surveying it? _____

_____

_____

Application I: Surveying

Survey at least four textbook chapters (either your own textbooks or the ones in this chapter: Practices A-3, A-4, B-2, G-3). Time yourself until you can survey a chapter and write down the three to six main ideas of that chapter in five minutes or less. Bring your survey results, including the main ideas you found, to class for discussion.

C. *Development of SQ3R Method*

1   Many books have been written on special skills useful in reading books. Some have emphasized increased speed of reading; others, techniques for getting the most stimulation from an author's ideas. Students, however, want a skill that will be particularly effective when reading school textbooks.

2   A new technique must be devised, since the methods of good students are too often inefficient and no one of the experiments previously discussed has found the perfect method. The findings of these experiments, however, did contribute a scientific foundation from which a higher-level study skill could be devised. They showed that a quick survey of headings and summaries before starting to read gave an orientation that speeded up reading and aided retention. They showed that asking a question before starting each section also helped reading. They showed that the very rapid forgetting that is so typical after reading can be markedly slowed by the simple expedient of forcing oneself to recite from memory after reading. Other experiments showed when the best timing of this self-recitation would be during the study period. Various studies emphasized the importance of understanding the larger meanings in the selection and of seeing their pattern of relationship. Outlining, relating the material to one's interests, and a brief review at the end of a reading session were shown to help with this understanding. Still other experiments showed the value of distribution of effort in studying.

3   The creation of a study skill that uses these findings, that satisfies the demands of school study, and that pleases the student with its efficiency is a challenge to the reading specialist. The student wants any suggested method to help him (1) select what he is expected to know, (2) comprehend these ideas rapidly, (3) fix them in memory, and later (4) review efficiently for examinations. The method must be more efficient and less time consuming than rereading lessons; and it should not be difficult to learn.

4   For years this writer has had students try out various methods that such experiments have suggested; such trials have led to further refinements and suggestions. One method has finally been devised that fits the criteria above. Further research may show other possible refinements, but it is felt that this now represents a higher-level skill of great effectiveness for schoolwork. The material that follows is devoted to a description of this study technique and to exercises directed toward developing such skill.

STEPS IN THE SQ3R METHOD

5   The title for this new higher-level study skill is abbreviated to make it easier to remember and to make reference to it more simple. The abbreviation SQ3R stands for the steps that the student follows in using the method. A description of each of these steps is given below.

6   **Survey 1.** Glance over the headings in the chapter to see the few big points that will be developed. Also read the final summary paragraph if the chapter has one. This survey should not take more than a minute

The SQ3R method of studying   **31**

and will show the three to six core ideas around which the discussion will cluster. This orientation will help you organize the ideas as you read them later.

7 **Question** 2.   Now begin to work. Turn the first heading into a question. This will arouse your curiosity and thereby increase comprehension. It will bring to mind information already known, thus helping you to understand that section more quickly. The question also will make important points stand out at the same time that explanatory detail is recognized as such. Turning a heading into a question can be done at the instant of reading the heading, but it demands a conscious effort on your part.

8 **Read** 3.   Read to answer that question, i.e., to the end of the first headed section. This is not a passive plodding along each line, but an active search for the answer.

9 **Recite** 4.   Having read the first section, look away from the book and try briefly to recite the answer to your question. Use your own words and cite an example. If you can do this you know what is in the book; if you cannot, glance over the section again. An excellent way to do this reciting from memory is to jot down brief cue phrases in outline form on a sheet of paper.

Now repeat steps 2, 3, and 4 with each successive headed section: that is, turn the next heading into a question, read to answer that question, and recite the answer by jotting down cue phrases in your outline. Read in this way until the entire lesson is completed.

10 **Review** 5.   When the lesson has been read through in this way, look over your notes to get a bird's-eye view of the points and their relationship and check your memory as to the content by reciting the major subpoints under each heading. This checking of memory can be done by covering up the notes and trying to recall the main points. Then expose each major point and try to recall the subpoints listed under it.

11   These five steps of the SQ3R method—survey, question, read, recite, and review—when polished into a smooth and efficient method should result in faster reading, picking out the important points, and fixing them in memory. The student will find one other worthwhile outcome: Quiz questions will seem familiar because the headings turned into questions are usually the points emphasized in quizzes. By predicting actual quiz questions and looking up the answers beforehand the student feels that he is effectively studying what is considered important in a course.

EFFECTIVENESS OF THE SQ3R METHOD

12   Evidence of the success of this method has been obtained from several studies. In one experiment several sections of a how-to-study class measured their reading ability (reading rate and comprehension accuracy) on a test that dealt with the

32   *Higher-level work skills*

history of Canada; they were then given practice in the use of the SQ3R method for several days, after which they took another comparable reading test. Before training, the average rate of reading for the sections was at the 34th percentile and after training it was at the 56th percentile; before training the average accuracy of comprehension was at the 43rd percentile; after training it was at the 53rd percentile. In another experiment an attempt was made to measure the effectiveness of this method for examination preparation. Two quizzes of equal difficulty were prepared; for the first quiz the students were permitted to study in their own way, but for the second quiz they were shown how to predict questions. The average number of errors on the first quiz was 15, but on the second quiz the average was only 6. One of the most convincing arguments for the method has been the comments of students who have tried the method and found that it works. Students have walked into class and said, "I predicted 15 of the 20 questions he asked" or "Boy, oh boy, I've been getting Ds in chemistry but I got a B yesterday" or "It looked as if he had picked the quiz questions from my list."

FURTHER DETAILS OF THE METHOD

13   A description that is an over-all picture of the method has been given. Experience in teaching its use, however, shows that certain typical errors may occur, usually because old study methods interfere (427). An indication of certain critical points, so the student can be particularly careful concerning them, is helpful in learning a skill. These cautions are arranged according to the steps in the method:

14   **1. Survey.**   A survey of headings in a lesson should take only a minute. Some students are so in the habit of reading on once they start that, until they have learned how, they need to make a conscious effort to look just at the headings and then to estimate what the lesson is about. It is worthwhile to practice this skill. Take some reading material on topics with which you are familiar, *e.g.*, newspapers, digest magazines, previously read textbooks, and so on. Glance at the headings in an article or a chapter and then make guesses as to what the material will actually say. Check to see how well you have done.

15   **2 and 3. Reading to answer questions.**   Changing a heading into a question should be a conscious effort to orient yourself actively toward the material to be read. You definitely should have in mind what you want to learn as you read each section and not read it passively line by line. Habits accumulated from reading fiction often make textbook reading difficult, for it has been found that most people read fiction in order to forget their troubles and not to remember what is in the book. Such an attitude of comprehending for the moment, when carried over into textbook reading, gives rise to a delusion that since the ideas are comprehended as they are read, they will, of course, be remembered and unconsciously organized as answers to questions. This is far from the truth. Reading a textbook is work; you must know what you are looking for, look for it, and then organize your thinking concerning the topic you have been reading about.

16   **4. Reciting.**   The tendency in reading is to keep going, but you should stop at the end of each headed section to see if you can answer the question asked at the start of the section. As indicated before, this procedure tends to act as a check on whether you have comprehended the material, and the recitation fixes the ideas in your memory. Furthermore, this insistence on answering the question makes it easier to force yourself to read with an active, inquiring attitude.

17   Self-recitation may consist of mentally reviewing the answer or of writing it out. The latter is more effective, since it forces the reader actually to verbalize the answer, whereas a mental review often may fool a reader into believing that a vague feeling of comprehension represents mastery. Furthermore, the more sensory channels are used in learning, the more effective they are; for example, in writing notes one receives visual and kinesthetic (muscle) cues as well as verbal imagery in thinking about the material.

18   It is very important that this note-taking require little time and energy; the notes should be exceedingly brief. It is at this stage, in fact, that many students have much difficulty with the SQ3R method. Some think they should use old habits of lengthy note-taking, in which all details are copied from the book, usually as complete sentences. This technique so disrupts the progress of reading that the train of thought is lost. Other students, when they see something important, are in the habit of stopping to copy it into their notes—with one finger marking each phrase as they look back and forth between book and notes. It truthfully can be said that many students copy a sentence into their notes without ever having read it for meaning.

19   The student will have to practice taking the type of "working notes," as they are called, recommended here. First, no notes should be written until the whole headed section is completely read. Second, the notes should be jotted down from memory and not from the book. And third, the notes should be taken in the student's own words and should be brief, *i.e.*, little more than a word or phrase. Just as a public speaker's notes usually consist of a list of topics as reminders of what to talk about, so the student's notes should include only cue words and phrases to demonstrate to his own satisfaction that he knows what points are included. The student, knowing a topic, can then easily supply an explanation of it. Such brief wording also keeps the notes in compact form so that they can be easily visualized later in review.

20   The following sample of working notes based on the preceding section shows how indentation makes points stand out and how brief wording makes visualization of the subpoints easier. The brief wording will not convey full meaning to a stranger—he should read the article—but to the student who made the notes, the cue phrases are sufficient reminders about what is in the article.

Notes on Previous Sections

A. Discovering new study methods
   1. To select what is important

34   *Higher-level work skills*

      a. Quick preview helps rate
      b. Previous questions help
         1. When?
            (a) Before whole lesson
            (b) Before each section
         2. Headings give questions
      c. Outlining
         1. Little value first trial
         2. Work notes help if trained

   2. To retard forgetting
      a. Not a wearing away
      b. Helped by
         1. Interest and intent to remember
         2. Selecting major points
         3. Recitation
            (a) Remember 80 vs. 20% after 2 weeks
            (b) Immediate recitation better
            (c) Best: brief note from memory after a section
         4. Distributed study

21   It is difficult to maintain an attitude of active attack on any type of work over a long period of time. In industry it has been found more efficient to alternate periods of working at different activities; the change of activity is less boring and one can start each new period with zest. In studying, an alternation of reading and note-taking makes it easier for the student to keep studying his lessons and to maintain an attitude of active searching for ideas. It is easier to keep reading until a headed section is finished than it is to complete the whole lesson. Therefore, breaks in attention are apt to come at logical places in the reading material and so do not disrupt the student's thinking too much. This alternation of tasks, in fact, helps make concentration much easier in studying lessons.

22   **5. Review.**   Review immediately after reading should be brief; probably not more than five minutes will be needed. This is certainly much faster than rereading the lesson. The total outline should be looked over to get an over-all, easily visualized picture, but the review should not be limited to this. As indicated earlier, self-recitation should be used to make sure that the material is fixed better in your memory. A good way to do this is to cover the notes, recite on the main points, and then check to see if you are correct. Then, cover up the notes again, recite on the subpoints under the first main point, and again check for accuracy. This system should be repeated with each major point. This method will help you to see the organization that exists between the various ideas, will help to indicate what is not yet mastered, and will help to fix known ideas more clearly in mind so they are forgotten more slowly.

23   Later reviews are also worthwhile because of the forgetting that takes place. The factors influencing the efficiency of these delayed reviews will be discussed in the next chapter.

The SQ3R method of studying   35

PRACTICE A-2: A Study Strategy: The SQ3R Method

Directions: This practice has a dual purpose. The first is to read the selection you just surveyed in Practice A-1. The second is to teach you the SQ3R study method by having you read it just as you would an assignment you know you will be tested on later. Return now to Practice A-1 and read "Development of SQ3R Method." When finished, return to the following questions and try to answer them without looking back.

1. List the steps in the SQ3R method: _____

   _____

   _____

   _____

2. How can you be certain of the effectiveness of the SQ3R method? _____

   _____

   _____

   _____

3. Making a preview of the headings in the chapter should take less than_____

   _____

4. Which is correct? (a) notes are written in your own words from memory; or (b) notes are written by jotting down important phrases and sentences from the chapter. _____

5. At what point in your reading should you take notes? _____

   _____

   _____

6. Why should you stop reading and recite at the end of each heading? _____

   _____

   _____

7. When should you review a chapter you have finished reading? _____

   _____

   _____

PRACTICE A-3: Applying SQ3R to a History Textbook Chapter

Directions: The following is a portion of Chapter Two, entitled "The Arrival of the Norse," from *Origins: Canadian History to Confederation*, 4th edition, by R. Douglas Francis, Richard Jones, and Donald B. Smith. Try applying the SQ3R technique to the selection to make certain you understand how to use what you just read. If you need to, review the information on SQ3R in Practice A-2. Then apply all five steps to the passage that follows.

THE ARRIVAL OF THE NORSE

R. DOUGLAS FRANCIS, RICHARD JONES, AND DONALD B. SMITH

1   Irish monks were probably the first European navigators both interested in voyaging westward and capable of reaching North America. They travelled in curraghs, wood-framed boats covered with sewn ox-hides, powered by oars and a square sail. In the early Middle Ages, tales circulated about the celebrated Irish saint, Brendan, who was said to have found new lands by sailing west in the sixth century. But no medieval claim that he reached lands to the west has ever been discovered.

2   From the ninth to the twelfth centuries, Scandinavia led the European sea powers with a commercial empire extending from Russia in the east to Sicily in the south and Normandy in the west. The Norse occupied small coastal areas on the southwestern coast of Greenland, as part of their voyages from the European mainland: first to the Faeroe Islands, roughly 300 km north of Scotland, by A.D. 800; then to Iceland, by A.D. 870; and finally to Greenland, by A.D. 985. Without compasses (introduced in the twelfth century), the Norse used a crude device to measure the location of the North Star and thus estimate their position at sea. At times, on their way home from Iceland to Norway, they landed by mistake in Ireland or Scotland.

3   Eric the Red (Eirikr Thorvaldsson) founded the Norse settlements in Greenland. Exiled from his native Norway as punishment for committing murder, he escaped to Iceland, only to become involved in a feud there. Banished for more killings, he fled farther west to a vast uninhabited subcontinent. On its west coast, this land had green, reasonably level pastures and impressive fiords and headlands, all of which reminded him of his native Norway. Rich in game animals, with a sea full of fish and large mammals such as seals and walrus, the land could support many Icelanders. Eric named the inviting, unoccupied country "Greenland." On returning to Iceland, Eric encouraged others to migrate with him to this promising land. Accompanied by fifteen shiploads of Icelanders, the Norse adventurer founded two settlements. The Icelanders persevered, raising cows, horses, sheep, pigs, and goats. Recent excavations of the remains of Eric's own farm revealed a surprisingly large and comfortable establishment, built with thick walls of stone and turf.

4   In A.D. 986, the second year of Eric's settlement of Greenland, Bjarni Herjölfsson, the owner of a ship that traded between Norway and Iceland, went to join Eric in Greenland. En route, he and his crew met with stormy weather, which drove them off course for several days. When the weather cleared they sighted a flat land covered with woods. As this country did not fit the description that he had of Greenland, Bjarni sailed north. Bjarni thus became the first known European to sight eastern North America (probably Labrador, only 800 km or roughly four days' sailing from Eric's Greenlandic settlements), although he never landed there.

5   Eric's second son, Leifr (or Leif) Eiriksson, grew up hearing tales about Bjarni's forested land to the south. In A.D. 1001, the 21-year-old Leif assembled a crew of 35 and set out to explore the lands southwest of Greenland. He sailed past Baffin Island, which he called "Helluland" (Flat Stone Land). Farther south, he landed in a forested area-probably the coast of central Labrador-that he called "Markland" (Wood Land). Continuing on, he reached an attractive location with a moderate climate, which he named "Vinland" (Wineland) for its plentiful "wineberries" (probably wild red currants, gooseberries, or mountain cranberries). Scholars have placed Vinland some-

where between Labrador and Florida. After wintering in Vinland and a summer of more exploring, Leif and his crew loaded a cargo of timber and "wineberries" and set sail for Greenland. They had not encountered any other humans during their stay.

6   In the opening decade of the eleventh century, the Norse sponsored several expeditions southwest from Greenland. Leif's brother, Thorvaldr, led the next voyage to Vinland. With his crew of 30 he reached the Vinland houses and settled there for the winter, catching fish to supplement provisions brought from Greenland. During the next two summers, Thorvaldr explored the coast to the south, meeting no one.

Comprehension Check

Directions: Answer the following questions.

1. The main idea of this selection is

    a. Irish monks, led by Brendan, were the first to sail west and sight new lands.

    b. Scandinavians, leaders in European sea power from the ninth to the twelfth centuries, were the first Europeans to settle in Greenland and explore the eastern coast of North America.

    c. Greenland was the centre for Scandinavian settlement and exploration of North America.

    d. "Vinland" (Wineland), somewhere between Labrador and Florida, was the most important Scandinavian settlement in the new world.

2. On what do modern archaeologists base their theories? _____

_____

3. What is "Helluland"? _____

4. What makes scholars conclude that Bjarni Herjölfsson was the first known European to sight eastern North America? _____

_____

5. How did the Norse navigate the seas? _____

6. Describe the vessels the Norse used. _____

_____

7. Summarize the experience of Liefr Eiriksson as set out in paragraph 5.

_____

8. Why did the Scandinavians meet no one on their first voyages to the new world?

_____

9. What circumstances in his own life led to Eric the Red reaching new lands?

_____

10. Why do you think the Norse chose not to settle permanently in Vinland?

_____

If you have any problems answering these questions, discuss them with your instructor. Make certain you fully understand the SQ3R method before going on to the next drill.

Vocabulary Check

Directions: Develop your own vocabulary test for this chapter by selecting ten words you don't know and writing them on vocabulary cards. After you write out the definitions, have a classmate test you on them.

Turn in the words to your instructor and record the results of your comprehension and vocabulary checks in the Student Record Chart in the Appendix.

Application 2: Using SQ3R with Your Textbook

Apply SQ3R to a textbook for another class. Briefly explain how you used each step of the process for that text. Include a list of the main ideas from your survey, a list of questions you developed, and a desccription of how you read, recited, and reviewed. Hand in your explanation to your instructor.

PRACTICE A-4: Modifying the SQ3R Method—A Health Textbook Passage

Directions: Some textbook passages, such as the one from the history textbook you just read, do not have many study aids such as headings, subheadings, learning checks, and the like. For such books, you may need to modify the SQ3R method to fit the text. The following passage is from *The Dynamics of Health and Wellness: A Biopsychosocial Approach* by Judith Green and Robert Shellenberger. There are no headings to survey or turn into questions here either. When such passages occur in your study-reading, form your questions by skimming the paragraphs looking for the topic sentence of each paragraph and for words and phrases set in italic or bold-face type.

Try following these steps as you work on the next passage:

1. Survey the selection by noticing the title and skimming each paragraph to get a general overview of the contents. Don't worry about what you don't understand at this point.

2. Compose the questions you want to answer based on what you skimmed, and write them here. _____

   _____

   _____

   _____

3. Now you are ready to read closely and make notes. Since there are no headings, you will have to decide how much you want to read before stopping to recite. You may need to stop after each paragraph or two. It depends on how well you are comprehending.

4. Remember that reciting can serve as an oral quiz. Cover up the passage and answer your questions (written above in point 2) or review your written notes. The main thing is to understand what you are reading as you go along.

5. Review the passage when you have finished, making sure that you have answered all your questions and any new ones that came up as you were reading.

Use what you learned in previous chapters about defining vocabulary in context and finding ideas and supporting details.

THE DYNAMICS OF HEALTH

JUDITH GREEN AND ROBERT SHELLENBERGER

1   Focus on the word **dynamic**. What comes to mind? Consider these examples: "She has a *dynamic* personality." "That is a *dynamic* program." The word *dynamic* comes from the Greek word *dynamis*, meaning "force." In physics, for example, dynamics refers to the forces that govern motion. Dynamic also means "changing," as opposed to "static." This meaning of dynamic refers to processes in which change occurs, such as growth—growth is a dynamic process, because continual change is part of the process. Dynamic also means "characterized by effective action" (*Random House Dictionary*, 1980). In this sense of the word, dynamic suggests that the change or process is for the better and involves conscious effort.

2   You can anticipate the meaning of "the dynamics of health and wellness."

3   Consider this example: "My friend finally regained her health after a traumatic illness." When we say that a friend "regained her health," we usually mean that she became free of injury or disease. "Mr. Wright regained his health" means that Mr. Wright became free of cancer. Freedom from illness and disease has been the most common meaning of health. This is exemplified in terms such as "health centre," "health care," and "health insurance," which actually refer to the treatment of disease and financial coverage of medical expenses. The fact that these activities are described as "health" activities, when the emphasis is on treatment of disease and illness, means that health is considered to be recovery from and absence of disease and illness.

4   Today we are experiencing a significant change in the meaning of "health," a redefinition that was first voiced in 1947 by the World Health Organization (WHO), a branch of the United Nations. WHO defined health as "a state of complete physical, mental, and social well-being and not merely the absence of disease and infirmity" (World Health Organization, 1947). Although this statement does not tell us what "well-being" is, it does say that health is not merely the absence of disease. A person is not healthy simply because he or she is not sick. A heart-attack victim cannot say, "I was healthy until the day I had my heart attack." This would be false because the physiological conditions that led to the heart attack, such as atherosclerosis or hypertension, developed over many years in which the victim was not well, although symptoms were not detected. We suspect that the belief that people are healthy if they are not obviously sick has promoted disease and death over the centuries and particularly in this one, by allowing people to continue destructive habits while believing that they are healthy. Smokers continue to smoke because they feel healthy and not sick; obese people consider themselves healthy because they are not sick. Obviously, a definition of health that promotes sickness is not a good definition.

5   Recognizing this fact, most health professionals agree that the definition of health must include lifestyle—a good diet, adequate exercise, coping effectively with stress, and freedom from addictions. Today, most health professionals would not consider you to be healthy just because you are not currently sick; your lifestyle is an integral part of your health. This means that if you have an "unhealthy" lifestyle, you are not healthy, even though you may have no physiological signs of disease.

6   In addition to freedom from sickness and living a healthy lifestyle, a third element must be included in the definition of health: physiological conditions that add no risk to health, such as low blood pressure and low blood cholesterol (Hamburg, Elliott, & Parron, 1982; Matarazzo, Weiss, Herd, Miller, & Weiss, 1984). Although a healthy lifestyle promotes physiological health, it is no absolute guarantee. A person could have a healthy lifestyle and also have high blood pressure or high blood fats, and therefore would not have a "clean bill of health." For this reason, we include physiological measures within ranges that indicate no risk to health in the definition of health.

7   In summary, you are healthy when: (1) you are free of illness and disease, (2) your physiological measures indicate no risk to health, and (3) you have a healthy lifestyle.

8   Because this three-part definition of health incorporates lifestyle, a significant and profound dimension is added—**self-responsibility**. Health is not a matter of chance or good luck, nor is it simply a matter of good genes. True health includes personal choice—the choice of adopting a lifestyle that promotes health or one that increases risk for sickness. Pro-health choices involve self-responsibility and self-regulation.

9   Health is not a simple matter, as you might have thought or hoped.

Directions: Now answer these questions without looking back.

1. What is the main idea of the passage? _____

_____

_____

2. What is meant by the "dynamics of health and wellness"? _____

_____

_____

3. What do the letters WHO stand for? _____

_____

_____

4. Today, what do most health professionals agree the definition of health must include? _____

_____

_____

5. Explain what self-responsibility has to do with health._____

_____

_____

_____

6. Explain why you were or were not able to answer most of the questions above.

_____

_____

_____

B.   Marking and Underlining Textbooks

In Part A, you learned that reciting is one of the three Rs in the SQ3R study method. While oral recitation was described, it was recommended that you take some form of notes during the Read-Recite cycle. It is strongly suggested that you use one of the methods described here and in the section for note-taking.

Basically, there are two ways to take notes as you read: (1) you can mark in your book, using the margins for your own remarks and underlining and circling important words and phrases; or (2) you can take notes from the text in a notebook. Section D will cover taking notes in a notebook. This section deals with marking and underlining correctly.

Take a look at the following passage and how it is marked:

It is now believed that the earth's outer layer of rock, called the lithosphere, is divided into large, rigid plates that fit together like pieces of a huge jigsaw puzzle. There are twelve major plates (and numerous subplates), each about sixty miles thick and some almost as wide as the Pacific Ocean. They float on a layer of dense, viscous rock called the asthenosphere, which, in turn, surrounds the earth's hot core.

How helpful are all those markings going to be when you review for a test? What do they mean? The act of underlining is not in itself a helpful comprehension or recall device.

Notice the same passage marked in a more sensible way:

lithosphere,
outer layer;
asthenosphere,
inner layer

It is now believed that the earth's outer layer of rock, called the lithosphere, is divided into large, rigid plates that fit together like pieces of a huge jigsaw puzzle. There are twelve major plates (and numerous subplates), each about sixty miles thick and some almost as wide as the Pacific Ocean. They float on a layer of dense, viscous rock called the asthenosphere, which, in turn, surrounds the earth's hot core.

Here, only the key points are highlighted. The student used what was learned about finding main ideas and supporting details. Thought went into what was to be marked for later review as well as what would be helpful for understanding the passage during the Read-Recite portion of SQ3R.

While there is no particular way to mark or underline, good note takers seem to follow two basic principles: (1) mark only the main points and (2) be consistent in the way you mark. Here are some suggestions for marking and underlining:

1. Use pen, not pencil. Pencil marks will fade and smear over time.
2. Underline main ideas and circle important words or phrases. Studies show that, when students were allowed to underline only one sentence in a paragraph, they took more time and underlined only important sentences, which produced better comprehension and recall.
3. Underline minor, yet important, points with broken lines. Later, during a review, such markings will make it easy for you to distinguish between main ideas and minor but relevant ones.
4. Use numbers in the margins to indicate a series of points or items being discussed.
5. Use the margins to write what you feel is important, questions you have for the instructor, or notes to yourself.

6. Draw rectangles around names or places that might be used in a test or quiz.

7. Jot key words on small Post-it notes, sticking them on the page and paragraph you want to remember.

8. From these Post-it notes, write notes on your computer. Propping your textbook on a book stand or music stand helps the process.

Remember that these are just suggestions. You may want to use your own type of marking. That's fine, as long as it is consistent and meaningful to you as you are marking and helps you later during reviews.

Marking and underlining are not as efficient as note-taking *unless* you take time to consider carefully what to underline and later review what you underlined. Underlining and marking are faster than note-taking, but it doesn't do you any good to underline if you don't actually study-read as you do it.

PRACTICE B-1: Marking and Underlining

Directions: Apply the SQ3R study strategy to the textbook passage on page 106, marking and underlining as described above when you get to the Read-Recite portion.

In the spaces provided, explain what you did for each step of SQ3R:

1. *Survey:* _____

_____

_____

_____

_____

_____

_____

_____

_____

_____

2. *Question:* _____

_____

_____

_____

_____

_____

_____

_____

_____

_____

_____

Cigarettes All cigarette packs sold in Canada carry messages such as: "Warning: Cigarette Smoking Is Dangerous to Your Health." Cigarette advertising has been banned on the radio and television. In 1988, U.S. Surgeon General C. Everett Koop declared that cigarette smoking was the chief preventable cause of death.

The percentage of adults who smoke has declined from 42.2 in 1966 to 26.5 in 1986 (Mansnerus, 1988). Nevertheless, about 350,000 still die from smoking-related illnesses each year in North America. This is seven times the number who die from motor-vehicle accidents (Cowley, 1988). Cigarette smoking can cause cancer of the lungs, larynx, oral cavity, and esophagus and may contribute to cancer of the bladder, pancreas, and kidneys. Cigarette smoking is also linked to death from heart disease (Epstein & Perkins, 1988), chronic lung and respiratory diseases, and other illnesses. Pregnant women who smoke risk miscarriage, premature birth, and birth defects.

So it's no secret that cigarette smoking is dangerous. In fact, in the 1980s, peer pressure seems to be favouring *not* smoking. Many people now look upon smoking as a form of "deviant behaviour" (Mansnerus, 1988).

Components of Tobacco Smoke: Where There's Smoke, There's Chemicals Tobacco smoke contains *carbon monoxide, hydrocarbons* (or "*tars*"), and *nicotine*.

Oxygen is carried through the bloodstream by **hemoglobin**. When carbon monoxide combines with hemoglobin, it impairs the blood's ability to supply the body with oxygen. One result is shortness of breath. Some **hydrocarbons** have been shown to cause cancer in laboratory animals.

Nicotine is the stimulant in cigarettes. Nicotine can cause cold, clammy skin, faintness and dizziness, nausea and vomiting, and diarrhea—all of which account for the occasional discomforts of the novice smoker. Nicotine also stimulates discharge of the hormone adrenaline. Adrenaline creates a burst of autonomic activity, including rapid heart rate and release of sugar into the blood. It also provides a sort of mental "kick." Nicotine is responsible for the stimulating properties of cigarette smoke, but its effects are short-lived. In the long run it can contribute to fatigue.

Physiological Dependence Nicotine is the agent that creates physiological dependence on cigarettes (Koop, 1988). Regular smokers adjust their smoking to maintain fairly even levels of nicotine in their bloodstream (Schachter, 1977). Symptoms for withdrawal from nicotine include nervousness, drowsiness, energy loss, headaches, fatigue, irregular bowels, light-headedness, insomnia, dizziness, cramps, palpitations, tremors, and sweating.

It has also been found that nicotine is excreted more rapidly when the urine is highly acidic. Stress increases the amount of acid in the urine. For this reason, smokers may need to smoke more when under stress to maintain the same blood nicotine level, even though they may *believe* that smoking is helping them cope with stress.

Truth or Fiction Revisited
It is true that cigarette smokers tend to smoke more when they are under stress. That is because nicotine is excreted more rapidly when they are under stress.

Hemoglobin The substance in the blood that carries oxygen.

Hydrocarbon Chemical compounds consisting of hydrogen and carbon.

Nicotine A stimulant found in tobacco smoke. (From the French name for the tobacco plant, *nicotiane.*)

3. *Read:*_____

_____

_____

_____

_____

_____

_____

_____

_____

4. *Recite:* _____

_____

_____

_____

_____

_____

_____

_____

_____

5. *Review:* _____

_____

_____

_____

_____

_____

_____

_____

PRACTICE B-2: More Marking and Underlining

Directions: Follow the directions for Practice B-1 in reading the selection that follows.

EMILY JENNINGS STOWE

R. DOUGLAS FRANCIS, RICHARD JONES, AND DONALD B. SMITH

1   Emily Jennings became the first female public-school principal in Upper Canada and, immediately after Confederation, the first Canadian woman to practise medicine openly. She was also one of the country's first suffragists.

2   Born near Norwich, Upper Canada, on May 1, 1831, Emily Jennings came from a Quaker background. Since the Society of Friends (Quakers) gave women the same status as men, she grew up in an atmosphere of complete gender equality. Her struggle to achieve equality for women began in 1852 when she applied for admission to Victoria College in Cobourg. Refused on the grounds that she was female, she then applied successfully to the Toronto Normal School. She graduated with first-class honours in 1854. She taught until her marriage in 1856 to John Stowe, owner of a carriage business in neighbouring Mount Pleasant.

3   Shortly after the birth of their third child in 1863, John Stowe contracted tuberculosis and had to leave the family for treatment. With the financial help of the Jennings family, and the support of her sister, Cornelia, who agreed to care for Emily's children, Emily prepared for a medical career.

4   Barred from medical school in Canada because she was female, Emily enrolled at the New York Medical College for Women, a homeopathic (or natural medicine) institution in New York City. She graduated in 1867. But when she returned to Canada, the College of Physicians and Surgeons refused to certify her. So for over a decade she practised medicine in Toronto without a licence. She was not prosecuted for doing so, but was charged in 1879 with having performed an abortion. In the lengthy trial that followed, she successfully defended her qualifications, skill, and professional conduct. After her acquittal, the College of Physicians and Surgeons granted her a medical licence.

5   Dr. Stowe helped to organize the Women's Medical College in Toronto (the forerunner of Women's College Hospital) in 1883. The same year, her daughter Augusta achieved her mother's own goal of 20 years earlier-she obtained a medical degree from the University of Toronto. Augusta Stowe became the first woman to receive a Canadian medical degree.

6   Emily Stowe treated her husband on terms of perfect equality. When John Stowe regained his health, she supported him while he retrained as a dentist. After his graduation, the Stowes practised side by side at 111 Church Street in Toronto, until Emily retired in 1893.

7   While in New York City as a medical student, Emily became interested in feminist causes. Upon her return to Canada she launched the Toronto Women's Literary Club, a pseudonym for a suffrage group, the first in Canada. It issued a magazine, the Citizen, that championed women's education and enfranchisement. In 1893, the group reconstituted itself as the Canadian Woman's Suffrage Association. Six years later, the group helped to form the Dominion Women's Enfranchisement Association. Dr. Stowe became its first president, a position she held until her death in 1903.

8   In a note she wrote in 1896, Emily Stowe provided her own best epitaph: "My career has been one of much struggle characterised by the usual persecution which attends everyone who pioneers a new movement or steps out of line with established custom."

Directions: Now answer the following questions in the spaces provided. Try not to look back at the reading selection.

1. Briefly describe the reason Emily Stowe was initially denied a medical licence in Canada. _____

_____

_____

_____

2. Discuss the various steps Emily Stowe had to take in order to achieve her goal of getting a medical licence. _____

_____

_____

_____

3. Who was the first woman to obtain a Canadian medical degree? _____

_____

_____

4. What does suffrage mean? _____

_____

_____

5. What was Emily Stowe charged with doing in 1879? _____

_____

_____

6. What is an epitaph? _____

_____

_____

If you had problems answering any of these questions, reread the sections of the passage that provide the answers. Make certain you are applying the SQ3R method properly and that your markings and underlining techniques are benefiting you. You may need to consult with your instructor. If you did well, go on to the next section.

C.   Scanning Graphic Aids

Scanning is what you do when you look for a friend's telephone number in the phone book. It is the technique used when locating a word in the dictionary, when seeking a page number in the index, or when checking to see what television programs are offered at eight o'clock. In all of these examples, you know what you are looking for before you begin to read. You have to use guides and aids to find what you want rather than reading everything on the page.

> Good scanning ability, then, depends on knowing what you want to find and knowing how the material to be read has been organized.

Scanning is something you already know how to do, but you may or may not be very proficient at it. In either case, the practices in this chapter will help you increase your scanning speed and become more aware of the organizational patterns in materials where scanning is best utilized.

Scanning graphic aids in textbooks is an important study skill. You need to learn how to scan charts, maps, graphs, indexes, and tables quickly in order to get the most information in the least amount of time. The following practice exercises are designed to help you become proficient at this skill. Try to keep to the time limits suggested.

As you do these practices, try finding a scanning technique that works well for you. Remember that you are not reading in the normal sense of the word; you are learning to develop a skill. Feel free to experiment and don't worry about mistakes. This is the place to make mistakes and to learn from them.

PRACTICE C-1: Charts

Directions: First take a minute to look at the chart below. Then scan the chart for the answers to the questions under the chart. Write your answers in the blanks provided. You should finish in less than three minutes.

CALORIES USED PER HOUR

	BODY SIZE		
	120 Pounds	**150 Pounds**	**175 Pounds**
Calisthenics	235–285	270–300	285–335
Running	550–660	625–700	660–775
Walking	235–285	270–330	285–335
Bowling	150–180	170–190	180–210
Swimming	425–510	480–540	510–600
Bicycling	325–395	370–415	395–460
Tennis	335–405	380–425	405–470
Golf	260–315	295–335	315–370

HOURS/MINUTES PER WEEK TO BURN 1,500 CALORIES

	BODY SIZE		
	120 Pounds	**150 Pounds**	**175 Pounds**
Calisthenics	5:16–6:23	5:00–5:33	4:29–5:16
Running	2:16–2:44	2:09–2:25	1:56–2:16
Walking	5:16–6:23	5:00–5:33	4:29–5:16
Bowling	8:20–10:00	7:54–8:49	7:09–8:20
Swimming	2:56–3:32	2:47–3:08	2:30–2:56
Bicycling	3:48–4:37	3:37–4:03	3:16–3:48
Tennis	3:42–4:29	3:32–3:57	3:11–3:42
Golf	4:46–5:46	4:29–5:05	4:03–4:46

Begin timing: _____

1. If you weigh about 120 pounds, what form of exercise burns the most calories?

    _____

2. If you weigh about 150 pounds, will you burn more calories if you swim or if you run? _____

3. If you weigh about 175 pounds, how long will it take you to burn 1,500 calories per week by walking? _____

4. What activity on the chart is the slowest way to burn calories at any weight?

    _____

5. If you want to burn as many calories as you can in order to lose weight, what activity should you do? _____

6. If you don't like the activity in the answer to question 5, what's the next best activity to do to burn calories? _____

7. If you weigh about 120 pounds, how many hours/minutes per week would you have to spend bowling in order to burn 1,500 calories? _____

   _____

8. Is bicycling a faster or slower way to burn calories than tennis?_____

   _____

Time: _____   **Number correct:** _____

PRACTICE C-2: Map, Graph, Chart

Directions: Using the map and charts on pages 112 and 113, scan for the answers to the following questions. Circle the letter of the correct response. Answers are provided as a learning tool. Don't read them until after you have scanned.

1. The city that has the fewest wet days per year is located in

   a. Newfoundland.

   b. Saskatchewan.

   c. Ontario.

   d. Alberta.

   The correct answer can be found by looking under the "Wet Days" column on the chart. The city is Regina with 109 wet days. To find the province in which the city is located, look on the map provided. The correct answer is Saskatchewan.

2. T/F The city having the least annual snowfall also has the highest average annual temperature.

   To find the correct answer you must compare two columns. Scan the columns that list average yearly snowfall and note the city that has the lowest snowfall. It is Victoria. Next scan the "Average High" column in the chart that lists average annual temperatures to determine which city has the highest average temperatures. The answer is Victoria. Therefore, the answer to question 2 is true.

3. The city having the lowest average temperature is

   a. Regina.

   b. Fredericton.

   c. Quebec City.

   d. Yellowknife.

   The correct answer can be found under the "Average Low" column in the "Average annual temperature" chart. The correct answer is Yellowknife with -9.7.

WEATHER CONDITIONS

	Wet days number	Snowfall cm
St. John's	217	322.1
Charlottetown	177	338.7
Halifax	170	261.4
Fredericton	156	294.5
Quebec City	178	337.0
Montreal	162	214.2
Ottawa	159	221.5
Toronto	139	135.0
Winnipeg	119	114.8
Regina	109	107.4
Edmonton	123	129.6
Calgary	111	135.4
Vancouver	164	54.9
Victoria	153	46.9
Whitehorse	122	145.2
Yellowknife	118	143.9

Adapted from the Statistics Canada Web site, http://www.statcan.ca/English/Pgdb/Land/Geography/phys08.htm.

AVERAGE ANNUAL TEMPERATURE

	Average high	Average low
	Celsius	
St. John's	8.6	0.8
Charlottetown	9.5	0.8
Halifax	10.7	1.4
Fredericton	11.0	-0.6
Quebec City	9.0	-1.0
Montreal	10.9	1.2
Ottawa	10.7	0.8
Toronto	12.6	5.2
Winnipeg	8.1	-3.4
Regina	8.9	-3.8
Edmonton	8.7	-1.5
Calgary	10.3	-2.6
Vancouver	13.5	6.1
Victoria	13.9	5.1
Whitehorse	4.1	-6.2
Yellowknife	-0.8	-9.7

Adapted from the Statistics Canada Web site, http://www.statcan.ca/English/Pgdb/Land/Geography/phys08.htm.

4. The average number of centimetres of snowfall in Charlottetown is
   a. 383.7
   b. 337.8
   c. 322.1
   d. 338.7

   Be careful with this question. Check the number carefully. Find Charlottetown on the chart that lists the number of wet days per year and the average snowfall in centimetres. Scan across to find the number 338.7. The correct answer is d.

5. The city with the highest average temperature is located in the province of
   a. Nova Scotia
   b. British Columbia
   c. Ontario
   d. Quebec

   The correct answer can be found by looking at the Average annual temperature chart. Under the column "Average High" look for the city that has the highest temperature. The answer is Victoria, with 13.9. Next, look at the map of Canada and find Victoria. You'll see that it is located in the province of British Columbia. Therefore, the correct answer is b.

6. The number of dry days per year in Winnipeg is
   a. 119
   b. 109
   c. 246
   d. 264

The correct answer can be found by finding the number of wet days per annum for Winnipeg. The answer is 119. Then, subtract that number from the total number of days per year, 365, from 119. The answer is 246, or c.

7. The city closest to the Pacific ocean had how many wet days?

   a. 118

   b. 153

   c. 217

   d. 170

   The correct answer can be found by first looking at the map and locating the city nearest the Pacific. Then look at the number of wet days on the chart to find the city. The city is Victoria and the correct answer is b.

8. The city having the most wet days had what average high temperature?

   a. 10.7

   b. 12.6

   c. 4.1

   d. 8.6

   The correct answer can be found by finding the city with the highest number of wet days. Next, find that city, St. John's, on the chart that lists the average annual temperatures. The average high temperature in St. John's is 8.6. Therefore, the answer is d.

9. The city appearing nearest the middle of the map is located in which province or territory?

   a. Manitoba

   b. Ontario

   c. Saskatchewan

   d. Nunavut

   The correct answer can be found by simply locating the middle point of the map and looking to see what city is nearest that point. It is Winnipeg, which is located in Manitoba.

10. The city farthest east on the map receives how many centimetres of snow per annum?

   a. 321.1

   b. 261.4

   c. 322.1

   d. 221.5

   The correct answer can be found by locating the city farthest east on the map. The city is St. John's, Newfoundland. Then look under the snowfall column on the chart to find the number of centimetres of snowfall. The correct answer is 322.1, or c.

PRACTICE C-3: An Index

Directions: Scan the index listing on page 117 for the answers to the following questions. Circle the letter of the correct answer. You should finish in less than three minutes.

Begin timing: _____

1. On what page(s) would you find information about Six Nations Confederacy?
   a. 193
   b. 124
   c. 411
   d. 229
   e. a and d above

2. On what pages would you find information about slavery in New France?
   a. 353–54
   b. 113–18
   c. 109–11
   d. 238–240

3. On what page(s) would you find information on the life of James Smith?
   a. 484
   b. 489
   c. 383
   d. a and b above

4. How many pages are listed for information on shipbuilding in the timber industry?
   a. 6
   b. 1
   c. 5
   d. 4

5. On what pages would you find information on Scottish immigrants?
   a. 221, 390
   b. 224, 368
   c. 177 only
   d. 198–99

6. Are Spanish settlers listed in the index?
   a. no
   b. yes
   c. can't tell

7. On what page will you find information about Elisabeth Tooker?

   a. 3790

   b. 17

   c. 11

   d. 156

8. How many pages are listed for the Seven Years' War?

   a. 1

   b. 2

   c. 3

   d. 5

9. Under what other listing besides "Toryism" could you find more information about it?

   a. Family Compact

   b. Prime Ministers

   c. Stanley, F.G.

   d. Taignoagny

10. How many pages are given to the smallpox epidemic?

   a. 1

   b. 2

   c. 3

   d. 5

Time: _____   Number correct: _____

From R. Douglas Francis, Richard Jones, and Donald B. Smith, *Origins: Canadian History to Confederation*, 4th ed., Harcourt 2000, p. 510.

D.   Taking Reading Notes

Some students don't want to mark or underline their textbooks because they want to sell them when the course is over. This is understandable, considering the cost of textbooks these days. Still, marking and underlining, if done correctly, are preferable to taking notes, for the reasons described in the previous section. But there are times when you must use books that are not yours, so a method for taking notes is needed.

> The main thing to remember about taking reading notes is not to copy word for word from the book. Rephrase what the author says in your own words as much as possible. Many students make the mistake of copying right from the book, thinking that they are doing a good job of studying. Such action usually produces no results. The purpose of taking notes is to make certain that you understand what you are reading at the time and to record it for later review.

As with marking and underlining, there is no single best way. But here are some guidelines for you to follow:

1. At the top of the notebook page, always write down the title of the book, the chapter title, and the pages your notes cover. There may be a time in the future when your notes aren't as helpful as you expected and you need to refer back to the book. This information will help you find the material in the book quickly.

2. Write the main ideas of the passage as your own heading, then list the supporting details under this heading. In effect, you are summarizing main ideas and supporting details just as you did in Chapter Two with paragraphs and essays.

3. Don't write anything down until you have studied a short passage and are sure you understand it. Let the writing patterns discussed in the last chapter help you sort out the key points. If an author is defining a term or concept, make certain your notes contain the definition. If the author is comparing or contrasting two items, make certain your notes reflect the comparison, contrast, and so on.

4. Remember, don't use the same words as the author unless it is necessary. If you do use the author's own words, make certain you know their meanings. Be sure to put quotation marks around words that are the author's and not yours.

5. Keep track of words you need to look up. If the vocabulary is difficult, you may need to look up some words in the glossary or in a dictionary before you can take notes.

6. Write down questions that you can't answer or that give you trouble so that you can ask your instructor about them at the next class.

Feel free to modify these suggestions. Just make certain that you are not going through the motions of taking notes without really understanding what you are writing down.

PRACTICE D-1: Taking Notes from a Political Science Textbook

Directions: Survey and form questions about the following short passage from *Great Political Thinkers,* a political science textbook. Then, as you read through it, mark key passages. In the space following the reading selection, write up a set of notes that summarizes the contents.

FROM "CHAPTER 1: THE GREEK FAITH IN REASON"

WILLIAM EBENSTEIN AND ALAN O. EBENSTEIN

1   The most memorable creation of Athenian civilization, of all of Greek antiquity, is not this or that idea, this or that sculpture or drama, but a person: Socrates (born in 469 B.C. and executed in 399 B.C.). Like Jesus, he never wrote a line, yet his influence on western thought, directly and indirectly through Plato, is second to none. One of the great teachers of all time, Socrates said of himself, "I have never set myself up as any man's teacher." He was ready at all times to converse with anyone who wished to do so, and "to answer questions for rich and poor alike."

2   In his youth he was strongly impressed with the philosophical and scientific ideas then current and generally accepted by the intellectuals throughout Greece. As he grew older, his interest shifted—like that of Greek thought generally—from the understanding of the outer world to the inner world of man. What was important (in fact, the only important thing) was the understanding and mastery of the inner life of individuals and their relations with others. He felt that just as knowledge unravelled the mysteries of physical nature, so it could lead to mankind's moral mastery. But this knowledge was not the specialized knowledge of the craftsman or expert in a particular field, but the knowledge of moral principles by which all are to be governed.

3   The method he used in the process of discovering these principles was not one of dogmatically laying down the truth in advance, followed by arguments in support. Socrates' method—and this is what makes him a teacher second to none—was to proceed by question and answer, helping the other person to use his own mind in finding answers to those questions that must be answered if life is to have meaning. Socrates liked to think of himself as merely fulfilling the function of an intellectual midwife, facilitating the birth of ideas already conceived in the mind of the other person.

4   The questions he asked were those that every person encounters in everyday living: What are the meanings of justice, courage, beauty, the good? By adducing practical examples of these abstract concepts, Socrates helped his fellow-debaters or interlocutors to gradually arrive at a general definition. Yet, he did not state he had final answers. He said that the only difference between himself and others was that, whereas they thought they knew, he at least knew he did not. If the moral life depends on knowledge, then virtue, or doing the good, and philosophy, or knowing the good, become identical. Living the right kind of life thus leads to an endless search for the knowledge of the right principles of living. Humankind's salvation from confusion and conflict lies, therefore, Socrates teaches, in a life-long quest for philosophical—and, consequently, moral—self-mastery. Humanity is saved, not (as in Christianity) by outside divine grace, but by inner rational and moral forces, provided these are mobilized and utilized properly.

5   Socrates was a profoundly religious man; yet his religion knew of no rewards and punishments, as in the Judeo-Christian theology. His innermost desire was to transcend the material temptations of life and to achieve a life of pure spirit on earth—to "practice immortality" in this life. He was not sure whether there was a life after death, but he faced death with equanimity whether death meant complete annihilation or the migration of the soul to another world.

6   Socrates was tried in 399 B.C., ostensibly on the charge of corrupting the minds of the young and of believing in deities of his own invention. In fact, the trial was

political. The Peloponnesian War between the two alliances of states—one led by Athens, the other by Sparta—had started in 431 B.C., and ended in 404 B.C. with the defeat of Athens, a defeat from which neither Athens nor Greece ever recovered. As a result of this defeat, an antidemocratic regime, led by Critias, a disciple of Socrates, was set up, and it committed many crimes of violence and tyranny. In 403 B.C. this unpopular tyranny was overthrown and democracy was restored.

7   Socrates was known as the spiritual guide and mentor of many of the antidemocratic faction and therefore something had to be done against him. In addition to this obvious political cause of the trial, there was also a deeper motivation: the fear of independent, unorthodox thinking. This was a fear not peculiar to democracy in ancient Athens. Had he asked for mercy or pity, there is little doubt Socrates would have received them from his judges. He also had the opportunity of escaping from his jail after he was sentenced to death. Yet Socrates used his trial (as described in Plato's *Apology*) not as means of saving his own life but as his last opportunity of serving his fellow citizens in the only way which he knew and thought was right, telling them again what his life was all about, what he believed in, and what it means to be a human. Possibly the most succinct summary of Socrates' thought, expressing both his intellectual and moral beliefs, is one brief statement during his trial: *"The unexamined life is not worth living."*

Write your notes in the space below and on the following page.

_____

_____

_____

_____

_____

_____

_____

_____

Compare your notes with these. Wording will vary, but yours should contain similar information:

Do your notes contain book and chapter titles? Page references?	From <u>Great Political Thinkers.</u> Chap. 1: The Greek Faith in Reason, pp. 12–13
Do your notes contain information about Socrates' life?	<u>About Socrates</u> (469 B.C. to 399 B.C.) —impressed with the philosophical and scientific ideas of his time as a youth —when older, concerned with the "inner man," "knowledge of moral principles" by which all men are governed —what's the meaning of justice, courage, beauty, good? —tried in 399 B.C. for corrupting young minds
Do your notes contain information about Socrates' teaching methods?	<u>Teaching Methods</u> —considered one of the greatest teachers of all time —never wrote —taught through questions and answers —intellectual midwife—birth to ideas
Do your notes contain information about his philosophy? Do your notes contain information that answers why Socrates is called the most memorable creation of Athenian civilization?	<u>His Philosophy</u> —believed humanity would be saved not by outside, divine forces but by inner rational and moral forces —moral life depends on knowledge —living the right kind of life leads to an endless search for the knowledge of the right principles of living. —"The unexamined life is not worth living." —He died for his principles (rather than saving his own life) by fighting for independent, unorthodox thinking.

<u>Class/Teacher Questions</u>
—How did Socrates die?

> ### Application 3: Taking Notes from Your Textbook
>
> Using a textbook from another class, develop a system of marking, under-lining, or taking reading notes. Explain your system and include a sample of your marking or note-taking from a chapter in that textbook. Compare your system with the system of a study partner in your class.

PRACTICE D-2: Mapping—Another Type of Note-taking

Directions: Mapping, a technique developed by an educator named M. Buckley Hanf, is a way to get your notes for an entire chapter on one or two notebook pages. The technique forces you to see a chapter as a whole rather than in pieces and helps you store what you read in your long-term memory. As with any study device, it is only as good as you make it.

Mapping works well with the SQ3R method. This practice will show you how to map a chapter as well as have you do some of it. Since you now know how to use SQ3R, learning how and why to map a chapter should make sense and prove to be another useful alternative for good studying.

Part A

First, survey the following passage, adapted from a communications text-book. As you carefully read the title and headings and look for study aids, count the number of major headings that divide the passage. When you are finished with your survey, go to Part B.

◆ CHANGING THE SELF-CONCEPT

◆ **The only person who behaves sensibly is my tailor. He makes new measurements every time he sees me. All the rest go on with the old measurements.**

George Bernard Shaw

Having read this far, you know more clearly just what the self-concept is, how it is formed, and how it affects communication. But we still haven't focused on what may be the most important question of all: How can you change the parts of your self-concept with which you aren't happy? Sometimes the answer involves changing your *self* (for example, getting a responsible job or losing weight), and sometimes it means changing your *beliefs* (recognizing your strengths or decreasing self-criticism). Neither of these processes is simple, for there's usually no quick method for becoming the person you'd like to be: Personal growth and self-improvement are lifelong activities. But there are several suggestions that can help you move closer to your goals.

52

"Changing Self-Concept" from *Understanding Human Communication*, 4th edition by Ronald B. Adler and George Rodman, copyright © 1991 by Harcourt, Inc., reprinted by permission of the publisher.

Have Realistic Expectations

It's extremely important to realize that some of your dissatisfaction might come from expecting too much of yourself. If you demand that you handle every act of communication perfectly, you're bound to be disappointed. Nobody is able to handle every conflict productively, to be totally relaxed and skillful in conversations, to ask consistently perceptive questions, or to be 100 percent helpful when others have problems. Expecting yourself to reach such unrealistic goals is to doom yourself to unhappiness at the start.

How committed are you to changing your self-concept? You can find out by responding to the steps that follow.

a. Choose a partner and for five minutes or so take turns making and listing statements that begin with "I can't..." Try to focus your statements on your relationships with family, friends, co-workers and students, and even strangers: whomever you have a hard time communicating with.

Sample statements:

"I can't be myself with strangers I'd like to get to know at parties."

"I can't tell a friend how much I care about her."

"I can't bring myself to ask my supervisor for the raise I think I deserve."

"I can't ask questions in class."

b. Notice the feelings you experience as you make each statement: self-pity, regret, concern, frustration, and so on; and share these with your partner.

c. Now go back and repeat aloud each statement you've just made, but this time change each *can't* to a *won't*. After each sentence, share with your partner whatever thoughts you have about what you've just said.

d. After you've finished, decide whether "can't" or "won't" is more appropriate for each item, and explain your choice to your partner.

e. Are there any instances of the self-fulfilling prophecy in your list— times when your decision that you "couldn't" do something was the only force keeping you from doing it?

Sometimes it's easy to be hard on yourself because all those around you seem to be handling themselves so much better than you. It's important to realize that much of what seems like confidence and skill in others is a front to hide uncertainty. They may be suffering from the same self-imposed demands of perfection that you place on yourself.

Even in cases where others definitely seem more competent than you, it's important to judge yourself in terms of your own growth, not against the behaviour of others. Rather than feeling miserable because you're not as talented as an expert, realize that you probably are a better, wiser, or more skillful person than you used to be and that this is a legitimate source of satisfaction. Perfection is fine as an ideal, but you're being unfair to yourself if you expect actually to reach that state.

Perception and the Self

Have a Realistic Perception of Yourself

One source of a poor self-concept is an inaccurate self-perception. As you've already read, such unrealistic pictures sometimes come from being overly harsh on yourself, believing that you're worse than the facts indicate. By sharing the self-concept list you recorded on page 27, you will be able to see whether you have been selling yourself short. Of course, it would be foolish to deny that you could be a better person than you are, but it's also important to recognize your strengths.

An unrealistically poor self-concept can also come from the inaccurate feedback of others. Perhaps you are in an environment where you receive an excessive number of "downer" messages, many of which are undeserved, and a minimum of upper messages. We have known many women, for example, who have returned to college after many years spent in homemaking where they received virtually no recognition for their intellectual strengths. It's amazing that these women have the courage to come to college at all, so low is their self-esteem; but come they do, and most are thrilled to find that they are much brighter and more competent intellectually than they suspected. In the same way, workers with overly critical supervisors, children with cruel "friends," and students with unsupportive teachers all are prone to suffering from low self-concepts owing to excessively negative feedback.

If you fall into this category, it's important to put the unrealistic evaluations you receive into perspective and then to seek out more supportive people who will acknowledge your assets as well as point out your shortcomings. Doing so is often a quick and sure boost to self-esteem.

Have the Will to Change

Often we claim we want to change, but we aren't willing to do the necessary work. You might, for instance, decide that you'd like to become a better conversationalist. Taking the advice offered in the next section of this book, you ask your instructor or some other communication adviser how to reach this goal. Suppose you receive two suggestions: first, to spend the next three weeks observing people who handle themselves well in conversations and to record exactly what they do that makes them so skillful; second, to read several books on the subject of conversational skills. You begin these tasks with the best intentions, but after a few days the task of recording conversations becomes a burden—it would be so much easier just to listen to others talk. And your diligent reading program becomes bogged down as the press of other work fills up your time. In other words, you find you just "can't" fit the self-improvement plan into your busy schedule.

Let's be realistic. Becoming a better communicator is probably one of many goals in your life. It's possible that you'll find other needs more pressing, which is completely reasonable. However, you should realize that changing your self-concept often requires a good deal of effort, and without that effort your good intentions alone probably won't get you much closer to this goal. In communication, as in most other aspects of life, "there's no such thing as a free lunch."

Elements of Communication

Have the Skill Needed to Change

Often trying isn't enough. There are some cases where you would change if you knew of a way to do so. To see if this is the case for you, check the list of can'ts and won'ts from the exercise on page 53, and see if any items there are more appropriately "don't know hows." If so, then the way to change is to learn how. You can do so in two ways.

First, you can seek advice—from books such as this one, from the references listed at the end of each chapter, and from other printed sources. You can also get suggestions from instructors, counselors, and other experts, as well as from friends. Of course, not all the advice you receive will be useful, but if you read widely and talk to enough people, you have a good chance of learning the things you want to know.

A second method of learning how to change is to observe models—people who handle themselves in the ways you would like to master. It's often been said that people learn more from models than in any other way, and by taking advantage of this principle you will find that the world is full of teachers who can show you how to communicate more successfully. Become a careful observer. Watch what people you admire do and say, not so that you can copy them, but so that you can adapt their behavior to fit your own personal style.

At this point you might be overwhelmed at the difficulty of changing the way you think about yourself and the way you act. Remember, we never said that this would be easy (although it sometimes is). But even when change is difficult, you know that it's possible if you are serious. You don't need to be perfect, but you can improve your self-concept if you choose to.

Perception and the Self

55

Part B

Your survey should have shown you that the selection is divided into four major headings. Read from one heading to the next, stopping to make notes about each of the headings in the spaces below.

Selection Title: _____

Heading #1: _____

_____

Heading #2: _____

_____

Heading #3: _____

_____

Heading #4: _____

_____

Rather than make reading notes as you just did, some students prefer the mapping technique. Look carefully at the map of the chapter below and compare it with your notes.

Notice how the chapter title appears in a rectangle in the center of the map. The four heading titles appear on lines drawn from each of the four quarters of the rectangle. The key points to remember about each of the headings appear on lines drawn under the appropriate heading. If there had been five headings rather than four, a different design might be drawn around the chapter title, to allow five lines, one for each heading. In other words, the design made around the chapter title can be drawn to fit the number of headings.

Also notice that each heading is written above or below a line depending on where you want the branches to fit. Frequently, students can map an entire chapter on one page, making it visually easy to review. In addition, mapping forces you to summarize key points.

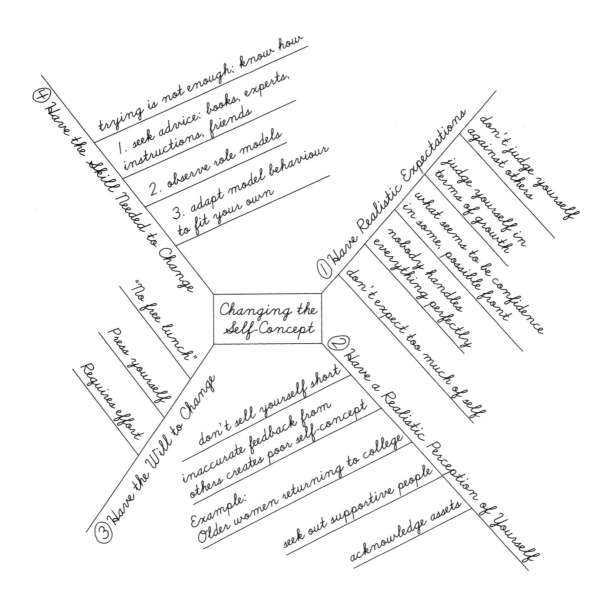

Part C

Directions: Go back to your notes for Practice D-1 on page 118. On a separate sheet of regular 8½" × 11" notebook paper, make a map for the information on Socrates. *Hint:* There are three headings you might have. Place the title of the passage in the middle of the page and draw a triangle around it. See what you can do from there. Turn in your map to your instructor when finished.

PRACTICE D-3: More Mapping Practice

Directions: There are four parts to this practice. Do them in order:

Part A

First, take just a minute or two and survey the following passage from a logic textbook. As you carefully read the title and headings, count the number of major headings that divide the chapter. When you are finished with your survey, go to Part B, which follows the textbook passage.

RECOGNIZING ERRORS IN REASONING

VINCENT RYAN RUGGIERO

1   The ten reasoning errors we will discuss in this chapter are not the only ones you will find in dialogues, but they are the most common ones. By becoming familiar with them, you will be able to identify where most arguments go wrong and determine how to set them right again.

EITHER-OR THINKING

2   The error in either-or thinking consists of viewing a particular reality solely in terms of opposing extremes when, in fact, other views are possible. It is often accompanied by the demand that people choose between the two extremes and the clear, if often unstated, suggestion that no third choice is possible. Here is an example of either-or thinking.

GERTRUDE: The real aim of religion is perfecting one's self. Nothing else but that matters.

HEATHCLIFF: That's not true. The real aim is loving one's neighbor. If your focus is in yourself, you simply aren't a religious person.

3   Now it may be that one or the other of these aims is the "real" aim of religion. But it may also be that religion has two or three or eighteen important aims. To discount that possibility even before considering it is unreasonable. Whenever you encounter either-or thinking, ask, "Why must it be one or the other? Why not both (or neither)?"

STEREOTYPING

4   Stereotyping is ignoring someone's or something's individuality and focusing instead on some preconceived notion about the person or thing. (It is one of the central features of prejudice.) There are stereotyped notions about Jews and blacks and atheists and political parties—in short, about many things. Here is an example:

> GERTRUDE: Are you going to that public lecture tonight, the one about the effects of exercise on stress? The local tennis coach is delivering it.
>
> HEATHCLIFF: I wouldn't waste my time listening to some dumb jock's simple-minded muttering.

5   Is the coach an authority on the subject he is lecturing on? Has he done research? Has he written articles or books? These are reasonable matters to inquire about. But Healthcliff's negative stereotyping smothers his curiosity and makes fair judgment impossible. Whenever you encounter such prefabricated assessments of an entire class of people or things, ask, "What evidence is offered that the assessment fits the individual in question?"

ATTACKING THE PERSON

6   Another error consists of disposing of an argument by attacking the person who advances it. It is not a reasonable approach because an argument's validity does not depend on the character of its advocates. A scoundrel may, on occasion, support a valid argument, and a saint an invalid one. Here is an example of attacking the person:

> GERTRUDE: Arthur Dean is organizing a group to protest the tearing down of the Hastings Mansion. He believes its historic value is too great to let it be sacrificed for a shopping center. I'm going to join.
>
> HEATHCLIFF: You're crazy to join. Dean is a real lowlife. He runs around with other girls behind his fiancée's back and uses his roommate's things without permission. Besides, he sponges off everyone.

7   Everything Heathcliff says about Dean may be accurate. And yet it sheds no light on whether the protest Dean is organizing is worthy of support. Whenever you find an attack on a person in a dialogue, ask, "Are the charges being made against the person relevant to the issue under discussion?" If they are not, refuse to consider them in your analysis.

CONTRADICTION

8   Contradiction occurs when a person makes two assertions that are logically inconsistent with each other. It is an error that occurs more often in long dialogues than in short ones and is more difficult to detect than other errors because the conflicting assertions seldom appear together. To detect contradiction you must remember each dialoguer's early assertions and recognize their relationship to later assertions. Here is an example of a contradiction dialogue:

> GERTRUDE: Morally, our nation is in big trouble. Let me give you an example. For centuries, the taking of a life was regarded as wrong. That's as it should be. No one is ever justified in taking a human life. Yet today books and articles are written defending so-called mercy killing and giving directions on how to commit suicide.
>
> [Later in the dialogue, after several exchanges with Healthcliff, Gertrude speaks again.]

GERTRUDE: I still say we've grown too casual about human life. The only situation in which the taking of a life is ever justified is self-defense.

9 First Gertrude says the taking of a human life is never justified. Then she says there is a situation where it is justified. That is a contradiction. Whenever you encounter a contradiction in a person's argument, ask, "Does the contradiction invalidate the person's entire argument or only a part of it? And if a part, which part?" A note of caution is in order here. Careful inspection of what at first glance appear to be contradictions will often reveal they are not contradictions at all. If, for example, Gertrude had said, "No one should ever be applauded for taking a human life," instead of "No one is ever justified in taking a human life," she could not fairly be charged with contradicting herself, at least until you knew what she meant by "applauded."

FAULTY ANALOGY

10 Analogy is a line of reasoning suggesting that things alike in one respect are also alike in other respects. Analogy is a very common kind of reasoning and there is nothing wrong with it as long as the similarities that are claimed are real. An analogy is faulty when they are not real.

11 Here is an example of faulty analogy:

GERTRUDE: I hear the government is requiring that stronger warnings be placed on cigarette packages and in advertisements.

HEATHCLIFF: Putting warnings on cigarette packages is as foolish as putting "Warning! Eating too much of this product may make you a fat slob!" on packages of spaghetti or "Warning! Careless use of this instrument may smash your fingers" on hammers.

12 Heathcliff's analogies are vivid, but faulty. Eating spaghetti is good for people; if done in moderation, it provides nutrition. Smoking cigarettes does no comparable good. Similarly, the hammer can do harm if used carelessly. But cigarettes have been shown to do harm no matter how carefully they are used. Whenever you encounter any analogy, say "Granted, these two things may be similar in certain aspects, but are there any respects in which they are dissimilar?"

FAULTY CAUSATION

13 Faulty causation may take either of two forms. The first is concluding that one thing caused another merely because of their proximity in time or space. For example, shortly after a black cat crosses someone's path, an accident befalls her, so she concludes that the cat's crossing her path caused her misfortune. This error occurs not only in everyday reasoning, but in formal reasoning as well. For many years the prevailing medical opinion was that damp night air causes malaria simply because the onset of the disease occurred after exposure to night air. (The real cause, mosquitoes, which happened to be more active in evening hours, was discovered much later.)

14 The other form taken by faulty causation is concluding that learning why people are interested in an issue is the same as evaluating their thinking about the issue. "Find the motivation," goes this reasoning, "and you have determined whether that argument is valid." This line of reasoning, which resembles attacking the person, is erroneous for a similar reason. A person's motivation for advancing an argument is never sufficient reason for approving or rejecting an argument. Noble motives may underlie bad arguments and ignoble motives good ones. Here is an example of this form of faulty causation:

GERTRUDE: Professor McCready told my class today he believes the way student evaluations are used on this campus doesn't provide effective evaluations of the quality of teaching. He said the questions themselves are OK, but the evaluation should be made at the end of the semester instead of during the tenth week. He blasted the administration, saying they are more concerned with suiting their schedules than getting meaningful input from students. He made a lot of sense.

HEATHCLIFF: Sometimes you're really naive, Gertie. Didn't you even wonder why he attacked the testing procedure? If you had done so, you'd know. It must be he got scorched by students on the evaluation last semester. If he'd received a good rating, he'd be praising the evaluation process. So much for his "sensible argument."

15   Perhaps Heathcliff is correct in what he says about the professor. Perhaps he did get a poor evaluation last semester. And perhaps that's what prompted him to take a critical look at the evaluation procedure. So what? That would be a normal reaction, yet it has no bearing on the validity of his argument about student evaluation of teachers. That argument can be appraised only by examining the evidence that supports or challenges it.

16   Whenever you encounter an assertion that one thing has caused another, ask, "Is the proximity in time or space evidence of a true cause/effect relationship or merely a coincidence?" Whenever you find an argument being approved or rejected because of a person's motivation, remember that motivation is irrelevant and test the argument against the evidence.

IRRATIONAL APPEAL

17   There are four common kinds of irrational appeal: appeals to emotion, to tradition or faith, to moderation, and to authority. Each of these is a misuse of a rational appeal and may be identified as follows:

An *appeal to emotion* is rational when it accompanies thought and analysis, and irrational when it substitutes for them.

An *appeal to tradition or faith* is rational when the particular practice or belief is regarded in light of the present circumstances, and irrational when it means "Let's continue to do (believe) as we have done merely because we have always done so."

An *appeal to moderation* is rational when the moderate approach is offered as the best solution to the problem or issue, and irrational when moderation is merely a convenient way to avoid offending someone or to evade the responsibility of judging.

An *appeal to authority* is rational when it acknowledges the fallibility of people and their institutions and the possibility of differing interpretations, and irrational when it disallows reasonable questions and challenges. (As used here, *authority* means not only eminent people, but also eminent books and documents, such as the Bible . . . and eminent agencies, such as the Supreme Court.) . . .

HASTY CONCLUSION

18   A hasty conclusion is one that is drawn without appropriate evidence. In other words, it is a conclusion chosen without sufficient reason from two or more possible conclusions. Hasty conclusions are especially tempting in situations where prior opinions compromise objectivity. These opinions make a person wish for a particular conclusion to be so, and wishing leads to uncritical acceptance. Here is an example of a hasty conclusion:

GERTRUDE: How did you make out with that part-time job you were applying for?

HEATHCLIFF: I didn't get it, and I know very well why, too. It's because I'm not black . . . and I'm not a woman.

GERTRUDE: How do you know that was the reason?

HEATHCLIFF: Come on, Gertie. You know perfectly well that minorities have an advantage in today's job market.

19   Even if Heathcliff were right about minorities having an advantage in the job market (and considerable evidence challenges that view), his conclusion about his failure to get the job is hasty. The fact that something is generally true is not sufficient evidence that it is true in a particular case. It is possible that Heathcliff was passed over because of lack of experience or a bad attitude or some other reason. Whenever you encounter any conclusion, ask whether the evidence is sufficient to warrant choosing it over other possible conclusions.

OVERGENERALIZATION

20   A generalization is a judgment about a class of people or things made after observation of a number of members of that class. Overgeneralization is generalization based upon insufficient observation. One of the most common errors in argument, overgeneralization may be explained by the natural human tendency to classify sensory data tidily, and by the difficulty of determining what, in any given situation, constitutes "sufficient evidence." Accordingly, people are often found making careless assertions about whole groups of people and things. Here are some examples:

GERTRUDE: Ever since I arrived on campus last month, I've been appalled by the manners of the students here. They're unbelievably boorish.

HEATHCLIFF: Yes, and the townspeople are so unfriendly, too. I don't know why I ever picked this college.

GERTRUDE: Oh, I'm not sorry I came here. The professors are very helpful and encouraging. They go out of their way to explain things.

21   We don't know how many students are enrolled in the college, what the population of the town is, or how many professors are on the college staff. But however small the college and the town are, it is unlikely that Gertrude and Heathcliff have had enough contact with people to justify their level of generalization. Whenever you encounter a statement about entire groups of people or things, look for evidence that the observations have been sufficient in number and that the person has demonstrated that what was observed is typical of the group in general. If that evidence is lacking in the dialogue, and your own experience does not provide it, you may conclude that you are dealing with an overgeneralization.

OVERSIMPLIFICATION

22   It is natural to want to simplify matters; simplification aids understanding and communication. For that reason, simplification is legitimate—as long as it does not distort the reality it describes. When it does that, it becomes oversimplification. The most frequent kind of oversimplification that occurs in dialogues is the presentation of only one side of a two-sided (or three- or four-sided) reality. Here is an example of such oversimplification:

GERTRUDE: I'm really looking forward to being a high school teacher someday. I only hope I can meet the demands of the profession.

HEATHCLIFF: Demands? High school teachers have it made. They're through at three o'clock every day and only work nine months of the year. The only cushier job I know of is the job of a college professor.

23   There is some truth in what Heathcliff says. The high school class schedule usually ends at 3:00 P.M. and the official work year, with holidays and summer vacation time considered, is nine months. But that is only part of the complex reality of high school teaching. Many teachers are responsible for five different classes each day, each of which requires preparation for lectures and discussions, and for the grading of homework. All that work must be done after 3:00 P.M. In addition, teachers are often expected to chaperone after-school activities and advise clubs and organizations. Finally, they are required to extend their knowledge of the subject matter they teach by pursuing graduate degrees in their spare time. To ignore all these duties is to oversimplify the reality of high school teaching.

24   There is no easy formula for detecting oversimplification. Your best approach is to be suspicious of any brief description of a complex reality. When you encounter one, ask, "Is it really this neat and simple? Is there another side of the reality that is not represented here?"

Part B

When you have finished your survey, answer the following questions:

1. What is the title of the chapter?_____

_____

2. How many headings does the chapter have? _____

_____

3. What do you think the chapter will cover? _____

_____

_____

Using this survey information, on a regular 8½" × 11" page in your notebook, place the title of the chapter in the middle of the page. Since there are ten headings to this chapter you may want to draw a circle around the title. Draw a line out from the circle and write in the title of the first heading so that your map will look like this:

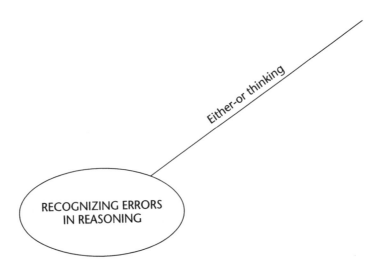

Note: Sometimes it is necessary to divide a chapter into two or more parts, depending on the length and number of headings. For instance, if you discover you need more room for notes, you might list only five headings on one map page and five on another.

Part C

You are now ready to turn each heading into a question, the second step in the SQ3R method. The first heading is "Either-Or Thinking." Turn the heading into a question, such as, "What is either-or thinking?" Then read until you get to the second heading. When you come to the second heading, come back here and answer the following questions.

1. What is "either-or thinking"? _____
_____
_____
_____

2. What is the main idea of the passage under the first heading? _____
_____
_____

3. What are some important supporting points you want in your notes from this section?_____
_____
_____

Now look at the following partial map and notice the information that has been written on the branch for the first heading. Your wording may be different but the main points should be the same.

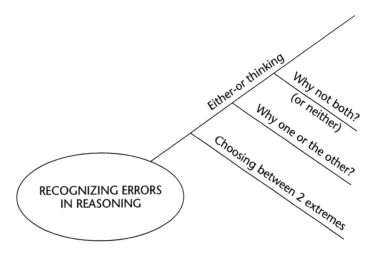

Part D

Now read from the second heading, "Stereotyping," to the third heading, then stop. Repeat the same process: draw another line or branch from the centre of your map, writing in the heading on the top of the line. List under that branch what you think are the key supporting points about stereotyping. Continue this process until you have read the entire chapter. Save your map: you will need it later.

Application 4: Creating a Chapter Map

In a textbook for another class, read a chapter or a long selection and develop a map. Compare your map with the map of your study partner.

E.   Test-Taking Strategies

When taking tests, it is important that you be able to read and interpret the questions correctly. It won't matter how well you studied if you can't show what you learned on a test.

Tests are usually classified as either *objective* or *subjective.*

- *Objective exams* include true-false, multiple-choice, matching and completion, or fill-in type questions. Your job on an objective exam is to choose the best answer from those provided. You may be asked to select a word or phrase that correctly completes a statement. Or you may need to recall on your own some fact, date, or figure to fill in a blank. Objective tests can be scored with an answer key and frequently are machine-scored.

- *Subjective exams,* on the other hand, usually require short to long written answers, usually called essay tests. Rather than a simple statement of fact, essay exams usually require that you demonstrate an understanding of the ideas learned rather than just a recall of facts and figures. Frequently, writing well is as important as knowing the answer in subjective tests.

Many students read the assignments, listen in class, and take good notes but can't put what they learned together for an exam. Here are some pointers to help you do better on tests.

Preparing for Exams

As almost any study skills book will tell you, preparing for exams begins the first day of class. Surveying your textbooks, using the SQ3R study method, taking lecture and reading notes, mapping, attending classes, and reviewing your notes frequently are all part of preparing for an exam.

Here are a few guidelines for more efficient use of time in preparing for exams:

1. *Ask your instructor about the exam:*

- Will the exam be objective or essay? If it will be an objective exam, you will need to memorize a certain amount of material. If it's an essay exam, you can practice writing some answers to the types of questions you think the instructor might ask.

- Can you bring a dictionary or outside materials?
- Will the exam be "open book," that is, can you use your text when writing the exam?
- Will the instructor provide paper or will you need to bring your own?
- Should the exam be done on a special form? Should you bring a "blue book" (exam booklet)?
- Should the exam be done in pen or pencil?
- Will the exam be primarily over lecture or textbook material?
- Will main ideas or details be emphasized? Will you be expected to remember dates or titles, for example?

2. *Review what has been covered in some methodical manner.* For tests that emphasize the textbook, try some of the following strategies:

- Skim over the assigned chapters in your textbook, making certain the headings make sense. Reread any sections that you may have forgotten.
- See if you can define any words in bold type or italics. Make flashcards of new terminology you can't immediately define, and study them.
- If there is a glossary in the book, make sure you can define those words. Frequently, objective tests are based on definitions given in the glossary.
- Skim over the sections of the textbook you have highlighted.
- Study the marginal notes you made while reading the assigned chapters.
- Make up summary sheets or maps of the chapters that will be covered in the exam, and review them.
- Answer, either in writing or out loud, any questions that appear at the end of the chapter. If you have trouble answering any of them, reread the section of the chapter that discusses the question.
- The index of your text is another good study tool. Look through the index for any names or events that appear in the chapters you will be tested on. If any name or event listed in those chapters looks unfamiliar, turn to that page in the book and reread that section.
- Form a study group composed of students who are willing to hold one or two study sessions. Each person in the group should be assigned a particular section of the material to be covered and either present a summary of the key points and supporting details and/or make up possible test questions to form a basis for group discussion of the test material.
- Make up a test and answer all the questions.

If the class and textbook emphasize solving problems (such as math, accounting, or chemistry), try some of the following study strategies:

- Redo problems, doing enough problems from each section to show that you understand pertinent concepts.
- Make up your own problems and work them. You could do this with a study partner and check each other's answers.
- Find a tutor if sections of the textbook still do not make sense to you. Don't just keep coming up with wrong answers; find out why they are wrong.

- Explain out loud the process for solving problems. Do you understand each step of the process?

If you know the test will be partially or primarily an essay test, try the following strategies:

- Make up essay questions and practice writing answers.
- Use study maps for key concepts in each chapter.
- Form a study group where each person in the group is responsible for discussing one section or one chapter, presenting both main ideas and details from that section or chapter.

For tests that emphasize class lecture notes, try the following strategies:

- Exchange photocopies of notes with other students. Use these other notes to fill in holes or misinformation in your own notes so that you have a complete set of class notes.
- Make summary sheets or maps of your class notes, and study them.
- Rewrite key terminology or key concepts from your notes in a blank column or on another piece of paper. Go over these terms or concepts and see if you can define them out loud or in writing. If you cannot, go back and study that section of your notes.
- Use study groups as described previously.

3. *Study for shorter periods of time but more frequently* . Research has shown that it's better to study for short periods of time rather than in long blocks. Long study periods may give you the feeling that you are studying diligently, but the result will be an overload. Many study skills experts even recommend that you not study the night before a test. If you have been preparing all along, a rested mind on the day of the exam will function better than a tired one.

   - Do you have short daily study periods for at least two weeks before a major test?
   - Do you have brief weekly reviews for each class, each week of the semester?
   - Do you have all major exams listed on a calendar so you can spread out your studying over a space of weeks rather than days?

Scoring Well on Objective Tests

When the day of the big test arrives, here are some things to keep in mind:

1. *Schedule your time properly.* Look over the entire exam before you begin to answer any questions. How long is it? How many parts are there? Is there a point system indicating that one section is more important than another? Some students plunge into one section of a test and spend more time on it than they should. Time runs out before there's a chance to answer other questions that could have given them more points for a higher grade.

2. *Answer the easy questions first.* By answering first the questions you know, you help refresh and stimulate your memory. When you finish the easy ones, go back and look again at the others. Chances are that, by answering the ones you did know, you will be able to remember answers to the more difficult ones. Don't spend too much time on any one question. You may want to leave some kind of mark by the tough ones and come back to them later if you have time.

3. *Look for clue words that will help you interpret the question.* In objective tests especially, clue words can make a question absolutely false or absolutely correct. The following words frequently make a statement false:

all	All objective tests are easier than essay exams.
every	Every objective test is difficult.
always	Objective tests are always difficult.
never	Objective tests are never easy.
best	Objective tests are the best kind.
worst	Objective tests are the worst kind.
none	None of the tests are easy.

When you see these words on test questions, read them very carefully to see what they are modifying. More often than not, these words produce a false answer.

Here are some clue words that tend to make a question frequently true:

some	Some objective tests are easier than essay exams.
often	Often, objective tests are easier than essay exams.
many	Many essay exams are easier than objective ones.
sometimes	Sometimes essay tests are easy.

There are clue words that can make an answer true or false depending on the point of the question. Read questions that contain these words very carefully:

generally	Generally speaking, essay tests are more difficult than others.
few	Few tests are more difficult than essay tests.
only	Only subjective tests should be given.

Just recognizing these clue words in a question will not automatically help you answer it correctly, but knowing how they sometimes work may give you an edge.

4. *If you don't know an answer, guess—intelligently.* Unless the test directions say that you will be penalized for wrong answers, don't be afraid to guess at an answer. Here are some clues to intelligent guessing:

a. Usually, true-false tests will contain more true answers than false ones. (That's *usually,* not always!)

b. Long statements tend to be false, because in order for a question to be true everything in it must be true. The longer the question, the more chance of a false statement. However, in multiple-choice answers, long statements tend to be the correct answer.

c. Don't change an answer unless you are absolutely sure you were wrong the first time you marked it.

d. With multiple-choice questions, "all of the above" tends to be a correct answer.

e. When answers to multiple-choice questions require a number, it's best to disregard the highest and lowest numbers and go for something in between.

f. If you are in doubt about an answer, think of your instructor. What would she or he probably want as an answer based on what has been said in class?

g. If a question uses double negatives, remove the negatives to see how the question reads. For example, take out the negatives in this statement.

It is *not un*advisable to guess when you don't know an answer on a test.

The statement then reads:

It is advisable to guess when you don't know an answer on a test.

This makes the statement true.

h. When taking a matching test with two columns, read both columns before marking any answers. Make a mark near the answers you use so that you don't use them twice.

Remember, these suggestions are not always going to work in your favour. But if you have studied carefully, chances are they can help you achieve a better grade.

PRACTICE E-1: Preparing for Objective Tests

Directions: Apply what you have just read about preparing for and taking objective tests to the following questions.

1. Which of the following is it recommended that you do before taking an exam?
    a. ask the instructor what type of exam it will be
    b. review what has been assigned in a methodical manner
    c. study for shorter but more frequent periods of time
    d. all of the above

2. Frequently, objective tests are based on _____ given in the glossary.

3. T/F It is never a good idea not to answer the easy questions first.
    a. True
    b. False because _____

4. List at least four clue words that frequently make a true-false question false.

    _____

5. List three clue words that frequently are used to make a true-false statement true.

    _____

6. Which of the following is not recommended as a method of reviewing for a test?
    a. using the textbook's index
    b. using the textbook's glossary
    c. forming study groups with responsibilities for each member
    d. cramming

7. Subjective exams are best described as those that require _____

    _____

Scoring Well on Essay Tests

Preparing for an essay test is not very different from preparing for an objective test. The big difference has less to do with how much you know and more with how well you can organize and write an answer. If writing itself is not one of your strong points, the best approach you can take is to practise writing some answers to questions you think might be on the exam.

There are at least three good sources to use in preparing for essay exam questions.

- First, some instructors will share previous test questions. Don't be afraid to ask if any are available. Seeing what type of questions will be asked can help you anticipate probable questions the instructor might ask.

- Another source for possible essay questions is the text itself. Frequently, instructors base their questions on those at the beginning or end of chapters in the course textbook. Chances are that, if you practice writing answers to those, you'll learn the information needed to answer the instructor's questions.

- A third source is the course syllabus. Students are often provided with hand-outs at the beginning of a course that list objectives and assignments and that often contain study-guide questions. Exam time is a good time to look again at such handouts.

Here are some guidelines for writing answers to essay questions:

1. *Read the questions carefully.* This seems obvious, but frequently students get involved in writing an answer to a question without regard for the total test. If directions aren't clear, ask the instructor to explain. Look for the following clue words that appear in essay exams, and make certain your answer states what is called for:

analyze	State the main ideas and show how they are related and why they are important.
comment on	Discuss, criticize, or explain (ask instructor for more specifics on this one).
compare	Show both similarities and differences, but your instructor may only want similarities.
contrast	Show differences.
criticize	Give your judgment or reasoned opinion, showing good and bad points.
define	Give a formal meaning or elaborate definition with supporting details.
describe	Give a detailed account or verbal picture in an organized or logical sequence.
discuss	Give details, discuss pros and cons.
enumerate	List main ideas one by one and number them.
evaluate	Give your opinion, showing advantages and disadvantages.
illustrate	Explain by giving concrete details, examples, or analogies.
interpret	Use examples to explain or give meaning through personal comments or judgments.
justify	Give proof or reasons.
list	List, usually by number, without details.
outline	Give a general summary using main ideas and skipping minor details.

prove	Use argument or logic to explain.
relate	Show the connection between one thing and another.
review	Give a summary or survey.
state	Provide the main points in precise terms.
summarize	Give a brief account of the main ideas.
trace	Show in chronology the progress of history.

Students often ignore these clue words and end up writing answers that are only partially correct or even totally miss the answer the instructor wants.

2. *Answer the easy questions first.* Usually you don't have to answer essay questions in their order on the test as long as you identify which questions you are answering. By writing answers to the easier questions first, you gain confidence and begin to call from memory other points you have studied.

3. *Write out a brief outline before you begin your essay answer.* Think through what you want to say before you begin writing your answer by making some type of outline. That way, if you run out of time, you can refer your instructor to your outline, which may contain parts of the answer you didn't complete and show that with more time you would have covered those areas in your answer.

   Making an outline may *seem* to take more time, but actually it is worth it to make certain your ideas are organized before you begin writing. It also helps you recall what you learned before trying to write it down in essay form.

4. *Get right to the question.* Don't waste time getting to the question. Let's say one of your essay questions is "Discuss the role Pierre Trudeau played in the development of *The Charter of Rights and Freedoms*." Don't waste time rewriting the question. Rather, turn the question into your first sentence:

   > Pierre Trudeau played an important role in the development of *The charter of Rights and Freedoms* in three important ways. One, . . .

   Then take each of the three important ways and discuss how he helped.

5. *As you write your answers, leave room for changes you may make.* It's best to use only one side of a sheet of paper. Leave margins and skip every other line in case you need to add or make changes. If you misspell a word, don't write over it; scratch through it and write it correctly in the space above the word.

   Remember that your instructor is going to be reading entire class sets of essay answers. A neat, clearly written essay will stand out. The easier you make it for the instructor, the better impression you make and the better your chances for a higher grade.

6. *Combat exam panic.* Sweaty palms, fast heartbeat, a sick feeling in the stomach, flushed face—all of these are common feelings at exam time. What can you do? Relax. Take a moment to sit up straight, close your eyes, and take some deep breaths. Let the tension out of your body. Slowly relax various parts of your body, working down from the head to the neck, to the shoulders, to your arms, upper torso, and so on down to your feet. Concentrate on your breathing; draw in a deep breath and then exhale slowly as you tell yourself you are forcing tension out of your body. Do this whenever you begin to feel tension building.

   Some students have success with *imaging.* They close their eyes and see themselves taking the test and writing excellent answers to the questions. They see themselves confident and prepared. Once they see this image of themselves at work, they open their eyes and apply the confidence they saw.

Success in exams depends on accepting those anxious feelings and learning to control them. It may take several practice sessions before you master your feelings.

PRACTICE E-2: Clue Words in Essay Tests

Directions: Define the following clue words frequently used in essay exam questions.

1. discuss _____

_____

2. contrast _____

_____

3. define _____

_____

4. describe _____

_____

5. list _____

_____

6. evaluate _____

_____

7. enumerate _____

_____

8. compare _____

_____

PRACTICE E-3: Practising Essay Question Answers

Directions: Answer the following question.

1. An essay question reads: "List the four major causes of the First World War." Read the following beginning answer to this question and in the space provided evaluate how well it starts.

> During the period prior to 1914, there were many problems confronting Europe. It began to look as though there were unresolved problems that could bring many countries to war. . . .

_____

_____

_____

_____

_____

_____

_____

_____

_____

_____

_____

_____

What to Do with Tests after You Get Them Back

Unless you learn to evaluate what you got right and wrong on a test, you will continue to make the same mistakes again and again. When you get a test back, take some time to figure out your strengths and weaknesses on that exam. The following questions will help you learn from your mistakes.

- Were the questions you missed from the textbook or the lecture notes?
- Did you misread any of the directions?
- Did you mostly miss main ideas or details?
- Were the questions you missed from one particular part of the chapter or notes (for example, are the missed questions often from the end of the class lecture)?
- Did you miss questions because you didn't know that information? If you didn't know it, why not?
- Were the test questions what you expected? If these weren't the test questions you predicted, why not?
- Did you miss questions because you didn't leave enough time to do one section of the test or you didn't finish the test?
- Is this the grade you predicted for yourself on this test? Why or why not?

> **Application 5:**
> **Using Test-Taking Strategies Before, During, and After a Test**
>
> Use the test-taking strategies explained in this chapter to prepare for, take, and evaluate a test in another class. Write up a brief explanation of the new test-taking strategies you used and the results you saw. Evaluate the results of your test-taking strategies by writing what you would do again (because it worked) and what you would change.

F.   Flexible Reading Rates

Another study skill you will find essential is developing reading-rate versatility. How fast a person reads is irrelevant if good comprehension doesn't match the speed. Yet, with a little training, most people can easily increase their reading rate without a loss in comprehension. Most people have never been trained in reading rate, yet college students are often hard pressed to keep up with assignments, and their concentration may wander when a textbook is open.

There are several factors to consider when discussing reading speed.

- First, not everything can be—or should be—read at the fastest rate. Your reading rate should depend on your *purpose* for reading. Surveying to get an idea of what you will be reading, looking for specific items, and reviewing for tests are purposes that allow fast reading rates. Some textbooks may be easy enough that faster rates are appropriate. Reading a poem in order to write an essay on it, for example, will take longer because you also have to analyze and interpret it. Reading rates vary with reading purposes.

- A second factor in reading speed has to do with your *concentration* as you read. The most intense concentration in difficult school tasks occurs in about twenty-minute segments. This does *not* mean you can only study for twenty minutes, but it does mean you will concentrate better if you set short frequent study sessions and change study activities more often. People who set long study periods ("I'll study all day Saturday") are usually deluding themselves. Are you aware of it when your concentration wanders? Is there a pattern to when you can and cannot concentrate? What is your shortest concentration span? your longest? The important point is *not* to sit with your book open while your mind drifts. The minute your mind wanders, turn away from that book immediately.

- A third factor affecting reading speed is lack of knowledge about how to read faster. Old reading habits are hard to break. Since most people are never trained to read quickly, reading habits learned early in life are never broken. Training in four areas can help you speed up your reading rate with no loss in comprehension:

1. *Reading for ideas and detecting patterns.* Untrained readers read as if every word is equally important in every kind of reading. Instead, you should read for ideas and think about what you're reading.

   (a) One exercise to help you read for ideas is *closure,* or the mind's ability to fill in blanks without seeing every detail. If I say, "Tom went to the _____ and bought a loaf of _____ ," your mind closes on the blank spaces, and you know he went to the store or bakery and bought a loaf of bread.

   Here is an exercise to help you understand how closure works. In the following paragraph from this section, twenty-five of the sixty-one words are crossed out, yet the meaning is still clear.

   Another study skill ~~you will find~~ essential ~~is developing~~ reading-rate versatility. How fast ~~a person reads is~~ irrelevant if good comprehension doesn't match ~~the~~ speed. ~~Yet,~~ with ~~a little~~ training, ~~most~~ people ~~can easily~~ increase ~~their~~ reading rate without ~~a~~ loss in comprehension. ~~Most~~ people read ~~as~~ slowly ~~as they do~~ because ~~they've~~ never ~~been~~ shown how to read faster.

   With twenty-five words crossed out, the paragraph now reads:

   Another study skill essential reading-rate versatility. How fast irrelevant if good comprehension doesn't match speed. With training, people increase reading rate without loss in comprehension. People read slowly because never shown how to read faster.

Do you see how you can get full meaning without stopping at each word? You can practise closure in your textbooks.

(b) The second exercise to help you read faster for ideas is to pick out main ideas, select supporting details, and detect paragraph patterns. These skills, which you learned in Chapter Two, will enable you to read faster with better comprehension.

Practise reading for ideas by seeing how quickly you can pick out main ideas and figure out the pattern of details in the following paragraphs.

As a technical writer, you need to remember these four ethical principles. First, don't leave out any vital information (such as safety hazards). Next, don't exaggerate (such as making claims for absolute success). Third, create a clear understanding of what the information means. Finally, respect copyrighted information. Don't knowingly download or distribute copyrighted information.

Where is the main idea? _____

_____

How many supporting details are there? _____

When interviewing for a job, don't ask about salary or bonuses during the first interview. Be prepared to ask questions that show your knowledge of the job or the company. Act as if you are determined to get the job. These are some of the tips to help you function most effectively in a job interview.

Where is the main idea? _____

_____

How many supporting details are there? _____

Here are the answers: In the first paragraph, the main idea in the first sentence and there are four major details (don't omit, don't exaggerate, be clear, respect copyrights). In the second paragraph, the main idea is the last sentence, and there are three major details (no salary questions, ask questions, be determined).

(c) Yet another skill to help you learn to read for ideas is to use the Q in SQ3R to develop questions before you read. Having a purpose in mind and questions to answer will help your rate and retention of the material.

Look at the first timed reading in this section, Practice F-1: "Cultural Messages about Time." Read the first comprehension question and see how quickly you can read the article just to get the answer to this question. For this practice, don't try to get anything from the selection except what you need to answer the question. This practice should give you an idea of how questions affect your rate and comprehension.

Now read all the rest of the comprehension questions before you start reading the selection. Keeping these questons in mind will help you set a purpose for reading the selection.

2. *Increasing vocabulary.* If a page has three or more unfamiliar words on it, you will not be able to speed-read it. You therefore need to continue the vocabulary strategies you learned in Chapter One. As your vocabulary grows, you will find more materials you can read quickly. If you want to read quickly, you need to learn the terminology first.

3. *Learning pacing strategies.* Untrained readers often find their minds wandering while they read. Training yourself to read at a forced rate with good concentration will take practice. Use an index card to cover each line as you read it, moving it down the page a little faster than you currently read. Another pacing strategy is to use your hand or a pen to keep you reading at a forced rate. Do not use your hand to trace each word or each line. Pull it straight down the page at a rate a little faster than your current rate.

4. *Practise fast reading rates.* The only way to learn flexible reading rates is to practise for a short time each day with fast rates. Find an easy, interesting book with no new vocabulary. Students have found it helpful to check out young juvenile literature from the library for this exercise. Work up to more difficult books as you feel more comfortable with fast rates.

   Start with five- to ten-minute practice sessions and work up to longer periods of time as your concentration and rate increase. If your concentration wanders, stop your practice session and turn away from your book.

   To figure your rate in a book, follow the following procedure:

   a. Count the number of words on an average page in the book (wpp).
   b. Count the number of pages you read in each practice session and multiply it by wpp. This is the total number of words you read.
   c. Write down the number of minutes you read.
   d. Divide the total number of words read by the minutes.

If your book has about 250 words per page and you read four pages, you have just read 1,000 words. Let's say it took you five minutes to read that. Divide a thousand by five, and you would get your rate of 200 wpm.

Keep the following chart. To estimate your comprehension, try to summarize out loud what you've just read. Sometimes students feel comprehension has dropped but their oral recall shows good comprehension. Your instructor will ask you to hand in this paper after a few weeks of practice.

Practice Fast Reading Rates

Date	Selection Read	WPM	Estimated Comprehension

Timed Reading Practice

The following articles are for timed reading practice. Remember that word—*practice.* They are provided to give you practice in reading faster, in developing your comprehension, and in learning vocabulary in context. In addition, some of the questions you will be asked to answer are designed to help you continue practising your skimming and scanning.

The articles deal with a variety of subjects. Some will be more interesting to you than others. Interest can affect your speed and your comprehension. In some cases, you may get "hung up" on the article's subject and forget you are practising reading skills. Other articles will be less interesting, and your comprehension may suffer because you are not concentrating. Try to remember that you are using these articles to develop your reading versatility. Use these drills to break old habits, not reinforce them.

- In all cases, read faster than you normally do, but not so fast that you don't get the main idea of the article. Speed is never more important than comprehension, but you are practising for faster speeds. Sometimes your comprehension scores may drop because of a faster reading speed. That's all right here because you are practicing. This is the place to make mistakes. The point is that the more you push yourself to read faster during practice, the faster you will read when you return to what you think is your "normal" reading rate.

- Learn from the errors you make in comprehension and vocabulary checks. Understanding why you miss a question is more important than missing it. Sometimes answer keys contain mistakes. Don't be afraid to challenge an answer. Often discussing the contents of an article or particular questions about the article helps develop comprehension skills.

- Use the vocabulary checks to continue developing your word power. Learning words in context is the best way to strengthen your vocabulary. See how the words are used, and make vocabulary cards for any new words you want to learn.

So remember, the following articles are intended for practice in rate, comprehension, and vocabulary development. As you record the results of your efforts on the Student Record Chart, don't be concerned if your scores go up and down; that is not unusual. What you learn about reading versatility is more important than the scores.

PRACTICE F-1: Speed Read

Directions: Practise new speed-reading strategies on the following 876-word selection. Start with a one-minute survey, making sure you look at the questions during the survey too. After the survey, use a pacing device (card, pen, or hand) and push yourself at a forced rate.

Begin timing: _____

CULTURAL MESSAGES ABOUT TIME

JOAN FLEET AND DENISE REAUME

A SOCIAL CONSTRUCT

1   A student who is a "New Canadian" was talking one day about the wonders of Canada. *"You know,"* he said, *"Canada is such a rich country. It has education, housing, lots of food in the stores and goods to buy. But the one thing that Canada is very short of is—TIME. Everyone here is in such a hurry. No one has much time to talk. They're always rushing off somewhere because they have so much to do. In my country the days were really long and slow. They seemed to go on forever."* Does this observation make you stop and think?

2   Canada is very typical of modern industrialized countries of the world. In its main population centres, the pace is fast and time is of the essence. How many people do you know who do not wear a wristwatch? It is probably a very small number. Getting one's first watch is almost what an anthropologist calls a "rite of passage." This is one of those events that indicate that we belong to a particular group. Learning to tell the time is such an important goal of our society that children are often given toy clocks and watches to facilitate early development of the concept of time through play. Even the name *"watch"* is a clear indication of what we expect to do with time!

3   Cultures differ in their beliefs and values about time. On a TV program about dance in religious ceremonies, a Nigerian was explaining the beautiful, gentle movements associated with dances of the old religion in Nigeria. The movements were very rhythmic and unhurried. He said, *"These movements parallel life. They represent patience. In our dealings with people in Nigeria, patience is a very important quality."* There are many other cultures, like that of Nigeria, in which the concept of time is slower than ours: where patience is practised and expected. Cultures have evolved over centuries and the concept of time has been constructed differently by the various societies. The Spanish word *"siesta"* for example, does not have an English equivalent and yet we all know what it means. The term *"afternoon nap"* hardly captures the meaning of the traditional respite from the heat of the day. We may not have the word "siesta" in our language, but how many people in North America experience that slowing down in the early afternoon, especially in the hot weather, as they try to maintain high productivity?

4   Cultures teach values, including values about time. For you to understand fully your own experience with time, it is important for you to put it into the context of the society in which you live. What has your society taught you about time management?

THE SOCIETY IN WHICH WE LIVE

5   Society sends clear messages about the role that time plays in people's lives. On some TV channels, time is on constant display and viewers can set their watches to within a micro-second. We live in a culture in which time matters and success if often measured by speed. For many people the few weeks of the year when they are on holiday and can enjoy the slower pace of unhurried living are a welcome change from the fast pace of work and school. Others even prefer to vacation at a fast pace and get bored quickly if there is a lull in activities. Whether we choose to fit with

society's expectations about time, choose to ignore them, or fight against them, society has influenced the way in which we all view and manage time.

Fast Is Better

6   A pervasive message from our own society is that "fast is better." With transportation, such as cars, trains, planes, bikes, skis and even roller blades, one of the major selling points is speed. How quickly can they get us from point A to point B? We expect tools to do the job as quickly as possible; office computers are getting aster all the time; touch telephones are rapidly making the telephone dial obsolete; the check-out counter at the supermarket uses computer scans to total the grocery bill; the instabank machine has replaced the line up at the bank. Fast is in and those who do not move or think fast can be left behind in our modern society.

Time Is Limited

7   We are also bombarded with the idea that "time is limited." How often do you see signs that proclaim *"for a limited time only," "weekly specials,"* or *"time is running out."* We get the message that we had better make up our minds quickly, otherwise we will miss the boat! As students, we live with the time limits of tests and exams. The academic testing situation evaluates far more than knowledge of the course content; it also tests our ability to work within time limits.

Time Is Money

8   The business concept of "time is money" directs us to save time because, when we waste time, we are wasting something of measurable value. Office desks are located with accessibility in mind. You may have set up your own workspace at home based on the same principle. Also, it costs a lot of money to be a student, and so students will often plan to graduate as quickly as possible for budget reasons. Saving time is always a most persuasive argument, for example, to rationalize driving the car to school instead of walking, cycling, or taking public transportation.

Finish timing. Record time here: _____ and use the Timed Readings Conversion Chart in the Appendix to figure your rate: _____ wpm.

Comprehension Check

Directions: Now answer the following questions.

1. The authors' main idea or thesis is that:
    a. time is important.
    b. time constricts one's ability to succeed.
    c. time is measured differently by different societies.
    d. Canadians obsess about time.
    e. c and d above

2. What do the authors mean when they say that "Even the name "*watch*" is a clear indication of what we expect to do with time"? _____

    _____

    _____

3. The authors state, "Whether we choose to fit in with society's expectations about time, choose to ignore them, or fight against them, society has influenced the way in which we all view and manage time." In what ways do the authors believe that our beliefs about time have been influenced by society?_____

_____

_____

4. T/F According to the authors, concern about time is beneficial to Canadians.

5. Explain why the authors do or do not believe that time is money.

_____

_____

6. What do the authors mean when they say that "The academic testing situation evaluates far more than knowledge of the course content . . ."?

_____

_____

7. According to the authors, would Canadians like to have a *siesta*? Explain.

_____

_____

8. What is the significance of the first paragraph of the essay?_____

_____

_____

9. According to the authors, we live in a culture in which time matters and

_____

_____

10. Explain what the title and subheadings mean. _____

_____

_____

Vocabulary Check

Directions: Define the underlined words in the following phrases and sentences from the article you just read.

1. Canada is very typical of modern <u>industrialized</u> countries (paragraph 2)

_____

2. children are often given toy clocks and watches to <u>facilitate</u> early development (paragraph 2) _____

_____

3. These movements <u>parallel</u> life. (paragraph 3) _____

_____

4. The term "*afternoon nap*" hardly captures the meaning of the traditional <u>respite</u> from the heat of the day. (paragraph 3) _____

_____

_____

5. Others even prefer to vacation at a fast pace and get bored quickly if there is a <u>lull</u> in activities. (paragraph 5) _____

_____

Turn to the Student Record Chart in the Appendix. Record your rate (wpm), comprehension, and vocabulary scores. Divide the number of correct answers by the number of questions in each check to determine your scores. Discuss with your instructor any questions or problems you may have. When you make mistakes, don't worry about them; learn from them. What you learn is always more important than what you record on your chart.

PRACTICE F-2: Speed Read

Directions: Now see if you can read the following 554-word selection 50 wpm faster than you read the last one. Start with a two-minute survey, be sure you've looked at the comprehension questions, and use a pacing device (a card, pen, or hand) to push yourself at a forced rate. As you read, look for the main ideas and supporting details. The following selection is entitled "Artifacts."

Begin timing: _____

ARTIFACTS

JULIA WOOD AND ANGELA HENRY

1   Artifacts are personal objects we use to announce our identities and heritage and to personalize our environments. We craft our image by how we dress and what objects, if any, we carry and use. Nurses and physicians wear white and frequently drape stethoscopes around their neck; professors travel with briefcases, whereas students more often tote backpacks. White-collar professionals tend to wear tailored outfits and dress shoes, whereas blue-collar workers more often dress in jeans or uniforms and boots. The military requires uniforms that define individuals in terms of the group. In addition, stripes and medals signify rank and accomplishments.

2   Artifacts may also define territories. To claim our spaces, we fill them with objects that matter to us and that reflect our experiences and values. Lovers of art adorn their homes with paintings and sculptures that announce their interests and personalize their private space. Religious families often express their commitments by displaying pictures of holy scenes and the *Bible*, the *Koran*, or other sacred texts. We exhibit artifacts that symbolize important relationships and experiences in our lives. For example, many people have pictures of family members in their offices and homes.

3   In her book *Composing a Life*, Mary Catherine Bateson (1990) comments that we turn houses into homes by filling them with what matters to us. We make impersonal

spaces familiar and comfortable by imprinting them with our artifacts. We use mugs given to us by special people, nurture plants to enliven indoor spaces, surround ourselves with books and magazines that announce our interests, and sprinkle our world with objects that reflect what we care about.

4   Artifacts communicate important relationship meanings. We use them to announce our identities and to express how we perceive and feel about others. Although clothing has become more unisex in recent years, once you venture off campus, gendered styles are evident. To declare gender, we dress to meet cultural expectations of men and women. Thus, women sometimes wear makeup, dresses that may have lace or other softening touches, skirts, high-heeled shoes, jewellery, and hose, all of which conform to the cultural ideal of women as decorative objects. Typically, men wear little, if any, jewellery, and their clothes and shoes are functional. Flat shoes allow a person to walk comfortably or run if necessary; high heels don't. Men's clothing is looser and less binding, and it includes pockets for wallets, keys, and so forth. In contrast, women's clothing tends to be more tailored and often doesn't include pockets, making a purse necessary.

5   We also use artifacts to establish racial identity. Jewellery and clothing are a common way to express a distinctive cultural heritage. Note the increase of ethnic artifacts that have reached the fashion markets in Canada.

6   Artifacts communicate our identity from an early age. Many hospitals still swaddle newborns in blue and pink blankets to designate sex, and even though many parents today try to be nonsexist, many still send gender messages through the toys they give their children. In general, parents, and especially fathers, give sons toys that encourage rough and active play (balls, trains) and competitiveness (baseball gloves, toy weapons), whereas they give daughters toys that cultivate nurturing (dolls, toy kitchens) and attention to appearance (makeup kits, frilly clothes) (Caldera, Huston, & O'Brien, 1989; Lytton & Romney, 1991; Pomerleau, Bolduc, Malcuit, & Cossette, 1990).

Finish timing. Record time here: _____ and use the Timed Readings Conversion Chart in the Appendix to figure your rate: _____ wpm.

Comprehension Check

Directions: Now answer the following questions.

1. Which of the following best states the main idea of the selection?

    a. Artifacts are personal objects that we use to define our territories, announce our identities, and personalize our environments.

    b. Artifacts help us perceive others.

    c. Men and women dress differently in order to make statements about their very different roles in society.

    d. From an early age, artifacts become important to us.

2. Describe how artifacts define territory. _____

    _____

    _____

    _____

3. According to Mary Catherine Bateson, why do we decorate our homes with artifacts?

_____

_____

4. T/F Women conform to the cultural ideal of their gender by wearing makeup, jewellery and dresses.

5. List ways in which artifacts communicate important relationships, according the authors. _____

_____

_____

6. List ways in which some professionals wear artifacts to create their identities.

_____

_____

7. What do gifts symbolize? _____

_____

8. List at least two cultural artifacts. _____

_____

_____

9. According to the authors, in what ways do we use artifacts to promote our racial identities? _____

_____

_____

10. Do you think that artifacts can promote gender stereotyping? Agree or disagree. Use examples to support your answer. _____

_____

_____

Vocabulary Check

Directions: See how well you understand the meanings of the following ten words from the reading selection. Write the letter of the best definition as used in the reading for each word in the left-hand column.

_____ **1.** heritage

_____ **2.** drape

_____ **3.** tote

_____ **4.** white-collar

_____ **5.** blue-collar

_____ **6.** adorn

_____ **7.** sacred

a. to specify or serve as a distinctive mark

b. to make beautiful or attractive

c. of or relating to wage earners whose jobs often involve manual labour

d. to represent or identify by a symbol

e. to haul

f. worthy of respect

g. to hang or rest limply

_____ **8.** symbolize

_____ **9.** perceive

_____ **10.** designate

h. of or relating to workers whose work usually does not involve manual labour

i. to observe or understand through one of the senses

j. object passed down from a preceding generation

Record your rate (wpm), comprehension, and vocabulary scores for this article on the Student Record Chart in the Appendix. Discuss any problems or questions you may have with your instructor. Feel free to share any improvements, too!

Don't forget to learn any vocabulary words you need to add to your repertoire.

Application 6: Speed Reading

Use the four speed-reading strategies on easy, interesting materials of your own choice. Keep a chart (title of selection, rate, comprehension) and practice five to fifteen minutes a day for two weeks, keeping track of your rate. Estimate comprehension by creating a map of the material you just read. Hand in your results.

G.   Putting It All Together

The following practices are provided to help you put all the information in this chapter to work. First, you will be asked to review your notes and maps from previous exercises in this chapter as a way to study for the tests in this section. Then, you will test your comprehension on a timed reading.

PRACTICE G-1: An Objective Test on "The Development of the SQ3R Method"

Directions: Review "The Development of the SQ3R Method," which you read earlier. Then look over your answers to Practice A-2. Once finished, answer the following questions without looking back.

Comprehension Check

1. The S in the SQ3R study method stands for

   a. selectively read   **c.** sample

   b. search   **d.** none of the above

2. The Q in the SQ3R study method stands for _____

3. The correct order for the 3R portion of the SQ3R method is

   a. recite, read, review   **c.** review, read, recite

   b. read, recite, review   **d.** none of the above

4. One of the reasons the SQ3R method is effective if done correctly is that it
   a. results in faster reading
   b. helps pick out important points
   c. aids memory of what is read
   d. all of the above

5. T/F Research does not prove that the SQ3R method works if done incorrectly.
   a. True
   b. False because _____

6. T/F The S portion of the SQ3R method should only take a minute or so.
   a. True
   b. False because _____

7. Changing a heading into a question takes a conscious effort on your part to become
   a. actively involved in the reading material
   b. passively involved in the reading material
   c. both of the above
   d. none of the above

8. T/F You should stop after reading from one heading to the next and question yourself on what you just read.
   a. True
   b. False because _____

9. The reciting part of the SQ3R study method can consist of mentally reviewing what was read or writing out notes. Which one is most recommended?

   _____

   _____

10. Reviewing should be done
    a. immediately after reading   c. at neither time
    b. at a later period   d. both a and b

Vocabulary Check

Directions: Define the following underlined words as they appear in context.

1. speeded up reading and aided <u>retention</u> (paragraph 2) _____

   _____

2. slowed by the simple <u>expedient</u> of forcing oneself to recite (paragraph 2)

   _____

3. try to recall the <u>subpoints</u> listed under it (paragraph 10) _____

   _____

4. took another <u>comparable</u> reading test (paragraph 12) _____

   _____

5. at the 34th <u>percentile</u> (paragraph 12) _____

_____

6. habits <u>accumulated</u> from reading fiction (paragraph 15) _____

_____

7. one receives visual and <u>kinesthetic</u> cues as well (paragraph 17) _____

_____

8. on the <u>preceding</u> section (paragraph 20)_____

_____

9. this <u>alternation</u> of tasks helps (paragraph 21)_____

_____

10. <u>self-recitation</u> should be used to make sure (paragraph 22)_____

_____

Record the results of the checks on the Student Record Chart in the Appendix.

PRACTICE G-2: An Essay Test on "The Development of the SQ3R Method"

Directions: On another sheet of paper to be handed in to your instructor, write an essay answer to the following question: "Discuss the effect that each main point of the SQ3R method has on the entire process."

PRACTICE G-3: Timed Reading

Directions: In Chapters Two and Three, you have learned to work on your reading rate by looking at the title, considering the familiarity of the topic, and reading the questions, before you start reading the selection. Here is another chance to practice these skills. The title of this selection, "Effective Memory," deals with a topic you know something about. Now look at the questions to see what your purpose is for reading this selection.

Recall that the next skill to help you increase reading rate is to find the main ideas or thesis of each article so that you can use that structure to help guide your reading. Unless you have these main ideas in mind as you read, you will end up with a lot of details you won't be able to remember. That is why untrained readers read every word but can't answer any of the instructor's questions in class the next day.

Notice that the first paragraph of this selection begins with a description of common memory problems to get you interested in the topic of memory. Look at it carefully. There are then four subheadings that appear to refer to different types of memory. While you are still learning to increase your reading rate, you might even find it helpful to write out the main idea and these four key points on a piece of paper before you start reading. The writing will help you remember the main ideas of this selection.

Now that you have looked at the title and the questions and identified the main idea and supporting details, you are ready to put your new speed-reading skills to work on the following 846-word selection. Push yourself to read it at least 50 wpm faster than you read the last selection.

Begin timing: _____

EFFECTIVE MEMORY

JOAN FLEET, FIONA GOODCHILD, AND RICHARD ZAJCHOWSKI

1   Students commonly report problems with memory. Many describe how they can understand new ideas, but later the information just doesn't stick. Students also commonly report that their friends can remember everything without any effort at all, and how they feel frustration with their own memory when a friend gets a higher grade without, seemingly, having studied much at all. While there are undoubtedly differences among students in the ease with which information is retained, there are strategies that can be applied that can improve retention over the long term. To be able to apply effective memory strategies, one needs first to understand some current theory about memory that can help to explain memory problems.

2   This chapter begins by examining how three types of memory are thought to operate together and what this implies for the learner. It then goes on to explore ways in which memory is stored to improve retrieval. The main purpose of this chapter is to have you relate the theory about memory systems to your own learning experience. As you read, ask yourself the following questions: "How does this theory reflect my own way of studying? In the light of these theories, what changes do I need to make to the way in which I study? What do I need to do to build these ideas into my own learning strategies?"

Memory Systems

3   Educators distinguish three memory systems operating together but each with distinct characteristics and functions. They are described very briefly here, focussing on the major implications for any learner wishing to take more personal control over the learning process. The three memory systems are:

- Sensory Memory
- Short-Term Memory
- Long-Term Memory

Sensory Memory

4   Our senses—sight, hearing, touch, taste, smell, and sense of position—register information from our environment. An important feature of the sensory-memory system is that the senses register information only for an instant. It is then either forgotten or is passed on to short-term memory as a conscious thought. How is this significant to you as a learner? Well, you might view sensory memory as a critical gateway through which information must pass in order to be available to your short-term memory. For information to register in short-term memory, you must attend to and concentrate on it.

5   In everyday life, if you could register all of the stimuli available to your sensory-memory system, your senses would become overloaded. When you sit at a desk processing some lecture notes, for example, you do not usually notice the pressure of your feet on the floor or hear background noises around you such as a fan or traffic outside. To be a Good Strategy User, you need to develop the ability to limit your attention to critical and necessary stimuli. Much of what your sensory memory does register is related to goals that you set. In other words, your immediate learning goals

have a profound effect on the information that passes from your sensory to your short-term memory.

Short-Term Memory

6   Short-term memory is sometimes referred to as working memory because it is here that you actively work to make sense of and respond to stimuli entering from the sensory memory environment or from knowledge you retrieve from long-term storage.

7   Two characteristics of short-term memory are critical to you as a learner. The first is that you lose information very quickly by forgetting unless you process the information further in some way (e.g., by reciting a telephone number over and over again in your head if something stops you from dialling the number immediately). The second is that it has limited capacity. When new information enters the memory, it often displaces what is already there in short-term memory. For example, switching between the simultaneous activities of listening and taking notes in a lecture can be very difficult if the lecture is fast paced. Unless you maintain some internal dialogue involving repetition of a critical phrase you wish to record, it is displaced by new information, and you quickly forget the important information.

8   If you are to minimize forgetting from short-term memory as you learn, you need to be very aware of situations that lead to overload and, whenever possible, apply strategies that will enhance storage into long-term memory. For example, reading a text commonly causes overload problems on your short-term memory. If you were to read many pages without pausing to apply strategies leading to long-term storage of the information, then the load on your short-term memory would increase to the point that you would forget much of what you had read.

Long-Term Memory

9   This is the component of memory that stores all the information an individual has learned. Much like a very large library or a computer with an 80-GB hard drive, it has an immense storage capacity. However, it also resembles a library in the sense that very careful storage and retrieval procedures are needed so that information is not lost inside the system. Unfortunately, many students do not have conscious and reliable procedures for information storage and retrieval. This results in forgetting information.

Finish timing. Record time here: _____ and use the Timed Readings Conversion Chart in the Appendix to figure your rate: _____wpm.

Comprehension Check

Directions: Answer the first five questions without looking back. The last five questions require scanning. More directions will be given when you get to them.

1. What is the thesis or main ideas of the essay? _____

    _____

    _____

2. T/F Many students do not have good procedures for storing information in their long-term memory.

3. Sensory memory is

   a. referred to as a working memory

   b. critical to learners

   c. like a large library in your mind

   d. none of the above

4. T/F Each memory system has distinct traits.

5. Explain what the following statement means: "In everyday life, if you could register all of the stimuli available to your sensory-memory system, your senses would become overloaded." _____

   _____

   _____

   _____

   _____

   Scan back through the article for the answers to the following five questions.

6. For a student to be a Good Strategy User (paragraph 3), the student must _____

   _____

7. Who is the author of "Effective Memory"? _____

   _____

8. How long are sensory images registered for? (paragraph 2) _____

   _____

9. What is one technique for increasing one's ability to remember information? (paragraph 5) _____

   _____

10. Why does memory have implications for a learner? (paragraph 1) _____

    _____

    _____

    _____

Vocabulary Check

Directions: Define the following underlined words from the article.

1. register information from our environment (paragraph 4) _____

   _____

   _____

2. memory as a conscious thought (paragraph 4)_____

   _____

   _____

3. a critical <u>gateway</u> through which information must pass (paragraph 4) _____

    _____

    _____

4. register all of the <u>stimuli</u> available (paragraph 5) _____

    _____

    _____

5. senses would become <u>overloaded</u> (paragraph 5) _____

    _____

    _____

6. goals have a <u>profound</u> effect (paragraph 5) _____

    _____

    _____

7. it has limited <u>capacity</u> (paragraph 7) _____

    _____

    _____

8. it often <u>displaces</u> what is already there (paragraph 7) _____

    _____

    _____

9. <u>simultaneous</u> activities of listening and taking notes (paragraph 7) _____

    _____

    _____

10. some internal <u>dialogue</u> (paragraph 7) _____

    _____

    _____

Once your answers have been checked and you understand any errors you may have made, record the results of rate, comprehension, and vocabulary checks on the Student Record Chart in the Appendix.

Questions for Group Discussion

1. Have each member of your group bring in a textbook from another class and explain how to adapt SQ3R to that particular textbook.

2. Develop a test (part objective and part essay) for this chapter, incorporating all the different sections of it.

3. Discuss which of the six study-reading strategies was most helpful to each member of your group and why.

4. Explain the differences between pleasure reading and study reading.

A Final Check

At the beginning of this unit, you looked at a diagram that illustrated the three facets of comprehension. The foundation for understanding, at the bottom of the triangle, is literal comprehension.

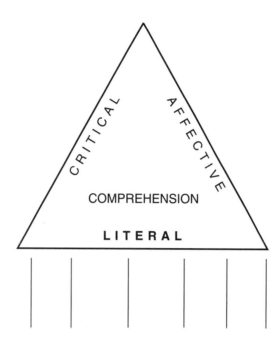

For the diagram above, fill in the blank lines in this section. Working with a partner or small group is acceptable if your instructor sets up groups. *Hints:* The first line corresponds to the first chapter and deals with words. The second and third lines correspond to the second chapter and deal with comprehension. The fourth, fifth, and sixth lines correspond to the third chapter and deal with study reading and flexible reading.

When you have finished, check your answers against the triangle at the beginning of Unit One.

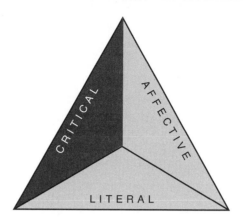

CRITICAL COMPREHENSION

Unit Two builds on what you learned in Unit One. A look at the cmprehension triangle below shows what you have learned about literal comprehension and what you will learn about critical comprehension in this unit. As you work through this unit, you will continue to develop your ability to read at the literal level, while learning to develop your ability to read critically.

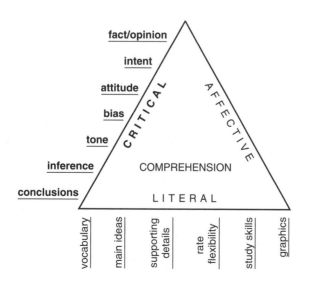

What Is Critical Comprehension?

Critical comprehension is that level of understanding that includes the following:

- the distinguishing of fact from opinion,
- the recognition of an author's intent, attitude, or bias,
- the drawing of inferences, and
- the making of critical judgments.

It's the second branch on the comprehension triangle explained in Unit One. Critical comprehension is a more sophisticated level of understanding than literal comprehension. A well-known reading expert, Dr. Francis Triggs, says that "Critical reading requires a contribution by both the author and the reader and an interplay which usually results in a new understanding." For instance, Jonathan Swift's *Gulliver's Travels* appeals to young people because at the literal level it reads like a fairy-tale adventure story about a man who lives with giants and miniature people. However, when the story is read at a more critical level of understanding, it is a very bitter satire on humankind. In other words, an understanding beyond the literal level is necessary for thorough comprehension.

What Does This Unit Cover?

There are three chapters in this unit, each one covering a different facet of critical comprehension.

- Chapter Four deals with separating fact from opinion. Exercises will call your attention to how we think we are dealing with fact when often we are accepting opinion.
- Chapter Five provides exercises for developing the ability to recognize an author's intent or real purpose in writing. Sometimes authors "disguise" their true purpose or thesis by the use of metaphor, satire, irony, or humour. At other times, authors use propaganda or present their evidence in a biased way. Chapter Five should help you analyze an author's actual intentions and evaluate bias.
- Chapter Six contains practices for discovering how both the author and the reader often draw inferences. Rather than coming right out and saying what they mean, authors sometimes imply or suggest what they want the reader to understand. Likewise, readers often draw inferences about what an author says. When you hear students talking about the "hidden meaning" of a work, or when you hear the statement "Read between the lines," drawing inferences is what is meant. This chapter also provides an opportunity to react to quoted statements, advertisements, and short articles, using what you learned in previous chapters to help you make critical judgments and draw conclusions.

A comment regarding reading rate is in order here. As you learned in Unit One, speed of reading is not as important as good comprehension. By now you should have realized that, although you can increase your overall speed, your reading rate fluctuates, affected by your interest in the topic, the length of the reading selection, your knowledge of the subject, the level of difficulty, and even how you feel on a certain day. That is natural. Some reading selections in this section of the book are timed, mostly for your own information. Most students developing their reading versatility like to have some idea how fast they are reading. That's fine. Go ahead and practise reading faster. Just remember not to let speed be your only goal. As you get to be a better reader, your reading speed will also increase.

What Should You Know after Completing This Unit?

Here are six objectives to work toward in this unit. By the time you complete this unit, you should be able to:

1. Distinguish fact from opinion.

2. Recognize an author's intent, attitude, and tone.

3. Recognize an author's bias and use of propaganda.

4. Recognize inferences being made by an author and make your own inferences from what you read.

5. Make critical judgments and draw conclusions by analyzing the author's diction, style, and use of figurative language.

6. Write a definition of critical comprehension.

If you have any additional objectives of your own, write them down below and share them with your instructor.

Personal reading objectives for Unit Two:

_____

_____

_____

_____

_____

_____

_____

For now, concentrate on objective 1, distinguishing fact from opinion, which is covered in the next chapter.

Distinguishing Fact from Opinion

Distinguishing fact from opinion is not always easy. A fact is usually defined as a truth, something that can be tested by experimentation, observation, or research and shown to be real. But even that is an elusive definition. For example, in 1930 it was generally accepted as fact that the atom was the smallest particle of an element and could not be split. With the advent of atomic power in the 1940s, scientists split the atom, making what was once thought to be a fact a fallacy. Today, physicists are just beginning to understand subatomic particles and refer to many of their findings as theory rather than fact. The point is that facts are sometimes "slippery."

An opinion, on the other hand, is often easier to distinguish. Your belief, feeling, or judgment about something is an opinion. It is a subjective or value judgment, not something that can be objectively verified. Even though you base your opinion on fact, others may not agree; an opinion cannot be proven to everyone's satisfaction. For instance, you may be of the opinion that Kiefer Sutherland is the greatest actor today, but there is no way to make your opinion fact. Others have their own favourite actors, while still others do not know who Kiefer Sutherland is. The only fact that you can prove is that Kiefer Sutherland is an actor.

Test your skill in recognizing fact from opinion by placing an *F* in the blank in front of any of the following statements you believe to be fact.

_____ **1.** Lester B. Pearson was a Prime Minister of Canada.

_____ **2.** Pearson was one of the best Prime Ministers Canada has had.

_____ **3.** Generally speaking, movies are more entertaining than books.

_____ **4.** *The Beaver* is a better magazine than *Maclean's*.

_____ **5.** Columbus, in 1492, was the first person to discover the Americas.

Now see how well you did.

- You should have marked the first one. It is a fact that can be verified objectively.

- The second statement, however, is not a fact. It is a subjective statement claiming "Pearson was one of the best." This claim is a value judgment; although we can prove that Pearson was a Prime Minister, historians may never agree that he was one of the best, even though he might have been. Words that give something value, such as *great, wonderful, beautiful, ugly, intelligent,* or *stupid,* make statements subjective opinions, not verifiable facts.

- The third statement is not fact; it is a value judgment. To say something is "more entertaining" or "better" or "worse" is to place a personal value on something. Value judgments may be based on facts, but they are opinions nonetheless.

- Number 4 is not a fact. You may believe one magazine is better than another; but *Maclean's* has a much larger circulation than *The Beaver,* so many readers disagree. However, the fact—and it *is* a fact—that *Maclean's* has a larger circulation than *The Beaver* does not mean it is any better either. The use of the word "better" needs clarification. Better in what way? Paper? Size? Cost? Contents? Again, "better" implies a value judgment.

- The fifth statement is one of those "slippery" facts. According to many sources, Columbus did discover the Americas in 1492. Yet, factually, he never actually landed on the continent; Vikings are said to have explored North America long before Columbus, and evidence indicates that native people inhabited the Americas over 25,000 years or more before Columbus. Obviously, he wasn't the first person to discover the Americas. It is a European viewpoint that many history books continue to express; yet many textbooks are now changing wording to clarify this historical point. As stated, number 5 is not an opinion; it is more an erroneous statement than anything else.

On the other hand, if someone were to claim that Columbus sailed to the New World in 1592 rather than 1492, it would be easy enough to consult historical records to show the correct date was 1492. Knowledge that we share and agree upon as a society is called *shared knowledge.* Agreed-upon facts, then, are generally referred to as objective. If we argue that Columbus was a better sailor than Magellan, we get into the subjective realm of opinion. Unless we can find objective evidence that one was better than the other, we can't speak factually.

Which of the following statements are based on objective evidence?

1. Coca-Cola tastes better than Pepsi-Cola.
2. The capital of Nunavut is Iqaluit.
3. The moon revolves around the earth.
4. Italians make great lovers.

- Both statements 1 and 4 are based on subjective evidence. You might get fifty people to say Coke tastes better than Pepsi, but you can get another fifty to say the opposite. The same goes for Italians as great lovers. These statements are opinions, not facts.
- Items 2 and 3 can be verified by checking agreed-upon information; thus they are facts based on objective evidence until such time as Iqaluit is no longer the capital and the moon quits revolving around the earth.

Just as our purpose for reading affects our speed and comprehension needs, it also affects how aware we must be of the differences between objective and subjective statements.

As a critical reader of all kinds of writing, you need to be able to distinguish between objective and subjective statements and then draw your own conclusions. The following drills will help you develop your ability to separate facts, opinions, and erroneous-sounding statements. If some of the answers seem "picky," just remember that the point is to sharpen your reading versatility.

A. Fact-Finding

PRACTICE A-1: Fact-Finding

Directions: Read each of the following statements and place an *F* in the blanks of those statements that you feel are *mostly* fact and an *O* in the blanks of those statements that are *mostly* opinion.

_____ 1. Four Canadian soldiers were killed during a training exercise near Kandahar, Afghanistan, when a United States Air Force jet dropped a bomb on them thinking they were enemy Al Qaida guerrillas. (From a Canadian Press release.)

_____ 2. People who graduate with a diploma from a community college are better off than those who complete university. This is because they have more practical knowledge that will lead more directly to a job.

_____ **3.** In most countries, roughly one out of 100,000 people has a problem with one of the eight enzymes that assemble haeme, the oxygen-carrying component of haemoglobin. The symptoms, which often don't show up until after puberty, can be aggravated by exposure to some foods and chemicals. (From *Discover*, April 2002, p. 25.)

_____ **4.** Compared to other captains of the Montreal Canadians, Saku Koivu isn't as fiery as Maurice "Rocket" Richard or as commanding as Jean Belliveau, but he still fits the mould of the legendary Hab captains, the proof being his willingness to fast-track his recovery from non-Hodgkin's lymphoma and suit up for the playoffs. (From *Maclean's*, April 22, 2002, p. 51.)

_____ **5.** A website should be designed so that users are never more than three clicks away from their desired end result. This is because most people who visit a website are looking for specific information, so navigation has to be quick and easy.

_____ **6.** The first Canadian comic book heroes, Nelvana, Johnny Canuck, and Canada Jack, emerged during the Second World War, when a foreign-exchange crisis led to a ban being placed on the importation of U.S. comics, including such popular titles as *Superman* (co-created by Canadian native Joe Shuster) and *Batman*. (From National Library of Canada, *Guardians of the North*.)

_____ **7.** With no conventional batteries or AC power whatsoever, the FR200 Radio, with its fine-tuning control of signal, provides superior crystal-clcar AM/FM/SW reception. (From Grundrig radio advertisement.)

_____ **8.** From the very moment of birth—even in the womb—Aboriginal children face infinitely more challenges than non-Native babies. Higher rates of smoking, alcohol, and polydrug use among Aboriginal mothers compromise the health and survivability of the fetus, as well as the child's long-term future. Almost twice as many Aboriginal babies die in infancy as other Canadian infants, despite a steady decrease in Aboriginal infant mortality over the last 40 years. (From Suzanne Fournier and Ernie Crey, "We can Heal: Aboriginal Children Today," *Visions of the Heart*, p. 305.)

_____ **9.** When an Iroquois war party attacked a French settlement on October 22, 1692, a fourteen-year-old girl named Madeleine de Verchères donned the attire of a French soldier and organized the defence of her settlement.

_____ **10.** The finest book published in the last year or so is *Churchill: A Biography*, by Roy Jenkins.

PRACTICE A-2: More Fact-Finding

Directions: Read each of the following statements. Circle the number of any that you think are primarily factual or can be objectively proven. Then underline any words in the statements that you feel are too subjective to be verified as factual.

1. Ringing in the ears is a form of tinnitus, the perception of sound that does not have an external source. Tinnitus can be constant or intermittent and can include buzzing, hissing, or sizzling. Many people experience momentary tinnitus, a high-pitched tone that last 5 to 30 seconds.

2. The transient sensation of tinnitus probably results from changes in blood flow or cellular activity within the inner ear. Acute tinnitus, which can last days or weeks, may be caused by infection, medication, head injury, accumulated earwax, or changes in blood pressure or chemistry.

3. There are still young persons who read for pleasure and who do well in school, but their number dwindles. The middle range of children muddles through high school and some go through college or university, but the general level of their academic achievement is significantly below what it was thirty years ago.

4. The NHL dominated hockey throughout the 1920s. It paid the average player $900 a year, with a few exceptional players earning upward of $10,000. Although interest in amateur trophies—the Allan Cup and the Memorial Cup—continued in the smaller centres, the focus remained on the NHL, even after the league shrank to six teams, with only the Toronto Maple Leafs and the Montreal Canadiens in Canada. Almost all the NHL players remained Canadian.

5. The games we played as kids were definitely more socially productive than the computer games played by kids today. Our games taught us the importance of respect and personal responsibility. We learned to value rules because we understood that they applied fairly to everybody. Loyalty was another principle that we learned through our games. How many life-long friendships were forged between the tattered nets of a hockey game no one can say.

6. Contemporary legends differ from legends of the past in that they claim to be factual rather than fantastic. These legends, although highly believable, are based on hearsay rather than fact. Some of them are horror stories reflecting urban fears, while some, like the trickster tales, are stories with a humorous, slightly ambiguous moral twist. An example of the first is the perennial legend of the Halloween candy poisoned by strangers that stirs up parental anxieties each October.

7. You climb for hours in the killer heat until you reach the alpine lake—serene, rainbow-coloured, backed by resplendent white peaks and practically deserted. Discover the natural beauty and majesty of the Waterton Lakes region in Alberta.

8. Research by Canadian economists suggests that, on average, unionized workers earn about 10 percent more than non-union workers do. Union members are also more than twice as likely to have pension plans provided by their employer, and unionized workers receive more paid vacations and holidays, and are more likely to have dental and medical plans and better job security than comparable non-union workers.

PRACTICE A-3: Fact versus Opinion

Directions: Each sentence is lettered in the following statements. On the line below each statement, write the letter of each sentence you think can be accepted as a statement of fact. The first one has been done for you.

1. (a) The last great Greek astronomer of antiquity was Claudius Ptolemy (or Ptolemeus), who flourished about A.D. 140. (b) He compiled a series of thirteen volumes on astronomy known as the *Almagest*. (c) Not all of the *Almagest* deals with Ptolemy's own work, for it includes a compilation of the astronomical achievements of the past, principally of Hipparchus. (d) In fact, it is our main source of information about Greek astronomy. (e) The *Almagest* also contains accounts of the contributions of Ptolemy himself. (From George Abell, *Exploration of the Universe*, 1982.)

a. although the phrase "last great" may not be fact b. c. d. e

2. (a) The July 2002 Almanac states that there are four West Coast species of salmon. This is incorrect. (b) There are five species. (c) The West Coast species belong to the genus *Oncorhynchus*. (d) Their common names are chinook, also called the spring or king salmon; the chum or dog salmon; the coho or silver salmon; the pink salmon; and the sockeye or red salmon.

---

3. (a) Women's suffrage and prohibition both gained support during the First World War. (b) Women reformers argued that men's aggressive nature had caused the worldwide cataclysm. (c) If women only had the right to vote and an opportunity to rule, wars would cease. (d) They also pointed out the inconsistency of fighting for democracy abroad when they were denied the vote at home. (From R. Francis *et al. Destinies: Canadian History Since Confederation*, Nelson, 2000, p. 245.)

---

4. (a) One teaching of Aboriginal people that is having an impact on the world is the Seventh Generation philosophy/prediction. (b) Simply put, it refers to how indigenous peoples make decisions with the Seventh Generation in mind. (c) The present generation is responsible for leaving future generations with a continuous cycle of resources and a habitable and safe environment. (d) This contrasts with Western planners, who once thought they were morally responsible only for a planning period, usually five years. (From S. Brascoupe, "Aboriginal Peoples' Vision of the Future: Interweaving Traditional Knowledge and New Technologies," *Vision of the Heart: Canadian Aboriginal Issues*, 2nd Edition, D. Long and O. Dickason, Harcourt Canada, 2000.)

---

5. (a) *The Glass Bead Game* by Hermann Hesse appeared in Switzerland in 1943. (b) It was his last major work of any importance. (c) It is also the best of all his novels, an "act of mental synthesis through which the spiritual values of all ages are perceived as simultaneously present and vitally alive." (d) It was with full artistic consciousness that Hesse created this classic work.

---

6. (a) Every television journalist soon learns that the picture comes first. (b) Words and other sounds, as well as the structure of a television news story, make an important contribution to the story's impact on the viewer, but only in a supporting role. (c) Without dramatic and eye-catching images, even the most important news story is difficult to convey on television; conversely, a relatively insignificant and routine event, such as a highway accident, fire, or incident of domestic violence, will rate prominence on television news if the camera has caught the action.

PRACTICE A-4: Interpreting "Facts"

Directions: Read the two passages below. They are accounts of the same historical event, written by two different historians at two different times. Notice how they both use facts and how they interpret those facts. Notice also the importance of their choice of words in conveying their respective messages.

   [T]he long ranks of the French were seen rapidly approaching the British position. . . . Another moment passed, the French paused, and from flank to flank poured a murderous and rapid fire upon the British line. . . . Wolfe [warned] his men to reserve their fire for a shorter and deadlier range. . . . And now the clear voice of Wolfe giving the word to fire rises over the field. . . . Numbers of French soldiers reeled and fell at once, others staggered for a moment, then dropped aside to die. . . . Scarcely fifteen minutes had passed . . . and already [their] battle was lost. Just then Wolfe was wounded . . . "Now, God be praised! I die happy," said the gallant soldier: and Wolfe, who had won a new empire for his race, passed from this material world to immortality. The loss of the British in the memorable battle of the Plains of Abraham amounted to 59 killed, and 600 wounded; . . . that of the French to 600 killed, and over 1000 wounded and taken prisoner. (From John M. McMullen, *The History of Canada From its Discovery to the Present Time,* McMullen & Co., 1892, pp. 192–194.)

The battle lasted less than half an hour. The two armies on the field were numerically equal, but the British had a force composed entirely of regular soldiers, while the French army included many badly trained militia members. The British held their fire until the French army was within 40m of them. Wolfe was ready: to ensure accurate and concentrated firepower, he had deployed three-quarters of his men in a single line confronting the French. Then the British officers gave the order, "Fire." The muskets roared, and a second volley followed, breaking the French attack and causing the French army to retire in disorder. Wolfe, leading a picked force of grenadiers, was shot down and died on the battlefield. . . . The British suffered about 650 casualties and the French roughly the same. On September 18 [1759], Quebec, short of provisions and soldiers . . . opened its gates and surrendered to the English. (From *Origins* 4E + *Destinies* 4E, 4th Edition by Francis © 2000. Reprinted with permission of Nelson, a division of Thomson Learning: www.thomsonrights.com. Fax 800-730-2215.)

1. What is the main idea of each paragraph? _____

    _____

    _____

2. List two supporting details that support the main idea in *each* of the paragraphs.

    _____

    _____

3. What facts reported in the first passage are also reported in the second one? Are there any differences in the reporting of facts? _____

    _____

    _____

    _____

4. Explain what would cause the differences in facts between these two passages.

    _____

    _____

    _____

5. How does each paragraph portray the death of General Wolfe? _____

    _____

    _____

PRACTICE A-5: Comparing "Facts"

Directions: Language is a storehouse of knowledge, customs, and traditions. Our thoughts and actions are influenced by the words and grammar that are supplied to us by our language. Two essays on the issue of disappearing indigenous languages are presented here. One author believes that the disappearance of a language is devastating, an event that has far-reaching effects on humanity. The other author argues that the loss of a language is not only common but also inevitable.

A DEAD END FOR HUMANITY

WADE DAVIS

About the author: *Wade Davis, a native of British Columbia, is best known for his writings on nature and environmental issues. He has also hosted and co-written television series on the environment.*

1   A hundred years from now, the 20th century will be remembered not for wars or technological innovations but as an era when people supported—or passively endorsed—the massive destruction of biological and cultural diversity. In the past 25 years alone, as many as one million species will have been driven to extinction. Yet, even as we mourn the loss of biological life, we ignore a parallel process of loss—the erosion of the ethnosphere, which might be defined as the sum of all thoughts, dreams, myths, and insights brought into being by human imagination since the dawn of consciousness.

2   Of the 6,000 languages spoken today, fully half are not being taught to children. Effectively, they are already dead. By the end of the 21st century linguistic diversity may be reduced to as few as 500 languages.

3   A language, of course, is not simply vocabulary and grammar; it's a flash of the human spirit, the vehicle by which the soul of a culture comes into the material realm. Each language represents a unique intellectual and spiritual achievement. Although many of the languages at risk are those spoken by small indigenous societies, their loss would be as great as that of any other language.

4   Even the most pessimistic biologist would not claim that 50 per cent of the world's biological diversity is currently at risk. And yet this represents the most optimistic cultural scenario. When we lose a language, as MIT linguistic professor Ken Hale says, it's like dropping a bomb on the Louvre.

5   Yet, even among those sympathetic to the plight of indigenous societies, there is a mood of resignation—as if these cultures, quaint and colourful though they may be, are somehow fated to fade away, reduced to the margins of history as the modern technological world moves inexorably forward.

6   To embrace this view, however, is to ignore the central revelation of anthropology—the idea that our own society is not absolute. Rather, it is just one model of reality, the consequence of one particular set of choices that our ancestors made generations ago. Whether it is the nomadic Penan in the forests of Borneo, Vodoun acolytes in Haiti, or Yak herders in Tibet, all of these people teach us that there are other ways of being and thinking and relating to the natural world.

7   I spent some time among the Penan of Borneo, one of the last nomadic peoples of Southeast Asia. For most of human history, we were all nomads, wanderers on a

Reprinted with permission of the author.

pristine planet. It was only 10,000 years ago, with the neolithic revolution and the rise of agriculture, that many of us succumbed to the cult of the seed. Among nomadic societies we see an image of what we once were.

8   In nomadic societies there is no incentive to accumulate possessions, because everything must be carried on your back. The wealth of a community is the strength of the relationships among its people. Sharing is an involuntary reflex; one never knows who will be the next to secure the food.

9   Different ways of life create different human beings, and there are profound lessons to be drawn from different world views. Today, in Canada, you might pass a homeless person on the street, and understand him to be the regrettable but perhaps inevitable consequences of the economic system. A Penan is raised to believe that a poor man shames us all.

10   I'm not suggesting a Rousseau view of indigenous people as noble savage conservationists; to suggest that is to deny indigenous people their legitimate place in the brutal struggle for survival. Life in the malarial swamps of New Guinea leaves little room for sentiment. Nostalgia is not a trait commonly associated with the Inuit. Nomadic hunters and gatherers in the Amazon have no conscious sense of stewardship.

11   What these cultures have, however, is a traditional relationship with the Earth, forged through time and ritual, and based not only on deep attachment to the land but on a far more subtle intuition-the idea that the land itself is breathed into being by human consciousness. Mountains, rivers, and forests are not perceived as mere props on a stage on which the drama of humanity unfolds. For these societies the land is alive, a dynamic force to be embraced and transformed by the human imagination.

12   A Kwakiut boy raised to revere the salmon forests of the Pacific Northwest as the abode of Huxwhukw and the Crooked beak of Heaven, cannibal spirits living at the North of the world, will be a different person than a Canadian child taught that such forests exist to be cut. A child raised in the Andes to believe that a mountain is the realm of a protective spirit will behave differently than a youth brought up to believe that it is an inert pile of rock ready to be mined.

13   Every view of the world that fades away, every culture that disappears, diminishes the possibilities of human life. We lose not only knowledge of the natural world but also intuitions about the meaning of the cosmos. We reduce the human repertoire of adaptive responses to the common problems that confront all humanity.

14   An anthropologist from another planet visiting contemporary North America would note wonders here, but would also perhaps be puzzled to see our environmental problems, or the fact that 20 per cent of our people control 80 per cent of the wealth, more than half of our marriages end in divorce, and that more than 90 per cent of our elders don't live with relatives. As we lose other models of living, we lose a vast archive of knowledge and expertise, the memories of countless elders, healers, farmers, midwives, poets, and saints.

15   How are we to value what is being lost? That we are losing the botanical knowledge of other cultures is obvious-and less than 1 per cent of the world's flora has been thoroughly studied by Western science. But how do we value less concrete contributions of other cultures? What is the worth of family bonds that mitigate poverty and insulate the individual from loneliness? Of diverse intuitions about the spirit realm? What is the economic measure of ritual practices that result in the protection of a forest?

16   Before she died, anthropologist Margaret Mead spoke of her singular concern that as we drifted toward a more homogenous world we were laying the foundations of a bland and generic modern culture that in the end would have no rivals.

17   The entire imagination of humanity, she feared, might become imprisoned within the limits of a single intellectual and spiritual modality. Her nightmare was the possibility that we might wake up one day and not even remember what had been lost.

18   One night, on a ridge in Sarawak, I sat by a fire with Asik Nyelit, headman of the Ubong River Penan. It was dusk and the light of a partial moon filtered through the branches of the canopy. Asik looked up at the moon and casually asked me if it was true that people had journeyed there, only to return with baskets of dirt. "If true," he asked, "why did they bother to go?"

19   It was difficult to explain a $1-trillion space program to a man who kindled fire with a flint. The proper answer to Ansik's query was that we did not go into space to secure new wealth but to experience a new vision of life itself.

20   The perspective of Earth we gained from space made us begin to understand the fragility of our biosphere. Now we must understand that there is an ethnosphere, and it too is fragile-and irreplaceable.

Directiions: Now answer the following questions.

1. Is this essay mostly fact or opinion? _____

_____

2. What is the author's main argument about language and culture?_____

_____

_____

3. Is the main argument based on facts? Explain. _____

_____

_____

4. Did the author convince you that it is important to preserve minority languages? Explain. _____

_____

_____

    The following essay offers the opposite opinion on the this same issue. As you read, underline any statements you feel are factual. Then answer the questions that follow the selection.

GET BEYOND BABEL

KEN WIWA

About the author: *Ken Wiwa is a Nigerian-born writer and journalist. He is the son of the Nigerian activist and writer Ken Saro Wiwa who was executed by the Nigerian government for his criticism of government policies.*

1   Earlier this week I received compelling evidence that I am doomed to extinction. According to figures released by the Worldwatch institute, half of the world's 6,800 languages face annihilation; that's because they are spoken by fewer than 2,500 people. Here in Canada, only three of 50 aboriginal languages may survive the coming cultural Armageddon. Lurking in the reaction to this news, I suspect, is the fear that we will end up speaking English in some monocultural flatland called "Disney."

2   There is an impassioned school of thought that says that unless we take active steps to preserve our "cultural diversity"—read "languages"—the human race is in

danger. When we lose a language, these doomsday prophets say, we lose its knowledge base and world-view; this, they assure us, impoverishes us all.

3   As a member of an indigenous people, and as someone actively concerned about the fate of my culture, I used to subscribe to this view. I'd soak up the arguments of philologists and writers I admired warning about the implications of losing our languages. I bought all these arguments. Then I started examining my own community's experience.

4   I am Ogoni. We number an estimated 500,000, and speak six mutually unintelligible dialects-languages, by now-on an overpopulated but fertile floodplain in southern Nigeria. The Ogoni languages and culture are threatened by Nigeria's socioeconomic realities. Our environment has been compromised by aggressive and irresponsible oil exploration. Unemployment, inadequate health care and neglect by the country's rulers has ripped out my community's heart.

5   The young, the energetic and the ambitious have no option but to leave in search of better opportunities. The community is left in the care of the old and the infirm. A whole generation of Ogoni is growing up elsewhere, speaking English, forgetting our languages, exiled from our villages and our traditions. When the elders die, they take our traditions, our folktales, our myths, our history and our cultural memories with them. As we say in Africa, "When an old man dies it is like a library has been burned down."

6   Which is why I started looking into Ogoni history, thinking about my language, trying to shoehorn our myths and folktales into a compelling story to keep them alive for another generation. But the more I study our history, especially the way our culture and our language has evolved, the more I suspect that those of us who have set out with the intention of reviving a culture by fixing it in time and space may actually be doing more harm than good.

7   Take the development of my language. According to one of our creation myths, the original Ogoni settlements was at a place called Nama. Here the first Ogoni people cleared the surrounding forest, left one tree standing and established our roots. Over time our community grew, and people migrated westward into the rain forests until there were 128 villages in Ogoni. Because these settlements were isolated, the language altered subtly. If you to go Ogoni today you can still hear the effects. In the eastern villages we speak a different dialect from the villages on the western fringes.

8   The point I am making here is that language is in constant flux. To fix it in a particular time and place is to arrest the movement and vitality that shapes a language's evolution. The more I examine the way my language has evolved, the more I believe that the best a language can do in response is to go with the flow. As far as I know, no Ogoni language has a word for "computer," but we do say *faa-bu-yon* (car of the sky)—or airplane.

9   Unless we make a huge effort to open up the language and the culture to embrace our experience of contact with other cultures and the modern world, we will always be vulnerable. To say that is not to diminish the past or our culture, but to acknowledge a simple truth: Indigenous peoples must not turn inward and cling to nostalgia for sustenance. Though we look back, we must always go forward.

10   For me, that's the great poetic insight in Gabriel Garcia Marquez's novel, *One Hundred Years of Solitude*. The community of Macondo begins amid vibrant energy, but ossifies into a parochialism trapped in a cycle of self-repeating prophecies that refuse to embrace or even acknowledge the passage of time. When Marquez delivers his verdict on Macondo (races condemned to 100 years of solitude do not get a second chance), it seems to me to be a warning of all the language curators and conservationists working to preserve our cultures in some cultural museum.

11   It is a warning that the guardians of the French language, the Academie Française, might heed. Once French was the international language of the world; thanks to the Academie's fastidious custody, it is becoming inflexible. English, on the other hand, has rarely been as neurotic about its purity. Most English words are borrowed from other languages; little Anglo-Saxon survives. Only an incurable romantic would attempt to revive Old English for general use. No, English has evolved, absorbed and adapted. Open to foreign influence, it borrows unashamedly. That's why English has more than 500,000 words in its vocabulary, while French has little more than 100,000.

12   For me the rise and preeminence of English is an example to all cultures about how a language survives and thrives. When Julius Caesar invaded Britain 2,000 years ago, English did not exist. Fifteen hundred years later, Shakespeare had a potential audience of only five million English-speakers. Over the next 400 years, English would come to be spoken by more than one billion people. According to *The Story of English* (by Robert McCrum and Robert MacNeil), English is now "more widely scattered, more widely spoken than any other language has ever been."

13   Thanks to its versatility, shameless habit of appropriation and the violence and aggression of its people, English is now the *lingua franca* of the world. What is more remarkable is that despite its mongrel nature, the English world-view has persisted. Through all the mutations and adaptations it has still managed to service and protect a small island's place in the world.

14   The English people and the English language have survived by picking up influences and adapting words from dead languages, like Latin and Ancient Greek, and grafting elements from their world-views, religions and philosophies onto the English trunk.

15   English is both a lesson and an obstacle to the development of other languages and cultures. Which is why it strikes me that to lament the death of languages and to prescribe a solution that freezes language in time is to condemn a culture and a language to certain extinction.

16   If cultural diversity is so vital to our survival as a race, we must understand how languages work over time. After all, it only took English 400 years to achieve its current status. Who is to say that in another 500 years English will not go the same way as Greek, Latin or French? There is one more lesson that leaps out from my reading of the story English. It is this: Languages and cultures don't die-they just get absorbed into something else.

Directions: Now answer the following questions.

1. Is this essay mostly fact or opinion? _____

_____

_____

2. What is the author's main argument about language and culture?_____

_____

_____

3. Is the main argument based on facts? Explain. _____

_____

_____

4. Did the author convince you that the loss of languages is not only common but also inevitable? Explain. _____

_____

_____

5. Have you changed your opinion after reading these two essays? Explain.

_____

_____

B.   Reading Opinions of Others

PRACTICE B-1

Directions: Take a few seconds to survey the following selection. Referring to the title, the headings, and your brief survey, write in the space below what you think the article will cover.

Probable coverage: _____

Now read the article, underlining factual statements. Then answer the questions that follow.

HOW GOOD ARE YOUR OPINIONS?

VINCENT RYAN RUGGIERO

1   "Opinion" is a word that is often used carelessly today. It is used to refer to matters of taste, belief, and judgment. This casual use would probably cause little confusion if people didn't attach too much importance to opinion. Unfortunately, most do attach great importance to it. "I have as much right to my opinion as you have to yours," and "Everyone's entitled to his opinion," are common expressions. In fact, anyone who would challenge another's opinion is likely to be branded intolerant.

2   Is that label accurate? Is it intolerant to challenge another's opinion? It depends on what definition of opinion you have in mind. For example, you may ask a friend "What do you think of the new Buicks?" And he may reply, "In my opinion, they're ugly." In this case, it would not only be intolerant to challenge his statement, but foolish. For it's obvious that by opinion he means his *personal preference*, a matter of taste. And as the old saying goes, "It's pointless to argue about matters of taste."

3   But consider this very different use of the term. A newspaper reports that the Supreme Court has delivered its opinion in a controversial case. Obviously the justices did not state their personal preferences, their mere likes and dislikes. They stated their *considered judgment*, painstakingly arrived at after thorough inquiry and deliberation.

4   Most of what is referred to as opinion falls somewhere between these two extremes. It is not an expression of taste. Nor is it careful judgment. Yet it may contain elements of both. It is a view or belief more or less casually arrived at, with or without examining the evidence.

5   Is everyone entitled to his opinion? Of course. In a free country this is not only permitted, but guaranteed. In Great Britain, for example, there is still a Flat Earth Society. As the name implies, the members of this organization believe that the earth is not spherical, but flat. In this country, too, each of us is free to take as creative a position as we please about any matter we choose. When the telephone operator announces "That'll be 95¢ for the first three minutes," you may respond, "No, it won't—it'll be 28¢." When the service station attendant notifies you "Your oil is down a quart," you may reply "Wrong—it's up three."

6   Being free to hold an opinion and express it does not, of course, guarantee you favourable consequences. The operator may hang up on you. The service station attendant may threaten you with violence.

7   Acting on our opinions carries even less assurance. Some time ago in California a couple took their eleven-year-old diabetic son to a faith healer. Secure in their opinion that the man had cured the boy, they threw away his insulin. Three days later the boy died. They remained unshaken in their belief, expressing the opinion that God would raise the boy from the dead. The police arrested them, charging them with manslaughter. The law in such matters is both clear and reasonable. We are free to act on our opinions only so long as, in doing so, we do not harm others.

OPINIONS CAN BE MISTAKEN

8   It is tempting to conclude that, if we are free to believe something, it must have some validity. But that is not so. Free societies are based on the wise observation that since knowledge often comes through mistakes and truth is elusive, every person must be allowed to make his own path to wisdom. So in a way, free societies are based on the realization that opinions can be wrong.

9   In 1972 a British farmer was hoeing his sugar beet field when he uncovered a tiny statue. It looked to him like the figure of a man listening to a transistor radio. In his opinion, it was a piece of junk. Yet it turned out to be a work of art made of gilt bronze in the twelfth century and worth more than $85,000. He was free to have his opinion. But his opinion was wrong.

10   For scores of years millions of people lit up billions of cigarettes, firm in their opinion that their habit was messy and expensive, but harmless. Yet now we know that smoking is a significant factor in numerous diseases and even does harm to non-smokers who breathe smoke-polluted air and to unborn babies in the wombs of cigarette addicts. Those millions of people were free to believe smoking was harmless. But that didn't make them right. Nor did it protect their bodies from harm.

KINDS OF ERROR

11   There are four general kinds of error that can corrupt anyone's beliefs. Francis Bacon classified them as follows: (1) errors or tendencies to error common among all people by virtue of their being human; (2) errors that come from human communication and the limitations of language; (3) errors in the general fashion or attitude of an age; (4) errors posed to an individual by a particular situation.

12   Some people, of course, are more prone to errors than others. John Locke observed that these people fall into three groups. He described them as follows:

   a.   Those who seldom reason at all, but do and think according to the example of others, whether parents, neighbours, ministers, or whoever else they choose or have implicit faith in, to save themselves the pain and trouble of thinking and examining for themselves.

b. Those who are determined to let passion rather than reason govern their actions and arguments, and therefore rely on their own or other people's reasoning only so far as it suits them.

c. Those who sincerely follow reason, but lack sound, overall good sense, and so do not have a full view of everything that relates to the issue. They talk with only one type of person, read only one type of book, and so are exposed to only one viewpoint.

INFORMED VS. UNINFORMED OPINION

13   In forming our opinions it helps to seek out the views of those who know more than we do about the subject. By examining the views of informed people, we broaden our perspective, see details we could not see by ourselves, consider facts we were unaware of. No one can know everything about everything. It is not a mark of inferiority but of good sense to consult those who have given their special attention to the field of knowledge at issue.

14   Each of us knows something about food and food preparation. After all, most of us have eaten three meals a day all our lives. But that experience doesn't make us experts on running a restaurant or on the food packaging industry. Many of us have played varsity sports in high school. But it takes more than that experience to make us authorities on a particular sport.

15   Some years ago the inmates of Attica prison in New York State overpowered their guards and gained control of the prison. They took a number of hostages and threatened to kill them if their demands were not met. Negotiations proceeded for a time. Then they were at an impasse. The situation grew tense. Finally lawmen stormed the prison and, before order was restored, a number of the hostages were killed. In the wake of the tragedy there were two difficult questions: Had the prisoners' demands been reasonable? And who was responsible for the breakdown in negotiations?

16   A number of people in public and private life offered their opinions. One newspaper editorial stated that the main fault lay with the prisoners, that they had refused to negotiate reasonably. A letter to the editor explained that the prisoners were unquestionably in the wrong simply because they were prisoners, and thus had forefeited all rights and privileges. A U.S. senator from another state declared that the blame lay with American life in general. "We must ask," he said, "why some men would rather die than live another day in America."

17   The governor of New York State issued this statement: "The tragedy was brought on by the highly-organized, revolutionary tactics of militants who rejected all efforts at a peaceful settlement, forcing a confrontation, and carried out cold-blooded killings they had threatened from the outset."

18   In a much less publicized statement, a professor at a small liberal arts college, an expert in penology (the study of prison systems), expressed sympathy with the prisoners, criticized the terrible conditions in the nation's prisons, agreed fully with many of the prisoners' demands, rejected a few as absurd, and explained some of the underlying causes of prison unrest.

19   Now all those opinions deserved some consideration. But which was most helpful in coming to an understanding of the issue in all its considerable complexity? Certainly the most informed opinion. The opinion of the expert in penology.

20   For all of us, whether experts or amateurs, it is natural to form opinions. We are constantly receiving sensory impressions and responding to them first on the level of simple likes and dislikes, then on the level of thought. Even if we wanted to escape having opinions, we couldn't. Nor should we want to. One of the things that makes human beings vastly more complex and interesting than trees or cows is their ability to form opinions.

21   This ability has two sides, though. If it can lift a man to the heights of understanding, it can also topple him to the depths of ludicrousness. Both the wise man and the fool have opinions. The difference is, the wise man forms his with care and, as time increases his understanding, refines them to fit even more precisely the reality they interpret.

Comprehension Check

Part A

Directions: Answer the following questions. Don't look back unless you are referred to a particular paragraph for an answer.

1. Circle the letter of the statement that best expresses the thesis of the article:

   a. We need to form our opinions with care.

   b. It is natural to form opinions.

   c. The word "opinion" is used carelessly today.

   d. Everyone has a right to his or her own opinion.

2. T/F The statement "Being free to hold an opinion and express it does not, of course, guarantee you favourable consequences" is a fact.

3. T/F Paragraph 9 is mostly factual in content.

4. Which of the following are mentioned as the kinds of errors that can corrupt anyone's beliefs?

   a. errors posed to an individual by a particular situation

   b. errors or tendencies to error common among all people by virtue of being human

   c. errors in the general fashion or attitude of an age

   d. errors that come from limitations of language

5. T/F In forming our opinions, it helps to seek out the views of those who do not know more than we do about the subject.

6. T/F "No one can know everything about everything" is an opinion.

7. In paragraph 19, the author claims the expert in penology was the most helpful in coming to an understanding of the prison riot issue. Why would this opinion be worth more than the others mentioned?_____

   _____

   _____

8. What is the difference between personal preference and considered judgment?

   _____

   _____

   _____

   _____

9. "One of the things that make human beings vastly more complex and interesting than trees or cows is their ability to form opinions," says the author. Is this a statement of fact or opinion? _____ Explain. _____

_____

_____

_____

10. Is the article mostly fact or opinion? _____ Explain. _____

_____

_____

_____

Part B

Directions: The preceding questions can be answered objectively. The following questions require subjective responses. Be prepared to explain your answers in class discussion.

1. "We are free to act on our opinions only as long as, in doing so, we do not harm others," says the author. Is this a good rule to follow?_____ Explain.

_____

_____

_____

_____

2. The author refers to a couple who took their diabetic son to a faith healer as an example of how acting on our opinions can be dangerous. Give an example of an opinion you hold or held at one time that could be dangerous in certain circumstances. _____

_____

_____

_____

3. Reread paragraph 12. In your opinion, do you fit any one of the three groups? Explain. _____

_____

_____

_____

4. Give an example of an opinion you once held but no longer do. Explain why you changed your viewpoint. _____

_____

_____

_____

_____

Vocabulary Check

Part A

Directions: Write a definition for each underlined word in the blank following each statement.

1. their <u>considered</u> judgment (paragraph 3) _____

_____

_____

2. it must have some <u>validity</u> (paragraph 8)_____

_____

_____

3. errors <u>posed</u> to an individual (paragraph 11) _____

_____

_____

4. some are more <u>prone</u> to errors (paragraph 12)_____

_____

_____

5. they have <u>implicit</u> faith in themselves (point a.) _____

_____

_____

Part B

Directions: Using the words from the list below, write the correct word in the appropriate blank.

overpowered   inmates   tense
impasse   proceeded

"Some years ago the **(6)** _____ of Attica prison in New York State **(7)** _____ their guards and gained control of the prison. Negotiations **(8)** _____ for a time. Then they were at an **(9)** _____. The situation grew **(10)** _____."

Record the results of the comprehension (Part A only) and vocabulary checks on the Student Record Chart in the Appendix. Discuss any problems or questions with your instructor before you continue.

PRACTICE B-2: Evaluating Differing Opinions

Part A

Directions: Some people believe that violence that happens in sports, especially in hockey, should be banned. Others feel that sports are not violent. Following are two different arguments about violence in sports. Before you read them, use the space below to write why you do or do not believe that violence in sports should be controlled.

YOUR OPINION ON VIOLENCE IN SPORTS: _____

_____

_____

_____

Now read the selection, separating facts from opinions.

GOONS: A LOVE STORY

JAY TEITEL

"I have no idea how I'd fare in a fight on the street. I don't fight on the street."
—Kris King

1   Reading about the Marty McSorley trial in the newspaper the other day reminded me of a discussion I had last spring with then Maple Leaf Kris King. McSorley, of course, is the Boston Bruin (ex-Edmonton Oiler, ex-L.A. King) defence-man who was charged with assault for hitting Vancouver Canuck tough guy Donald Brashear over the head from behind with his stick last spring, felling him like an oak. I was as repelled by McSorley's apparent thuggery as anyone, even more so when he subsequently pleaded, "But I just wanted to fight!" The whole incident seemed like a welcome last straw to a hockey aberration I considered lethal to the sport. But the next night I heard Eddie Shack, of all people, on CBC Radio, delivering a weirdly compelling explanation of why Brashear should have fought, or known he was required to fight, according to the Byzantine tough-guy code of hockey violence. And it occurred to me that it might be a good idea to talk to an articulate exponent of that code before I smugly consigned the entire species of tough guys to extinction.

2   Which is how I found myself, a few days later, standing in front of Kris King's cubicle in the Leafs locker room at the Air Canada Centre after a Maple Leafs prac-tice, pondering three surprises: one, how small, or at least normal-sized, King looked for a tough guy; two, how fast he shed his equipment (always a revelation with pro athletes); and three, not just how articulate he was, but how matter-of-factly he was able to convey a totally novel point of view—how logical he was in talking about a passion I had never considered. If Kris King is typical—and there's ample evidence he is—hockey's "goons" may be not only the most interesting players in the game today, but the custodians of its soul.

3   Exhibit A in my conversion was the first thing King said to me: "Frankly, it's a shitty job." Actually what he said was, "Frankly, it's a shitty job, which is probably why the guys who are willing to do it are also the guys who love hockey more than anyone else. They have to be, because they're setting aside part of their dream to do it. No one dreams of being an enforcer. I came into the league as a top goal-scorer from Junior, but I had to learn another `trade' to make it to the NHL. And it is a skill you have to learn. I was so naive that during my first fight I kept my gloves on. The situation was similar for a lot of guys: Bob Probert, Rick Tocchet. Even Tie Domi." And for Ken Baumgartner and Bill Berg (both of whom are also unusually articulate).

4   This is the key to the reality of the "modern goon," the thing most fans don't think about when they see the nightly ritual bloodletting on the NHL highlights. The majority of tough guys in the league today aren't players who were necessarily

identified as such in Junior, but skilled players (Bob Probert scored forty-eight goals in his last full year in Junior hockey) who aren't quite skilled enough to make it as "everyday" players in the NHL and who are asked to drastically change their style, and their dream, if they want to stick. Not everyone is willing to make the trade. Andre Hidi, a talented young forward in the Washington Capitals system, was told by the team that he'd have to fight to make it in the NHL. He said no thanks and went to get his MBA at Stanford instead. The choice in the old city neighbourhoods was criminal or cop; in the new NHL, it's more likely to be goon or graduate school.

5   And in large part, the choice today's tough guy makes reveals the singularity of his heart. What do we decry most as fans, after all, but the spoiled behaviour of over-paid athletes who appear to love money more than the game? Enforcers are the dia-metric opposite. Like other mature adults, they accept disillusionment in pursuit of a higher loyalty. So Kris King learned to take his gloves off in a fight, and to duck his head into his shoulder for protection against enforcers twenty pounds heavier and four inches taller than him, and to get his helmet off quickly, "which you probably want to do because the chinstrap is choking you." And to put on a visor because his kids wanted him to after Bryan Berard's accident, but to remind himself to take it off if he fights, so that his opponent won't hurt his hand on the plastic. And in his spare time to watch Mats Sundin and Jaromir Jagr play the game he loves.

6   Because in the end the question is one of love, the nature and size of it. Critics of hockey fighting—me included—will complain that the fights are so predictable as to be deadening. But it's exactly that lack of spontaneity that makes the bargain tough guys strike so curious: they agree to play the least spontaneous game in the world in order to bask second-hand in the glow of the most spontaneous. By necessity, tough guys have to live the examined life, to be thoughtful about what it is they do in a way that a merely talented hockey player does not.

7   "There are five main reasons for a fight to occur," King says. "One, in response to ill-treatment of a skilled player on your team; two, in response to abuse of the goalie; three, to change the momentum of a game; four, to draw the other team into taking an extra penalty; five, because you don't like someone." King's list of reasons, which places proletarian emotion a poor fifth, is almost Talmudic in its logic. In fact, there's a passage in the Talmud that King might have penned himself: There are three reasons for not going into a ruin: it may cave in on your head; your reputation could suffer; there could be evil spirits lurking there.

8   It takes discipline, compassion, and a self-awareness that comes close to sadness to write something like that, whether you're a tough guy or a rabbi. Would Pavel Bure be up to it? For that matter, would Mats Sundin stay in hockey if he had to fight to stick? Would Wayne Gretzky have squared off to play the sport? Or more precisely: you can hate fighting in hockey, and think what Marty McSorley did was plenty ugly, but if they get rid of all the goons, who will be left to cherish the game the way you do?

Directions: Now answer the following questions.

1. What is the main idea of the essay? _____

_____

_____

2. Is the essay mostly fact or opinion? _____

_____

_____

3. What is the author's main argument against stricter penalties for violent activity while playing sports? _____

_____

_____

_____

_____

4. Is the main argument based mostly on facts? _____ Explain. _____

_____

_____

_____

_____

5. Did the author convince you of his argument? _____ Explain. _____

_____

_____

_____

_____

Part B

Directions: The next essay offers the opposite view on violence in sports. As you read, separate fact from opinions. Then answer the questions that follow the reading selection.

TACKLING VS. VIOLENCE—WHERE DO WE DRAW THE LINE?

JOHN VERRAN

1   The recent high-profile incident involving NHL star Marty McSorley and the subsequent rulings by the courts and the NHL have caused many of us to think long and hard about the topic of violence and its place in society, particularly in the area of sports.

2   As a hockey coach, educator, and parent, I have an incredible internal struggle with this issue. I grew up living the game of hockey and believe that there is no other sport that better teaches our children the lessons of hard work, commitment to a goal, and the value of teamwork. In my opinion, hockey is the greatest game on the face of the earth. However, this is not to say it is without its problems.

3   Hockey, by its very nature, is a physical game and should not be compared to other sports and activities that don't involve this form of contact. It requires high-speed and protective gear that covers participants from head to toe. Even with this protection, injuries still prevail whether the game is being played by the rules or not. In today's game, bigger, stronger, and faster is what coaches are looking for. This often results in more injuries for the participants.

4   In my many roles, I am constantly talking to young people about ways to solve conflict without using physical or verbal aggression. I believe all individuals need to learn how to resolve their differences in a non-aggressive manner.

Used by permission of Canadian Association for Health, Physical Education, Recreation and Dance.

5   Discussions around the topic of violence in hockey often stimulate a wide range of opinion. This is apparent by just opening any daily newspaper to the sports section or watching a sport telecast on television. Clearly, there is a very fine line between playing a hard physical game of hockey and being violent on the ice. However, in my opinion, there is no room in this game for violent attacks that deliberately put the safety of another in jeopardy.

6   As parents, we pack our children up every morning and send them off to school believing they are going to a safe and caring environment. We expect that teachers, administrators, and educational assistants will treat them with respect and will help them with any problems that they have during the day. We should expect no less when we send our children off to the local arena, swimming pool, or dance studio. Instructors and coaches have a responsibility to make children's experiences safe and caring ones.

7   In hockey, youth must be taught to respect the safety of their opponents. This does not mean participants shouldn't play hard or aggressively. It simply means they must be taught, at an early age, that it is wrong to take advantage of any opponent who is in a vulnerable position.

8   Coaches work hard to get their players to play with emotion. This can be a challenge, since there is a very fine line between playing with emotion and losing control. When players lose control, violent acts often occur. Coaches must make a continuous effort to work with their players, helping them to learn to stay in control, to play fair, and to demonstrate respect for both their teammates and opponents.

9   Sport governing organizations have influenced many changes to the rules of hockey in recent years to demonstrate their commitment to reduce its level of violence. Infractions like high-sticking now carry much stiffer penalties. All minor hockey players must wear a stop sign patch on the back of their sweaters to remind all participants of the dangers associated with hitting from behind.

10   The NHL has a responsibility to be a leader in the development of fair play and violence-free sport. After all, minor hockey players and coaches often learn from professional sport heroes and coaches. There must be more emphasis on skill development and less on intimidation tactics.

11   Incidents like the McSorley one often give the game of hockey a bad rap. And unfortunately these incidents are on the rise. It is important to remember, however, that every day, all year long, many young players are learning valuable lessons by participating in hockey and other activities. These players benefit from an environment that is safe and caring and results in positive experiences for all. As coaches and teachers, let's help our participants learn from the negative incidents that we hear about and promote to our kids the appropriate ways to play. We can all play a role in reversing this negative trend and image, helping our players to develop into highly skilled athletes and citizens that are grounded in the principles of integrity, fairness, and respect.

Directions: Now answer the following questions.

1. What is the main idea of the essay? _____

_____

_____

_____

2. Is the essay mostly fact or opinion? _____

_____

_____

3. What is the author's main argument for stricter rules against violent behaviour in sports? _____

_____

_____

_____

_____

4. Is the main argument based mostly on facts? _____ Explain._____

_____

_____

_____

_____

5. Did the author convince you of his argument? _____ Explain._____

_____

_____

_____

_____

6. Reread your stated opinion on the subject (page 184). Then explain why you have or have not changed your mind after reading these two essays. _____

_____

_____

_____

_____

7. What would it take to change your opinion? _____

_____

_____

_____

_____

PRACTICE B-3: Quick Quiz on Fact/Opinion

Part A

Directions: In the space provided, explain the differences between fact and opinion.

_____

_____

_____

_____

_____

_____

_____

_____

_____

_____

_____

Part B

Directions: Place an *O* in the blank in front of all statements of opinion, an *F* if a statement is fact or can be verified.

_____ **1.** Potatoes are served in 77 different ways on the dinner menu at Morton's Spud-o-rama.

_____ **2.** We can no longer get along in our present society without telephones.

_____ **3.** It is important for college students to have good study skills if they are to succeed in the academic world.

_____ **4.** Delta-9 tetrahydrocannabinol or THC, the main psychoactive constituent of marijuana, is said to have a wide variety of therapeutic properties.

_____ **5.** The two most interesting things in the world, for our species, are ideas and the individual human body, two elements that poetry uniquely joins together.

_____ **6.** Last year, as a result of the worldwide collapse of oil prices, the Mexican economy shrank 5 percent, and underemployment reached 50 percent. Things are worse in El Salvador.

_____ **7.** After the terrorist attacks on the United States on September 11, 2001, the Canadian government was unfairly criticized for having immigration policies and procedures that were too lenient.

_____ **8.** War against the Plains Indians in the early nineteenth century was a hopeless proposition for Europeans armed with swords, single-shot pistols, and breech-loading rifles. The Indians were infinitely better horsemen and could loose a continuous fusillade of arrows from beneath the neck of a pony going at full tilt.

_____ **9.** The Queen Mother lived for 101 glorious years, during which time she earned the love and devotion of all her subjects in the Commonwealth.

_____ **10.** Your jeweller is the expert where diamonds are concerned. His knowledge can help make the acquisition of a quality diamond of a carat or more a beautiful, rewarding experience.

Part C

Directions: In the space provided, explain what kind of evidence you would have to gather to prove the following statements as facts.

1. The viewing of violence on television has created a more violent society.

   _____

   _____

   _____

   _____

2. City slums breed crime. _____

   _____

   _____

   _____

   _____

3. Solar energy is the most efficient way to heat homes in some parts of Canada.

   _____

   _____

   _____

   _____

4. A postsecondary education provides better job opportunities._____

   _____

   _____

   _____

   _____

5. If you are rich, you probably won't get convicted of a crime as easily as you would if you were poor. _____

   _____

   _____

   _____

Hand in the quiz to your instructor.

Name _____ Section _____ Date _____

C.   Detecting Propaganda

Before you begin this section on propaganda, answer the following questions.

1. Using your dictionary to define *propaganda.* _____

_____

_____

2. Does the word *propaganda* have a positive or negative connotation for you? Explain. _____

_____

_____

3. Give some examples of the use of propaganda. _____

_____

_____

_____

4. Do you think you are always aware of propaganda when it is being used? Explain.

_____

_____

_____

Now read the following information, comparing your definition and examples of propaganda with those provided here.

Propaganda is a deliberate attempt on the part of a group or an individual to sway our opinions in their favour. Contrary to what many people think, propaganda is not merely a tool used by dictatorial governments. We are exposed to various propaganda techniques nearly every day of our lives. Politicians use propaganda, along with other devices, to ge0t us to accept their opinions and vote for them. Newspapers and magazines use propaganda techniques to influence our opinions on political and social issues. Religious leaders use propaganda to influence our opinions on morality. Advertisers, through television, radio, newspapers, and magazines, use propaganda techniques to get us to buy things we often don't need or to change the brand of soap we use.

Propaganda techniques usually appeal to our emotions or our desires rather than to our reason. They cause us to believe or do things we might not believe or do if we thought and reasoned more carefully. When we are too lazy to think for ourselves, we become potential victims of propaganda. Propagandists are usually not concerned with good or bad, right or wrong. They are more concerned with getting us to believe what they want us to believe. The techniques they use can range from outright lies to subtle truths.

The power of propaganda cannot be overestimated. While some propaganda may be socially beneficial, it can also be harmful. Through propaganda techniques, our opinions can be changed to be "for" or "against" certain nations, political rulers, races, moral values, and religions. What we must guard against is having our opinions formed for us by others. We must not let ourselves be used or fooled, even for good causes.

Those who investigate the way propagandists work have identified seven basic techniques that are used frequently:

1. *Name calling:* using names that appeal to our hatred or fears; if the propagandists know a group fears communism, they might call an opponent a "commie" or a "red" to get the group to distrust the opponent.

2. *Glittering generalities:* using words that appeal to our emotions such as *justice, freedom fighters, love,* or *loyalty* are vague but have positive connotations that appeal to us; they are often used because propagandists know we are touched by such words.

3. *Transfer:* linking something we like or respect to some person, cause, or product; if we respect the flag or the Christian cross, our respect for the symbol is transferred to whatever use it is being associated with.

4. *Testimonial:* using well-known people to testify that a certain person, idea, or product is "the best"; if we admire Robert Redford and we see him in advertising for a particular product or politician, we then buy the product or vote for the person because of our respect for Redford, even though he may not be an authority on the subject.

5. *Plain folks:* a device used by politicians, labour leaders, businesspeople, clergy, educators, and advertisers to win our confidence by appearing to be just plain folks like ourselves.

6. *Card-stacking:* stacking the evidence against the truth by lying, omitting, or evading facts, underplaying or overemphasizing issues, telling half-truths, or stating things out of context; advertisers might say their product "helps stop bad breath," leading us to think it *does* stop it.

7. *The bandwagon:* appealing to our desire to be on the winning side, to be like or better than everyone else and follow the crowd or be one of the gang and "in on the latest fad."

Most of these devices work because they appeal to our emotions, our fears, our ignorance, or our desire to do the "right thing." But by sorting facts from opinions, and by recognizing these propaganda techniques when used, we won't become victims, but rather thoughtful readers and thinkers.

PRACTICE C-1: Detecting Propaganda Techniques

Directions: Read each of the following items and in the space provided write in which propaganda technique is being used and why you think so.

1. "My opponent, Ms. Glick, has a record of being soft on crime at a time when we need to be strong." _____

   _____

2. "Mr. Cluck cares what happens to the farmers; he cares for the future of the Canadian tradition of prosperity. He'll put this country back on track!"

   _____

3. "Wayne Gretzky—Knows Aspirin works for arthritis pain!" _____

   _____

4. "M Lotion helps skin keep its moisture . . . discourages tired-looking lines under eyes." _____

_____

5. "Over 8,000,000 sold! Why would anyone want to buy anything else?" _____

_____

_____

6. "Buy Banhead. It contains twice as much pain reliever." _____

_____

_____

7. "Mayor Naste has shown time and again he's for the little guy. You don't see him driving a big limo or wearing fancy suits. No, sir. You'll find him out talking to us folks to see how he can serve us better." _____

_____

_____

8. "Buy the Sportsman's Shaving System, appointed the exclusive skin care system for the Winter Olympics." _____

_____

_____

9. "Yes, I lied. But I did it for my country. As God is my witness, I felt in my heart—and still do—that what I did was right, and the people of this country who want to preserve its freedom will thank me some day." _____

_____

_____

10. "Drive to class reunions with this new Fone-E antenna on your car, and even Mr. Most-Likely-to-Succeed will be envious. Everyone will assume you have a cellular phone—*the* mark of success!" _____

_____

_____

Application I: Recognizing Propaganda at Work

Find an example of one of the seven propaganda techniques used in a current magazine or newspaper advertisement. Write a brief explanation of how the technique is being used, attach it to the ad, and share it in class.

D.   Putting It All Together

The next two practices give you an opportunity to use what you have learned about critical comprehension, to distinguish fact from opinion, read the opinions of others, and detect propaganda. Review your scores on the Student Record Sheet in the Appendix and try to match or do better than your scores for the previous reading selections. If you make mistakes, analyze your errors and figure out how to improve the next time. The first practice follows an introduction to the author Neil Bissoondath; the second practice is timed.

Now, read about the following author, Neil Bissoondath, to understand more about how life affects opinions and about the process of writing. His views may inspire you to develop different views. Another way to find current information, quotations, or pictures of Neil Bissoondath is to use the World Wide Web. Using a search engine such as go2net.com, Google, or AltaVista, type the name under Search.

INTRODUCING NEIL BISSOONDATH

Neil Bissoondath is a Trinidad-born Canadian writer who has won great acclaim for his fiction. His work includes short stories, novels, and essays. Many of his stories deal with social and political upheaval. *The New York Times* has said that his work is filled with issues of "exile, estrangement, and dislocation." He currently lives in Quebec City and had this to say recently about his writing:

I have no problems with inspiration: I get it from my life: newspapers that I read, magazines, the news. I get it from talking with people. . . .

My writing process is an instinctive one. I never decide what I'm going to be writing. A novel or short story will just suddenly sit up and be there-I can't really explain why or how this happens. It just usually happens when I'm not thinking about anything: I'll be washing the dishes or in the shower and suddenly there'll be a character there, and a sense comes that there's something here, and a scene will shape around it.

It's only once I finish [writing] a book that I can step back and look at it as a reader and see the themes. But none of it's planned, it just sort of emerges. I think it's lethal and dangerous for the imagination to write a novel with an agenda.

Bissoondath also teaches creative writing at Laval University in Quebec. "I enjoy teaching," he says. "The class is all about what I do. I enjoy finding students who have talent and help them along."

PRACTICE D-1

Directions: Read the following book excerpt. As you read, look for the main argument, underline facts, and be aware of opinions.

MARGINALIZATION

NEIL BISSOONDATH

1   To be simply Canadian, untinged by the exoticism of elsewhere, seems insufficient, even unacceptable, to many other Canadians. The fact clearly stems, in part, from the simple human attraction to the exotic. But it seems to me that it also has much to do with a wider issue: the uncertainty we feel as a people.

From *Selling Illusions: The Cult of Multiculturalism in Canada* by Neil Bissoondath. Copyright © 1984 by Neil Bissoondath. Reprinted by permission of Penguin Books Canada Ltd.

2   We reveal this uncertainty in a variety of ways, including our newly minted concern for traditions, but particularly through that quintessential (and possibly eternal) Canadian question: Who are we? The usual answer—"Well, we're not like the Americans . . . "—is insufficient: a self-perception cast in the negative can never satisfy (although it can obsess: in John Robert Colombo's *The Dictionary of Canadian Quotations*, "Canada" requires fewer than nine columns while "Canada & the United States" fills more than seventeen). . . .

3   There are many visions of us, many answers to that question of who we are, some complimentary, some critical. And so, ourselves lacking a full and vigorous response ("A Canadian," the English essayist J.B. Priestley once remarked, "is lost when he asks himself what a Canadian is") we search for distinctiveness—exoticism—wherever we can find it. And we find it most readily in our compatriots most recently arrived.

4   For people I think of as "professional ethnics"—they who enjoy the role of the exotic and who depend on their exoticism for a sense of self—this is not an unpleasant state of affairs. But for those who would rather be accepted for their individuality, who resent being distinguished only by their differences, it can prove a matter of some irritation, even discomfort. The game of exoticism can cut two ways: it can prevent an individual from being ordinary, and it can prevent that same individual from being accepted.

5   Trudi Hanley, a twenty-one-year-old black woman who works in a field—modelling—where exoticism can reasonably be expected to be an advantage, once spoke to a reporter of the excuses used by those reluctant to hire her: "My nose was too big. I was too black. I was too different. We have enough ethnics. I heard them all."

6   But the finest example of this exclusion remains the sprinter Ben Johnson. Within a shattering twenty-four-hour period in Seoul, Korea, Mr. Johnson was transformed in media reports from being the Canadian who had won Olympic gold through effort to the Jamaican immigrant who had lost it through use of drugs. The only thing swifter than Mr. Johnson's drug-enhanced achievement was his public demotion from "one of us" to "one of them." The exotic multicultural concept of the everlasting immigrant has come to function as an institutional system for the marginalization of the individual: Ben Johnson was, in other words, a Canadian when convenient, an immigrant when not. Had he, success or failure, been accepted as being simply Canadian and not "Jamaican-Canadian," it would have been difficult for anyone to distance him in this way.

7   Thus the weight of the multicultural hyphen, the pressure of the link to exoticism, can become onerous—and instead of its being an anchoring definition, it can easily become a handy form of estrangement. Dr. John Polanyi, born elsewhere, is the *Canadian* Nobel-prize-winning chemist. Michael Ondaatje, born elsewhere, is the *Canadian* Booker-prize-winning novelist. Valery Fabrikant, born elsewhere, is the *Russian émigré* murderer.

8   This hyphen, even when it is there in spirit only, is a curious beast. It appears to mean so much and is yet so often indicative of so little.

9   Ali Sharrif, a Somali immigrant who freelances for *NOW* magazine in Toronto, began wondering why the city's black community had failed to come to the aid of Somalis in conflict with long-time residents of six apartment buildings in Toronto. He telephoned a man identified only as a "well-known Toronto black activist" and was told, "You see, it's hard to place the Somalis. They really are not black in the true sense of the word." He explained that the black community in North America saw Somalis and other people from the Horn of Africa as Muslims and Arabs first, Africans second. Somalis, who to those without the distinguishing eye bear a strong resemblance to Ethiopians, are Muslims but not Arabs, Africans but not black, and in Metro Toronto

they find acceptance and support difficult to obtain. Sharrif ends his article on a note that is part plaintive, part angry: "Most of the Somalis I know, casual acquaintances and friends, really want to be part of the black community. But their fate might be that they are considered black, but not black enough to be really black."

10   Too much of this, not enough of that: it is a problem. There are people of African descent, born in the Caribbean, immigrants to Canada, who describe them-selves as African-Canadians, a phrase now deemed more acceptable than "coloured" or even "black." Yet I cannot help wondering how, say, former South African president F.W. de Klerk would be described should events force him to flee his country for a Canadian haven: would he too be an African-Canadian? And what about, say, Muammar al-Qaddafi? Libya too is in Africa. I am uncertain, then, as to the precise meaning of phrases such as African-Canadian or Italian-Canadian or Greek-Canadian, particularly when applied to people whose experience of these foreign lands is most likely historical, touristic or anecdotal: what conclusions are to be drawn from them? Their principal effect, I would suggest, is not to define the word "Canadian" but to mark a distance from it, the hyphen that links them a sign of an acceptable marginal-ization.

11   If the questions of degree of race and ethnicity, and of that troublesome hyphen, unsettle me, it is because they strike close to home—as they strike close to home for the growing number of Canadians whose personal relationships entail a commingling of ethnicities. It is a realm that must be entered with care, for the very language we use is a minefield of offence.

12   One of my favourite *New Yorker* fillers—those little nuggets of linguistic curios with which the magazine rounds out its articles—concerned a U.S. newspaper that reported on the restructuring program instituted by a faltering company. Not only would the plan save jobs in the long run, the newspaper reported, but it was expected eventually to put the company's books back in the African-American.

13   Back in the *what*?

14   The newspaper subsequently ran a correction explaining that it had meant to say that the company's finances would be back in the—uhh—black. It blamed overzealousness on the part of a copy-editor.

15   The trend to more specific ethnic self-identification is a complex one. What is one to make, for instance, of Sir Peter Ustinov, he of the Russian surname, the British manner (Jacques Parizeau with a sense of humour and no chip on the shoulder) and a family history that ties together influences from Russia, Italy, France, Germany, Switzerland and, by virtue of a great-great-grandmother, Ethiopia (which may qualify him as a person of colour)?

16   A similar deconstruction would make of me an Indian-West-Indian (or, more accurately, an Indian-Trinidadian-West-Indian) by birth and an Indian-Trinidadian-West-Indian-Canadian by choice. My companion's ethnicity is less complex. She would be a Franco-Québécoise-Canadian (barring possible confirmation of a family legend that tells of an infusion of native blood somewhere in the distant past).

17   But what then of our daughter?

18   With her mixture of heritages, should she one day be asked to define her ethnic-ity, she would be obliged to take a deep breath before replying that she is "a Franco-Québécoise-First Nations-Indian-Trinidadian-West-Indian-Canadian." Or something of the sort. (I am assuming here that the actual order of the ethnicities is not subject to political considerations, but I may be wrong.) I do shudder, though, for the children she may one day have should she choose to have a family with someone of different but equally complex composition.

19   There is an interest here, it seems to me, in a certain simplicity, a simplicity that my daughter might find in moving away from an ethnic concept of self-definition

(without abandoning the knowledge of it) towards a self-definition based on her homeland. But, as I found out after the publication of an article I wrote on the subject, even the word "homeland" is problematic.

20   I had written in the article of the many young men, born and bred in Canada of parents from Croatia, who had returned to that unhappy land to take up arms in its defence. I was puzzled by their actions, concerned about the implications for Canada, saddened by the thought of young men eager to go off to war. The following week, a Montreal writer and editor named François Hébert penned a reply to my piece in which he defended the right of these young men to go to the aid of, as he put it, their homeland. I had not questioned their right, but what struck me in the reply was the defining of Croatia as the "homeland" of these young men.

21   My understanding of the word would have defined Croatia as the homeland of these young men's parents or grandparents, while their homeland would be Canada, the land of their birth and upbringing. I felt that to view their *ancestral* land as their homeland was to wilfully distance them, to make them marginal to the Canadian context. It was to define the belonging of others through the prism of one's own personal and political needs, in a way not very different from the historical view of that young woman on the phone-in show in Washington.

22   To consider the ancestral land as the true homeland is to risk engaging a dizzying absurdity, for it would mean that my homeland is India, a place I have never visited and have little wish to. It would mean that Lucien Bouchard's would be neither Quebec nor Canada but France; Brian Mulroney's would be Ireland, David Suzuki's Japan, Nino Ricci's Italy and so on. Only aboriginals, then, could claim Canada as their homeland—unless it is true that they happen to have migrated here thousands of years ago from another continent, in which case they're out of luck. And what is one to make of the homelands of people like Pierre-Marc Johnson, Claude Ryan, Jeanne Blackburn and others complicated by history?

23   And what of my daughter's homeland? Does she have two, India and France? How much time must go by, then, how many cultural changes are required, before one's homeland is no longer that of one's ancestors? Is there a moment when one stops being, in the eyes of others, an alien, an exile, an immigrant?

24   It seems to me vital that, as unfashionable or as outdated as it may seem to some in their rush both to claim and to impose narrow ethnicity and tribal exoticism, that my daughter should grow up to think of her homeland as simply Canada and of herself as simply Canadian. In this way, there will be no other "homeland" to which others can wilfully consign—and therefore distance—her, alienating her from the mainstream and thereby withholding her rightful place in the land of her birth.

25   There is also a strong element of marginalization in the Sikh-turban issue. The controversy of turbans in Legion halls and in the RCMP is in itself an indication of the failure of multiculturalism programs to go beyond superficiality in explaining us to each other. To view the turban as just another kind of hat, with no significance beyond sheltering the head, is to say that a cross worn on a chain is of no significance beyond a decoration for the neck: it is to reveal a deep ignorance of the ways and beliefs of others. To ban either in any context is to revel in that ignorance and to alienate the wearer by rejecting an intimate and fundamental part of his or her self.

26   The marginalization to which we so easily subject one another comes frequently in times of economic hardship. The stresses of unemployment—the difficulty of the present and the unimaginable idea of a future—create a need for scapegoats: we need something or someone to blame. We can rail against politicians, taxes, corporations—but these are all distant, untouchable.

27   No one is more easily blamed for the lack of opportunity than the obvious "foreigner" cleaning tables in the local doughnut shop or serving behind the counter at

McDonald's. Maybe he has brown skin, maybe he speaks with an accent: clearly he is out of place here, filling a paid position that should by rights have gone to a "real" Canadian. All differences, always so close to the surface, are seized upon, turned into objects of ridicule and resentment, the psychology of exoticism once more cutting both ways.

28   Encouraging people to view each other as simply Canadian, discouraging the use of the marginalizing hyphen, would not solve such problems—humans, in times of fear and anger, have a unique ability for seeking our bull's-eyes in each other—but it might help deflect some of the resentment, so that in expressing our pain we do not also alienate our fellow citizens. Differences between people are already obvious enough without their being emphasized through multiculturalism policy and its growing cult of racial and ethnic identity.

Comprehension Check

Directions: Now answer the following questions.

1. State one fact the author mentions about himself in the article. _____

_____

2. What is Bissoondath's main argument about Canada? _____

_____

3. Is the following statement fact or opinion? "The exotic multicultural concept of the everlasting immigrant has come to function as an institutional system for the marginalization of the individual. . . ." _____

_____

4. List one of the facts he gives to support his argument. _____

_____

5. List another fact he uses to support his argument. _____

_____

6. According to Bissoondath, what are some of the problems Canadians face when they insist on hyphenating their nationalities (e.g., Jamaican-Canadian)?

_____

_____

_____

7. What is Bissoondath's overall opinion of Canadians' tendencies to "hyphenate" their cultural identities? _____

_____

_____

8. List one or two of the facts he uses to support this opinion. _____

_____

_____

9. Are Bissoondath's arguments in this article based more on fact or on opinion? Explain. _____

_____

_____

_____

10. Does the author convince you of his argument? Explain. _____

_____

_____

_____

_____

_____

_____

Vocabulary Check

Directions: Define the following underlined words.

1. To be simply Canadian, underlined untinged (paragraph 1)_____

_____

2. of who we are, some complimentary (paragraph 2) _____

_____

3. works in a field—modelling—where exoticism (paragraph 3)_____

_____

4. it can be a handy form of estrangement (paragraph 6) _____

_____

5. sign of an acceptable marginalization. (paragraph 9) _____

_____

6. It blamed overzealousness (paragraph 12) _____

_____

7. legend tells of an infusion of native blood (paragraph 14)_____

_____

8. to view their ancestral land as their homeland (paragraph 18) _____

_____

9. to which others wilfully consign (paragraph 21) _____

_____

10. create a need for scapegoats (paragraph 23) _____

_____

Record your comprehension and vocabulary scores on the Student Record Chart in the Appendix.

PRACTICE D-2: Timed Reading

Directions: Before reading the following 980-word selection, survey the article and the questions in about one minute. Then time yourself as you begin reading the article. As you read, notice the author's opinion on education and grades.

Begin timing:_____

IN PRAISE OF THE F WORD

MARY SHERRY

1   Tens of thousands of 18-year-olds will graduate this year and be handed meaningless diplomas. These diplomas won't look any different from those awarded their luckier classmates. Their validity will be questioned only when their employers discover that these graduates are semiliterate.

2   Eventually a fortunate few will find their way into educational-repair shops—adult-literacy programs, such as the one where I teach basic grammar and writing. There, high-school graduates and high-school dropouts pursuing graduate-equivalency certificates will learn the skills they should have learned in school. They will also discover they have been cheated by our educational system.

3   As I teach, I learn a lot about our schools. Early in each session I ask my students to write about an unpleasant experience they had in school. No writers' block here! "I wish someone had made me stop doing drugs and made me study." "I liked to party and no one seemed to care." "I was a good kid and didn't cause any trouble, so they just passed me along even though I didn't read well and couldn't write." And so on.

4   I am your basic do-gooder, and prior to teaching this class I blamed the poor academic skills our kids have today on drugs, divorce, and other impediments to concentration necessary for doing well in school. But, as I rediscover each time I walk into the classroom, before a teacher can expect students to concentrate, he has to get their attention, no matter what distractions may be at hand. There are many ways to do this, and they have much to do with teaching style. However, if style alone won't do it, there is another way to show who holds the winning hand in the classroom. That is to reveal the trump card of failure.

5   I will never forget a teacher who played that card to get the attention of one of my children. Our youngest, a world-class charmer, did little to develop his intellectual talents but always got by. Until Mrs. Stifter.

6   Our son was a high-school senior when he had her for English. "He sits in the back of the room talking to his friends," she told me. "Why don't you move him to the front row?" I urged, believing the embarrassment would get him to settle down. Mrs. Stifter looked at me steely-eyed over her glasses. "I don't move seniors," she said. "I flunk them." I was flustered. Our son's academic life flashed before my eyes. No teacher had ever threatened him with that before. I regained my composure and managed to say that I thought she was right. By the time I got home I was feeling pretty good about this. It was a radical approach for these times, but, well, why not? "She's going to flunk you," I told my son. I did not discuss it any further. Suddenly English became a priority in his life. He finished out the semester with an A.

7   I know one example doesn't make a case, but at night I see a parade of students who are angry and resentful for having been passed along until they could no longer

By Mary Sherry, as published in *Newsweek*.

even pretend to keep up. Of average intelligence or better, they eventually quit school, concluding they were too dumb to finish. "I should have been held back," is a comment I hear frequently. Even sadder are those students who are high-school graduates who say to me after a few weeks of class, "I don't know how I ever got a high-school diploma."

8   Passing students who have not mastered the work cheats them and the employers who expect graduates to have basic skills. We excuse this dishonest behaviour by saying kids can't learn if they come from terrible environments. No one seems to stop to think that—no matter what environments they come from—most kids don't put school first on their list unless they perceive something is at stake. They'd rather be sailing.

9   Many students I see at night could give expert testimony on unemployment, chemical dependency, abusive relationships. In spite of these difficulties, they have decided to make education a priority. They are motivated by the desire for a better job or the need to hang on to the one they've got. They have a healthy fear of failure.

10   People of all ages can rise above their problems, but they need to have a reason to do so. Young people generally don't have the maturity to value education in the same way my adult students value it. But fear of failure, whether economic or academic, can motivate both.

11   Flunking as a regular policy has just as much merit today as it did two generations ago. We must review the threat of flunking and see it as it really is—a positive teaching tool. It is an expression of confidence by both teachers and parents that the students have the ability to learn the material presented to them. However, making it work again would take a dedicated, caring conspiracy between teachers and parents. It would mean facing the tough reality that passing kids who haven't learned the material—while it might save them grief for the short term—dooms them to long-term illiteracy. It would mean that teachers would have to follow through on their threats, and parents would have to stand behind them, knowing their children's best interests are indeed at stake. This means no more doing Scott's assignments for him because he might fail. No more passing Jodi because she's such a nice kid.

12   This is a policy that worked in the past and can work today. A wise teacher, with the support of his parents, gave our son the opportunity to succeed—or fail. It's time to return this choice to all students.

Finish timing. Record time here: _____ and use the Timed Readings Conversion Chart in the Appendix to figure your rate: _____ wpm.

Comprehension Check

Directions: Now answer the following questions.

1. What is the author's thesis or main point? _____

_____

_____

_____

2. What does the author mean by the term *educational-repair shops*? _____

_____

_____

3. T/F The author is a high school English teacher.

4. Before teaching her present classes, what things did she blame for the poor academic skills of students? _____

_____

_____

5. What does she now feel is a major cause of poor academic performance by students? _____

_____

_____

6. What, according to the author, is wrong with passing students on who have not mastered the course work? _____

_____

_____

7. Most of the author's students have what she calls a "healthy fear of failure." What does she mean? _____

_____

_____

_____

8. T/F The author feels that most young people generally don't have the maturity to value education the way adults do.

9. Why does the author believe flunking students as a regular policy has merit?

_____

_____

_____

_____

10. What does she feel it would take to make her policy work? _____

_____

_____

For every question you missed, find the place in the article that contains the correct answer. Try to determine why you missed the questions you did. If you read faster than you normally do, a score of 60 percent correct is considered good. As you get used to faster speeds, you will discover your comprehension scores will improve.

Vocabulary Check

Part A

Directions: Define the following underlined words or phrases as they appear in the article.

1. their <u>validity</u> will be questioned (paragraph 1) _____

_____

2. drugs, divorce, and other <u>impediments</u> to concentration (paragraph 4)

_____

3. don't put school first on their list unless they perceive something is at <u>stake</u> (paragraph 8) _____

_____

4. expert testimony on unemployment, <u>chemical dependency</u>, abusive relationships (paragraph 9) _____

_____

5. a dedicated, caring <u>conspiracy</u> between teachers and parents (paragraph 11)

_____

Part B

Directions: Select from the right-hand column the best definition for each word in the left-hand column. Write the letter of the correct definition by the word.

_____	**6.** radical (paragraph 6)	**a.**	calmness, tranquillity
_____	**7.** priority (paragraph 9)	**b.**	favouring extreme change
_____	**8.** flustered (paragraph 6)	**c.**	confused, befuddled
_____	**9.** steely-eyed (paragraph 6)	**d.**	favouring more important things over less important
_____	**10.** composure (paragraph 6)	**e.**	a hard or severe look

Record your rate (wpm), comprehension, and vocabulary scores for this article on the Student Record Chart in the Appendix. An average score is around 250 wpm with 70 percent comprehension. Discuss any problems, concerns, or questions you have with your instructor.

Questions for Group Discussion

1. As a group, discuss the author's opinion about education and grading.
2. Present an argument for an opposite opinion about education. Have your group come up with several reasons to support your opinion.
3. Decide as a group why you agree or disagree with each opinion.
4. Do you feel you worked as hard as you could when you were in high school? Why or why not?

CHAPTER FIVE

Recognizing Tone, Figurative Language, and Point of View

A.   Recognizing Intent, Attitude, and Tone

In addition to distinguishing fact from opinion, critical reading requires an awareness of an author's *intent, attitude,* and *tone.*

- An author's **intent** is not always easy to recognize. An author's intent may be to satirize a problem or condition, to amuse readers, to make them cry by arousing sympathy, pity, or fear, to argue a point that another writer has made, or to accuse someone of something. But whatever an author's intent may be, you, as a critical reader, need to be absolutely certain that you understand what it is.

- An author's treatment of a subject reflects an **attitude** toward it. The intent may be to satirize a problem, but the author's attitude may be serious. An author's attitude, then, is the author's personal feeling about a subject. Attitudes can range from sad to happy, angry to delighted, sympathetic to unsympathetic, tolerant to furious.

The language an author uses is frequently a clue to that writer's attitude both toward his or her subject and toward the reader. In his book *Preface to Critical Reading,* Richard Altick provides a good example of how paying attention to the language a writer uses can help you see intent and attitude:

> Compare the two ways in which a person could express the desire [intent] to borrow some money: (1) "Hey, good buddy, how about loaning me a ten for a few days? I'm in a bind. You'll get it back on Friday." (2) "I'm very sorry to impose on you, but I'm in a bit of a predicament, and I need ten dollars just until payday. I'd be extremely grateful." The language of the first appeal suggests that slang is the normal means of expression for this speaker. The meaning of the second appeal is identical, and the general approach is the same. But whereas the first speaker is forthright and unembarrassed, the other seems hesitant and apologetic. The personalities of the two seem as different as the connotations of *bind* and *predicament.*

In other words, the intent of both the appeals in the example is the same; both speakers want to borrow money. But the attitudes are different. Critical reading requires the ability to distinguish such differences.

How an author uses language creates what is called a **tone.**

> Tone in writing is similar to what we call a tone of voice. For instance, the phrase "Thanks a lot!" can have different meanings based on the tone of voice used to express it. If we are truly grateful, we will say it one way; if we want to be sarcastic, we'll say it another way; and if we are angry or disgusted, we'll say it still another way.

When reading, however, we can't hear an author's tone of voice. But as critical readers, we must be able to recognize the true tone intended by the author.

The following practices will help you learn to recognize intent, attitude, and tone in various types of writing.

PRACTICE A-1

Directions: Read the following magazine article, looking for fact, opinion, intent, attitude, and tone. Then answer the questions that follow it.

SIMPLIFYING LIFE

FIONA HEATH

1   It seems that many Canadians are discovering the truth of what comedian Lily Tomlin observed years ago: "the trouble with the rat race is that even if you win, you're still a rat." In a 1999 Health Canada survey, researchers found that one in three Canadians experienced a high level of work–family conflict, half the respondents reported high levels of stress on the job, and one quarter complained of feeling "burnt out."

2   While it's difficult to gauge the number of people turning to the voluntary simplicity movement in search of more time and less stress, best-selling books, an ever-growing Web network, and rapidly developing organizations are all signs pointing to an increasing interest in simplicity.

3   Advocates of voluntary simplicity argue that the good life is not to be found in an endless accumulation of wealth and striving for status, but within ourselves and in the quality of our relationships. Duane Elgin, author of the classic 1983 text *Voluntary Simplicity*, calls it "a manner of living that is outwardly more simple and inwardly more rich, a way of being in which our most authentic and alive self is brought into direct and conscious contact with living."[1]

4   "The objective is not dogmatically to live with less," Elgin says, "but it is a more demanding intention of living with balance in order to find a life of greater purpose, fulfillment, and satisfaction."

5   Simple living is not a set of rules, but a loose framework that can lead people to a better understanding of their true needs and a more conscious way of life. Janet Luhrs, author of *The Simple Living Guide*, suggests that to live simply is to live deliberately, to consider the consequences of choices made. What impact does your lifestyle have on you, your family, others, and the planet? Does your daily activity reflect your goals, values, and sense of purpose?[2]

6   Both Elgin and Luhrs emphasize that the actual expression of simple living is a personal matter, dependent on each individual's circumstances. But there are recurring themes: searching for community, wanting more personal time, spending less, and avoiding overconsumption. Rural homesteaders may identify with simple living, following an ethic of self-sufficiency, but so do urban condo dwellers, tired of the fast lane, who support local and fair-trade businesses.

7   People turn to simple living to find ways to work less and have more time for the things that matter to them. They may reduce their work week, become a one-income family, or work part-time. And those who choose to have more control over their time are inevitably led to question their relationship to money. Books such as *Your Money or Your Life* by Vicki Robin and Joe Dominguez help people control their spending habits. Following the advice found in this best-seller, you can reduce your spending by 20 percent and move towards financial independence by learning to live on a small stable income from investments.[3]

From *Alternatives*, Spring 2001, pp. 38–39. Reprinted by permission of the author.

8   Simple living may also be a way to live in a more socially just and ecologically sound manner. By reducing meat consumption and automobile use, buying second-hand goods and patronizing locally owned businesses rather than big box stores controlled by multinationals, people can take a step back from the worst excesses of consumer society. Not all of these choices are cheap or even convenient, but they are firmly grounded in a recognition that we are interdependent with others. By consciously choosing to live with less amidst great material wealth, by choosing fair trade and ecologically sound products, simple living becomes an ethical act.

9   While some people focus on the practical aspects of living a less consumer-oriented life, others view voluntary simplicity as a path of personal transformation. Canadian Mark Burch, author of *Stepping Lightly*, argues that simplicity is a way to develop mindfulness, an awareness of ourselves as belonging to the earth and the "divine being."[4] He sees simplicity as a primarily psychological process in which we reconnect with our authentic identity and orient ourselves to a deeper meaning.

10   In terms of its impact on consumer society, however, simple living has clear limitations. Indeed, the idea of simplicity may be in danger of being co-opted by the mainstream, as suggested by glossy magazines such as *Real Simple*, extolling the delights of walking in the rain wearing a five-hundred-dollar raincoat. Moreover, many people find they can only simplify their lives to a certain point before they are discouraged by serious inconveniences: unsupportive workplaces, limited public transportation, or consumer goods that cannot be repaired, recycled, or re-used.

11   A vigorous complementary movement to address social and political conditions could address these limitations. For the moment, however, the main goal of the nascent simple living movement is to provide a network of support for individuals trying to make the transition to a simpler life. A developing infrastructure of loosely formed local groups and Internet-based communications supports grassroots action that sidesteps traditional organizing.

12   The Centre for a New American Dream, a non-profit organization in the United States with the motto "more fun, less stuff!," illustrates the low-key organizing techniques typical of the movement. True to its own principles, instead of a conventional (and consumptive) mass mail out, the group conducted a successful membership drive by relying on the networking abilities of existing members and Internet connections.

13   Simplicity circles, the brainchild of Cecile Andrews, author of *The Circle of Simplicity*, provide another support mechanism for those tempted by the prospect of a simpler life.[5] Based on the practice of study circles, a model of participatory education developed in Sweden, simplicity circles give small groups an opportunity to discuss ways to live more simply. Circles are facilitated by members rather than by an "expert," encouraging people to take responsibility for their lifestyle.

14   Though it is primarily a white, middle-class movement, simple living does reach people across all ages, income levels, and political perspectives, embracing both fundamentalist Christians and urban hippies. This demonstrates the wide appeal of the movement and gives it a robust diversity that can only strengthen it over time.

15   The simple living movement is still in formation. Within its loose, community-oriented framework, reliance on personal choice and emphasis on the non-material aspects of life lies a vision of a better way of living.

NOTES

[1] Duane Elgin, *Voluntary Simplicity* (New York: William Morrow, 1983).
[2] Janet Luhrs, *The Simple Living Guide* (New York: Broadway Books, 1997).
[3] Joe Dominguez and Vicki Robin, *Your Money or Your Life* (New York: Viking, 1992).
[4] Mark Burch, *Stepping Lightly* (Gabriola Island: New Society Publishers, 2000).
[5] Cecile Andrews, *The Circle of Simplicity* (New York: Harper Collins, 1992).

Directions: Now answer these questions.

1. T/F The opinions in this article are mostly based on fact.

2. Which of the following is the best statement regarding the article's intent?

   a. to define a simple life

   b. to encourage simpler lifestyles in North Americans

   c. to say that many people are leading simpler lives

   d. to objectively report the findings of a simple lifestyle

3. Which of the following best describes the author's attitude towards simple lifestyles?

   a. concerned

   b. open-minded

   c. humorous

   d. serious

   e. none of the above

4. The tone of the article is

   a. objective

   b. apologetic

   c. humorous

   d. formal

5. Based on what is presented in the article, do you believe a simple life is a better way to live for most people? Explain. _____

   _____

   _____

PRACTICE A-2

Directions: Read the following newspaper article, also about consumerism. As you read, consider the author's opinion, attitude, intent, and tone. You will also want to be thinking about how this article on consumerism compares and contrasts with the previous article.

STRUGGLING FOR SIMPLICITY

AIDEN S. ENNIS

1   So I've been thinking about simple living. A primary motive is clarity. I like to drink beer in a glass because I can see what I'm drinking. In the same way, I have this urge to pile all of my stuff in the middle of a room and look at it—the same way I did when I moved to Winnipeg as a university student 13 years ago.

2   But now if I wanted to pile all of my stuff into a room, I'd need a room the size of two two-car garages. If I stop to think about it, this makes me sick—in a dull malaise kind of way. I'm becoming that middle-class consumer I despised in my uni-

versity years. (I'm sure I wasn't the only one who read portions of Walden and said, "All I'll ever need in life is what I can pack into my car.")

3   Baby steps. I don't need to reach my simplicity goal overnight, I can chip away at it by taking teeny tiny baby steps. So, instead of just talking, talking, talking, I persuaded my partner (in two minutes) that we should take both our vehicles off the road for the duration of the year 2000. We made this decision while in our VW van, driving through Los Angeles last summer. We can slow down our pace of life, offer less pollution to the environment, and save some money at the same time.

4   To make it through 52 weeks in Winnipeg without a car, I needed to make a few other structural changes. I decided to quit my weekly, 10-kilometre pilgrimage (a 20-minute drive) to our suburban church. Now I'm walking eight minutes to one in the neighbourhood. I'm on no committees (which lifts a load of obligation off my idealistic shoulders), and I only go when my soul says so (I hope I still get to heaven).

5   And I changed dentists, from one across town that made me feel bad for waiting so long to replace the temporary filling that fell out, to one I see who is not far from my house and asks no questions.

6   Our room, which has a hardwood floor, is two flights of stairs above the main entry, where the vacuum cleaner sits under the coats. That means dust balls get pretty big and swirly under my bed. Fortunately, I'm mildly allergic to dust, so I have to vacuum at least once every month or two, before the balls either get lodged in my nostril one night, or I trip over them one morning.

7   So, in an attempt to simplify my life, I had to add another thing: For the sake of convenience, we now have a second vacuum cleaner in the closet in our third-floor bedroom. (I found it in a dumpster and, after replacing the hose, it's fine. Actually, it's cool—a real kitschy steel turquoise Electrolux, which means I still pay attention to quality and colour—two attributes that fit into my simplification program, uh, lifestyle.)

8   Simplification has made other demands. I've recently noticed a chronic pattern in my behaviour—dropping stuff around the house. I come home from work and drop stuff near the door. I find bills, papers and photos and drop them on my desk. When I even think about doing a fix-it job, I drop tools and stuff on my workbench. My outer life consists of a pile of things to do in almost every room. I have no place to hide.

9   So I decided to take action in at least one room: the bedroom. Take everything out that is not related to relaxing. This is going to be my haven. Fortunately, my partner was also interested in giving the room a good cleaning. I removed all the letters, receipts, to-do lists, and stale toothpicks (thanks to the dentist). We cleaned the dressers and the closet, putting "maybe" stuff in a blue plastic bin with a lid. (We took the whole thing to the thrift store four months later, and now we have room for a vacuum cleaner and hose up there.) It's nice to see the sun shine on the floor, and rediscover the colour of our baseboards.

10   Having tasted the serenity of simplicity in one room, I'm tempted to work on the others. But this is going to require some inner housecleaning. The discipline required to defeat chronic consumptive behaviour doesn't come from one or two impulsive cleaning binges-as cathartic as they are.

11   I need to really change from within. But I don't tell anybody this. Hoping for such change is too optimistic for most people around me. There seems to be a default contentedness with clutter and business. So, quietly, and on my own, I practise my breathing: inhale and . . . exhale. I remind myself to focus. Wash dishes, and think about dishes. Turn the background radio off, well, wait, the news is coming soon. This simplification stuff is harder than it seems.

12   I guess one of my biggest temptations is to solve important problems with a new gadget (I think this comes from being exposed to one too many ads). For example, I could co-ordinate all this activity and inactivity with a portable digital daytimer. Life would be simpler, wouldn't it? I could keep all my addresses, to-do lists, and memos in one handy little spot. I could even answer e-mails from the palm of my hand! But it just doesn't feel right. I don't think my road to simplicity and contentment is adorned with more computer-type stuff.

13   Although, if I had a little palm-top computer, I could compile a list of recently bought books, which might possibly keep me from buying a third copy of *Voluntary Simplicity*.

Directions: Now answer these questions.

1. T/F The opinions in this article are mostly based on factual studies and reports.

2. What is the author's opinion about "stuff" at his house? _____

   _____

   _____

3. Which of the following best describes the author's attitude toward stuff?

   a. concerned

   b. open-minded

   c. humorous

   d. sarcastic

4. Give at least one example from this article that shows the author's tone.

   _____

   _____

5. Based on what is presented in the article, do you believe that Canadians are cutting down on consumption and turning toward a simpler life? Explain.

   _____

   _____

   _____

   _____

Questions for Group Discussion

1. Explain some of the differences between these two articles and their approach to consumerism and living a simpler life.

2. Which article did you find more convincing? Why?

3. Do you believe you have become more or less of a consumer in the past year? Why?

B.   Recognizing Figurative Language

Frequently, writers use **figurative language** to express their tone. Figurative language is used in an imaginative way rather than in a literal sense. For instance, when a writer says, "her eyes flashed fire," the intent is not for us to imagine real fire coming from someone's eyes but to realize that the character is angry. Or, when we read that a lawyer "dropped his client like a hot potato," we are given to understand that the lawyer's actions were quick, just as we'd be quick to drop a hot potato.

Figurative language is familiar to everyone. A great deal of our slang and ordinary speech is based on figurative language, as well as a great many works in literature. Without figures of speech our language would be dull and mechanical. It becomes important, therefore, in developing reading comprehension to know the difference between literal and figurative language. It also becomes important to know the difference between literal and figurative language in developing your aesthetic understanding of what you read.

- One form of figurative language is the **metaphor.** A metaphor is a comparison of two things without the use of the words "like" or "as." For instance, when you say someone "clammed up and wouldn't talk," you are comparing the person's closed mouth with the tightness of a closed clam. When you say someone has a "stone face," you are comparing the unchanging expression with the immobility of stone.

    Dead metaphors are metaphors that have been used so frequently that we accept them almost literally. Terms such as "a tenderfoot," "hands" on a watch, the "head" of a cane, a "run" in a stocking, or an engine "knocking" are all dead metaphors, yet they help us convey meaning that is seldom misunderstood. S. I. Hayakawa says that metaphors are probably the most important of all the means by which language develops, changes, grows, and adapts itself to our changing needs.

- A **simile** is another form of figurative language. It, like a metaphor, compares one thing with another but uses the word "like" or "as." Examples of similes are: "out like a light," "sparkles like a lake," "sounds like a machine gun," "cool as spring water," and "phony as a three-dollar bill."

- When metaphors and similes are overused, they turn into **clichés.** Clichés are worn-out figures of speech such as "a blanket of snow covered the hill," or "the silence was broken," or "my old lady." Such terms have been used so often in speech and writing that they lose their real effectiveness and seem stale.

- Still another type of figurative language is **hyperbole.** Hyperbole is a deliberate exaggeration or overstatement used to emphasize a point being made. For instance, if a friend tells you she can't go to the movies because she has "mountains of homework" to do, she is using hyperbole. If someone tells you that the story was "so funny he almost died laughing," he's using hyperbole. If you "love someone to pieces," know someone who "talked your arm off," or couldn't get your work done because "the phone rang ten thousand times," then you have been dealing with hyperbole. Like overused similes and metaphors, hyperbole can become clichéd, too.

Recognizing how authors use figurative language helps us clarify whether or not an author's attitude is serious, playful, sympathetic, outraged, sarcastic, bitter, humorous, and so on. Thus, attitude and tone are closely allied through the use of figures of speech.

PRACTICE B-1: Identifying Literal versus Figurative Language

Directions: The following statements are either literal or figurative. Place an *F* in the blank next to each statement that uses figurative speech. If you want more practice identifying figurative language, see Chapter Eight, Practice A-2.

_____   **1.** Mr. Timpkin went through the ceiling when his son told him that he had wrecked the car.

_____   **2.** Alyce waited eagerly for the show to start.

_____   **3.** Doreen's checks are bouncing all over town.

_____   **4.** The crowd was getting increasingly angry waiting for the musicians to show up.

_____   **5.** That battery is dead as a doornail.

_____   **6.** Prices are being slashed to rock bottom.

_____   **7.** Mom really stuck her neck out for you this time.

_____   **8.** I find myself out on a limb.

_____   **9.** When Jimmy screamed, her hair stood on end.

_____   **10.** The Blue Jays were defeated 18–4 in the last game.

PRACTICE B-2: Recognizing Tone through Figurative Language

Directions: Read the following paragraphs and answer the questions that follow them.

1. My job was really starting to get to me. It seemed a dead end, a treadmill taking me nowhere. If I was to keep from blowing a fuse, I had to somehow shatter my negativity toward my work or go for broke and resign. After what seemed centuries of indecisiveness, one day I plunked myself down at the typewriter, quickly tossed off my resignation, and boldly signed it with great flair. So I wouldn't chicken out at the last minute, I sailed into my boss's office and slapped it down on her desk.

    a. The tone of this passage is best described as

    _____ one of relief   _____ frustration

    _____ fear of losing a job   _____ indecision

    b. The phrase "go for broke" here means _____

    _____

    _____

    c. T/F "My job . . . seemed a dead end, a treadmill" is an example of a metaphor.

2. Eventually I moved to Ottawa and Montreal, where I further discovered that to grow up Native in Canada is to feel the sting of humiliation and the boot of dis-

crimination. But it is also to experience the enviable security of an extended family and to learn to appreciate the richness of the heritage and traditions of a culture most North Americans have never been lucky enough to know. (From Carol Geddes, "Growing Up Native," *Pens of Many Colours*, p. 168.)

a. T/F The author uses two metaphors in the above passage.

b. The tone of the paragraph is best described as

_____ serious	_____ sarcastic
_____ morbid	_____ apathetic

c. T/F The intent of the passage is to convey *only* the hardship caused by racism in Canada toward Natives.

3. My father never saw Paris. Never read Yeats. Never stayed out with the boys drinking too much. Never flew to New York on a whim. Nor turned over in bed and slept in, rather than report to work. Never knew a reckless love. What did he hope for? What did he want? Beyond peace and quiet, which he seldom achieved, I have no idea. So far as I know he never took a risk or was disobedient. At his angriest, I once heard him silence one of his cousins, a cousin bragging about his burgeoning real estate investments, saying, "You know how much land a man needs? Six feet. And one day that's all you'll have. Ha, ha!" (From Mordecai Richler, "My Father's Life," *Pens of Many Colours*, p. 202.)

a. T/F The father's words at the end of the paragraph show he had a dry sense of humour.

b. T/F The author's intent in this passage is to show disrespect toward his father.

c. The tone of this passage can best be described as

_____ ironic	_____ sad
_____ apathetic	_____ serious concern

PRACTICE B-3

Directions: Read the following essay looking for intent, attitude, tone, and figurative language. Then answer the questions that follow.

IF YOU DROP A STONE . . .

HUGH MACLENNAN

1   If you drop a stone into the ocean the impact is as great as if you drop it into a farmer's pond. The difference is that the ocean doesn't seem to care. It swallows the stone and rolls on. But the pond, if the stone is large enough, breaks into waves and ripples that cover its surface and are audible in every cranny along its banks.

2   So it is with life in a metropolis and life in a small town. It takes a colossal event to affect a city. After the bombing of Hamburg in which eighty thousand people were killed, the city was functioning within a few days. Grief did not paralyse it because, to the survivors, most of the casualties were people they had never met. But a single

murder can convulse a small town for the reason that in such a community people care who lives and who dies. They care because they know each other. All knowledge is relative to our capacity to grasp its details, and no matter what the communists and industrial organizers may say, no man can think humanly if he thinks in terms of masses. In the small town, and not in the metropolis, human life is understood in fundamental terms.

3   Because I grew up in a smallish town, this idea struck me with the force of a shock the first time I saw a play in London about London life. I marvelled how any audience could believe in it. Apparently, I thought, Londoners don't know each other and the playwright has taken advantage of their ignorance. A play as superficial as this, I said to myself when I left the theatre, could never succeed in Halifax.

4   My youthful reaction was naïve, but it was not stupid. I did not know then, as I have learned since, that practically no creative ideas have ever originated in a megalopolis. The prelude to creation, as every parent knows, is intimacy. I had come straight to London from an intimate town, and what we knew about each other in that town could have kept a Balzac supplied with material for life. Small-town gossip may be notorious, but by no means all of it is malicious. It has one virtue which its metropolitan imitators, the newspapers, cannot claim. Most of it has personal significance for the people who listen to it.

5   We knew in our town, for example, and we knew in detail, how our wealthiest citizens had made their money. Although we did not know a neurosis from a psychosis, we understood, and made allowances for, the family conditions which caused one man to be aggressive and another subservient, one woman to be charming and another to be a shrew. We had a sixth sense which the more intelligent city-dwellers lack—a sense of time. We knew that a family, like Rome, is not built in a day.

6   We would look at one family and remember hearing about the grandfather, now dead, who used to sit in his galluses on a stool outside the livery stable chewing a straw and occasionally reaching up with the thumb of his left hand to scratch his head. It had been a matter of interested speculation whether he scratched because he was nervous or because he was lousy. The father, still with us, was a middle-aged man doing fairly well in a hardware business. He never scratched his head, but it was noticed that he had a curious habit of stopping suddenly while walking down the street to lift the right leg of his trousers and scratch the back of his calf. As the hardware merchant was certainly not lousy, this gesture was assumed to be hereditary; as such, it cleared the grandfather's reputation from all suspicion of uncleanliness. The merchant's son raised the family one notch higher. He went to college, did well, and now was laying the foundations of a solid career in the administration in Ottawa. Perhaps he might even rise to cabinet rank and make us all proud, for rumour had it that the Prime Minister's eye was on him. Incidentally, he was never seen to scratch himself at all.

7   This kind of small-town knowledge may seem petty, but the sum of it is vast. Through a multitude of intimate details people come to know the best and the worst about each other, and concealment of character is impossible over a lifetime. A ruthless or a cunning man can ride roughshod over his neighbours and cop most of the money in the place. In every small town there are always a few who try this, and at least one who succeeds. They make bad bargains, for they spend the rest of their days knowing exactly what their neighbours think and say about them. In the small town, since everyone knows the sins of everyone else, each man must live as best he can with the knowledge that his faults and weaknesses are part of the lore of the whole community. That is what I mean by saying that in a small town people know life as it really is. That is why Halifax or Peterborough has a better chance of producing a Balzac than London or New York, and why a little place like Bermuda, where the

stakes are really high, could produce a second Shakespeare if some Bermudian had the genius and the nerve to write as Shakespeare did.

8   But for the past two hundred years the small towns have failed in what should be their mission, which is the illumination of life. Only to a very small extent has their unrivalled knowledge of life been used for artistic purposes. They have given the world nearly all its famous writers and artists, but the moment their gifted children are ready to produce they are compelled to leave home and emigrate to the city. "Appearances must be maintained," a small-town friend said to me not long ago; "otherwise life couldn't go on." But to maintain appearances is the one thing no creative artist can ever do. If he tries, his work shows as much liveliness and veracity as the average obituary column. So, for freedom's sake, he moves to the big city and there he tends to stay. That is why for the past two hundred years art has always been associated in people's minds with the life of the metropolis.

9   But the metropolis—London, Paris, New York, Rome—does not nurture art. It merely gives the immigrant artist or writer freedom to paint or write as he pleases. And it exacts a bitter price for this freedom, the loss of the small-town intimacy from which all life-knowledge derives. That is why so many writers over the past two hundred years have done their best work before they were forty. In their early years in the big city, they availed themselves of the freedom it offered to be themselves. They wrote, generally, of the life they had lived in their native regions. But as they grew older they inevitably consumed their vital material, and in middle age they tended to run dry. The metropolis which was now their home failed to provide them with the life-giving material they required.

10   The very freedom the big city grants is based on a kind of indifference to the individual, an indifference that springs from ignorance. The city has no real gossip. In the city a man is a name or a career, a unit in a factory or the occupant of an office desk. There is no universal folk-memory of the grandfather who scratched his head or the son who hoisted his trouser to scratch the back of his leg. The emotional upheavals which shatter families are swallowed up by the city as the ocean swallowed the *Titanic*, and to the onlooking artist they seem almost as meaningless as traffic accidents because he cannot possibly know, much less feel, the forces which caused them.

11   When modern writers attempt to use metropolitan life as the material for tragedy their work is usually cold and dry. This has been especially notable in the English-speaking centres of London and New York. It is true that Dickens was a Londoner; it is equally true that he saw only the surface of things. As for New York, in the whole of American literature not a single great book has been based on its life.

12   How could it be? In New York, who cares who commits suicide? The crowds massed in the street to see if the stranger will jump from the skyscraper window are not interested in the man, because they do not know him. They are interested only in the spectacle. In New York, who cares who cheats whom? Or who survives through endurance? Or who, by a denial of himself, wins spiritual greatness? This does not imply that New York is less noble than a small town. It merely implies that in terms of art it is too large for any individual artist to handle.

13   Far different was the situation in the days when no cities were immense and a few small or medium-sized towns were the life-centres of a whole people. Ancient Athens at the height of her glory had a voting list somewhat smaller than that of modern Halifax. But she had a spirit which Halifax and all modern smallish towns entirely lack—she preferred excitement to caution and greatness to respectability. She invented tragic and comic drama, the art of history, and the democratic method of government. All these stupendous inventions arose out of her own experience. The

characters in her great comedies were living Athenian citizens, and when Socrates was satirized in *The Clouds* by Aristophanes he rose in the theatre so that everyone would know that he was enjoying the play, too. Plato's *Republic* had its origin in a dinner party which assembled after a late-afternoon walk just as casually as Joe Smith gets together his cronies for a poker game by the simple expedient of walking the length of the main street from the barber shop to the Maple Leaf Hotel.

14   It has always been the same—without intimacy, there can be no creation. Republican Rome was a relatively small town. Florence, Genoa, Venice, and Pisa, in the days of their glory, were about a quarter the size of Ottawa. In Shakespeare's London everyone who mattered knew everyone else, and we can be pretty certain that the characters who live in Shakespeare's plays were modelled on people the playwright knew personally or had heard about from the intimate gossip of others who did.

15   But these wonderful small towns had one thing in common besides the intimate knowledge of life which all small towns share. It never occurred to them that their knowledge should be repressed "in order that life might go on." There was no conspiracy of silence when it came to writing books and plays. The citizens were not afraid of gossip. In such communities a man like Mackenzie King could never have become Prime Minister, nor would a generation of public servants have admired his theory that a leader should veil his thoughts in the stuffiest language possible lest the public become sufficiently interested to make an effort to find out what he was talking about.

16   It seems to me, thinking along these lines, that the cultural future of Canada is opposed only by fear of what the neighbours will say. For Canada, by and large, is still a nation of small towns. Toronto, for all its sprawling size, has a small-town psychology. So, when it comes down to it, does Montreal; in this city we still have a great deal of the intimate small-town knowledge of life which New York and London lack. It has made us shrewder than we realize. We know, for example, that our present material prosperity does not mean, in itself, that we are a great country. We know intuitively that we will become great only when we translate our force and knowledge into spiritual and artistic terms. Then, and only then, will it matter to mankind whether Canada has existed or not.

Comprehension Check

Directions: Now answer the following questions.

1.   The best statement of the thesis of this article is:

   a. The ancient Athenians were a spirited and creative people who laid the foundations of what we know as Western culture.

   b. Smalls towns are full of quirky, eccentric characters whose lives become the subject of great art.

   c. Gossip in small towns is notorious, but it is rarely malicious; gossip in large metropolises has no significance for those who listen to it.

   d. Small towns, not large cities, are better settings to understand the basic questions confronting humanity and can provide a better knowledge of life for artistic purposes.

2.   According to the author, what words describe the modern writer's attempt to use life in a big city? _____

3. Which of the following best characterizes life in a small town?

    a. intimate knowledge of others' lives

    b. horrible gossip about others' lives

    c. aggressive neighbours

    d. all of the above

4. Hugh MacLennan's attitude toward life in a big city is

    a. critical

    b. positive

    c. indifferent

    d. sympathetic

5. MacLennan's intent is to

    a. persuade readers to move to small towns from big cities

    b. entertain readers with anecdotes about small town life

    c. discourage people who live in big cities from engaging in damaging gossip

    d. make people realize that life that life in a small town is more conducive to artistic creation than life in a big city

6. Words and phrases in this article about big cities tend to be negative while words and phrases about small towns tend to be positive. List at least one positively charged phrase about life in a small town and one negatively charged phrase about life in a big city. _____

    _____

    _____

7. T/F The ocean "swallows the stone and rolls on" is an example of a metaphor.

8. Explain what the figurative language in question 7 means. _____

    _____

9. Explain the following figurative language: "The emotional upheavals which shatter families are swallowed up by the city as the ocean swallowed the *Titanic* . . . "

    _____

    _____

10. What does MacLennan say about Toronto and Montreal? _____

    _____

    _____

Vocabulary Check

Directions: Develop your own vocabulary test for this practice by selecting ten words you don't know and writing them on vocabulary cards. After you have had a chance to write the definitions, have a classmate test you on them.

Turn in the words to your instructor and record the results of your comprehension and vocabulary checks on the Student Record Chart in the Appendix.

> ### Application I: Finding Figurative Language in Other Materials
>
> In magazines, newspapers, or textbooks, find at least two examples of metaphors or similes and underline them. Write a sentence about how the figurative language shows the author's tone and attitude, and bring this exercise to class.

C.   Comparing Biased Points of View

A writer's attitude toward a subject may not be ours. However, as critical readers, it is important not to let either the author's **bias** or our own interfere with critical comprehension.

> Being biased means being prejudiced about or having a special leaning toward something. For instance, you may be biased about the type of music you listen to. Maybe you have no patience with classical music and prefer hard rock. That is a bias.

Everyone is biased about something, whether it's music, food, religion, politics, or people. Many of our biases are unconsciously learned from parents, friends, people we admire, or teachers. Reading critically can help us examine our own biases for their value.

While we are free to make up our own minds about a subject, we must still examine carefully the arguments and reasons of an author with opinions different from ours. We must recognize those biases of the author and not allow our own biases to interfere with or shut out those of the author. Once we critically examine what we read, we should reflect on its worth before accepting or rejecting it.

Most of us tend to accept readily the ideas of writers who have the same biases we do, and we tend to reject the views of those we have biases against. To do so is to have a closed mind. As critical readers, we must be willing to make critical judgments based on reason rather than emotion.

As you learn to read critically, you need to recognize bias in writing. If you don't, you may become the victim of an author's propaganda. You may miss seeing how an author takes facts and misrepresents them. You may not see that an author is being more subjective (using personal opinions) than objective (using undistorted facts). Or you may be unaware of how one-sided some writing is.

Sometimes recognizing an author's bias is easy; at other times it isn't. Bias is apt to be present in advertisements, newspaper and magazine editorials, and religious and political pamphlets. You generally pay little attention to an author's bias when it matches your own. When you don't agree with an author, the reverse is true. To read critically requires real involvement in the text and in thinking through what is being read. In effect, critical reading *is* thinking.

The following passage appeared in *Consumer Reports,* a publication of Consumers Union, a nonprofit organization. Read it and then answer the questions that follow.

The letter, marked "confidential," was from the R.I. Research Special Human Being Laboratory in New York City and was signed by one Dr. Roger Grimstone. It informed the recipient that, based on the date and hour of her birth, she was an extraordinary individual, "apart from the rest of humanity," a "Beyonder."

"Owing to some cosmic quirk," the letter went on, "your destiny operates independently of any stars. . . . Why have you suffered so much? *Why has true happiness, true love, wealth, a happy home always been out of your reach? Why have the things you've yearned for most been snatched away?*"

Simple. According to the good Dr. Grimestone, it's because the recipient has yet to send him 20 bucks for something entitled "The Guide."

The reader who sent us Dr. Grimstone's solicitation has a different theory, however. He believes that his daughter, the recipient of the letter, has yet to find happiness, companionship, and financial security because she is only four months old. (Copyright © 1987 by Consumers Union of U.S., Inc., Yonkers, NY 10703-1057, a nonprofit organization. Excerpted with permission from the September 1987 issue of *Consumer Reports* for educational purposes only. No commercial use or photocopying permitted. To learn more about Consumers Union log onto *www.ConsumerReports.org*.)

1. What is the intent of the "confidential" letter sent by the R.I. Research Special Human Being Laboratory?_____

   _____

   _____

   _____

2. What is the intent of the article from *Consumer Reports*?_____

   _____

   _____

   _____

3. What attitude toward the recipient is implied by the originators of the letter?

   _____

   _____

   _____

4. What is the attitude of *Consumer Reports* toward the laboratory? _____

   _____

   _____

   _____

5. What is the tone of the letter sent by Dr. Grimstone?_____

   _____

   _____

6. What is the tone of the passage from *Consumer Reports*? _____

   _____

   _____

Your answers to the questions may be worded differently from the following, but see if they don't match up.

- The answer to the first question is to sell "The Guide" for twenty dollars by appealing to the recipient's "uniqueness" and desire for more wealth, happiness, and health, things almost all of us want more of.
- The intent of *Consumer Reports,* the second question, is to expose the "Laboratory" as a fraud.
- The third question can be answered by looking at such phrases as "apart from the rest of humanity," "owing to some cosmic quirk," and "Beyonder."
- The laboratory believes there are enough people (suckers?) who believe in astrology and who are dissatisfied enough with their lives (or curious enough) that they are willing to spend twenty dollars to find "the answer." *Consumer Reports's* attitude is that the whole thing is phony.
- The tone of the letter is tied in with attitude. The letter's tone, based on what quotes are given, seems serious about wanting to help. Even the "doctor's" name is serious sounding—Grimstone (or is it a subtle touch of humour on the sender's part?).
- *Consumer Reports's* tone is humorous. Waiting until the end of the passage to let us know that the "confidential" letter was sent to a four-month-old makes us chuckle. We realize that phrases such as "the good Dr. Grimstone" and "20 bucks" provide a light, playful tone.

Critical reading requires identifying an author's point of view and motives. Nearly all controversial subjects are written from a particular point of view or bias. By their very nature, such controversial subjects cannot be written about with complete objectivity. For instance, if a Catholic priest were to write about abortion, chances are his point of view would reflect opposition by the very nature of his training and religious beliefs. On the other hand, a social worker who has seen many teenage lives destroyed because of unwanted pregnancies might very well speak in favour of abortion. Even though the priest and the social worker have different points of view, their motives are the same—to convince us their particular viewpoint is the correct one. As critical readers—and thinkers—we need to consider as many points of view as possible before making up our own minds on controversial issues. Then we need to examine the reasoning used to support those viewpoints.

Here are a few guidelines to follow so that you don't fall victim to poor reasoning. Watch out for:

1. Statements that oversimplify or distort the issue being discussed.
2. Irrelevant or unsupported evidence.
3. Left-out or suppressed information or evidence.
4. Appeals to the emotions rather than reasonable evidence.
5. Mudslinging, or attacks on people or groups rather than discussing the issue itself.
6. References to or quotations from the Bible or historical figures even though there is no connection to the issue.

These are the most frequent, although not all, of the devices used to sway people to accept a particular point of view. They appear in advertisements, political campaigns, newspaper and magazine columns, editorials, and television commentaries.

Now read the following essay using the six previously listed guidelines that outlined what you should watch for when reading about controversial issues. Then answer the questions that follow the essay.

BETTER DEAD THAN READ? AN OPPOSING VIEW

TIMOTHY FINDLEY

In 1978, a committee in Huron County, Ontario, attempted to ban Margaret Laurence's The Diviners *from school libraries. In a response to an article that supported the committee, Timothy Findley eloquently defended the right of authors to be free of censorship. Findley's words apply equally today, as debates over book censorship in schools continue in many parts of Canada.*

1   The whole of this current movement concerned with the censorship and banning of books, whether in schools or libraries or courts of law, is riddled with false moral indignation and fake concern for the hearts and minds of our children. It stems, in my opinion, from a truly evil manipulation of people's genuine fear and uncertainty about the world we live in. And the society we've created. And the children we've borne. The [censorship supporters] speak often of their children and of hopes for their moral and spiritual character. Well, those are the same concerns of the books these people want to ban and of the men and women who wrote them. Why are we so afraid of our own children that we want to close their hearts and minds to the fund of compassion they would find in these books? *Who Has Seen the Wind?, Lives of Girls and Women, The Diviners, One Day in the Life of Ivan Denisovitch, The Diary of Anne Frank, Huckleberry Finn.* The list goes on and on, and it grows and grows every year....

2   Has nothing been learned? Of course, it has been argued that these books have "only been banned in the high schools. Anyone can read them after that." Wrong. Once banned in schools books will always be read without respect for their true qualities. Even now children riffle the pages of these books wherever they may find them looking for "the dirty bits." This is not the book's fault. Nor the fault of its writer. It is the fault of those who have condemned the book as "obscene" or "pornographic" or "filled with profane language." Literature is being locked away with the truly obscene, as much as to imply that Margaret Laurence is an advocate of "child abuse." And this, of course, is nothing less than intellectual blasphemy.

3   It is an artist's privilege to see what others cannot see. Sometimes this is not a happy privilege. Sometimes what is seen is very hard to bear, and equally difficult to voice. But if it is the artist's privilege to see, it is also his job to tell what he sees. As W.H. Auden did, looking over his shoulder into Europe in 1939 and writing: "Intellectual disgrace stares from every human face, and the seas of pity lie locked and frozen in each eye."

4   These days, he wouldn't even have to look over his shoulder. But I don't want to close on that note, any more than Auden did. His poem, from which those lines are taken, was about the death of a poet, W.B. Yeats. Its last verse makes a far better epigraph for the idea I have tried to express here, which is the idea that a false issue is being raised by people who, for motives of their own, want to prevent certain books from reaching the minds that most require them, minds that can make the future better than the present and infinitely better than the past. What Auden wrote is as fine a definition of the desired effect of an artist's work as anyone will ever give. And, like it or not Huron County, it applies to Margaret Laurence's *The Diviners:*

In the deserts of the heart,
Let the healing fountain start,
In the prison of his days
Teach the free man how to
praise.

Directions: Now answer the following questions.

1. What is the author's point of view toward censorship? _____

   _____

2. What is his intent in writing this essay? _____

   _____

3. T/F The article is mostly based on fact.

   a. True because _____

   b. False because _____

4. T/F The author's assertion that the current movement concerned with banning books in high schools "stems . . . from a truly evil manipulation of people's genuine fear and uncertainty about the world we live in" is an example of mudslinging rather than dealing rationally with the issue.

   a. True because _____

   b. False because _____

5. Circle any of the following that you feel the author does:

   a. makes irrelevant or unsupported statements

   b. appeals to the emotions rather than reason

   c. refers to the Bible for authority.

   d. oversimplifies the problem and the solution

6. For each of the items you circled in question 5, find a passage in the essay that serves as an example. _____

   _____

   _____

It's not too difficult to answer the first question. The first sentence of paragraph 1 is a strongly worded denunciation of those who seek to ban certain books from the high school curriculum. As we read through the essay, we notice that his emotion intensifies, and his intent is to stop the censorship of books in schools everywhere.

Although the author may stand in defence of principles that many of us share, his argument is based solely on emotion. He uses no facts to substantiate any of his points; thus, regardless of whether or not we agree with his point of view, we can argue that his lack of factual statements to support his claims weakens his argument. Emotional appeals for change may be effective, but we cannot allow ourselves to be swayed by our emotions all the time. Factual support for an argument is always something that we should include in our own writing, and it is always something that we should look for when reading. The answer for question 2 is False, and the answer to question 5 is b.

It's important to note that Findley may be right or wrong. What we as critical readers must do is recognize his point of view or bias, then see what facts he provides to support his thesis. If his facts or supporting arguments are valid, then we should consider his point of view before making up our minds, especially if we disagree with him. If we already agree with him, but have no more facts or reasons to support our point of view than he has, then we need to evaluate critically our own reasons for having the views we do. One of the primary reasons for reading a wide range of viewpoints is to acquire, broaden, and strengthen intelligent views of our own.

Too often we tend to accept the views of others we trust or admire without examining the logic or reasoning behind them. Many people follow the teachings of others, no matter how extreme, not because they have examined these ideas but because others have told them that they are right. Many people have been elected to office not because they are the best qualified but because they make a good impression in public. Many countries have gone to war not because it was the right thing to do but because people were led to believe it was the only solution to a problem.

The next set of practices will help you develop your critical reading skills in these areas.

PRACTICE C-1: Comparing Two Authors

Directions: Skim back over "Simplifying Life" on page 206 and "Struggling for Simplicity" on page 208. You may want to look over the answers to the questions that follow the two essays. Then answer the following questions.

1. Do you think the two authors would agree on the subject of consumerism? Explain. _____

    _____

    _____

2. Which essay has more facts to support its thesis? Explain. _____

    _____

    _____

    _____

3. Which author do you agree with? _____

    Why?_____

    _____

    _____

4. Which essay is more convincing? Explain. _____

    _____

    _____

    _____

    _____

5. What is your bias based on?_____

_____

_____

_____

_____

Practice C-2:   The Question about Marijuana

Directions: Read the following essay (actually a letter to the editor). Look for the author's stand on marijuana and the supporting points, intent, attitude, and bias.

BOGART THAT JOINT

1   Before your 17-year-old waves yesterday's *Globe and Mail* in your face and says, "See, man: marijuana doesn't make you stupid," prepare yourself by reviewing the evidence. Yesterday's report, of a study by Peter Fried, a psychology professor at Carleton University in Ottawa, actually found considerable harm done to intelligence levels among heavy marijuana users. The key is that the harm exists only during the period that they are using marijuana regularly, and not over the long term. Provided they stop.

2   By smoking five or more joints a week, users are lopping four points off their IQ—which is roughly the effect felt by children whose mothers smoked crack cocaine when they were pregnant, or consumed three alcoholic drinks a day.

3   As long as they habitually smoke weed, they have every bit as good a jump on life as a former crack baby, or someone growing up with fetal alcohol syndrome. Like the rest of this luckless fraternity, they're now at much higher risk of dropping out of school or being fired from their job. And they may discover the brutal joys of addiction—scientists now believe that today's highly potent marijuana (roughly five times as strong as that sold on the street 30 years ago) can be psychologically and physically habit-forming.

4   Why did any of the heavy users in Dr. Fried's study quit? They told him that their short-term memory and attention span were suffering. Whether that effect lasts, Dr. Fried doesn't know. As he stressed in his report, he didn't measure these other crucial elements of cognition.

5   Noteworthy, too, is that Dr. Fried's sample of heavy users was small, only nine people. Keep in mind that lab tests on rats have found lasting brain damage in about five per cent of those heavily dosed with marijuana. Regular teenage users, whose numbers have been growing sharply in the past few years, should know that they are dumbing themselves down, in more ways than one.

From *The Globe and Mail*, April 3, 2002. Reprinted by permission of *The Globe and Mail*.

Directions: Now answer the following questions.

1. T/F The opinions in this article are mostly based on fact.

2. Which of the following is the best statement regarding the article's intent?

a. to question validity of reports claiming that marijuana usage is harmless

b. to report the facts about the effects of long-term marijuana usage on people's IQs and short-term memory

    c. to question psychological data

    d. to report facts about marijuana

3. Which of the following best describes the author's attitude toward heavy users of marijuana?

    a. concerned   **c.** determined

    b. open-minded   **d.** sarcastic

4. The tone of the article is

    a. objective   **c.** humorous

    b. apologetic   **d.** bitter

5. Based on what is presented in the article, do you believe that smoking marijuana is harmless? Explain. _____

_____

_____

PRACTICE C-3

Directions: The following essay is a response to the essay you read in Practice C-2. Look for the author's stand on marijuana and the supporting points, intent, attitude, and bias.

WHY DECRIMINALIZATION IS THE WISEST COURSE

1   Walk into any large Canadian high school, on any afternoon, and chances are a small percentage of the students will be high from puffing on marijuana during their lunch break. If the use is constant, long-term consequences can be severe, measured in health risks and short-term memory loss that can devastate the learning process.

2   Worse, soft-drug use among Canadian teenagers appears to be on the rise, as is drinking. A recent study by Ontario's Addiction Research Foundation found that in 1999, 29 per cent of students from Grades 7 to 13 in the province admitted smoking cannabis at some time in their lives, compared with 13 per cent in 1993.

3   Those are the kinds of statistics the 30,000-member Canadian Police Association had in mind when it voiced opposition 10 days ago to any loosening of the country's drug laws, a proposal rekindled by the creation of an all-party House of Commons committee to examine the issue. Legalizing or decriminalizing marijuana—two very different approaches—would send out entirely the wrong message to young people, the CPA believes. Nor is the union persuaded that decriminalizing marijuana use would significantly reduce law-enforcement costs.

4   Both arguments hold some water. Relegating small-scale marijuana possession to the level of a parking ticket would, rightly, be interpreted as an acknowledgment that it is a relatively trivial offence. As well, budgetary savings for police would be small since, for most, chasing marijuana-smokers has long ceased to be a priority. Under the federal *Controlled Drugs and Substances Act*, fingerprinting is not mandatory for users found with less than 30 grams. In plenty of jurisdictions, police often ignore the laws against simple possession. When charges are laid, courts routinely dismiss them with a warning.

From *The Globe and Mail*, June 4, 2001. Reprinted by permission of *The Globe and Mail*.

5   At the same time, thousands of Canadians are still convicted each year of possessing cannabis, and saddled with a criminal record that may be far more injurious than any cannabis they have ingested. That's one reason such influential figures as Toronto Police Chief Julian Fantino (rarely accused of pandering to criminals) favour more lenient cannabis laws. The RCMP, too, is open to the idea, provided the move is in concert with educational and preventive programs. The Canadian Medical Association takes a similar stance.

6   That view is rooted in the recognition that cannabis, smoked by an estimated 1.5 million Canadians, is an unwanted but unalterable fact of modern life. We are awash in marijuana, we export countless tonnes of it to the United States each year, and the laws against simple possession don't work.

7   But would decriminalization not encourage wider abuse? It might. That is why looser laws have to be accompanied by intelligent, credible drug-education programs emphasizing that while cannabis will not kill you, it may make you seriously stupid. Most teenagers yearn to be cool and to be in charge of their lives. A reminder of why drugs are also known as "dope" is the most cogent argument against using them.

8   But is not cannabis the gateway to other, far more dangerous substances? That too holds a grain of truth. Virtually all users of heroin or cocaine begin by smoking a marijuana joint, or a pipeful of hashish.

9   But that doesn't mean most joint-smokers are necessarily vulnerable to the allure of hard drugs. Data from the Netherlands, where drugs of all kinds have long been available, show that while cannabis use among young people is roughly the same as in other European countries, heroin use is extremely rare. Why? Dutch drug experts believe that in a country where "harm reduction" is the mantra, most teenagers understand clearly that not all drugs are the same, and that lumping them all together is a major mistake.

10   For Canada, as for the Dutch, outright legalization of marijuana is not currently an option. Hostility from south of the border would be acute. Decriminalization, on the other hand, is feasible. The grey legal terrain that would open up would not be especially satisfactory. But it would be better than the status quo.

Directions: Now answer the following questions.

1. T/F The opinions in this article are mostly based on factual studies and reports.

2. What is the author's opinion about legalizing marijuana? _____

_____

_____

3. Which of the following best describes the author's attitude toward decriminalizing marijuana?

   a. concerned

   b. open-minded

   c. determined

   d. sarcastic

4. Give at least one example of the author's attitude toward decriminalizing marijuana. _____

_____

_____

5. Based on what is presented in this article, do you believe that decriminalizing marijuana usage is a viable option?

_____

_____

Questions for Group Discussion

1. Discuss some of the implications for decriminalizing marijuana.

2. As a group, come up with solutions that might appease both sides of the marijuana debate—those that think it should be legal, and those that think it should remain illegal.

3. Which article do you agree with more? Discuss why you agree with that article with the members of your group.

D. Putting It All Together

The next two reading selections provide practice in what you have learned in this chapter and previous ones. First, read about the following author, George Elliott Clarke, and how his life has helped shape his writing. Another way to find current information, quotations, or pictures of this author is to use the World Wide Web. Using a search engine such as go2net.com or Google, type the author's name under Search.

INTRODUCING GEORGE ELLIOTT CLARKE

George Elliott Clarke was born in Windsor, Nova Scotia, in 1960 and is a poet, anthologist, essayist, playwright, and professor. His books of poetry include _Whylah Falls_ (1990), which won the Archibald Lampman Award, _Beatrice Chancy_ (1999), and _Execution Poems_ (2002). Much of his work deals with Black history in the Maritimes. George Elliott Clarke is himself a seventh-generation African-Canadian. In an interview, Clarke has described the importance that the stories in his own family have had on his work:

> . . . I was literally sitting in people's living rooms, writing down what they had to say—stories, jokes, sayings, proverbs—and trying to weave it into longer poems or keeping it as a short snippet in longer pieces of prose. . . . If I can sum this up, _Whylah Falls_ was for me a kind of falling into consciousness, not merely racial consciousness, which was always there, but a poetic consciousness, an understanding finally that while there was a great world of Anglo-American poetry out there, there was this Black Nova Scotian, "Africadian" poetry that was rooted in the voice and in these shared jokes, stories, proverbs. If I really wanted to be a strong poet, I felt that's the material I had to work with.

In addition to writing about Black experiences in Canada, George Elliott Clarke creates awareness about Black history. In the following essay, "Honouring African-Canadian Geography: Mapping the Black Presence in Atlantic Canada," Clarke shows us how traditional notions of Canadian history as being settled by "white, pristine" people is incorrect.

PRACTICE D-1

Directions: Read the following essay by George Elliott Clarke. Look for his thesis, supporting points, intent, attitude, and tone.

HONOURING AFRICAN-CANADIAN GEOGRAPHY: MAPPING THE BLACK PRESENCE IN ATLANTIC CANADA

GEORGE ELLIOTT CLARKE

1   African-Canadian geography! Hardly are those words out when, to paraphrase Yeats, a lost image out of *The Geography of Canada* anoints my sight: somewhere in frost-accursed Nova Scotian fields, a white clapboard church in the shape of a man, its eyes black and faithful as the river, kneels in deep prayer, while all about it, African Baptists, in black robes, wheel, shout and testify.

2   The image confronts the consensual understanding of Canada as a white, pristine land settled by pristine whites, with only a few, docile First Nations peoples providing incidences of local colour. Official multiculturalism has not dislodged this popular conception of Canada, one to which even that minstrel of liberal (in)tolerance, Mr. Neil Bissoondath, subscribes.

3   Yet, even in the period of the European invasion of the space now named Canada, non-indigenous people of colour were present. A Black Portuguese, Matthieu de Costa, translated the Mi'kmaq tongue into the French of Samuel de Champlain, thus enabling him to inaugurate the New World French Empire at Port Royal (Annapolis Royal, Nova Scotia). Later, the French imported Africans from the continent, from the Caribbean and even from New England to serve them in the capital of New France, Quebec, in Montreal and even at Louisbourg, the great, threatening fortress that flaunted French power over Cape Breton and the North Atlantic. But we do not remember that Marie-Joseph Angelique, a slave, started a fire that incinerated much of Montreal in 1734. (Where is her rue in the city?) Nor have we constructed any memorial to the slaves who toiled and died in Louisbourg. Yet, both Montreal and Cape Breton were (as they still are) Black spaces. (Indeed, early in our current century, African Americans and West Indians, especially Bajans, "returned," so to speak, to Cape Breton to mine its coal and to work at the steel mills. They also organized a Garveyite church—and at least one cricket club. Cape Breton's not just Rita McNeil country!)

4   Within a year of founding Halifax, whose mile-deep, ice-free harbour made it a strategic counterweight to Louisbourg, the British settlers imported slaves from Boston and sold them on the nascent city's waterfront, thus colouring Halifax as a chocolate-ripple city from its inception. For all its history since 1749, Halifax has been a secret "Black Atlantic" site, attracting Black merchant and naval sailors, sol-

diers, refugees, exiles and adventurers from around the Diaspora. (My paternal grandfather, whose name may have been Morris Clarke and who came to Halifax in the mid-1930s from either Barbados or Jamaica, worked aboard one of the Canadian National Railways-owned "Lady" ships that plied the waters between Halifax and the West Indies.) The city's status as yet another piece of Black Canadian "real estate" prospered when, in 1783, some 3,000 African Americans arrived, numbering some 10% of all the Loyalists who came to British North America after the American Revolutionary War. Having answered the British call to resist the rebellious Yankees, in exchange for land and liberty, the African-American exiles soon found themselves consigned to atrocious properties and reduced, in consequence, to a species of servitude in what they—and others—soon began to dub "Nova Scarcity." Conditions were so bad that, in Shelburne, some Black Loyalists lived in caves. By 1792, then, more than a thousand of the Black Loyalists were more than ready to vacate Nova Scotia for Sierra Leone, in West Africa, which they did. But those who stayed in Nova Scotia constructed all-Black, rural communities in places like Weymouth Falls, near Acadie, and in Tracadie, on the road to Cape Breton.

5   Black Loyalists also dropped anchor in New Brunswick (where folklore reports that slaves were chained to walls) and even Prince Edward Island. (Here, in 1789, Thomas Williams was murdered by his white boss at a site which has been tagged, ever since, "Nigger Point".) Some Loyalists also went to Quebec, where they joined the historical Black population in the recently conquered colony.

6   The cessation of the Maroon insurgency in Jamaica saw 600 of these take-no-prisoner guerrillas dispatched, by the British, to Halifax in January 1796, where they helped to build the fortifications of the Citadel, the star-shaped fortress which rendered the city "the Warden of the North." (Leon Trotsky was briefly imprisoned in the Citadel in 1917). In 1800, the Maroons, detesting the hostile whites and the hostile climate, demanded to be removed from Nova Scotia. They were then sent to Sierra Leone, where they arrived, ironically, just in time to help the colonial authorities quell the first rebellion, on African soil, against European domination. Nevertheless, they left some progeny in Nova Scotia, partly as a result of Governor John Wentworth's adultery with a Maroon woman. (Members of North Preston's Colley clan trace their lineage from the Wentworth connection.)

7   The War of 1812 contributed even further to the creation of a "Black Maritimes." Some 2,000 African-American slaves, liberated by British forces in land engagements against the Americans, were transported to Nova Scotia and New Brunswick between 1813 and 1815. My maternal ancestors, African Americans from the Chesapeake Bay region, arrived in Nova Scotia in this way in 1813. First landed in Liverpool, their children later migrated to Three Mile Plains (70 km NW of Halifax), where my mother was born in 1939 and where I followed in 1960. Three Mile Plains was like many other rural Afro-Nova Scotian—or "Africadian" (my neologism)—communities. Folks laboured as primary producers—as woodlot woodcutters, as dirt-poor gypsum miners and as hardscrabble farmers, or as domestics and servants in mainly white towns (such as Windsor, the town closest to the Plains). Their schools were segregated and minimal; their roads were unpaved. The central communal institution was the church, generally African Baptist (the African United Baptist Association of Nova Scotia was founded in 1854). Their favourite music was (as it still is) country and western, though they also liked gospel and rhythm and blues. (Academics like York University's Rinaldo Walcott need to spend some time in the countrified Black spaces of this nation: Maestro Fresh Wes and the Dream Warriors do not represent the full spectrum of Black Canadian musical expression!) They were apt to say things like, "Hand me the thingamajig, thingabob," to talk about hotcombs and "good" hair, to grow potatoes and raise chickens, to enjoy step-dancing, fiddle

music, molasses and some condiment called "green tomato chow-chow" and to make their own—very dangerous—beer and dandelion wine. To escape Nova Scotia, they'd go to Montreal or "the Boston States"; some would even go to Toronto, but they preferred Montreal—its always-multicultural Black community, its jazzy night life, its halfway-decent French people! (I note that Dr. Charles Drew, the pioneer African-American surgeon, received his training at McGill University.)

8   Of the once 44 Black communities scattered around Nova Scotia, Africville is now the best known, precisely because it no longer exists; the City of Halifax bulldozed it into history, between 1964 and 1970, in the name of a specious integrationism. It was the Black Refugees of 1812–1815 who first gave Africville its start. Developing as a rural enclave on the north edge of the city, its wood-frame, colourfully-painted, shingled homes faced the Bedford Basin from a spit of land called "Negro Point." (The city completed its erasure of Africville in 1995 by eliminating this place name from city maps.) Numbering some 400 people by the time of its demolition in the 1960s, Africville had its own church, school, community store and post office. (Once upon a time, you could mail a letter to "Africville, Nova Scotia"!) Villagers (and I insist that it was a village, not a "slum") worked as labourers, as domestics, as factory workers (Africville was hemmed in by factories and, beginning in the 1950s, by the city dump). They paid taxes to the City of Halifax but received no city services in return, mainly because city officials never accepted the existence of Africville. Though some residents held title to their properties, the city zoned Africville as industrial land. Villagers could petition city council for services as much as they wished; the city viewed them only as squatters. In the end, villagers lost their land, their homes and, in some cases, their health, their dignity, and their sanity, for the city and its allies—social workers and urban planners—insisted that the preservation of a distinctive Black community contradicted their liberal objective to obliterate it in favour of integration. But, as it turned out, "integration" meant that Africvillers went from being homeowners to being renters of slum housing in principally Black portions of North End Halifax. Eventually, many Africvillers were relocated to public housing projects that conjoined poor whites and Blacks—but without trees, without grass, without hope.

9   Not only Africville has disappeared. Out-migration has reduced the historical African-Islander population of P.E.I. to a footnote in the province's history. Many Africadians have abandoned familial properties in the countryside to move to Halifax and further afield. Indeed, many have "gone down the road" to cities like Toronto, whose own historical Black population dates back to the slavery era as well as to the Underground Railroad which funnelled tens of thousands of African Americans into Upper Canada (Ontario), Lower Canada (Quebec), and British Columbia (mainly Victoria and Saltspring Island), between 1850 (the passage of the iniquitous Fugitive Slave Bill in the U.S.) and the outbreak of the Civil War in 1861.

10   In the cities and towns of southern and eastern Ontario, especially, in the middle of the last century African Americans put down roots. The great slave liberator, "General" Harriet Tubman, lived for eight years in St. Catharines; other Blacks moved to Toronto, where they founded First Baptist Church (still on Huron St.) and saw one of their number, William Peyton Hubbard, rise to become acting-mayor of the city. Ottawa, Kingston and Cornwall received African-American fugitives, as did that swath of territory extending from Chatham to Windsor. Here Blacks formed farming communities, centred on the British Methodist Episcopal Church, such as Buxton, North Buxton, and Amherstburg. (Howard McCurdy emerged from this region to become Canada's second Black member of Parliament [1984-1993]). Chatham is

where Mary Anne Shadd became a crusading abolitionist newspaper editor and publisher and near where Josiah Henson, the purported model for Harriet Beecher Stowe's Uncle Tom, maintained his farm. It is also the site where Martin Robinson Delany authored the first African-Canadian novel, *Blake; or, The Huts of America,* between 1859 and 1862. Happily, a "Freedom Trail" has been established, with provincial funding (inaugurated by the former NDP Government of Bob Rae), to allow interested tourists to retrace the Underground Railroad route into Ontario. (I have met African Americans who have toured the province for this reason alone.)

11   Further west, in the early twentieth century, African Americans in Oklahoma and the South, fleeing intense persecution from the diabolical Ku Klux Klan, migrated to Canada and homesteaded in northern Alberta and Saskatchewan. At least one all-Black community, Amber Valley, was constructed in Alberta (roughly 120 km North of Edmonton). Before this period, during the Klondike Gold Rush, some African Americans even made it as far as the Yukon, where a few remained after the gold gave out.

12   This impressionistic canvas of African-Canadian geography should put to rest the Big Lie that the African presence in Canada is both recent and urban. It is neither. African Canadians have been part of this country, in all its immensity, since its settlement commenced. Though whites often thought that we would perish because of the climate (which is, in places, downright miserable), we have remained; we have even prospered. We have become hockey players and figure skaters; we have mined nickel in the freezing cold of Sudbury; we have fished on the frigid North Atlantic; we have even endured the epochal cold of Ottawa (the world's second-coldest capital—after Ulan Bator, Mongolia). Canadian nature, climate and weather are second nature to us.

13   I'll speak for myself. I grew up in Halifax, but I returned frequently to Three Mile Plains and Windsor, the gateway to the Annapolis Valley. Everybody knows Margaret Atwood's "Survival" thesis and it does apply to Nova Scotia (and to African Canadians). But the Annapolis Valley is one of the lushest, most temperature climates in Canada. Lookit, in the springtime, in May, you can ride for fifty miles under apple blossoms. There's even a village called—no kidding—"Paradise." As a Black, as an Africadian, I claim this landscape for my own. It was watered by the slave blood of all those Black people who preceded me and I now water it with my tears. I confess that Tom Thomson and the Group of Seven—white boys all—speak to me; but so do Benjamin Chee Chee and Tomson Highway. Can't help it. I've looked upon the Annapolis River, to paraphrase Langston Hughes, and I've seen its blossomed bosom turn all goldorange in the sunset. I know sad woodsmoke and acrid harmonicas and chopped wood and slain horses and mouldered barns and hanged Black men. (Two of my second cousins, George and Rufus Hamilton, were hanged in Fredericton, new Brunswick, in 1949. And what is the story of that Black man who was hanged in Stratford, Ontario, in 1905, for raping Mary Peake?) The sound of bagpipes can make me cry. I, too, sing, Canada. This land is my land.

14   To turn to the future, I think that we need to map—and to understand—the African odyssey in Canada. It didn't start and it doesn't stop in Toronto. Nope. We need, for instance, to understand the deep importance of the railway in African-Canadian life, for it bridged our far-flung communities. We also need to rediscover the profound philosophical and sexual intercourse that occurred between Africans and First Nations peoples in this country. (I am part Mi'kmaq.) We also need to appreciate the folkways that enabled the first Black Canadians to survive and to plan for our arrivals. We owe them this.

Comprehension Check

Directions: Now answer the following questions.

1. The author's thesis or main point is _____

_____

_____

2. The author's attitude toward history is _____

_____

_____

3. The author's intent in this essay is _____

_____

_____

4. Is the essay mostly fact or opinion? _____

_____

_____

5. Why does the author include personal history in the essay? _____

_____

_____

6. List at least two major reasons why Blacks have settled in Canada. _____

_____

7. What was Africville? _____

_____

8. T/F African-Canadian history is recent.

9. What does George Elliott Clarke think we need to do in the future? _____

_____

_____

_____

10. Why does the essay end with the sentence "We owe them this"? _____

_____

_____

_____

Vocabulary Check

Directions: Define the following underlined words.

1. Canada anoints my sight (paragraph 1) _____

_____

2. <u>docile</u> First Nations peoples (paragraph 2) _____

_____

3. The <u>cessation</u> of the Maroon (paragraph 6) _____

_____

4. <u>insurgency</u> in Jamaica (paragraph 6)_____

_____

5. left some <u>progeny</u> in Nova Scotia (paragraph 6)_____

_____

6. the colonial authorities <u>quell</u> the first rebellion (paragraph 6)_____

_____

7. my <u>neologism</u> (paragraph 7) _____

_____

8. Africville was <u>hemmed</u> in (paragraph 8)_____

_____

9. their liberal objective to <u>obliterate</u> (paragraph 8) _____

_____

10. to the <u>Underground Railway</u> which funnelled (paragraph 9) _____

_____

Record the results of both checks on the Student Record Chart in the Appendix. Make certain you understand any problems you may have had before going on.

PRACTICE D-2: Timed Reading

Directions: Read the following essay about poverty by Emma LaRocque, looking for the author's thesis, facts/opinions, intent, attitude, and tone. This will be a timed reading, so take about three minutes to preview this 877-word selection and questions. Be sure you push yourself, trying to read faster than your last timed reading.

Begin timing: _____

A PERSONAL ESSAY ON POVERTY

EMMA LAROCQUE

1   Liberalism has made much of poverty in our last decade. Statistics on poverty have been flying around from all directions. And as I mentioned before, Native people have been closely associated with it; so closely in fact that some very significant questions have been bypassed.

2   What is poverty anyway? Is it the failure to reach beyond that magical Poverty Line established by the Economic Council of Canada? Or is it "...relative to the living standard the rest of society enjoys." And more important, what is so sacred about what the majority enjoys?

3   To me it seems obvious that poverty is relative all right; but not necessarily relative to the wealth of the majority, but rather to one's own perceptions of material possessions.

4   My two brothers, one sister and I grew up in a one-roomed but well-managed log cabin. Many of our clothes were handsewn by my very resourceful mother. All our wooden furniture (two beds, one table, a cupboard, several night stands, three chairs and a bench) was put together by my practical father. Our diet consisted of a large variety of wild meats, berries, bannock, potatoes, some vegetables and herbal teas and so on, all of which were usually cooked with originality and imagination.

5   At the age of nine, against my father's perceptive advice, I howled my way into school. He knew only too well that sooner or later I would come home with new desires. As predicted, a few months later I wanted juicy red apples, oranges, bananas, trembling jello, bread and even red-and-white striped toothpaste! Once, my father teasingly wondered what I could possibly do with toothpaste and brush because my teeth were falling out! Toothless or not, I found the pictures at school powerfully suggestive.

6   Other school pictures also played with my mind. I saw Dick, Jane and Sally's suburban home and their grandparent's expansive and, oh, so clean farm. Not for a long time was I to appreciate my home again.

7   The point is, I had been perfectly content to sleep on the floor, eat rabbit stew and read and play cards by kerosene lamp until my perceptions were swayed at school. Neither had I suffered spiritual want. I had been spellbound by my mother's ability to narrate Cree legends and enriched by my father's dreams, until the teacher outlawed Cree and made fun of dreams.

8   From then on I existed in poverty; not with reference to our log cabin, our food and our small wood-stove as compared to the brick schoolhouse, its food and its huge, coal-burning pot-belly stove, but because I was persuaded by my teacher's propaganda and the pictures.* The teacher's authoritarianism, coupled with his failure to reinforce whatever world we came from, effectively weakened our respect for our parents.

9   Still, there is more to poverty than its relativity. Even if I had believed in my home and its simple beauties, it is true that I had no money. And without that commodity, eventually I could not be mobile. And to be immobile in any society is to be quite choiceless. It is at this point that equal opportunity becomes meaningless.

10   It is psychologically cathartic to know that one has a choice. Ultimately, poverty in the North American context is not having enough money to choose among alternatives. Poverty exacts its toll on people not always because of a mere lack of material possessions, but often because of choicelessness.

11   Today, there are hundreds of urban dwellers who are suffering from "cabinitis." Come Friday afternoon there is a mass and speedy exodus to the "simple" life of their cabins. These people are often happy there because they are there by choice. They feel a sense of self-direction.

12   People may be "culturally deprived" perhaps only in that they are deprived of choice. In this sense then, most of us are "culturally deprived" in some area because most of us cannot choose everything we want out of life.

13   Now I live in a city, and I often see children playing on concrete, at artificial playgrounds and in overcrowded parks or swimming pools. I always feel a profound sense of sadness that these children cannot have what I had as a child. No spruce

branch from which to master a Tarzanian swing. No soft moss to land on if you fall. No moonlight rendezvous beside a creek, watching a beaver tirelessly build his dam. No place to build an honest-to-goodness, creaking, but functioning, ferris wheel! No pond or lake or river to try out a self-made raft, row boat or canoe. Or to skinny-dip in. No green space to just run and run and run. No wooded meadow in which to lie and sleepily feel akin to the lethargic clouds. No crocuses, wild roses, tiger lilies or bluebells to sniff.

14   Cultural deprivation?

15   Yes, we must work towards equal opportunity for all. We must help people reach a sense of self-direction and mobility. We must lift people to the place of choice. But we cannot, we must not, dictate what people should choose.

* It must be said that this teacher meant well. He was by nature a disciplinarian but not malicious. Apparently, he sincerely believed that his ways were for the good of the Native children.

Finish timing. Record time here: _____ and use the Timed Readings Conversion Chart in the Appendix to figure your rate: _____ wpm.

Comprehension Check

Directions: Now answer the following questions.

1. Circle the best statement of the main idea or thesis of this essay.

   a. Poverty is a terrible problem that our society must deal with.

   b. The author had lots of fun growing up in rural Canada.

   c. True poverty can best be defined not as a lack of material possession but as a lack of choices.

   d. Native people in Canada continue to suffer from outrageous poverty and discrimination.

2. The author's attitude toward poverty can best be described as

   a. sarcastic

   b. reflective

   c. serious

   d. unsympathetic

3. T/F The author displays a bias against urban dwellers, who feel a strong need for "the simple life of their cabins."

   a. True

   b. False because _____

4. Is the essay mostly fact or opinion? Explain._____

_____

_____

_____

5. Which of the following supporting points does the author include? (Select all that apply.)

    a. Her teacher's attitude weakened the author's respect for her parents.

    b. The author grew up in a one-room log cabin.

    c. The author now lives in a city.

Vocabulary Check

Directions: Write the letter of the correct definition (right-hand column) by the word it defines (left-hand column).

_____ **1.** liberalism (paragraph 1)	**a.**	in comparison with
_____ **2.** relative (paragraph 2)	**b.**	a flat bread made of oatmeal
_____ **3.** bannock (paragraph 4)	**c.**	deep, poignant
_____ **4.** resourceful (paragraph 4)	**d.**	freeing, invigorating
_____ **5.** suggestive (paragraph 6)	**e.**	oppression, tyranny
_____ **6.** authoritarianism (paragraph 9)	**f.**	evocative, stimulating further thought
_____ **7.** cathartic (paragraph 10)	**g.**	practically imaginative
_____ **8.** profound (paragraph 13)	**h.**	politically progressive thinking
_____ **9.** lethargic (paragraph 13)	**i.**	determine, direct, control
_____ **10.** dictate (paragraph 14)	**j.**	slow-moving, lazy

Be sure to record your rate and comprehensive and vocabulary scores on the Student Record Sheet in the Appendix. Understand any errors before you go on.

Questions for Group Discussion

1. Underline facts in the previous two essays and discuss the impact these facts have on each member of the group.

2. Find examples of figurative language in both essays. Does your group find other meanings in the essays when you look at the patterns of figurative language?

3. Discuss your opinions about families and about poverty. As a group, decide if either essay changed your mind.

CHAPTER SIX

Recognizing Inferences and Drawing Conclusions

A. Recognizing Inferences

Each of the skills you have been practicing in this unit is a basis for making critical judgments. You have been learning to recognize an author's attitude, intent, tone, and bias. Here's another important aspect of reading critically: recognizing **inferences**. For instance, when people smile, we infer that they are happy. We base our inference on the fact that most smiles express happiness or pleasure. A frown, we know from experience, generally indicates displeasure or pain. Thus, when someone frowns, we infer that the person is displeased.

An inference is a conclusion or an opinion drawn from reasoning based on known facts or events.

Our inferences are based on experience and/or knowledge.

Drawing inferences is something we do every day. For instance, if you met a woman wearing a large diamond necklace and three platinum rings with rubies and pearls, you would no doubt infer that she is wealthy. You might not be right; the jewellery could belong to someone else or it could be fake. But because we know from experience that the type of jewellery she is wearing is expensive, it is natural to assume she is wealthy. It's a good **educated guess** based on experience and knowledge. Without experience or knowledge, however, any inferences we make are built on shaky ground.

Complete the following statements by drawing inferences from what is known in each case:

1. We may infer from the boy's crying and a melting ice cream cone on the ground that the boy _____

2. We may infer from a woman's grease-stained hands and fingernails that she probably has been _____

3. We may infer from the many whitecaps on the ocean that sailing would be

_____

4. We may infer from the way the man threw his food on the floor and refused to pay the restaurant bill that he was_____

_____

5. We may infer from an F grade on a test that we _____

_____

Let's look now at some of the possible inferences.

• As to the first item, we can assume the boy dropped his ice cream cone; however, we don't know for a fact that this is what happened. Someone may have knocked it out of his hands, or even thrown it at him. But based on the circumstances described, a good inference to draw is that he dropped it and is unhappy.

- In the second item, we can infer that the woman has been working on something mechanical, such as an oily engine. Since we know that our hands and fingernails get greasy from such work, it's a good inference to make.

- The circumstances in item 3 lead us to believe that sailing conditions might be rough, since whitecaps are caused by strong winds. However, a good sailor might like the conditions and think of it as a challenge. Of course, if you have never been around the sea, whitecaps might provide no information for drawing any kind of inference.

- The man in item 4 might be angry, drunk, or "high" on something. We might further infer that he didn't like the food, didn't get what he ordered, or hated the service. Most of us don't make a habit of throwing our food on the floor and making a scene, so we can infer that something is greatly upsetting him to cause him to act this way.

- In the last item, we probably infer that we failed. But is that technically an inference? The F grade is a symbol for failure. No inference need be drawn. But *why* did we fail? Maybe we didn't study hard enough, misunderstood the directions, studied the wrong material, the test was a poor one, or the instructor made a mistake.

Drawing inferences while we read critically is no different from the kind of thinking done in the preceding examples. Read the following passage and then answer the questions that follow.

> If we compare college textbooks of just two decades ago with those of today, we see a dramatic decrease in the number of words, vocabulary level, and specificity of detail, but a sharp increase of graphics and, particularly, illustrations. Such textbook pictures can scarcely convey as well as words the subtle distinctions that emerge from scholarly or scientific work.

1. What is being compared in this paragraph? _____

    _____

2. What inference can be drawn about the author's attitude toward college textbooks today? _____

    _____

3. What inference can be drawn about today's college students? _____

    _____

    _____

Notice that the first question has nothing to do with inference, but it serves to remind you that in order to read critically you also have to use your literal comprehension skills.

- The paragraph contrasts college textbooks of today with those published twenty years ago. In order to draw inferences, you have to understand that first.

- The answer to question 2 is that the author's attitude is negative. We can infer that from the last sentence of the paragraph.

- The answer to question 3 is that the reading levels of today's college students are probably lower than those of students twenty years ago.

Because of the decrease in words, lower vocabulary level, and more numerous pictures, we can infer that today's students don't read as well. We could also infer instead that publishers are merely changing their way of publishing, but chances are that's not the author's intent here.

Here's a passage taken from a short story. Read it and answer the questions that follow.

In walks these three girls in nothing but bathing suits. I'm in the third checkout slot, with my back to the door, so I don't see them until they're over by the bread. The one that caught my eye first was the one in the plaid green two-piece. She was a chunky kid, with a good tan and a sweet broad soft-looking can with those two crescents of white just under it, where the sun never seems to hit, at the top of the back of her legs. I stood there with my hand on a box of HiHo crackers trying to remember if I rang it up or not. I ring it up again and the customer starts giving me hell. She's one of those cash-register-watchers, a witch about fifty with rouge on her cheekbones and no eyebrows, and I know it made her day to trip me up. She'd been watching cash registers for fifty years and probably never seen a mistake before. (John Updike, "A & P" from *Pigeon Feathers and Other Stories*. Reprinted by permission of the author and Alfred A. Knopf, a Division of Random House, Inc., Copyright © 1962.)

Based on the information provided, answer the following questions by drawing inferences:

1. How old and what sex is the narrator or person telling the story? _____
   What makes you think so? _____
   _____
   _____

2. Where is the story taking place? _____

3. T/F People in bathing suits coming into the place where the narrator is working is not an everyday occurrence.
   a. True because _____
   b. False because _____

4. T/F The narrator is not distracted by the girls.
   a. True because _____
   b. False because _____

5. T/F The narrator is very observant.
   a. True because _____
   b. False because _____

As we find out later in the story, the answer to the first question is a nineteen-year-old male. But we can guess from the passage that the narrator is male because of his reaction to the girls, because of the language he uses, and because of his comments about the "witch about fifty" who catches his mistake. The tone has a youthful, informal quality about it.

It's not too difficult to infer that the story is taking place in a supermarket of some type, probably a grocery store. He is working at a checkout slot ringing up HiHo crackers, and he comments that the girls were "over by the bread" before he saw them. These are clues to us.

Question 3 is probably true, making question 4 false. He is distracted by the girls. No doubt girls come into the store all the time, but in this case they are wearing "nothing but bathing suits," making this an unusual event. It causes him to forget whether he has already rung up the crackers.

Question 5 is true; he is very observant. His description of the one girl and the "cash-register-watcher" are full of details, reflecting an observant person.

The word *critical* often connotes finding fault with something. But making valid critical judgments, in its strictest sense, implies an attempt at objective judging so as to determine both merits and faults. Critical reading is thoughtful reading because it requires that the reader not only recognize what is being said at the literal level but also distinguish facts from opinions, recognize an author's intent, attitude, and biases, and draw inferences. A reader who is reading critically is actively involved.

PRACTICE A-1: Drawing Inferences

Part A

Directions: An inference, remember, is "a statement about the unknown made on the basis of the known." Complete the following statements, drawing inferences from what is known.

1. We may infer from the smile on the professor's face as he passed back the exams that _____

2. We may infer from the large turnout at our college orientation session that

   _____

3. We may infer from the fact that a student in a college English class is consistently late for class that _____

   _____

4. We may infer from the number of Academy Awards a movie won that

   _____

5. We may infer from the extreme thinness of some current models and actresses that _____

Part B

Directions: Read the following passages and answer the questions that follow them.

1.   The word *concerto* originally meant a group of performers playing or singing together, as "in concert," or making a "concerted effort" of entertaining. The Gabrielis of sixteenth-century Venice called their motets, scored for choir and organ, *concerti ecclesiastici*. Heinrich Schultz, a seventeenth-century German composer, titled his similar works *Kleine geistliche Konzerte*.

   a. What is the intent of this paragraph?_____

   _____

   b. T/F The German word *Konzerte* probably means concerto.

   c. T/F We can infer that the author probably knows some history of music.

2. He had a direct and unassuming manner and a candid way of speaking with a soft French-Canadian accent. The interviewer rushed right in with questions, but he turned all the questions around and wanted first to know some things about the interviewer. She had a hard time getting the conversation centred on him—until he was ready. He was a bright, insightful man who seemed oblivious to his genius.

    a. What words best describe the man in the preceding passage? _____

_____

    b. T/F The man is important or famous.

    c. T/F The interviewer was impressed with this man.

    d. T/F We can infer the man is talkative and open.

3. Infer as much as you can from each of the following statements:

    a. The evening has proved to be most entertaining. I extend my deepest appreciation. _____

_____

    b. Tonight's been a real blast! Thanks a bunch. _____

_____

    c. Like, I mean, funwise, this night has blown me away, babe. _____

_____

4. There are all kinds of rumours about Giao Li. Some say, no matter how dangerous, he'd enter any mountain to light the dynamite, and manage to walk out every time. Others say he could drive a peg into a rail faster than any of the big railway men. Others say he could quote long passages of Confucius. And still others claim he had the eyes of a cat and faster hands. Most all who knew him claim he was the last of the labourers.

    a. What was Giao Li's occupation? _____

    b. T/F Based on the rumours, most people seem to admire him.

    c. T/F Li probably lived somewhere in the western provinces.

    d. What can we infer about Li if it is true that he could quote long passages of Confucius? _____

    e. Why would a man such as Li be interested in Confucius? _____

_____

5. During the Middle Ages many scholars regarded printed books with apprehension. They felt that books would destroy the monopoly on knowledge. Books would permit the masses to learn to improve their lives and to realize that no man is better than another. And not too long ago, slaves were strictly forbidden to learn to read and had to pretend that they were illiterate if they had learned how. Societies based on ignorance or repression cannot tolerate general education.

    a. T/F The first sentence is fact.

    b. What is the author's attitude toward education? _____

_____

    c. What is the intent of the statement? _____

_____

B. Recognizing Inferences and Facts

When inferences are based on facts, much useful information can be obtained. Scientists and historians, to name a few, have been able to infer from facts and observation most of the knowledge we have today. Below is a passage based on fact with many inferences that are probably true. As you read, note the inferences and the facts.

1   Archaeologists believe that the ancestors of the Native peoples of the Pacific coast had resided there for thousands of years before European contact. The linguistic complexity of the coastal region, with its nineteen distinct languages, suggests that it is an "old area," and thus the most likely starting point for migrations of successive groups to the east and south.

2   The coastal inhabitants relied on the abundant fish for their livelihood: herring, smelt, oolichan (candle-fish), halibut, and several species of cod. In addition, they hunted sea mammals, such as whales, seals, sea lions, porpoises, and sea otters. Salmon, which they speared, netted and trapped in large quantities, then sun-dried or smoked, became their basic, year-round staple. Such an abundant food supply made the Pacific coast region the most densely populated area in Canada.

3   The Northwest Coast peoples used the giant cedars and firs of the coastal rain forest to build houses and to make dugout canoes and woodwork, such as carved boxes, bowls, dishes, and ladles. They lived the year round in villages located in sheltered island coves or on channels near the mouths of rivers. Each village was self-contained, but on occasion, particularly in times of war, several settlements joined together. Their communal activities included the potlatch, a large ceremonial feast, which they used to mourn the dead, to celebrate the investiture of new chiefs, or to mark the completion of a new house.

From *Origins* 4E + *Destinies* 4E, 4th Edition by Francis © 2000. Reprinted with permission of Nelson, a division of Thomson Learning www.thomsonrights.com. Fax 800-730-2215.

Directions: Now answer these questions.

1. T/F The first sentence of paragraph 1 is fact.
2. T/F The information in the last sentence of paragraph 1 is mostly fact.
3. T/F The first sentence of paragraph 2 is mostly inference.
4. T/F The last sentence of paragraph 2 is mostly fact.
5. T/F Paragraph 3 is mostly inference.
6. T/F Chances are that someday this information will prove to be wrong.

The answer to question 1 is false; it's mainly inference based on facts or evidence that, when put together, lead scientists to believe that these conditions existed thousands of years ago. We have no way of knowing for certain.

Question 2 is true. While it can be proven easily enough that this region of the country was home to nineteen distinctive languages, the observation that it was "most likely the starting point for migrations of successive groups to the east and south" is an inference made from this fact.

Question 3 is true. Again, no one was around to verify these statements, but the inference here is probably based on recent observations or archaeological evidence.

Question 4 is true—more or less. While we might be able to prove that it was the most populous region by checking archaeological artefacts or other data, we can only infer that it was the abundance of food and not some other mitigating factors that made this region the most populous.

The answer to question 5 is true. All of the information contained in paragraph 3 is inference. Unless we could send a team of archaeologists back in time to observe these rituals and practices, we won't know for certain if any of this information is fact.

Question 6 is false; it's possible, but highly unlikely because of present-day facts and remains. However, in the future, this might be a "slippery fact," like the atom being thought of as the smallest particle at one time. But based on all the known facts we have at present, the best answer is false.

You can see that much of what we call "fact" today is based on inferences. When scientists agree on inferences that are drawn from what is known, we tend to accept as fact their conclusions until such time that more evidence can show the inferences drawn are wrong.

The following practices will help you to recognize the difference between facts and inferences.

PRACTICE B-1: Drawing Inferences from Facts

Directions: Read the following passages and answer the questions that follow them.

1. During the 1970s, women began making major breakthroughs in the male domains of business and finance professions and medicine and dentistry. These trends continue, for in 1999 women made up close to half of the workers in these occupations. They have also made gains in other high-status occupations, and in 1999 made up 35 percent of managers. How does this compare with other advanced industrial countries? The general category of managerial work in the United States and Australia was over 40 percent female by the early 1990s, well ahead of Japan (9 percent), Germany (19 percent), and Mexico (20 percent). This selective comparison suggests that labour markets and cultural barriers to women may be more resistant to change in some countries than in others.

   However, a detailed analysis of the managerial category reveals that women are clustered in the least responsible and lowest-paying jobs. By reviewing detailed occupational titles contained in the 1996 Census, we learn that women accounted for 8 percent and 17 percent, respectively, of senior managers in key goods-producing industries and in business and distributive service industries. Looking more closely at the latter sector, a study of women in Canada's investment industry (investment dealers) found that gender stereotyping, exclusion from informal networks and role models, and a lack of family-friendly policies were major barriers to women advancing into senior management positions (Women in Capital Markets, 2001). Moreover, few women have entered management positions in natural sciences and engineering or in the mining and oil sector—all economic activities dominated by men. Conversely, women managers are concentrated in predominantly female enclaves within organizations, such as office administration, personnel, and sales. In conclusion, despite women having entered management in sizable numbers in North America and Europe, real power and decision-making authority continue to be exercised by male corporate executives and directors. (From *Work, Industry, and Canadian Society* by Krahn/Lowe, © 2003. Reprinted with permission of Nelson, a division of Thomson Learning: www.thomsonrights.com. Fax 800-730-2215.)

    a. The intent of this passage is to _____

_____

    b. T/F The first paragraph is mostly factual.

    c. T/F Women's employment status has increased recently.

    d. T/F We can infer that the author believes that women deserve better treatment in the workforce.

    e. T/F The last sentence of the second paragraph is factual.

2.   I raised my head, squared my shoulders, and set off in the direction of my dorm, glancing twice (and then ever so discreetly) at the campus map clutched in my hand. It took everything I had not to stare when I caught my first glimpse of a real live football player. What confidence, what reserve, what muscles! I only hoped his attention was drawn to my air of assurance rather than to my shaking knees. I spent the afternoon seeking out each of my classrooms so that I could make a perfectly timed entrance before each lecture without having to ask dumb questions about its whereabouts.

    The next morning I found my first class and marched in. Once I was in the room, however, another problem awaited me. Where to sit? . . . After much deliberation I chose a seat in the first row and to the side. I was in the foreground (as advised), but out of the professor's direct line of vision.

    I cracked my anthology of American literature and scribbled the date on the top of the crisp ruled page. "Welcome to Biology 101," the professor began. A cold sweat broke out at the back of my neck. (From Evelyn Herald, "Fresh Start," *Nutshell* magazine.)

    a. Where can we infer that the event described in the passage is taking place?

_____

How can you tell? _____

_____

    b. T/F The narrator telling the story is female. Explain. _____

_____

_____

_____

    c. T/F We can infer from the author's tone that the author has a sense of humour. Explain. _____

_____

_____

    d. Why did the author break out in a cold sweat when the professor greeted the class? _____

_____

_____

    e. T/F We can infer that the author is trying not to conceal his or her true feelings. Explain. _____

_____

_____

_____

3.   From the seller's viewpoint, advertising is persuasion; from the buyer's viewpoint, it is education. No single group of people spends as much time or money per lesson to educate the masses as do the creators of ads.

Ads participate in a feedback loop. They reflect a society they have helped to educate, and part of the advertising reflection is the effect of the advertising itself. Every ad that exploits a personality hole educates the audience toward using a particular product to fill that hole. Just as drug ads teach a crude and sometimes dangerous form of self-medication, psychosell ads teach a form of self-analysis and cure for psychological problems.

An ad that stirs a hidden doubt, that causes a person to ask, "Why does no one love me?"; "Why don't I have more friends?"; "Why am I lonely?" invariably goes on to suggest a partial cure—use our product. Suppose an announcer for Pepsi were to appear on screen and say:

> Are you lonely? Do you feel left out? Do you sometimes feel that everybody else has all the fun in life? Are you bored and isolated? Well, if you are, drink Pepsi and find yourself instantly a part of all those energetic, joyful, young-at-heart people who also drink Pepsi.

Such an ad would be greeted as either laughable or insulting by the viewing audience. Yet the old "Pepsi generation" campaign used pictures and a jingle to make exactly that point.

The danger in psychosell techniques is not that people might switch from Coke to Pepsi in soft-drink loyalties or abandon Scope for Listerine. The danger is that millions learn (especially if the message is repeated often enough, as ads are) that problems in self-acceptance and boredom can be alleviated by corporate products. Which brand to buy is secondary to ads as education; the primary lesson is that the product itself satisfies psychological needs. (From Jeffrey Schrank, *Snap, Crackle and Popular Taste: The Illusion of Free Choice in America,* Delacorte Press, 1977.)

a. What is the intent of the author? _____

_____

_____

b. Is the passage primarily fact or opinion? _____ Explain. _____

_____

_____

c. T/F The author thinks ads may be silly and repetitive, but are basically harmless. Explain. _____

_____

_____

d. T/F The author believes that some advertising is a dangerous form of education because it brainwashes us into thinking we can solve many of our personal problems by buying corporate products. Explain. _____

_____

_____

_____

e. T/F The author's bias is easy to identify. Explain. _____

_____

_____

4.   Evolution has been made to appear a religious issue by two opposing groups of religious fundamentalists, each proposing a single-lens view of reality. The biblical fundamentalists, interpreting the creation narratives of Genesis as historical and scientific records dictated by God, are compelled to reject any scientific theory which, like evolution, appears to contradict what God said. Never mind that their biblicism flies in the face of a century of biblical scholarship and is rejected by the majority of religious denominations whose traditions stem from the same biblical witness. This only reinforces their conviction that they are the righteous few who will be saved. Never mind that, like the churchmen who refused to look through Galileo's telescope, they must deny an enormous body of scientific evidence for evolution. This only proves that scientists are the tools of Satan, using the theory of evolution to spread vice and corruption everywhere. Never mind that many scientists see an evolving universe as an even more magnificent tribute to a Creator than a static one. They are lying, for only atheists "believe in" evolution. Salvation for us all lies in conversion to, or legal enforcement of, the biblical fundamentalists' tribal myth, with its unquestionable morals and mores.

The opposite extreme of religious fundamentalism is represented by the "secular humanists." Their creed is the Humanist Manifesto, I and II. Since they are neither secular nor humanistic, in the traditional sense, and their basic premise seems to be that science has displaced religion as the only valid way of acquiring knowledge of the real world, a better name for them might be "scientific fundamentalists." This group does not seem bent on proselytizing, perhaps because it assumes that those who can leave behind the religious myths (read "fantasies") of mankind's childhood will be limited to the enlightened few. Their biases appear as gratuitous snipes at religion, such as sometimes mar the otherwise lucid writings of Isaac Asimov. (From Anne Marie Brennan, "Biblical Fundamentalists vs. Scientistic Ones: The Creationist Controversy," *Commonweal*, October 22, 1982. Reprinted by permission of the Commonweal Foundation.)

a. The intent of the paragraphs is to _____

_____

b. T/F The author is more biased against the "biblical fundamentalists" than the "secular humanists." Explain. _____

_____

c. T/F The author believes that only atheists "believe in" evolution. Explain.

_____

d. T/F The author seems biased against Isaac Asimov's writings. Explain.

_____

_____

e. T/F The author shares the views expressed in the Humanist Manifesto, I and II. Explain. _____

_____

_____

f. Do you agree or disagree with the views revealed in the passage? Explain.

_____

_____

PRACTICE B-2: Inferences in Advertisements

Directions: Study the advertisement for 3M Innovation shown on page 250. Then answer the following questions.

1. In advertisements, every word counts because there is only enough space for a few words. What are the double meanings for "on a roll" and "popped up"?

   _____

   _____

   _____

2. What purpose does the picture of the rolls serve in the ad? _____

   _____

   _____

3. What is the effect of the numbers (1 and 2) in the ad?_____

   _____

   _____

   _____

   _____

4. What inferences do you make about the Pop-up Tape Strips from the visual of the device on the hand? _____

   _____

   _____

   _____

5. Look carefully at the written description (under point #2) of this innovation and decide what inferences are being taught through these words._____

   _____

   _____

   _____

6. What is the main purpose of the ad? Explain your answer. _____

   _____

   _____

   _____

7. Who is the primary audience for this ad? Be specific, and explain your answer.

   _____

   _____

   _____

Reprinted by permission of the 3M Corporation.

C. Drawing Conclusions Using Induction and Deduction

A big part of critical reading is being able to draw conclusions based on the information authors provide. Once you understand the thesis or main idea of a reading selection, can distinguish fact from opinion, and understand intent, attitude, and inference, you almost automatically draw conclusions of your own. In fact, some of the questions you have been answering in the last practices require drawing conclusions based on the evidence provided.

Drawing conclusions is based on making **reasoned judgments.** Reasoned judgments usually come from two basic methods of reasoning: **deductive reasoning** and **inductive reasoning.** Deductive reasoning occurs when you begin with a general statement of truth and infer a conclusion about a particular specific. For instance, the old standby definition of deductive reasoning is shown through a **syllogism,** a three-step statement that begins with a general statement recognized as a truth and moves to a specific statement:

> All men are mortal.
> Bryan Adams is a man.
> Therefore, Bryan Adams is mortal.

Deductive reasoning is the subject of formal logic courses and involves a process of stating a series of carefully worded statements, such as the Adams example just given, each related to the other statements. Deductive reasoning begins with a generalization:

> *All dogs are animals.   *or*   *Athletes are physically strong.

The next statement identifies something as belonging (or not belonging) to that class:

> _____is a dog.

What would be a second statement for the athlete generalization?

_____

For the first example, you should have given the name of a dog you know or a famous dog. For example, Lassie is a dog. For the second statement, you should have named an athlete. "Mario Lemieux is an athlete" would be one example.

The third statement of deductive reasoning is the inference you arrive at if the first two statements are true:

> All dogs are animals.   Athletes are physically strong.
> Lassie is a dog.   Mario Lemieux is an athlete.
> Lassie is an animal.   Mario Lemieux is physically strong.

Fully understanding deductive reasoning takes a lot of study but, for the purpose of this introduction, you should be aware that you start with a generalization and use a careful reasoning process to arrive at a conclusion.

> You can make errors with deductive reasoning if you start with faulty generaliza-tions or premises. If you started with the generalization that "all college students have high IQs" you would be starting with a false premise. Some college students have high IQs; others may be conscientious workers with average IQs.

Inductive reasoning works the opposite way from deductive reasoning. With inductive reasoning, you begin with observing specifics and draw a general conclusion. You might move to a new town and notice that every time you see police officers they are wearing bright green uniforms. After seeing no police offi-cer wearing anything other than this color, you might inductively reason that in this particular town the official police uniform is bright green.

Inductive reasoning is often used when you can't examine all the data but need to come to conclusions based on what you know. Political polls do this when they look at some voters and base conclusions on what "the people" want by that sample. You may come to inductive conclusions based on sensory observations (what you see or hear), lists or groups, cause-effect thinking, or pattern recognition.

* *Sensory observation:* Using your eyes, ears, taste, or smell involves sensory observation. The police uniform example in the previous paragraph is an example of sensory observation.
* *Lists or enumeration:* Often we look at lists of items and come to conclu-sions based on those lists. You may look at lists of what prevents heart problems and decide you will not smoke and will exercise every day.
* *Cause-effect:* When two events happen, we may decide that the first one was one cause of the second one (effect). Historians use this kind of reasoning. Cause-effect thinking means you notice that every time you run a red light you are almost in an accident. The cause (running the red light) has a certain effect (near accident).
* *Pattern recognition:* Pattern recognition involves looking at parts and draw-ing conclusions. A professor may notice one student who is rarely in class, doesn't turn in work, and flunks the midterm. That professor is likely to conclude that the student is a poor college student.

The conclusion you draw in inductive reasoning is usually called a hypothe-sis. Scientists use this method all the time.

> As with deductive reasoning, you can make many errors with inductive rea-soning. Some of these are listed in Practice C-4 of this chapter and include such obvious errors as oversimplification and using the wrong facts to come to your conclusion.

Perhaps the best way to explain these two types of reasoning is to quote Robert M. Pirsig in a passage from his book *Zen and the Art of Motorcycle Maintenance*:

> If the icycle goes over a bump and the engine misfires, and then goes over another bump and the engine misfires, and then goes over another bump and the engine misfires, and then goes over a long smooth stretch of road and there is no mis-firing, and then goes over a fourth bump and the engine misfires again, one can logically conclude that the misfiring is caused by the bumps. That is induction: reasoning from particular experiences to general truths.

Deductive inferences do the reverse. They start with general knowledge and predict a specific observation. For example if, from reading the hierarchy of facts about the machine, the mechanic knows the horn on the cycle is powered exclusively by electricity from the battery, then he can logically infer that if the battery is dead the horn will not work. That is deduction.

We use these two types of reasoning every day, often without even knowing it.

To look more closely at how we draw conclusions, read the following passage and then answer the questions that follow.

> In 1832, a twenty-four-old Englishman named Charles Darwin, aboard the HMS *Beagle* on a surveying expedition around the world, was collecting beetles in a rain forest near Rio de Janeiro. In one day, in one small area, he found over sixty-eight different species of small beetles. That there could be such a variety of species of one kind of creature astounded him. In his journal he wrote that such a find "... is sufficient to disturb the composure of an entomologist's mind...." The conventional view of his day was that all species were unchangeable and that each had been individually and separately created by God. Far from being an atheist, Darwin had taken a degree in divinity in Cambridge. But he was deeply puzzled by his find. (Adapted from James Burke, *The Day the Universe Changed,* Little, Brown & Co., 1985, p. 267.)

1. T/F We can draw the conclusion that Darwin was not actually out searching for what he found.
2. T/F The evidence provided for our conclusion is based partly on Darwin's journal.
3. T/F What Darwin discovered was contrary to the beliefs of his day.
4. T/F Darwin's later "theory of evolution," that species were not fixed forever, probably began with his discovery about the beetle.

All of the answers to these questions are true.

- Darwin's journal statement that the find was "sufficient to disturb" his composure, the statement that he was "deeply puzzled," and the fact that what he found was contrary to what he had been taught to believe, all provide evidence to support our conclusion that he was not looking for what he found.
- Even though no one living today was with Darwin in 1832, his journal notes leave evidence to help answer question 2 as true.
- As to question 3, if Darwin had a degree in divinity from Cambridge, he would have been taught to believe what was accepted as "fact" in his day: that God individually and separately created all species. The fact that he found sixty-eight different species is contrary to such a belief.
- Question 4 is true, but unless you have knowledge of what Charles Darwin's "theory of evolution" is, you might have difficulty drawing such a conclusion. If you know that he continued to pursue the suspicion in his mind that all species were not fixed forever, and that he eventually wrote *On the Origin of Species by Means of Natural Selection,* then there's no problem in answering this question as true.

The following practices are designed to help you develop your ability to draw conclusions from what you read.

Reprinted by permission of the Canadian Magazine Publishers Association.

PRACTICE C-1: Drawing Conclusions from an Ad

Directions: Study the advertisement for the Canadian Magazine Publishers Association, reproduced on page 254. Then answer the following questions.

1. What is the intent of the ad? _____

_____

_____

_____

2. Most of the text on the ad is located on a label because _____

_____

_____

_____

3. T/F The creators of the ad probably believe that the shock value of the picture will get your attention.

   a. True because _____

   b. False because _____

4. What facts from the ad give you information about its intent? _____

_____

_____

_____

_____

_____

5. To understand this ad, do you use inductive or deductive reasoning? Explain.

_____

_____

_____

_____

_____

PRACTICE C-2: Drawing Conclusions from Paragraphs

Directions: Read the following paragraphs and answer the questions that follow them.

1.   Look for a moment at the situation in those nations that most of us prefer to label with the euphemism "underdeveloped," but which might just as accurately be described as "hungry." In general, underdeveloped countries (UDCs) differ from developed countries (DCs) in a number of ways. UDCs are not industrialized. They tend to have inefficient, usually subsistence agricultural systems, extremely low gross national products and per capita incomes, high illiteracy rates, and

incredibly high rates of population growth. . . . Most of these countries will never, under conceivable circumstance, be "developed." They could accurately be called "never-to-be-developed" countries. (From Paul and Anne Ehrlich, *Population, Resources and Environment.*)

a. The intent of the passage is to _____

_____

_____

_____

b. T/F The authors of the passage have drawn the conclusion that UDCs exist because they are not industrialized, have poor agricultural systems, high illiteracy rates, low incomes, and too much population growth.

c. T/F If a UDC has a population growth that is too high for its agricultural system, we can draw the conclusion that it will never become a DC.

d. T/F We can draw the conclusion from the information in the passage that the authors feel UDCs can eventually become DCs.

e. Identify what kind of reasoning (inductive or deductive) is required to answer *d.* _____

_____

_____

_____

2.   Science is sometimes confused with technology, which is the application of science to various tasks. Grade-school texts that caption pictures of rockets on the moon with the title, "Science Marches On!" aid such confusion. The technology that makes landing on the moon possible emerged from the use of scientific strategies in the study of propulsion, electronics, and numerous other fields. It is the mode of inquiry that is scientific; the rocket is a piece of technology.

Just as science is not technology, neither is it some specific body of knowledge. The popular phrase "Science tells us that smoking is bad for your health" really misleads. "Science" doesn't tell us anything; people tell us things, in this case people who have used scientific strategies to investigate the relationship of smoking to health. Science, as a way of thought and investigation, is best conceived of as existing not in books, or in machinery, or in reports containing numbers, but rather in that invisible world of the mind. Science has to do with the way questions are formulated and answered; it is a set of rules and forms for inquiry created by people who want reliable answers. (From Kenneth R. Hoover, *The Elements of Social Scientific Thinking*, 3rd edition, St. Martin's Press, 1984, pp. 4–5.)

a. The intent of the passage is to _____

_____

_____

_____

b. T/F According to the author, some grade-school textbooks contribute to the confusion between science and technology.

c. T/F The author does not think there is much difference between the terms *science* and *technology.*

d. T/F The author does not believe that science is something that cannot be written down.

e. T/F The author would agree with the statement, "Science has proven that too much sun causes skin cancer."

f. T/F The author has respect for scientific thinking.

g. What kind of reasoning (inductive or deductive) did you use to answer *f*?

_____

_____

3. Some years ago, I ran into an economist friend at the University of Michigan in Ann Arbor who told me, with concern bordering on shock, that assembly-line workers at the nearby Ford plant in Dearborn were making more money than an assistant professor at the University. It occurred to me that quite a few at Ford might prefer the more leisured life of a young professor: Certainly there seemed no need to fear any major movement of academic talent from Ann Arbor to the noisome shops in Dearborn. (From John Kenneth Galbraith, "When Work Isn't Work," *Parade* Magazine, February 10, 1985.)

a. T/F The author's economist friend believes that a university professor should be paid more than an assembly-line worker.

b. T/F The author agrees with his friend.

c. T/F The author feels that a university professor's work is easier than factory work.

d. T/F Because the pay is better for factory work, many professors will probably leave the university to seek factory jobs.

e. T/F The author probably believes the usual definition for "work" can be misleading when comparing various types of jobs.

PRACTICE C-3

Directions: Read the following essay to further develop your understanding of inductive reasoning and some of the errors that may be associated with it.

THE FAILURE OF OBJECTIVITY

WILLIAM BROAD AND NICHOLAS WADE

1   Cyril Burt, one of the pioneers of applied psychology in England, was a man of brilliance and great culture. He became professor of psychology at University College, London, and was the first psychologist to receive a knighthood for his services. The American Psychological Association gave him its Thorndike prize in 1971, the first time that the high honour had been awarded to a foreigner. When he died, the same year, the obituaries proclaimed him "Britain's most eminent educational

psychologist" and even "dean of the world's psychologists." "Everything about the man," wrote Arthur Jensen of Stanford University, "—his fine, sturdy appearance; his aura of vitality; his urbane manner; his unflagging enthusiasm for research, analysis and criticism; . . . and, of course, especially his notably sharp intellect and vast erudition—all together leave a total impression of immense quality, of a born nobleman."

2   But the man who impressed Jensen with his nobility of intellect possessed a grievous intellectual flaw: he was a cheat. He invented data out of whole cloth to support his own theories and confound his critics. He used his mastery of statistics and gift of lucid exposition to bamboozle alike his bitterest detractors and those who acclaimed his greatness as a psychologist.

3   What was more remarkable still, Burt attained a great part of his eminence in the field of IQ testing not because of any thoroughgoing program of research, of which he did little worth the name, but through his skills of *rhetoric*. If a real scientist is one who wants to discover the truth, Burt was no scientist, because he already knew the truth. He used the scientific method with great effect, but not as an approach to understanding the world. In Burt's hands the scientific method can be seen most clearly for its utility as a purely rhetorical device, a method of argument with which to assume a position of moral superiority, to pretend to greater learning or diligence. According to his biographer L. S. Hearnshaw, "He was fond of accusing his opponents of basing their criticisms 'not on any fresh evidence or new researches of their own, but chiefly on armchair articles from general principles.' 'My co-workers and I,' on the other hand, were engaged in on-going research. It was a powerful argument with which to belabour the environmentalists; but to sustain it there had to be co-workers, and these co-workers had to be currently engaged in data collection." But there were no new data, and no co-workers. The lonely and embattled Burt sat in his armchair, summoned both data and co-workers from the vasty deep of his tormented imagination, and clothed them so well in the semblance of scientific argument that the illusion fooled all his fellow scientists for as much as thirty years.

4   Burt's work was influential, in different ways, on both sides of the Atlantic. In England, he served as a consultant to a series of blue-ribbon committees that restructured the English educational system after the Second World War. The crux of the new system was a test applied to children at the age of eleven, the results of which determined their assignment to a higher- or lower-quality education. The 11+ exam, as it was called, was based on the assumption that a child's educability and future potential can fairly be assessed at that age. Burt cannot be held responsible for the 11+ exam, which was the decision of many people, but his persuasive insistence that intelligence is more than 75 percent a fixed, inherited ability was certainly influential in shaping the climate of opinion among English educators from which the 11+ was born.

5   The 11+ exam and the selective system of education that was based on it began to come under heavy attack in the 1950's, after Burt had retired from his professorship at University College, London. To defend his theory against the critics, Burt started to publish a series of articles in which striking new evidence for the hereditarian view was produced. The new evidence, Burt explained, had mostly been gathered during the 1920's and 1930's when he was the psychologist for the London school system. It had been updated with the help of his co-workers, Miss Margaret Howard and Miss J. Conway. The pearl of Burt's impressive IQ data was that derived from separated identical twins, the largest single such collection in the world. With the same heredity but different environments, separated identical twins afford uniquely ideal subjects for testing the interplay of the two effects on intelligence. Burt's data on twins and other kinship relations "were widely quoted, widely accepted as valid, and were

among the strongest piece of evidence for the preponderantly genetic determination of intelligence," says Hearnshaw.

6   In 1969, after the 11+ had been abolished and England's selective education replaced with a comprehensive system, Burt published an article purporting to document a decline in educational standards. The intention of the article was clearly to influence educational policy.

7   Meanwhile, the authority and crispness of Burt's new twin data was attracting the eager attention of hereditarian psychologists in the United States. Arthur Jensen made considerable use of Burt's findings in his 1969 article in the *Harvard Educational Review,* a furiously debated tract in which he argued that since the genetic factor determines 80 percent of intelligence, programs of compensatory education addressed to lower-class black and white children were useless and should be scrapped. Burt's twin data were relied on even more heavily by Richard Herrnstein of Harvard in his September 1971 article in *The Atlantic* arguing that social class is based in part on inherited differences in intelligence. "The measurement of intelligence," the Harvard psychologist proclaimed in his widely influential article, "is psychology's most telling accomplishment to date." Pride of place was given to Burt's twin studies.

8   When Burt died in October 1971, at the age of eighty-eight, his theories were at the peak of their influence in the United States, even if educational policy in Britain had turned away from them. His oeuvre crumbled only after his death, and the collapse was quite sudden, because the edifice was a mere façade of scholarship. The man who had eyes to see the emperor's outrageous state of undress was Leon Kamin, a Princeton University psychologist who had never ventured into the IQ field until a student urged him to read one of Burt's papers in 1972. "The immediate conclusion I came to after 10 minutes of reading was that Burt was a fraud," says Kamin.

9   Kamin noticed first that Burt's papers are largely innocent of the elementary trappings of scholarship, such as precise details of who had administered what tests to which children and when. This peculiar vagueness is evident in Burt's first major summary of his IQ and kinship studies, an article published in 1943; and continues thereafter. But in Burt's twin studies, Kamin spotted something much more serious.

10   Burt published the first full report on the IQ of his separated identical twins in 1955, when he claimed to have located twenty-one pairs. A second report in 1958 mentioned "over 30" pairs, and the final accounting in 1966 cited fifty-three pairs, by far the largest collection in the world. The correlation between the IQ scores of the separated twins, Kamin noticed, was given as 0.771—*in all three studies.* For a correlation coefficient to remain unchanged, to three decimal places, while new members are added to the sample on two occasions, is highly improbable. But it was not the only case. The correlation in IQ of identical twins reared together struck at 0.944 through three sample sizes. All together there were twenty such coincidences in a table of sixty correlations. Kamin summarized his study of Burt's work in a book published in 1974. His review was biting, ironic, and devastating. He concluded, in words that will always be part of the history of psychometrics, "The absence of procedural description in Burt's reports vitiates their scientific utility. . . . The marvelous consistency of his data supporting the hereditarian position often taxes credibility; and on analysis, the data are found to contain implausible effects consistent with an effort to prove the hereditarian case. The conclusion cannot be avoided. The numbers left behind by Professor Burt are simply not worthy of our current scientific attention. . . ."

11   Despite the unchallenged statements published by Kamin and Jensen two years earlier, the actual charge of fraud evoked spasms of indignation from psychologists on both sides of the Atlantic. The very suggestion, said Herrnstein, "is so outrageous that I find it hard to stay in my chair. Burt was a towering figure of 20th century psychology.

I think it is a crime to cast such doubt over a man's career." Hans Eysenck, a leading IQ expert at the Institute of Psychiatry in London, wrote to Burt's sister that the whole affair "is just a determined effort on the part of some very left-wing environmentalists determined to play a political game with scientific facts. I am sure the future will uphold the honour and integrity of Sir Cyril without any question."

12   In effect, the task of deciding exactly what had gone wrong was left to Leslie Hearnshaw, professor of psychology at the University of Liverpool. Hearnshaw, an admirer of Burt's, had given the eulogy at his funeral, as a result of which he had been commissioned by Burt's sister to write a biography. To his growing amazement as he continued his research, Hearnshaw found that Burt had indeed invented data in several of his crucial papers. "As I read Burt's correspondence I was surprised, and shocked, by his contradictions and demonstrable lies—lies which were not benign, but clearly cover-ups," Hearnshaw says. The evidence from Burt's detailed personal diaries showed that he had not carried out the research he claimed to have done. "The verdict must be, therefore, that at any rate in three instances, beyond reasonable doubt, Burt was guilty of deception," his official biographer concluded.

13   Published in 1979, Hearnshaw's study of Burt is a sympathetic and subtly drawn portrait. It shows a man of great gifts, but with a pathological streak in his character that found expression in his jealous treatment of critics, rivals, and even former students. Introverted, private, ambitious, there was a duality in Burt's nature that allowed his talents to be bent to demeaning ends. His twin data are at least partly spurious, Hearnshaw believes, because he could not have added twins to his collection after his retirement in 1950, yet the papers of 1958 and 1966 state this to be the case. Burt may once have worked with the elusive Misses Conway and Howard, but not in this period: he had no co-workers and did no research. For the same reason, his paper of 1969 purporting to document a decline in educational standards over the period 1914 to 1965 must also be fictitious, at least in part. The third case of proven falsification, in Hearnshaw's view, lies in Burt's claim to have invented the technique of factor analysis. Although Kamin suspects that possibly everything Burt did was fraudulent, right from his first research paper in 1909, Hearnshaw believes that the earliest work there is any reason to doubt dates from 1943. "From 1943 onwards Burt's research reports must be regarded with suspicion," he concludes.

14   "The gifts which made Burt an effective applied psychologist," observes Hearnshaw, ". . . militated against his scientific work. Neither by temperament nor by training was he a scientist. He was overconfident, too much in a hurry, too eager for final results, too ready to adjust and paper over, to be a good scientist. His work often had the appearance of science, but not always the substance." How could a man who had only the appearance of being a scientist rise to the height of his academic profession, to the senior chair of psychology in Britain? If science is a self-policing, self-correcting community of scholars, always checking one another's work with rigorous and impartial skepticism, how could Burt get so far and stay undetected for so long?

15   If Burt's fraud is taken as starting in 1943, he remained undetected for thirty-one years, until Kamin's book of 1974. For psychology as a discipline, the point is not so much that the fraud itself passed unnoticed, but that the glaring procedural and statistical errors—there for whatever reason—were not picked up earlier. During the sixteen years that Burt was editor of the *British Journal of Statistical Psychology*, numerous articles signed by pseudonyms (such as Conway) appeared and in unmistakably Burtian style heaped praise on Burt and criticism on his opponents. At least from 1969 onward, his data occupied a central position in controversy, in a subject that is presumably no less rigorous than other disciplines. Why did journal editors and referees not require that

he report his results in scientific form? Why did scholars reading his papers not spot the flaws? . . .

16   The most plausible answer . . . is that many scientific communities do not behave in the way they are supposed to. Science is not self-policing. Scholars do not always read the scientific literature carefully. Science is not a perfectly objective process. Dogma and prejudice, when suitably garbed, creep into science just as easily as into any other human enterprise, and maybe more easily since their entry is unexpected. Burt, with the mere appearance of being a scientist, worked his way to the top of the academic ladder, to a position of power and influence in both science and the world beyond. He used the scientific method as a purely rhetorical tool to force the acceptance of his own dogmatic ideas. Against such weapons, the scientific community that harboured him was defenseless. Against rhetoric and appearance, the scientific method and the scientific ethos proved helpless. Against dogma disguised as science, objectivity failed.

Comprehension Check

Directions: Now answer the following questions.

1. Explain the meaning of the title, "The Failure of Objectivity." _____

   _____

   _____

   _____

2. Is this essay primarily about inductive reasoning or deductive reasoning? Explain.

   _____

   _____

   _____

   _____

3. Which of the following are Burt's original ideas on IQ or intelligence? (Select all that apply.)

   a. 11+ exams in England are valid tests for knowing which students are college material.

   b. Intelligence is primarily a fixed, inherited ability.

   c. Twin studies show heredity is more important than environment for IQ.

   d. Special education programs are useless since IQ is set and cannot be changed.

4. The psychologist who finally realized Burt was a fake was

   a. Jensen

   b. Kamin

   c. Herrnstein

   d. Thorndike

5. T/F Cyril Burt faked data, made up statistics, and lied about co-workers.

   a. True

   b. False because _____

6. Why do the authors believe it took so long to uncover Burt's lies?_____

_____

_____

7. Who confirmed Kamin's findings?

    a. Hearnshaw, Burt's biographer

    b. Jensen, a Stanford psychologist

    c. Eysenck, a London IQ expert

    d. Burt's co-workers

8. What was the primary intent of this article?

    a. to dispute the notion of IQ as a fixed trait

    b. to amuse current readers with scientific history

    c. to expose scientific deceit

    d. to narrate a story about Cyril Burt

9. What is the 11+ exam?

    a. eleven or more questions that can reliably predict IQ

    b. an American test given to eleventh graders to determine college entrance

    c. a difficult exam that gives data about eleven aspects of IQ

    d. a test of eleven-year-olds that determines their future education

10. T/F Ideas about IQ or intelligence are generally well accepted and well-known.

    a. True

    b. False because _____

Vocabulary Check

Directions: Define the following underlined words from the essay.

1. Burt's <u>urbane</u> manner (paragraph 1)_____

_____

2. Burt's vast <u>erudition</u> (paragraph 1) _____

_____

3. gift of <u>lucid</u> exposition (paragraph 2) _____

_____

4. his skills of <u>rhetoric</u> (paragraph 3) _____

_____

5. the <u>crux</u> of the new system (paragraph 4)_____

_____

6. published an article <u>purporting</u> to document a decline (paragraph 6) _____

_____

7. programs of <u>compensatory</u> education (paragraph 7) _____

_____

8. his <u>oeuvre</u> crumbled only after his death (paragraph 8)_____

_____

9. the <u>edifice</u> was a mere facade of scholarship (paragraph 8) _____

_____

10. lies which were not <u>benign</u> (paragraph 12)_____

_____

Record the results of the comprehension and vocabulary checks on the Student Record Chart in the Appendix.

Logical Fallacies

Of course, we can make mistakes in our reasoning. Sometimes we make statements that draw the wrong conclusions. There are called **logical fallacies.** Here are some of the more common fallacies that you should avoid making and that you should look for when you are reading:

1. *Either-or thinking* or *oversimplification* occurs when a simplistic answer is given to a large problem: "You want to get rid of poverty? Just make everyone get a job!" Either-or thinking is also oversimplifying issues: "Let's either get rid of all the nuclear weapons in the world, or learn to live with the bomb." Such thinking ignores or covers up other possible answers to a problem.

2. *Stereotyping* ignores individuality. There are stereotypes about political parties (Conservatives are pro-rich people; New Democrats are pro-poor people), stereotypes about ethnic groups (an Irish temper), stereotypes about races (better athletes, good at math), and so on. Stereotyping disallows looking at people, groups, or ideas on individual merit.

3. *Attacking a person's character* (the Latin term is *ad hominem*) to discredit someone's views is also a faulty way to reason: "Sure, Premier Walker favours taxes on softwood lumber. Why shouldn't he? He's in cahoots with the President of the U.S."

4. *Non sequiturs* (just a fancy Latin name for "it does not follow") occur when a logical reason is not provided for the argument being made. It's a contradiction when a person says, "Keanu Reeves would make a good cop; his action movies show you how tough he'd be on the beat." The two assertions don't logically follow, since one has nothing to do with the other.

5. *Arguments because of doubtful sources* occur when an unknown source or a source lacking authority is cited: "The government doesn't want us to know about UFOs, but the *National Enquirer* has been providing a lot of evidence that proves contrary." While it might be true that the government is hiding something, the *National Enquirer*'s reputation for sensationalism does not make it a good source to use as a convincing argument. Also, be cautious when you read that a story comes from an unnamed "high-level official."

6. *Begging the question* occurs when something that has already been proven as a truth is used to argue a point. Arguing that drunken drivers are a menace is begging the question, since it has already been proven that they are.

7. *Irrational appeal* occurs when appeals to our emotions, to our religious faith, or to authority are made rather than appeals or reasons based on logic. "Of course you'll vote Liberal; our family always has." "I'll get even. The Bible says 'an eye for an eye.' " "My country, right or wrong."

8. *Mistaking the reason for an occurrence* happens when we fail to see that there may be other causes or we are misled. "John is a naturally brilliant student." (Is John brilliant, or does he do well in school because his parents make him study more than others? Maybe he's trying to impress a girl in his class.) "Karla is absent from class again. She must not be a serious student." (Maybe Karla has a health problem, or a small child to look after, or lacks transportation to campus on certain days.)

If you have already read Chapter Three, you might want to review Practice D-3. If you haven't read that part of the book yet, you may want to read it now and compare these examples with the ones in Practice D-3. That practice is based on a chapter from a textbook that deals with logical fallacies.

There are many kinds of faulty reasoning, but the ones described in this chapter are some of the more common ones you should begin to look for and avoid using when you draw conclusions or make inferences.

PRACTICE C-4: Identifying Logical Fallacies

Directions: Read the following dialogues and determine which of the following logical fallacies or errors in reasoning appear in the argument. There may be more than one type in a dialogue.

a. either-or thinking
   (oversimplification)
b. stereotyping
c. attacking character
d. non sequitur
   (contradiction)
e. doubtful sources
f. begging the question
g. irrational appeal

1. SAM: There's only one real aim of education—to learn all you can while going to school.

   GEORGE: Nonsense. Today, the only real reason to go to college is to get the skills necessary for a good job.

   Error in reasoning: _____

   Explain: _____

   _____

   _____

   _____

2. HARRY: George is forming an organization to protest the dumping of toxic waste near the bird and wildlife sanctuary. He really seems concerned about this. Quite a few people I know are joining with him. I think I will, too.

   SALLY: Don't be a sucker: George is just doing it to bring attention to himself. He plans to run for president of the student body next term and wants to look good. Anyway, I dated him once and he came on too strong for me.

Error in reasoning: _____

Explain: _____

_____

_____

_____

3. KIP: You going to vote for Sally? She'd make a good school representative on the board of education. She gets As in all her classes.

PIP: You kidding? What does she know about politics? Anyway, a female's place is in the home, not running for office.

Error in reasoning: _____

Explain: _____

_____

_____

_____

4. DALE: Did you hear that Sue is moving to the East Coast? She's convinced a major earthquake is going to hit us any day now.

FRED: She may be right. Have you been reading that series on natural disasters in the local newspaper? They predict an 8.8 earthquake will occur here in the next two years. The Maritimes are a lot safer, that's for sure.

Error in reasoning: _____

Explain: _____

_____

_____

_____

5. RAUL: Did you read about the junior high kid who stabbed and killed his friend after they watched the movie *Friday the 13th* on TV?

PAM: Isn't that terrible? Maybe now they'll stop showing that worthless junk on television. Everybody knows what a big influence TV viewing has on kids.

RAUL: But how will this incident change anything?

PAM: Now there's proof of the harm.

Error in reasoning: _____

Explain: _____

_____

_____

_____

PRACTICE C-5: Quiz on Intent, Attitude, Bias, and Inference

Directions: As you read the following selection, look for the author's intent, attitude, bias, and inferences.

BIG WHITE

SKIP ROZIN

1   A strange calm settled over me as I stood before the large white vending machine and dropped a quarter into the appropriate slot. I listened as the coin clunked into register. Then I pressed the button marked "Hot Chocolate." From deep inside a paper cup slid down a chute, crackling into place on a small metal rack. Through an unseen tube poured coffee, black as night and smoking hot.

2   I even smiled as I moved to my customary place at the last table, sat down, and gazed across to the white machine, large and clean and defiant. Not since it had been moved in between the candy machine and the sandwich machine had I known peace. Every morning for two weeks I had selected a beverage, and each time the machine dispensed something different. When I pushed the button for hot chocolate, black coffee came out. When I pushed the button for tea with sugar, coffee with half and half came out. So the cup of coffee before me was no surprise. It was but one final test; my plan had already been laid.

3   Later in the day, after everyone else had left the building, I returned to the snack bar, a yellow legal pad in my hand and a fistful of change in my pocket. I approached the machine and, taking each button in order, began feeding in quarters. After the first quarter I pressed the button labeled "Black Coffee." Tea with sugar came out, and I recorded that on the first line of my pad. I dropped in a second quarter and pressed the button for coffee with sugar. Plain tea came out, and I wrote that down.

4   I pressed all nine of the buttons, noting what came out. Then I placed each cup on the table behind me. When I had gone through them all, I repeated the process, and was delighted to find the machine dispensing the same drinks as before.

5   None was what I had ordered, but each error was consistent with my list.

6   I was thrilled. To celebrate, I decided to purchase a fresh cup of chocolate.

7   Dropping in two dimes and a nickel and consulting my pad, I pressed the "Coffee with Sugar and Half and Half" button. The machine clicked in response, and a little cup slid down the chute, bouncing as it hit bottom. But that was all. Nothing else happened. No hot chocolate poured into my cup. No black coffee came down. Nothing.

8   I was livid. I forced five nickels into the slot and punched the button for black coffee. A cup dropped into place, but nothing more. I put five more nickels in and pushed another button, and another cup dropped down—empty. I dug into my pocket for more change, but found only three dimes. I forced them in, and got back a stream of hot water and a nickel change. I went berserk.

9   "White devil!" I screamed as I slammed my fists against the machine's clean enamel finish. "You white devil!"

10   I beat on the buttons and rammed the coin-return rod down. I wanted the machine to know what pain was. I slapped at its metal sides and kicked its base with such force that I could almost hear the bone in my foot crack, then wheeled in agony

on my good foot, and with one frantic swing, sent the entire table of coffee-, tea-, and chocolate-filled cups sailing.

11   That was last night. They have cleaned up the snack bar since then, and I have had my foot X-rayed and wrapped in that brown elastic they use for sprains. I am now sitting with my back to the row of vending machines. I know by the steadiness of my hand as I pour homemade hot chocolate from my thermos that no one can sense what I have been through—except, of course, the great white machine over against the wall.

12   Even now, behind me, in the space just below the coin slot, a tiny sign blinks off and on:

13   "Make Another Selection," it taunts. "Make Another Selection."

Directions: Now answer the following questions.

1. What is the author's general intent?

    a. to make us hate vending machines

    b. to share an experience with us

    c. to satirize the machine age

    d. to satirize the power of machines and human reactions

2. What is the author's attitude toward "Big White"?

    a. frustration   **c.** defeat

    b. hate   **d.** all of the above

3. T/F The author seems to be biased toward the vending machine.

4. T/F We can infer from paragraph 2 that the author has had trouble with "Big White" before.

5. T/F We can infer from paragraph 4 that the author thinks he has outfoxed the machine.

6. What type of reasoning does the author use to outfox the machine?

    a. inductive

    b. deductive

7. T/F From paragraph 11, we can infer no one knows the author was responsible for the mess he created the night before.

8. T/F We can infer from the last three paragraphs that the author hates "Big White."

9. T/F We can conclude that the author has given up trying to outwit "Big White."

Hand in the quiz to your instructor.

Name _____ Section _____ Date _____

Application I:
Recognizing Attitude, Bias, and Inference in Other Materials

From a magazine, newspaper, or textbook, choose a selection and come up with your own questions about attitude, bias, and inference (at least one question about each). Bring the selection and questions to class and exchange with a classmate. Each of you should answer the other's questions. Discuss what you learned from each article by using critical reading skills.

D.   Putting It All Together

The word *critical* often carries a connotation of finding fault with something. But as you have seen in this unit, reading critically implies an attempt at objective judging so as to determine both merits and faults. Critical reading is thoughtful reading because it requires that the reader recognize not only what is being said at the literal level but also facts, opinions, attitudes, inferences, and bias. A reader who is not actively involved is not reading critically.

Whether you are aware of it or not, you make critical judgments all the time, from deciding what type of toothpaste to buy to choosing a topic for an English theme. The trick is to always be aware of your critical judgments and to know the reasoning behind your decisions.

Making critical judgments is a two-way street. As a reader you must be aware of the judgments the author is making and you must also be aware of the judgments you make, based on evidence rather than bias. For instance, you may dislike the subject of history so much that you have a bias against anything you read before you even get started. Your mind is already partly closed to the author. On the other hand, you could be biased in favour of what you read and accept what is being said simply because you already agree with the author. True critical reading should leave you a little wiser, a little better informed, and less biased than before—both about the subject and yourself.

Use the following practices to help you develop the critical reading skills taught in this unit.

PRACTICE D-1

Directions: Read the title and the first paragraph of the following essay. Then, in the space provided, write what you think the essay will discuss.

_____

_____

_____

_____

Now, as you read the essay, apply all the reading techniques you have been learning. Then answer the questions that follow.

CONSEQUENCES OF JOB SATISFACTION AND DISSATISFACTION

HARVEY KRAHN AND GRAHAM LOWE

1   "It the job's so bad, why don't you quit?" Many of us may have thought this about an unsatisfying job, but fewer have actually done so. There may be some features of the job-pay, hours, location, friendly workmates—that make it palatable, despite the absence of other work rewards. In addition, unless other jobs are available, most employees simply cannot afford to quit. Even during a period of relatively low unemployment in 2000, the CPRN national survey found 41 percent of Canadian workers agreeing that it would be difficult to find another job as good as their current job. Two-thirds (67%) agreed that it would be difficult to cope financially if they lost their job. Thus, job dissatisfaction will not necessarily translate into quitting behaviour, although there is some research evidence linking the two (McEvoy and Cascio 1985; Akerlof et al. 1988). But dissatisfied workers are more likely to call in sick or come in late (Clegg 1983).

2   Studies have also shown a relationship between job dissatisfaction and overt acts of employee deviance, such as theft of company property, or the use of drugs and alcohol on the job and away from work (Mars 1981; Martin and roman 1996). Dissatisfaction with work is also correlated with the number of complaints and grievances filed in unionized work settings. As for nonunionized workers, surveys have shown that those dissatisfied with their work are more likely to view unions positively and are more likely to join a union, if given the chance.

3   From an employer's perspective, however, the critical issue is whether increases in job satisfaction will boost productivity. If dissatisfaction leads to tardiness, absenteeism, deviance, or quitting, will improvements in the quality of working life lead to a happier and more productive workforce? Although one can find examples of research showing such a relationship, the safest answer to the question would be "don't count on it." Research has consistently shown that the relationship between satisfaction and productivity is very weak, or is only present in some work settings.

4   There are several possible explanations for this. First, productivity is more often a function of technology and workers' skills than of their attitudes. Thus, even if high levels of satisfaction are evident, low skill levels, inadequate on-the-job training, or obsolete technology will limit opportunities for productivity increases. Second, work-group norms and expectations must be taken into consideration. Managers and consultants who have introduced job enrichment programs or high-performance work practices, and have perhaps even found higher levels of satisfaction as a consequence (Berg 1999), have frequently been disappointed when productivity increases did not follow. They failed to realize that workers might view an improved quality of working life as their just reward, or that informal work norms and long-standing patterns of behaviour are difficult to alter (Macarov 1982: 71).

5   Finally, it may be that productivity can be influenced by job satisfaction, but only under certain conditions. Our earlier discussion suggested that workers in low-level jobs might report job satisfaction because they were assessing their work with a limited set of alternatives in mind. Workers in higher-status jobs might, on the other hand, report satisfaction because of tangible work rewards. If so, perhaps productivity

increases due to job satisfaction might only be expected in the latter group. In fact, a review of over 40 studies on this topic supports this hypothesis, demonstrating that the productivity-satisfaction link is strongest among professional, managerial, and supervisory workers (Petty et al. 1984).

Comprehension Check

Directions: Now answer the following questions.

1. What is the thesis of this essay? _____

    _____

2. What is the authors' attitude toward employee job satisfaction?

    a. Canadians are unhappy workers.

    b. Links between employee satisfaction and productivity are tenuous.

    c. Productivity varies depending on the type of job.

    d. None of the above.

3. The primary intent of this essay is to

    a. make employees realize that they are most often unhappy.

    b. demonstrate that employees are fickle and must understand that productivity is essential to successful business.

    c. suggest that blue-collar workers are treated unfairly.

    d. present research that links productivity and employee satisfaction conflicts.

4. What is the authors' bias in this essay? _____

    _____

    _____

5. Is this essay based primarily on facts or opinion? Explain. _____

    _____

    _____

    _____

6. Does this essay primarily use inductive or deductive reasoning? Explain. _____

    _____

    _____

    _____

7. T/F One inference made by the authors is that most employees can afford to quit their jobs.

    a. True because _____

    b. False because _____

8. T/F One conclusion we can make from paragraph is that Krahn and Lowe believe that employees aren't treated very fairly.

    a. True because _____

    b. False because _____

9. The authors believe that employee satisfaction is

    a. possible.

    b. impossible.

    c. rare.

    d. important.

    e. None of the above.

10. Why do the authors conclude that managers/supervisors are happier than other workers? _____

_____

Vocabulary Check

Directions: Define the following underlined words or phrases from the essay.

    1. . . . pay, hours, location, friendly workmates—that make it <u>palatable</u> . . . (paragraph 1) _____

_____

    2. . . . it would be difficult to <u>cope</u> financially if they lost their jobs. (paragraph 1)

_____

    3. But <u>dissatisfied</u> workers are more likely to call in sick . . . (paragraph 1)

_____

    4. Dissatisfaction with work is also <u>correlated</u> with . . . (paragraph 2) _____

_____

    5. . . . increases in job satisfaction will <u>boost</u> productivity . . . (paragraph 3)

_____

    6. If dissatisfaction leads to <u>tardiness</u> . . . (paragraph 3) _____

_____

    7. First, productivity is more often a <u>function</u> of technology . . . (paragraph 4)

_____

    8. . . . report satisfaction because of <u>tangible</u> work rewards. (paragraph 5)

_____

    9. . . . job satisfaction might only be expected in the <u>latter</u> group. (paragraph 5)

_____

    10. . . . over 40 studies on this topic supports this <u>hypothesis</u>. (paragraph 5)

_____

Record the results of both checks on the Student Record Chart in the Appendix. Make certain you understand any problems you may have had with any of the questions before going on.

The following reading selection can be used to practise increasing your reading speed of comprehension. You may want to look at your Student Record Chart to review your rate and comprehension scores from the last timed readings you did. You may want to just use this one as reading comprehension practice and not time yourself. It's up to you and your instructor.

The next reading practice contains comprehension and vocabulary checks that require using all the skills taught in this and the first unit of the book. Remember that you are competing against yourself. Try to learn from any mistakes you may make so that you can do better on each consecutive practice.

PRACTICE D-2: Timed Reading

Directions: Take about one minute to preview the following 959-word selection and questions. After your preview, time yourself on the reading.

Begin timing: _____

AN IMMIGRANT'S SPLIT PERSONALITY

SUN-KYUNG YI

1   I am Korean-Canadian. But the hyphen often snaps in two obliging me to choose to act as either a Korean or a Canadian, depending on where I am and who I'm with. After 16 years of living in Canada, I discovered that it's very difficult to be both at any given time or place.

2   When I was younger, toying with the idea of entertaining two separate identities was a real treat, like a secret game for which no one knew the rules but me.

3   I was known as Angela to the outside world, and as Sun-Kyung at home. I ate bologna sandwiches in the school lunch room and rice and kimchee for dinner. I chatted about teen idols and giggled with my girlfriends during my classes, and ambitiously practiced piano and studied in the evenings, planning to become a doctor when I grew up. I waved hellos and goodbyes to my teachers, but bowed to my parents' friends visiting our home.

4   I could also look straight in the eyes of my teachers and friends and talk frankly with them instead of staring at my feet with my mouth shut when Koreans talked to me.

5   Going outside the home meant I was able to relax from the constraints of my cultural conditioning, until I walked back in the door and had to return to being an obedient and submissive daughter.

6   The game soon ended when I realized that it had become a way of life, thatt I couldn't change the rules without disappointing my parents and questioning all the cultural implications and consequences that came with being a hyphenated Canadian.

7   Many have tried to convince me that I am a Canadian, like all other immigrants in the country, but those same people also ask me which country I came from with great curiosity, following with questions about the type of food I ate and the language I spoke. It's difficult to feel a sense of belonging and acceptance when you are regarded as "one of them." "Those Koreans, they work hard. . . . You must be fantastic at math and science." (No.) "Do your parents own a corner store?" (No.)

Reprinted by permission of the author. Sun-Kyung Yi is a documentary filmmaker in Toronto.

8   Koreans and Canadians just can't seem to merge into "us" and "we."

9   Some people advised me that I should just take the best of both worlds and disregard the rest. That's ideal, but unrealistic when my old culture demands a complete conformity with very little room to manoeuvre for new and different ideas.

10   After a lifetime of practice, I thought I could change faces and become Korean on demand with grace and perfection. But working with a small Korean company in Toronto proved me wrong. I quickly became estranged from my own people.

11   My parents were ecstatic at the thought of their daughter finally finding her roots and having a working opportunity to speak my native tongue and absorb the culture. For me, it was the most painful and frustrating $2\frac{1}{2}$ months of my life.

12   When the president of the company boasted that he "operated little Korea," he meant it literally. A Canadianized Korean was not tolerated. I looked like a Korean, therefore I had to talk, act, and think like one, too. Being accepted meant a total surrender to ancient codes of behaviour rooted in Confucian thought, while leaving the "Canadian" part of me out in the parking lot with my '86 Buick.

13   In the first few days at work, I was bombarded with inquiries about my marital status. When I told them I was single, they spent the following days trying to match me up with available bachelors in the company and the community.

14   I was expected to accept my inferior position as a woman and had to behave accordingly. It was not a place to practice my feminist views, or be an individual without being condemned. Little Korea is a place for men (who filled all the senior positions) and women don't dare to speak up or disagree with their male counterparts.

15   The president (all employees bow to him and call him Mr. President) asked me to act more like a lady and smile. I was openly scorned by a senior employee because I spoke more fluent English than Korean. The cook in the kitchen shook her head in disbelief upon discovering that my cooking skills were limited to boiling a package of instant noodles. "You want a good husband, learn to cook," she advised me.

16   In less than a week I became an outsider because I refused to conform and blindly nod my head in agreement to what my elders (which happened to be everybody else in the company) said. A month later, I was demoted because "members of the workplace and the Korean community" had complained that I just wasn't "Korean enough," and I had "too much power for a single woman." My father suggested that "when in Rome do as the Romans." But that's exactly what I was doing. I am in Canada so I was freely acting like a Canadian, and it cost me my job.

17   My father also said, "It doesn't matter how Canadian you think you are, just look in the mirror and it'll tell you who you *really* are." But what he didn't realize is that an immigrant has to embrace the new culture to enjoy and benefit from what it has to offer. Of course, I will always be Korean by virtue of my appearance and early conditioning, but I am also happily Canadian and want to take full advantage of all that such citizenship confers.

18   But for now I remain slightly distant from both cultures, accepted fully by neither. The hyphenated Canadian personifies the ideal of multiculturalism, but unless the host culture and the immigrant cultures can find ways to merge their distinct identities, sharing the best of both, this cultural schizophrenia will continue.

Finish timing. Record time here: _____ and use the Timed Readings Conversion Chart in the Appendix to figure your rate: _____ wpm.

Comprehension Check

Directions: Now answer the following questions.

1. What is the thesis of the essay? _____

    _____

2. What is the author's attitude toward being a Korean-Canadian?

    a. She's concerned that people don't respect her.

    b. She thinks it confuses people.

    c. She believes that having two separate identities is fun.

    d. She knows that it's difficult to merge two cultures that are dissimilar.

3. The primary intent of this essay is to

    a. create awareness of cultural issues.

    b. raise concerns about immigration, especially as it relates to children.

    c. call for better understanding in the Korean-Canadian community.

    d. show others the difficulties people of mixed cultures experience within their own communities.

4. Is this essay based primarily on facts or opinions? Explain. _____

    _____

    _____

5. T/F We can infer from what the author says that she does not respect her parents.

    a. True because _____

    b. False because _____

6. Explain the statement that "the hyphen often snaps in two." _____

    _____

    _____

7. Why does the author raise the point that she could look into her teachers' eyes?

    _____

    _____

8. What inference can we draw from the last paragraph? _____

    _____

    _____

9. What are some of the challenges faced by "hyphenated" Canadians? _____

    _____

    _____

10. When the author says, "Koreans and Canadians just cannot seem to merge into 'us' and 'we'," what does she mean? _____

    _____

Vocabulary Check

Directions: Define the underlined words in the following phrases.

1. When I was younger, <u>toying</u> with the idea . . . (paragraph 2) _____

   _____

2. . . . <u>obliging</u> me to choose to act. (paragraph 1) _____

   _____

3. . . . relax from the <u>constraints</u> of my . . . (paragraph 5) _____

   _____

4. . . . obedient and <u>submissive</u> daughter. (paragraph 5) _____

   _____

5. . . . <u>disregard</u> the rest. (paragraph 9) _____

   _____

6. . . . with very little room to <u>manoeuvre</u> . . .(paragraph 9) _____

   _____

7. . . . became <u>estranged</u> from my own people. (paragraph 10) _____

   _____

8. . . . the president of the company <u>boasted</u> . . . (paragraph 12) _____

   _____

9. . . . Korean was not <u>tolerated</u>. (paragraph 12) _____

   _____

10. . . . I was <u>demoted</u> because . . . (paragraph 16) _____

    _____

Record your rate, comprehension, and vocabulary scores on the Student Record Chart in the Appendix. Discuss your results with your instructor.

Questions for Group Discussion

1. Discuss what can be inferred about the author's bias in the article by Yi.
2. Find examples of logical fallacies in other materials. Decide the effect of these fallacies on your understanding of the material.
3. Discuss the conclusion the author intends in either of the articles in "Putting It All Together." Now take another side and support that conclusion.
4. Did anyone's opinions change because of either of the articles? As a group, explain why or why not.

A Final Check

At the beginning of this unit, you looked at a diagram that illustrated the three facets of comprehension. Now you have completed the unit that is represented by the left side of the triangle.

For the diagram below, fill in the blank lines in this section. Working with a partner or small group is acceptable if your instructor sets up groups.

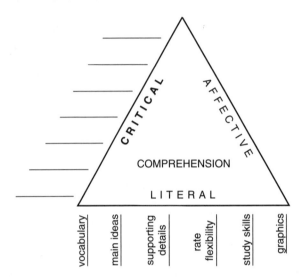

Hints: The first line has to do with information and judgments. The next four lines have to do with the author's worldview and how it influences our reading. The sixth line has to do with reading between the lines. The seventh line deals with what the reader does based on the information given.

When you have finished, check your answers against the triangle at the beginning of Unit Two.

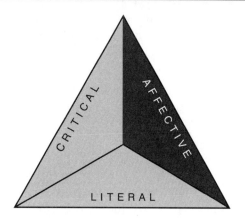

AFFECTIVE COMPREHENSION

What Is Affective Comprehension?

Knut Hamsun wrote that "One must know and recognize not merely the direct but the secret power of the word." This unit is about the "secret power of the word," or affective comprehension.

> Affective comprehension, most simply put, is your reaction to what you read at the literal and critical levels of understanding. It is your intellectual and emotional response to what you read.

Why, for instance, do some people prefer to read factual materials rather than fiction? Why do some people react favourably and others negatively to a novel such as *Moby Dick*? Why do some people read fiction merely for recreation, whereas others find it personally enlightening? These differences are based on people's affective reaction to the type of material that they read.

The purpose of this book is not just to present you with various reading skills. While the development of skills is important, it is just as important that you understand the distinction between the different kinds and levels of reading. As Frank Jennings says in his book *This Is Reading:*

We read to learn. We read to live another way. We read to quench some blind and shocking fire. We read to weigh the worth of what we have done or dare to do. We read to share our awful secrets with someone we know will not refuse us. We read our way into the presence of great wisdom, vast and safe suffering, or into the untidy corners of another kind of life we fear to lead. With the book we can sin at a safe distance. With Maugham's artists in *The Moon and Sixpence,* we can discommit ourselves of family responsibility and burn our substance and our talent in bright colours on a tropical isle.

Unless we react at an affective level, a personal, meaningful level, reading becomes dull and uninteresting. It becomes nothing more than a series of isolated drills where you read and answer questions to plot on a chart.

Once you have mastered the basic reading skills, it is important to move into the world of facts and opinions, ideas, and feelings. As a good reader, you will become your own teacher, using the skills you have learned to rebuild and reorganize your thoughts and beliefs. That can only happen when affective reactions to what you read take place.

As you can see from the diagram below, affective comprehension and its components complete the comprehension triangle you have been building in the previous two units.

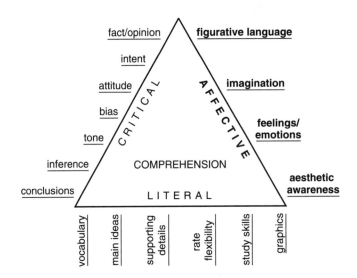

Affective comprehension also has to do with our tastes and appreciation of the skills involved in writing. For instance, some people like to read *Reader's Digest* because it takes a collection of readings from a variety of sources and condenses them for easier and faster reading. What they end up reading is seldom the original work; in fact, the language is frequently changed or written at a lower level. This may be a convenient way to read from many sources, but some readers prefer reading the original works. It's a matter of preference and taste.

Our tastes in reading often change as we ourselves change. For example, as a college student you may be required to read a book that is considered a classic. At the time in your life that you are reading it, you may be bored by the work and wonder what all the praise is about. Years later, a rereading of that book may provide you with the answers to your own questions, answers that you weren't ready for during college. Does your present lack of appreciation for, say, Herman Melville's *Moby Dick* mean you lack taste? Do you have poor affective comprehension? Will you "appreciate" it when you're eighty years old? Why do critics think it's such a great work? Answers to these questions are all part of developing affective comprehension.

Some people try to rely solely on their intellect as a way to see and respond to the world. While reason is important, it is just as important to stay in touch with our feelings; it's what makes us human. When we lose touch with our feelings, we lose a part of our humanity, the part of us that lets us know we're alive. To react affectively is to react openly, to share our feelings with others, and to know that others can, have, and will feel as we do.

What Does This Unit Cover?

Much of our affective reaction has to do with our feelings. Someone once said that our feelings are our sixth sense, the sense that interprets, analyzes, orders, and summarizes the other five senses. Whether or not we feel and appreciate the fear, joy, shock, or passion an author wants us to feel through words depends on our ability to feel them in real life. The inability to react to what we read with appropriate feelings is to miss a large part of what total comprehension is all about.

This unit contains two chapters.

- The first practices in Chapter Seven, through the use of pictures, advertisements, and expository writings, will help you understand your affective reaction to a variety of materials. The second set of practices develops your ability to see how figurative language is used to create images and analogies as used in poetry. You have already done some drills in figurative language in Unit Two; this chapter will explore your affective reactions to words at the literal, critical, and affective levels of comprehension.

- Chapter Eight provides practices in reading short fiction. Reading fiction requires a different approach from expository writing. Just as painters deal with different colours and designs to give us an image of how they see things, writers similarly paint pictures with words. They stimulate our senses—taste, touch, smell, sight, and sound—with word images. How well a writer can create impressions and emotional reactions for us often depends on his or her use of figurative language.

In this unit it is important to discuss some of the questions in class. Only through interacting with others, sharing your feelings and listening to those of others, will you begin to develop your affective levels of comprehension. Good discussions are frequently frustrating because there often doesn't seem to be a "correct" answer. (It's especially frustrating to instructors who want all questions to have right or wrong answers in order to make grading your responses easier!) But sometimes there are no "right" answers; it's important to listen to others as their sixth sense (feelings) interprets their literal and critical thought processes.

What Should You Know after Completing This Unit?

As in previous units, there are some objectives you should strive to accomplish by the time you finish this unit. You should be able to:

1. Recognize how writers use figurative language to stimulate our senses.

2. Recognize images in both fictional and factual writings.

3. Write a definition of affective comprehension.

4. See how closely literal, critical, and affective levels of comprehension are tied together.

5. Approach the various types of literature with an awareness of what is expected of you as a reader in each case.

6. Know all three facets of the comprehension triangle.

If you have personal objectives of your own, write them below and share them with your instructor.

Personal reading objectives for Unit Three:

_____

_____

_____

_____

_____

CHAPTER SEVEN

Developing Affective Awareness

A.   Responding Affectively

One important element involved in developing reading comprehension is your affective or emotional involvement with what you read. Some things, such as scientific and historical facts, may be presented and received with little or no affective reaction. But the whole range of human emotions is also communicated through the written word. The concern of this chapter is your affective reaction to what you read.

- There are both negative and positive affective reactions. You may begin reading a poem, story, or essay with a positive attitude, only to discover that what you are reading isn't really interesting or moving or agreeable to you. This legitimate type of negative response comes about because of the literature itself, not because of a prereading judgment on your part. It is also possible to approach something you read with a preconceived bias, or to let your emotional reaction to what you read warp your critical judgment. Only when your affective reaction is based on critical evaluation and judgment is it a valid reaction.

- Everyone reacts affectively. The idea is to develop your awareness of why your affective reaction is what it is, to investigate the reasons behind your emotional and intellectual responses. For instance, many readers lack interest in fiction and its literary effects and values. They just want the facts, the quick bottom line. They think that reading fictional literature is useless and unproductive, perhaps even slightly immoral. Many people think that reading literature is too pleasure-oriented, too elitist, or only for a select few oddballs. Some even feel that because literature is "made-up," it is not related to real life; it's untrue, humourless, and boring. These are all affective reactions, but they all are based on an unaware, undeveloped sense of aesthetics and reflect poor affective understanding. If nothing else, literature is a reflection of life, and because of the affective involvement necessary for reading fiction, it often teach us more about ourselves and others than factual writings.

The point of this chapter is to help you open up to affective communication. Practices include reacting to pictures as well as to words in order to help you understand what affective comprehension is, give you more ways to develop your affective reactions, and expose you to a variety of affective experiences.

Reading and Reacting to Advertisements

You are surrounded by advertisements—on television, in magazines and newspapers, and on the radio. These ads influence us in both subtle and not-so-subtle ways. If you see twenty ads a day that encourage you to value new cars as a path to a better life, you are prone to think you need a new or different car.

We often don't think of "reading" ads, yet this is certainly one of the most common reading tasks people do. Learning how to read ads is the subject of a full course, but this section will show you how two strategies can help you become more effective and affective readers of advertisements.

- One way advertisements and pictures work is by leading you to *evaluations*, or examinations and judgments. You evaluate when you decide one course is better than another, when you choose one brand of pizza over another, or when you decide how to spend your free time. Evaluations are a part of your everyday life, but they can also be a problem when you make evaluations without thinking, being aware of, or analyzing them. Advertisements may lead you to these unconscious evaluations by playing on your feelings. You may not think you're paying any attention to the advertisements or you may ignore the effect they have on you—but that doesn't undo their impact on you. You can learn to examine ads for evaluations and then decide whether you agree with that evaluation. What words will help you examine or judge the effects of an ad? If the ad talks about being happy, for example, what sort of evaluation of happiness are you getting? What does the ad imply will make you happy?

• A second way advertisements work is through their *use of language.* Ads tend to use few words, and each word usually has multiple *connotations,* or meanings that are associated with or underlie the dictionary definitions or *denotations.* Words such as *pleasure* or *good times* carry many connotations for most of us. You probably get a feeling of positive emotions when these words appear. If you see a female in a picture and one person refers to her as a "girl" while the other person refers to her as a "lady," what are the different connotations you would get from these words? One has the connotation of youth or inexperience, and the other connotes an older woman of a certain refinement.

Do the first two practices to increase your awareness of how ads function and how you "read" them. The other practice (A3) helps you develop affective reactions to a modern fable.

PRACTICE A-1: An Ad

Directions: Answer the following questions about the advertisement on page 284 for Newfoundland and Labrador that shows the coastline.

1. In the ad, the picture carries much of the message. Jot down a few words that express your first evaluation of the picture of the coastline and lighthouse.

   _____

   _____

2. What do you assume is the intended audience for this ad (gender, age, other)? Why do you make this assumption? _____

   _____

   _____

3. The text "The yawn and stretch of a new day" uses figurative language. Explain.

   _____

   _____

4. What does the text imply about Newfoundland and Labrador? What is the ad motivating the reader to do? _____

   _____

   _____

Reprinted by permission of the Newfoundland and Labrador Department of Tourism.

5. What besides promoting Newfoundland and Labrador is the ad "selling"?

_____

_____

6. After examining the entire ad more carefully, now what is your affective reaction
to the ad? _____

_____

_____

PRACTICE A-2: Another Ad

Directions: Look at the ad for BoxLot reproduced on page 286. Then answer the following questions.

1. Jot down a few words that express your first reaction to the ad. _____

_____

_____

2. How do you evaluate the woman in the ad from the bicycle she has bought and
the clothes she is wearing? _____

_____

_____

_____

3. Who is the ad directed to? Explain your evaluation of audience here. _____

_____

_____

_____

4. The text "Now, my life is complete" equates a "complete life" with what? Explain.

_____

_____

_____

5. What are the connotations you associate with the first line of text: "What would it
take to make you happy?" How would you answer that question? _____

_____

_____

_____

6. What is the intent of this ad? _____

_____

_____

7. How does the text "Finders. Keepers." play on familiar refrains? What is the effect
of the period between the two words? _____

_____

_____

_____

8. After examining the ad carefully, what is your reaction to the ad now?

_____

_____

PRACTICE A-3: A Modern Fable

Directions: Read the following fable and then answer the questions that follow.

THE PRINCESS AND THE TIN BOX

JAMES THURBER

1   Once upon a time, in a far country, there lived a king whose daughter was the prettiest princess in the world. Her eyes were like the cornflower, her hair was sweeter than the hyacinth, and her throat made the swan look dusty.

2   From the time she was a year old, the princess had been showered with presents. Her nursery looked like Cartier's window. Her toys were all made of gold or platinum or diamonds or emeralds. She was not permitted to have wooden blocks or china dolls or rubber dogs or linen books, because such materials were considered cheap for the daughter of a king.

3   When she was seven, she was allowed to attend the wedding of her brother and throw real pearls at the bride instead of rice. Only the nightingale, with his lyre of gold, was permitted to sing for the princess. The common blackbird, with his box-wood flute, was kept out of the palace grounds. She walked in silver-and-samite slippers to a sapphire-and-topaz bathroom and slept in an ivory bed inlaid with rubies.

4   On the day the princess was eighteen, the king sent a royal ambassador to the courts of five neighbouring kingdoms to announce that he would give his daughter's hand in marriage to the prince who brought her the gift she liked the most.

5   The first prince to arrive at the palace rode a swift white stallion and laid at the feet of the princess an enormous apple made of solid gold which he had taken from a dragon who had guarded it for a thousand years. It was placed on a long ebony table set up to hold the gifts of the princess's suitors. The second prince, who came on a gray charger, brought her a nightingale made of a thousand diamonds, and it was placed beside the golden apple. The third prince, riding on a black horse, carried a great jewel box made of platinum and sapphires, and it was placed next to the diamond nightingale. The fourth prince, astride a fiery yellow horse, gave the princess a gigantic heart made of rubies and pierced by an emerald arrow. It was placed next to the platinum-and-sapphire jewel box.

6   Now the fifth prince was the strongest and handsomest of all the five suitors, but he was the son of a poor king whose realm had been overrun by mice and locusts and wizards and mining engineers so that there was nothing much of value left in it. He came plodding up to the palace of the princess on a plow horse and he brought her a small tin box filled with mica and feldspar and hornblende which he had picked up on the way.

7   The other princes roared with disdainful laughter when they saw the tawdry gift the fifth prince had brought to the princess. But she examined it with great interest

and squealed with delight, for all her life she had been glutted with precious stones and priceless metals, but she had never seen tin before or mica or feldspar or hornblende. The tin box was placed next to the ruby heart pierced with an emerald arrow.

8   "Now," the king said to his daughter, "you must select the gift you like best and marry the prince that brought it."

9   The princess smiled and walked up to the table and picked up the present she liked the most. It was the platinum-and-sapphire jewel box, the gift of the third prince.

10   "The way I figure it," she said, "is this. It is a very large and expensive box, and when I am married, I will meet many admirers who will give me precious gems with which to fill it to the top. Therefore, it is the most valuable of all the gifts my suitors have brought me and I like it the best."

11   The princess married the third prince that very day in the midst of great merriment and high revelry. More than a hundred thousand pearls were thrown at her and she loved it.

12   *Moral: All those who thought the princess was going to select the tin box filled with worthless stones instead of one of the other gifts will kindly stay after class and write one hundred times on the blackboard "I would rather have a hunk of aluminum silicate than a diamond necklace."*

Directions: Now answer the following questions.

1. Which prince did you think the princess would choose? _____

   Why?_____

   _____

   _____

   _____

   _____

2. Why is it important to the story that the poorest prince be described last?

   _____

   _____

   _____

   _____

3. Much of the humour in this piece comes from the author's use of incongruity, things that don't fit or are illogical, such as the language the princess uses compared with the fairy-tale setting. What are some other incongruous aspects of the story, in language use or otherwise? _____

   _____

   _____

   _____

   _____

4. Satire is used to poke fun at things. Here the author pokes fun at our human frailties. Is he satirizing the princess, the reader, or both? Explain. _____

   _____

   _____

   _____

5. If you were the princess, which prince would you have selected and why?

_____

_____

_____

_____

6. What does the moral at the end of the tale imply? _____

_____

_____

_____

_____

B.   Recognizing Images and Analogies in Affective Language

In literature, **imagery** is a term used to refer to the use of words to compare ideas, things, or feelings with something else. A writer might say, "She looks very unhappy," or "Her face looks like she learned she only has twenty-four hours to live." The first statement is a literal one; the second an _analogy_. The second statement allows us to _imagine_ (from which the term imagery comes) how the person feels rather than just telling us. Because we can imagine what it might feel like to learn we don't have long to live, our feelings are tapped by the author through the analogy.

Imagery is important in fiction and nonfiction. Almost all good writing uses imaginative or figurative language, but it is especially important in writing poetry, short stories, or novels. It often requires that a writer carefully select words that provoke strong connotative feelings in us. In the example above, "only twenty-four hours to live" connotes death within a day's time. In turn, that connotes a negative image, one we are supposed to feel.

To see more closely how this works, read the following short poem.

THE DEATH OF THE BALL TURRET GUNNER

RANDALL JARRELL

From my mother's sleep I fell into the State
And I hunched in its belly till my wet fur froze.
Six miles from earth, loosed from its dream of life,
I woke to black flak and the nightmare fighters.
When I died they washed me out of the turret with a hose.

Directions: Now answer the following questions as best you can.

1. Write the denotative and connotative meanings in the words from the poem in the spaces provided.

	Denotation	**Connotation**
a. mother	_____	_____
b. sleep	_____	_____
c. State	_____	_____
d. fur	_____	_____

2. What is the analogy being drawn between "my mother's sleep" and waking to the "black flak and the nightmare fighters"? _____

_____

_____

_____

3. What images are created in the following lines from the poem?

   a. "From my mother's sleep I fell into the State" (Why is "State" capitalized?)

   _____

   b. "I hunched in its belly" _____

   _____

   c. "my wet fur froze" _____

   _____

   d. "Six miles from earth" _____

   _____

   e. "washed me out . . . with a hose" _____

   _____

4. What is the tone of the poem? _____

_____

_____

5. What is the author's attitude toward his subject? _____

_____

_____

6. Write a one-sentence literal statement that says what the poem implies.

_____

_____

_____

Let's look at question 6 first. While wording will be different for everyone, the basic idea behind this poem is that "War is hell," or "In war, death is common and indiscriminate," or "Some lives are treated as expendable in war." But rather than say such things at a literal level, the author chooses to make us *feel* the hell of war or the death of innocent people forced into a situation that is not of their choosing. How do we know this?

The author knows that the word *mother,* literally the female parent, generally connotes feelings of love, security, warmth, and home life. *Sleep* connotes quiet peacefulness, especially when the author says "my mother's sleep." It's a pleasant image; but it's quickly lost when he falls "into the State." The capital on the word causes us to think about government, an institution that has sent him to war. But the word also can refer to his state of mind, the change from a pleasant, safe home environment to now being at war in the belly of an airplane. It's a rude awakening from "my mother's sleep." It's also a strong analogy the author draws between the safety of home and the "black flak and the nightmare fighters." He has gone from pleasant dreams to nightmares.

Likewise, fur is soft. We use it for warmth and decoration on our clothes. But the use of the word *fur* could also remind us of the animals from which we get fur. Is the author implying through this image that man becomes animal-like by going to war? There's irony in this image. The image of "my wet fur froze" implies or suggests he may be sweating from fear. At the literal level, his perspiration freezes at six miles up in a bomber plane.

From the image, "From my mother's sleep I fell into the State," we then feel for this young man who recently was safe at home suddenly finding himself at war in a bomber (State could also refer to the actual plane itself). The image "hunched in its belly" conveys a cramped feeling, like an animal hiding; in this case, he is both the hunter, looking for the enemy, and the hunted, being chased by an enemy. The word "belly" literally refers to the ball turret under the bomber where men operated machine guns to shoot down fighter planes. But "belly" (perhaps his mother's womb) is made analogous to the airplane's "womb." One is safe and one isn't; thus more contrast is made between the safety of home and the dangers of war six miles high.

The image of the last line is ugly. We are left with him dead and the callousness of washing his remains out of the turret in order to make room for the next person. When we put all these things together, we can say that the tone of the poem is ghastly, grim, deadly. The attitude of the author toward war is obviously negative, but more than that, he wants us to see and feel for the innocent victims of the folly of war. By using figurative language, the author creates images that are hard to forget and affect us at a level that a plain, literal statement could never touch.

The following practices will help you see how authors use affective language in a variety of ways.

PRACTICE B-1: Lines from Poetry

Directions: Below are some short passages from poetry and some quotations. Read each one and in the blanks provided write what you think is the *literal* meaning of the passage.

1. "The pen is mightier than the sword." (Edward Bulwer-Lytton) _____

_____

_____

_____

2. "The Lord is my shepherd; I shall not want." (Psalm 23:1) _____

_____

_____

_____

3. "Was this the face that launched a thousand ships,

And burnt the topless towers of Ilium?" (Christopher Marlowe) _____

_____

_____

_____

4. "There is no frigate like a book

To take us lands away." (Emily Dickinson) _____

_____

_____

_____

5. "God's in his heaven—

All's right with the world!" (Robert Browning)_____

_____

_____

_____

6. "A little learning is a dangerous thing." (Alexander Pope) _____

_____

_____

_____

7. "But love is blind." (William Shakespeare) _____

_____

_____

_____

PRACTICE B-2: Images in a Poem

Directions: This short poem, written by Maureen Hynes, was published in her collection of poetry entitled *Harm's Way*. It has as its theme tulips, but as you read the poem, see if you determine any other themes that the poet raises.

SIX TULIPS

MAUREEN HYNES

Six tulips, seven kisses; nine days
they've lasted. A yellow flame at the core
of each red star brightened in my living room
as the first days collected; the petals
5 softened wider, lacking an embrace

to hold them still, fix
them into this room. The air
has bruised the petals a slow purple
at their edges. This affliction called time,
10 I complain to them.
Nine days' absence
and I am searching for the messages
written with this reaching
and shrivelling: all these curled petals,
15 deeply red, scattered around the glass of water,
and six green stalks, ready as pencils
to mark this paper
with their crow-black pollen.

Reprinted by permission of Brick Books and the author.

1. List all the colours the poet uses in her poem. _____
_____
_____

2. What is happening to the tulips as the poem progresses? _____
_____
_____

3. What other themes does the author touch on in this short poem? _____
_____
_____

4. Explain your reaction to the poet's description of the tulips. _____
_____
_____

5. Why do you think she says that the tulips "softened wider, lacking an embrace / to hold them still"? What do you usually think of when you hear the word "embraced?" _____
_____
_____

6. What is the significance of the tulip stalks being used to mark the paper?
_____
_____

7. What emotion do you think the narrator of the poem is feeling? Explain.
_____
_____

The next poem you will read is by Dionne Brand. First, read about Dionne Brand's life and accomplishments. Then see what she has to say about poetry before you read one of her poems. A way to find current information, quotations or pictures of this author is to use the World Wide Web. Using a search engine such as go2net.com or Google, type the author's name under Search.

INTRODUCING DIONNE BRAND

Dionne Brand is a poet, novelist, filmmaker, and essayist. She has been nominated for many literary awards, including the Governor General's Award and the Trillium Award. Her poetry publications include *Chronicles of the Hostile Sun, No Language is Neutral,* and *Land to Light On.* At the age of seventeen, Brand moved to Canada from Trinidad. Early on in her career she was heavily involved in Black Power movements and was a member of the Communist party. Now, much of her activism is channelled through her writing. Indeed, her writing is political: many recurring themes in her work deal with issues of oppression, particularly as they relate to race and sexuality. "She has insisted that poetry is dependent on politics-it must be 'relevant, charged, politically conscious, memorable' " (quoted in *Canadian Contemporary Biographies*).

In an article in *The Globe and Mail,* Brand had this to say about her writing:

> If you live your life in your mind, and that's what you do as a writer, it's your job. I don't want to glorify writing by saying it's a calling, and by now I've been doing it so long that I don't know the distinction. It's certainly a need with me—I have to do it. I write in all kinds of shapes, prose as well as poetry; for me, it's what I have to do.

An excerpt from Brand's poem "Through My Imperfect Youth and Life and Way," from her collection, *Land to Light On,* appears in the following practice. Don't be afraid to try your own "brave interpretation" after reading it aloud two or three times.

PRACTICE B-3: Intent and Attitude in a Poem

Directions: Read the following poem, looking especially for the author's intent and attitude. As with all poems, this one should be read aloud two or three times before you even try to decipher the meaning.

THROUGH MY IMPERFECT YOUTH AND LIFE AND WAY

DIONNE BRAND

I know you don't like poems, especially mine
and especially since mine never get told when
you need them, and I know that I live some
inner life that thinks it's living outside but
5   isn't and only wakes up when something knocks
too hard and when something is gone as if gazing
up the road I miss the bus and wave a poem at
its shadow. But bus and shadow exist all the same
and I'll send you more poems even if they arrive
10 late. What stops us from meeting at this place
and imagining ourselves big as the world and broad
enough to take it in and grow ancient is fear and
our carelessness, and standing in the thrall
of the wicked place we live in and not seeing

15 a way out all the time and never clearly all at once
and not at the same time and abandoning each other
to chance and small decisions, but if I ever thought
that I could never recover the thought struggling
to live through my imperfect mouth and life and way,
20 if I thought that I could do nothing about the world
then . . . well, and we've hung on to old hurts as if
that was all there was and as if no amount of sadness
would be enough for our old, insistent,
not becoming selves; and as if sadness should not end,
25 so for this I'll send you more poems even if they
only wave and even if I only look up late to see
your shadow rushing by.

From *Land to Light On* by Dionne Brand. Used by permission, McClelland and Stewart, Ltd., *The Canadian Publishers.*

Directions: Now answer these questions.

1. Whom is the speaker addressing in this poem? _____

_____

2. Rather than end sentences with punctuation, Brand uses the co-ordinating con-
junction "and" a lot. What effect does this have on the poem? _____

_____

_____

3. Brand's intent in this poem is to

   a. convince us that poetry is a waste of time.

   b. convince the reader that poetry helps us understand the world.

   c. to get the love of a former lover back.

   d. None of the above.

4. List three images that the poet uses in the poem. _____

_____

_____

5. Explain the meaning and effect of the last three lines of the poem. _____

_____

_____

6. The attitude of the speaker is

   a. happy because _____

   b. angry because _____

   c. sad because _____

   d. none of the above because _____

7. Have you ever persevered with something you loved when others thought it was a
waste of time? _____

_____

_____

PRACTICE B-4: Quick Quiz

Directions: Answer the following questions as thoroughly as you can. There are two parts to the quiz.

Part A

Below are some quotations and short passages from poetry. In the blanks provided, write what you think is the literal meaning of the passage.

1. "... ignorance is bliss." (Thomas Gray) _____

_____

_____

_____

_____

2. "Where liberty dwells, there is my country." (John Milton) _____

_____

_____

_____

_____

3. "The truth is rarely pure, and never simple." (Oscar Wilde)_____

_____

_____

_____

_____

_____

_____

4. "Knowledge comes, but wisdom lingers." (Alfred Lord Tennyson)_____

_____

_____

_____

_____

_____

_____

5. "All the world's a stage." (William Shakespeare) _____

_____

_____

_____

_____

_____

Part B

Define the following terms.

1. imagery _____

_____

2. metaphor _____

_____

3. simile _____

_____

4. figurative language _____

_____

5. "the secret power of the word" _____

_____

6. affective comprehension _____

_____

Hand in the quiz to your instructor.

C. Putting It All Together

The following practices will help you put to use the information from this chapter and all the previous ones. As you work through them, apply all the reading skills you have learned so far.

PRACTICE C-1: An Essay

Directions: Quickly read the title and first paragraph of the following essay, then answer the questions here.

1. What do you think the essay will discuss? _____
   _____
   _____

2. Do you think you will enjoy reading the essay? _____
   Why? _____
   _____
   _____

Now read the essay, applying all the skills you have learned.

THE CASE FOR CURLING UP WITH A BOOK

CAROL SHIELDS

1   Some years ago a Canadian politician, one of our more admirable figures, announced that he was cutting back on his public life because it interfered with his reading. His reading[—]notice the possessive pronoun, like saying his arm or his leg[—] and notice too, the assumption that human beings carry, like a kind of cerebral brief case, this built-in commitment to time and energy[:] their reading.

2   I'm told that people no longer know how to curl up with a book. The body has forgotten how to curl. Either we snack on paperbacks while waiting for the bus or we hunch over our books with a yellow underliner in hand. Or, more and more, we sit before a screen and "interact."

3   Curling up with a book can be accomplished in a variety of ways: in bed for instance, with a towel on a sunlit beach, or from an armchair parked next to a good reading lamp. What it absolutely requires is a block of uninterrupted time, solitary time and our society sometimes looks with pity on the solitary, that woman alone at the movies, that poor man sitting by himself at his restaurant table. Our hearts go out to them, but reading, by definition, can only be done alone. I would like to make the case today for solitary time, for a life with space enough to curl up with a book.

4   Reading, at least since human beings learned to read silently (and what a cognitive shift that was!) requires an extraordinary effort at paying attention, at remaining alert. The object of our attention matters less, in a sense, than the purity of our awareness. As the American writer Sven Birkerts says, it is better, better in terms of touching the self within us, that we move from a state of half-distraction to one of full attention. When we read with attention, an inner circuit of the brain is satisfyingly completed. We feel our perceptions sharpen and acquire edge. Reading, as many of you have discovered, is one of the very few things you can do only by shining your full awareness on the task. We can make love, cook, listen to music, shop for gro-

ceries, add up columns of figures all with our brain, our self that is, divided and distracted. But print on the page demands all of us. It is so complex, its cognitive circuitry so demanding; the black strokes on the white page must be apprehended and translated into ideas, and ideas fitted into patterns, the patterns then shifted and analyzed. The eye travels backward for a moment; this in itself is a technical marvel, rereading a sentence or a paragraph, extracting the sense, the intention, the essence of what is offered.

5   And ironically, this singleness of focus delivers a doubleness of perception. You are invited into a moment sheathed in nothing but itself. Reading a novel, curled up with a novel, you are simultaneously in your arm chair and in, for instance, the garden of Virginia Woolf in the year 1927, or a shabby Manitoba farmhouse conjured by Margaret Laurence, . . . participating fully in another world while remaining conscious of the core of your self, that self that may be hardwired into our bodies or else developed slowly, created over the long distance of our lives.

6   We are connected through our work, through our familial chain and, by way of the Internet, to virtually everyone in the world. So what of the private self which comes tantalizingly alive under the circle of the reading lamp, that self that we only occasionally touch and then with trepidation. We use the expression "being lost in a book," but we are really closer to a state of being found. Curled up with a novel about an East Indian family for instance, we are not so much escaping our own splintered and decentred world as we are enlarging our sense of self, our multiplying possibilities and expanded experience. People are, after all, tragically limited: we can live in only so many places, work at a small number of jobs or professions; we can love only a finite number of people. Reading, and particularly the reading of fiction (perhaps I really do have a sales pitch here) lets us be other, to touch and taste the other, to sense the shock and satisfaction of otherness. A novel lets us be ourselves and yet enter another person's boundaried world, to share in a private gaze between reader and writer. Your reading, and here comes the possessive pronoun again, can be part of your life and there will be times when it may be the best part. . . .

7   [A] written text, as opposed to electronic information, has formal order, tone, voice, irony, persuasion. We can inhabit a book; we can possess it and be possessed by it. The critic and scholar Martha Nussbaum believes that attentive readers of serious fiction cannot help but be compassionate and ethical citizens. The rhythms of prose train the empathetic imagination and the rational emotions. . . .

8   Almost all of [us are] plugged into the electronic world in one way or another, reliant on it for its millions of bytes of information. But a factoid, a nugget of pure information, or even the ever-widening web of information, while enabling us to perform, does relatively little to nourish us. A computer connects facts but cannot reflect upon them. There is no depth, no embeddedness. It is, literally, software, plaintext, language prefabricated and sorted into byte sizes. It does not, in short, aspire; it rarely sings. Enemies of the book want to see information freed from the prison of the printed page, putting faith instead in free floating information and this would be fine if we weren't human beings, historical beings, thinking beings with a hunger for diversion, for narrative, for consolation, for exhortation.

9   We need literature on the page because it allows us to experience more fully, to imagine more deeply, enabling us to live more freely. Reading, [we] are in touch with [our best selves], and I think, too, that reading shortens the distance we must travel to discover that our most private perceptions are, in fact, universally felt. Your reading will intersect with the axis of my reading and of his reading and of her reading. Reading, then, offers us the ultimate website, where attention, awareness, reflection, understanding, clarity, and civility come together in a transformative experience.

Comprehension Check

Directions: Now answer the following questions.

1. Which of the following best states the thesis of this essay?

    a. Reading is good for people.

    b. Reading opens up a world of possibilities.

    c. Reading allows people to experience other cultures.

    d. All of the above

2. The tone of the essay is mostly

    a. humorous   **c.** sarcastic

    b. serious   **d.** angry

3. The author's intent is to _____

    _____

    _____

4. T/F We can infer from the essay that the author reads a lot.

5. What does the author mean when she writes, "Either we snack on paperbacks while waiting for the bus or we hunch over our books with a yellow underliner in hand?" _____

    _____

    _____

6. T/F We can infer that the author thinks people need to travel more to experience other cultures.

7. T/F By sharing her enjoyment of reading, she reveals her bias.

8. According to the author, curling up with a book requires _____

    _____

9. What does the author means when she writes, "this singleness of focus delivers a doubleness of perception"? _____

    _____

10. Based on what the author tells us in this essay, what advice do you think she would give to people who don't enjoy reading? _____

    _____

    _____

Vocabulary Check

Directions: Define the following underlined words or phrases.

1. . . . a kind of <u>cerebral</u> brief case . . . (paragraph 1) _____

    _____

2. . . . is a block of uninterrupted time, <u>solitary</u> time . . . (paragraph 3) _____

    _____

3. . . . (and what a <u>cognitive</u> shift that was!) . . . (paragraph 4) _____

_____

4. You are invited into a moment <u>sheathed</u> in nothing . . . (paragraph 5) _____

_____

5. . . . which comes <u>tantalizingly</u> alive under the circle of the reading lamp (paragraph 6) _____

_____

6. . . . and then with <u>trepidation</u>. (paragraph 6) _____

_____

7. . . . we are not so much escaping our own <u>splintered</u> and <u>decentred</u> world as we are enlarging our sense of self . . . (paragraph 6) _____

_____

8. . . . we can love only a <u>finite</u> number of people. (paragraph 6) _____

_____

9. There is no depth, no <u>embeddedness</u>. (paragraph 8) _____

_____

10. . . . language <u>prefabricated</u> and sorted into <u>byte</u> sizes. (paragraph 8) _____

_____

Record your scores on the Student Record Chart in the Appendix. Make certain you understand any errors before going on to the next drill.

PRACTICE C-2: A Poem

Directions: Read the following short poem. Remember to read the poem out loud two or three times. Then take a moment to think about the poem and your reactions to it before answering the questions that follow it.

This poem, by Mi'kmaq poet Rita Joe, discusses the impact that the construction of buildings has on the land and those people who used to inhabit it.

YOUR BUILDINGS

RITA JOE

Your buildings, tall, alien,
Cover the land;
Unfeeling concrete smothers,
    windows glint
Like water to the sun.
No breezes blow
Through standing trees;
No scent of pine lightens my burden.
I see your buildings rising skyward,
    majestic,
Over the trails where once men walked,
Significant rulers of this land

Who still hold the aboriginal title
In their hearts
By traditions know
Through eons of time.
Relearning our culture is not difficult,
Because those trails I remember
And their meaning I understand.
While skyscrapers hide the heavens,
They can fall.

Reprinted with permission of the author.

1. Explain the line, "No scent of pine lightens my burden." Paraphrase what the line means. _____

_____

_____

2. Why do you think the title of the poem is "Your buildings?" Why not "Our buildings?" _____

_____

_____

3. Throughout the poem, the buildings are described in many ways. In the space below, note the words that are used to describe the buildings. _____

_____

_____

4. What impact do the buildings have on the environment? _____

_____

_____

5. What effect have the buildings had on the men who once walked the land?

_____

_____

6. Do you think that the buildings are a metaphor for something? If yes, explain. If no, why? _____

_____

_____

7. What would you say is the attitude of the narrator toward development?

_____

_____

8. Explain the effect of the last two lines. _____

_____

_____

9. What image from the poem stands out the most in your mind? _____

_____

_____

Discuss these answers in class. There are no right or wrong answers to these, although some may be more thoughtful than others. It's important to see how others responded to these questions. (To tell the truth, your authors feel questions such as the preceding one are more important than trying to answer questions such as "What does this poem mean?")

Now acquaint yourself with the author of the next selection by reading the following introduction to David Adams Richards. A way to find current information, quotations, or pictures of this author is to use the World Wide Web. Using a search engine such as dogpile.com or Google, type the author's name under Search.

INTRODUCING DAVID ADAMS RICHARDS

David Adams Richards is a prolific Maritime writer who, throughout his career, has won numerous literary awards, including the Giller Prize for his latest novel *Mercy Among the Children*. His stories often discuss poverty, murder, alcoholism and violence. Richards assures his readers, though, that his stories are often filled with joy. For his novel *Nights Below Station Street*, William French of *The Globe and Mail* commented, "We watch in awe as [the characters] stumble through their grim lives, struggling for their own kind of dignity and respect, sometimes achieving redemption." This book won the Governor General's award. Adams has also adapted his stories for film. He hopes that by watching the film adaptations of his work, people will be inspired to read his books. When asked in an interview whether he was an interested reader as a child, David Adams Richards said:

> I never read much when I was a young kid. When I was about eight I wondered how anyone could read a book without pictures, and that stuck with me until the time I started reading seriously at about fourteen. After I read *Oliver Twist*, I wanted to be a writer, and that's all there was to it. I never thought of doing anything else.

The following article from *Saturday Night* magazine reveals how David Adams Richards is at ease writing about his personal life to an anonymous reader.

PRACTICE C-3: Exposition

Directions: Quickly survey the following selection, reading the title, the first paragraph, and last paragraph, and the questions. Then time yourself as you read the 4,003-word selection.

Begin timing: _____

BRILLIANT MAN'S WEAKNESS

DAVID ADAMS RICHARDS

1   When I was four, my grandfather, who'd been drunk for days, bought my sister a horse—a bowed, wobbly draft he brought to the front of our bungalow. We were at the door watching as my mother went out to meet him. She was pregnant again, and

Reprinted by permission of Ann McDermaid & Associates Ltd.

an outsider among her in-laws; an outsider in our town of Newcastle, New Brunswick, in which we as a family were also, in a certain way, outsiders.

2   Though we were willing to care for the horse—house it in the garage, feed it beets—my mother broke our hearts by telling him we couldn't accept it. This was quite an insult in front of the men he drank with, who talked him into buying it. So he cursed her in front of those men.

3   We did not get the horse. Nor did we know we were part of a power play Grampie had concocted, silly little dupes for the grown-up world. My mother, putting her foot down on the edge of our dry lot, quashed the grandeur he had tried to obtain by spending my grandmother's money.

4   My grandfather came to our house at breakfast the next day to continue his tirade, and my father, with shaving cream still covering half his face, came out of the bathroom and told him to leave. There was a shoving at the door, but my father, though uniformly a pacifist, was as strong as a bull. So my grandfather left, hat and suit askew, railing abuse at us all.

5   My father didn't drink, for he had seen what it had done to his stepfather—our Grampie. I could see my father shaking as he came inside, in anger and bewilderment. Bewilderment for his uncles, who were numbered among the town drunks. They were men of my blood.

6   Not only was there drinking in our family, we employed drinkers as well, at our theatre. The ones I admired were dutiful-minded; there was something great about their affliction—drawn to our theatre and each other, they had the mark of genuine humanity. They watched Bogie thwack the bad guys, drive a boat blind in fog, grin through his whisky and cigarette smoke.

7   Back in the fifties, when these men were in their twenties, they ran projection machines and took tickets, chewed peppermints to mask the smell of wine, stood waiting for drives home at dark in freezing weather without hats or mitts, more like Bogie than they would ever know. Sooner or later they drifted off or moved away.

8   Drink surrounded me, coaxed me gently with its timeless serenade, told me that it would wait, bide its time, and be there whenever I turned to embrace it.

9   When I was eight years of age my family moved to a section of town called "the Rocks," that overlooked the crystal Miramichi River. It was a harsher and wilder part of town, with families not only blue-collar but desperately poor. Here, on May nights filled with the whiff of snow, prostitutes as young as sixteen would wait for strange foreign sailors, accepting in payment foreign utterances of devotion and a bottle of wine. I passed them lying down on cardboard boxes in the flare of fires as I walked up the small pathway with my little sister. We saw men sitting out on the banks to drink who had, like my great-uncles, been shot up in the first War or been gassed at Ypres. I knew them by name, and was conscious of a certain decayed splendour they had.

10   By twelve I began to hear my name called by those who mocked what they considered, in error, my father's money and my lame left side, lame because of a fall my mother had had when she was seven months' pregnant with me. Because of this I was always something of an outcast. I understood that I was different and I supposed I was alone.

11   All of this was diligent recruitment for the bottle. Yet as a boy I could never picture myself with a drink in my hand. The only thing my father ever requested of me, on one of our trips to Saint John, was for me not to drink. Still, I knew it was near me. Sometimes it came into the house with the cold, off the breath of some playful uncle, and slapped me on the knee and laughed. Or it coursed through the veins of certain bleary-eyed men my father did business with in Saint John. (I accompanied him only so I could go to a restaurant and have an elevator ride.)

12   At first on occasion, and then on a more regular basis, I began to see drink in youngsters I knew. They drank in caves or shacks overlooking the river, their faces drenched white by their breath or the light from weak light bulbs. I knew that soon something would be required of me.

13   The first two people my age I saw drunk were the son of a judge and a boy that judge had put in jail. They offered me a beer. I shook my head no. They mocked me. I went home. Thinking of the reputation it carried within my family, I promised myself I would never drink. I made that promise in October of 1964, when I was fourteen. I began to drink that December, at the time I began to read books. I was given a beer on Christmas Eve. Flushed with lights and joyous celebration, all seemed possible. I was also given a copy of *Oliver Twist* that same Christmas, and my love of books and writing was born.

14   By fifteen I was drinking now and again, a bottle of beer or a quart of wine. Sometimes I bought it myself, staring at the bottle as a foreigner. Often the beer tasted like potato peelings, or the wine was too sweet. We drank in groups on special occasions. After a time there was no need for special occasions—whenever we managed to find something to drink, well, that was special enough.

15   Looking back now, I see I drank with many kids whose families had histories of drink. We were establishing ourselves as the next generation. From the first, I didn't drink naturally—but neither did any of my friends. We came from a hard-drinking river, though, and after a certain period we all drank heavily, continuing until we quit or were killed or found ourselves chronic alcoholics. I was discernibly different from most of my friends in one way. I loved to drink alone. If I were still drinking, I still would.

16   The town library had three floors, and on the top floor was a locked room. It was the French room, with French books, and a friend of mine had obtained a key. No one else ventured up there, and with the door locked it made a comfortable place to while away the afternoons when I was thought to be in school. I had no use for school, but, as I mentioned, I loved books. And many of these French texts had side-by-side English translations. So I drank wine and read François Villon in the old nineteenth-century manse. When the librarian locked the front door and left for home, I would venture into the rooms downstairs and read until well after dark. I also started to write my own sketches there.

17   As my drinking and skipping school became more frequent, I became more of a problem. I rebelled in a violent, almost anarchic way. I came to class late or snuck in a bottle with me. I would fight at the least provocation. Finally I was suspended, then expelled. I was told the only way I'd be allowed back in school would be if I saw a psychiatrist and took the strap. I was in a funny position, forced to see a psychiatrist and take the strap in order to be allowed access to someplace I never wanted to be.

18   However, I did graduate and was accepted by St. Thomas University. There I drank more, and partied harder. It was there that a friend took me aside and cautioned me one afternoon. If I was invited to his parents' house he wanted me sober. It was the first time anyone had ever said anything to me about my drinking, and it provoked me. I did not go to his house or visit him again.

19   During these years a number of friends and acquaintances I had grown up with were killed. Most of them died, in one way or another, because of drink. I wanted to write about all of this, and I started a novel.

20   But my writing seemed like everything else in my life. No one thought me much good. So I quit university and went to Europe. There I drank every day. I got drunk only once, but I came back home with an appreciation for the morning drink.

21   At twenty-one I got married to the girl who had stood beside me during my high-school visits to the psychiatrist. We lived at first in a room in Fredericton, with a hot plate and a single cot. The bathroom was two flights up. We got our own little apartment on King Street some months later, and it was there I wrote what would become my first published novel, *The Coming of Winter*. After that was done, we moved to another apartment, on Saint John Street, where I started my second novel, *Blood Ties*.

22   I was twenty-three, twenty-four years old. I was drinking almost every day and taking downers (which I thought were a great complement to a drink, and had gotten from the second psychiatrist I was asked to see). By now I was aware that I could not stop drinking. This was fine, because I did not want to stop. But it did cause problems. I was a far heavier drinker than most of my friends from university, and certain of them began to shun me. My wife, Peggy, left on two or three occasions. Each time I would straighten out and tell myself, and her, that I would stop drinking.

23   After *Blood Ties* was finished, Peggy and I left for Europe.

24   I felt alienated among the other Canadian artists and writers I met there. I was not the kind of liberal that was in vogue in the seventies; my work seemed to be in direct opposition to the communal spirit of the time, which I felt was bogus. Drink protected me from these ideals I could not take seriously, while hiding my belief in a kind of individual anarchism. It let me pretend to be like others while the whole course of my life cried out for me to be something else. I could hide in the bottle, and there was always another bottle after that.

25   Back in Canada, Peggy decided we must do something about my drinking. So we tried the geographical cure. She picked a spot on the map and we went there, literally to the other side of Canada—Victoria.

26   We rented an apartment and bought a card table from the Salvation Army. I set up my typewriter and went out for a walk. This was the first of many "walks" in which I would disappear from home, sometimes for days—drinking. Every time I told myself that I would have only one drink. But of course that never happened. The first drink led to more and more. I would start for home but never make it. After I'd been on an almost continuous seven-month drunk, we headed back to New Brunswick. I had completed one story in all that time. I believed I was washed up as a writer, and many of my writing friends were available to tell me this was so—because if you make your name young, like Billy the Kid, there is a price on your head.

27   It would take well over three years to write my next book, *Lives of Short Duration*. During this time Peggy and I moved again, to the worst place possible for me—our hometown.

28   The blackouts became regular. Each time I drank there would be hours, even days I could not remember. I would start to work and manage to get three pages done. Then, thinking three pages was a wonderful amount, I would go to the bookshelf where I kept my bottle of rum and have one drink, then two. I would leave the house before Peggy got home from work. The night stretched out before me, and many times the next day.

29   We went back to Europe. For a while Peggy tried to keep up with my drinking. She would sit with me sometimes, and we'd drink through the night. But one night would never do it for me. So Peggy would go to bed, and I would find myself at the bar at nine in the morning drinking beer. Of course, beer was nothing more than piss, so I would drink a few and then buy rum.

30   I decided that a three-day drunk was nothing to be ashamed of. After all, I was a writer—and all the writers whose work I cared for drank. All the writers I knew drank, in fact, and I was younger than most of them by ten or twenty years.

31   At a point in my life when I had begun to drink alone in earnest, Peggy provided me with the twenty questions. Answer three in the affirmative and you are an

alcoholic, she said. I checked yes to nineteen out of twenty. The only one I did not answer yes to was "Does alcohol cause problems between you and fellow workers?" Of course not. I had no fellow workers.

32   Yet now, when I really wanted to stop, when I prayed to be able to drink normally, I could not. Nor could I control anything I did or said once I started drinking. It was a terrible feeling, not knowing what was to happen to me once I went outside. Three-day drunks became three-week drunks, and then three-month drunks.

33   I would return to my wife and my study in tremors, filled with remorse. I would look at my manuscript in progress and realize I hadn't put a word to paper in weeks. I would, as my sister-in-law once told me, stink of booze. I would remember snatches and snippets of conversation, realizing that I had been somewhere, had spoken about something. I would remember railing and ranting at someone—perhaps a friend—and then I would hear that I had threatened someone, or someone had threatened me.

34   I would vow not to drink again.

35   I lay on the couch, holding a Bible in my hand (I'm still not sure why), and drifted in and out of horrors. I almost always saw dragonflies flying about the room. I would hear my name being called, and I would sit up, sweat pouring off me, waiting for an intruder who never came.

36   After a few days, with some proper food and rest, the shaking and the itching would go away. The demons would recede. I would go back to work for a day or two. Then, seeing my chance (an argument with Peg or something else), I would go downtown once more, sure that I would only have a drink or two and be home in time for supper.

37   But from the time I was twenty-three, a drink or two never happened. Worse for me was the fact that certain people believed I wrote terrible things about the Miramichi. The idea many had was that I sent Peg out to work so I could drink and write "dirty books." They were right about one thing—I had earned no money in years.

38   I had descended pretty much into hell. It took a long while to get out, for a writer is a strange beast, and so many of my plans revolved around drinking. Drinking is good for the creative mind, I told myself. Drinking liberates you from the mundane and the pedestrian. Drinking is a brilliant man's weakness. Those who don't drink are uninspired, callow cogs. Better dead than becoming one of those artificial, church-going, gossip-slinging mannequins.

39   Those vague absolutes were hard to get rid of. I wrecked our car and did not rid myself of them. I was thrown in jail and they did not loosen their hold upon me. My friends turned away from me. Still my central idea of drink as romantic and inspirational continued.

40   The greatest fear of all, of course, was failure. I could do nothing else in life but write. How, then, could I face up to failure as a writer? Bad enough to face up to being a failure as a husband or a human being. But as a writer, like poor Scott Fitzgerald, you could still be called a brilliant failure. If I chose to quit drinking, I would have no crutch to lean on when I failed. And by the time I was thirty, everything pointed to my failure.

41   That idea, compounded by the feeling that my drinking friends were the wisest and most brilliant people I knew, put me in a Catch-22. If I quit, what would they say about me? Did I want them to talk about me as a teetotaller? Never. For what had I said about teetotallers myself? Yet weeks would go by and no friend would call. And in my house, bottles were hidden for those occasions when the demons visited.

42   The December I was thirty-one, swollen up to 189 pounds, I borrowed $1,000 from the bank for presents. I did not buy one present. I bought cocaine and rum and beer, and I started to drink and snort coke midway through the month. Christmas had never been a particularly joyous occasion for me. Worse, my new book, *Lives of Short*

Duration, had arrived, and I hated the cover. I was frightened of the pending reviews. I was also bothered by the fact that Peg had bought us skis that year. How could I ski with a bad leg? What would people say when they saw me trying? Better to get drunk and stoned and forget it. Or to go skiing drunk and high on coke. I could always write about it later.

43   Peggy celebrated Christmas alone, went to midnight Mass by herself.

44   On Boxing Day, my rum and cocaine gone, I sat at the kitchen table with a case of beer, nursing a hangover. Everything in our house seemed desolate. Then Trapper, a friend I had not seen in months, came to the door. He sat on one side of the table, Peg on the other. I sat in the middle piling beer into myself, looking at both of them.

45   I had never thought of AA. And when Trapper starter speaking to me about it, I had exactly the same feeling that many others have had—What in hell does this guy know about life compared to me?

46   The thing was, he didn't say he knew more about life than me. He just said: "You're using booze to fight booze. You hit the bottle, it will always hit you back."

47   Then he said he had been sober for three months. Three months was an eternity. I looked at him and almost laughed. I didn't believe him.

48   "How in hell did you stay sober for three months?"

49   "Just come to a meeting," he said.

50   "You want me to go to a meeting?" I asked Peg.

51   "I think you should," she answered.

52   That, too, was surprising. I had thought she would say, no, you're not that bad yet.

53   So I told him I would go—but that I wanted to go there the back way. There must be a route we could take where no one would see me? But what was worse, the meeting was that night. He told me he would come and get me at a quarter to eight.

54   It all seemed too much too soon. For the rest of the day I tried to find some way out. I blamed Peg for getting me into it. But that day I could not get sober and I could not get drunk. I was stuck in no man's land. At quarter to eight Trapper arrived, and I angrily left the house with him.

55   I had passed the building we arrived at 2,000 times without knowing it was an AA hall. But from the first words of the first speaker at my first meeting, I realized that someone else had felt all the things I had, and had done most of them himself, and I felt at home.

56   I went to AA every second day. I did not drink for one whole month—the longest I had been sober since I was fifteen. Then I went to Ontario on a reading tour. In Ottawa I decided to have a glass of wine. Peggy asked me not to. Don't be ridiculous, I told her. I had not had a drink in a month, and one drink would not hurt. I picked up the wine. I looked at it. I closed my eyes as I drank it. It was seven o'clock on January 26. I would not draw a sober breath until April.

57   The demons came back. But for some terrible reason, now they were ten times worse—just as the people at AA had told me they would be. Feeling there was no hope, I decided I would drink until I died. I went for drives dead drunk, closing my eyes for snatches of sleep while doing sixty miles an hour. I would wake up in strange places, drive 100 miles for a drink at a bar where no one knew me. The drunk went on and on and on. It was a deadly drunk in which I tried to kill myself and threatened to kill others. I snuck about town at night, kept myself hidden all day. I drank and did coke with abandon. Finally, I found myself at the hospital door, dropped off by someone I had been drinking with.

58   When they started to admit me, I, ashamed and scared, balked and went home.

59   The house was empty. It was desolate as always. We had not bought a new piece of furniture in years because I drank up almost everything. Peggy was at work, and

the humming of the fridge almost drove me catatonic. So I telephoned Trapper. Once again he came, 220 pounds of muscle and a sweet smile on his face. I remembered how he and I and another friend had gone on week-long benders, how he had arrived in the Gaspé in a hearse, and how I had thrown a knife through the foot of our drinking buddy. I remembered how Trapper, on a binge, had taken a taxi to Newfoundland, how he had knocked a man cold for a drink of wine. He had once been one of the toughest men on the river. That night he sat down and watched me as I paced the floor. I couldn't sleep, couldn't eat, couldn't do anything but shiver, hot and cold, seeing shadowy figures and hearing my name called. The horrors went on and on. I looked and felt like a man on the way to the gallows.

60   "Think you'd like to go to a meeting?" he said.

61   I went back to AA. It was April 2, 1982. I thought people would feel superior to me. But when I walked in, people smiled at me and shook my hand. I hung around. But it wasn't easy. It wasn't easy at all. Sometimes it still isn't. It took months before I felt human, and three years before I was able to complete another book. But since then I have written ten more. Since then, by luck and by God, and though I have been sorely tempted, I have never taken another drink.

Finish timing. Record time here: _____ and use the Timed Readings Conversion Chart in the Appendix to figure your rate: _____ wpm.

Comprehension Check

Directions: Now answer these questions, applying a mixture of literal, critical, and affective comprehension.

1.   What is the significance of the anecdote about the horse that is described in the opening paragraph? _____

_____

_____

2.   Cite three other "scenes" that the author describes in the story. _____

_____

_____

3.   What is the chronological order of the main events in the story? _____

_____

_____

4.   How would you describe Richards' relationship with Trapper? _____

_____

5.   What role does Richards' father play in this story? _____

_____

_____

6.   In several places, Richards uses very specific details to describe an event. List two of them. _____

_____

7. Place a check mark in front of each statement that you believe is an example of figurative language:

_____ **a.** "Drink surrounded me, coaxed me gently with its timeless serenade, told me that it would wait, bide its time, and be there whenever I turned to embrace it."

_____ **b.** "I knew them by name, and was conscious of a certain decayed splendour they had."

_____ **c.** "If I chose to quite drinking, I would have no crutch to lean on when I failed."

_____ **d.** "I almost always saw dragonflies flying about the room."

_____ **e.** "We had not bought a new piece of furniture in years because I drank up almost everything."

8. T/F "You hit the bottle, it will always hit you back" is an example of a metaphor.

9. T/F "I looked and felt like a man on the way to the gallows" is an example of a simile.

10. What is the point of this narrative essay? _____

_____

_____

Vocabulary Check

Directions: Define the following underlined words from the story.

1. . . . <u>quashed</u> the grandeur he had tried to obtain. . . (paragraph 3) _____

_____

2. . . . to continue his <u>tirade</u>. . . (paragraph 4) _____

_____

3. . . . this was <u>diligent</u> recruitment for the bottle. (paragraph 11) _____

_____

4. . . . or found ourselves <u>chronic</u> alcoholics. (paragraph 15) _____

_____

5. . . . almost <u>anarchic</u> way. (paragraph 17) _____

_____

6. I felt <u>alienated</u> among the other Canadian artists. . . (paragraph 24) _____

_____

7. . . . filled with <u>remorse</u>. (paragraph 33) _____

_____

8. Those who don't drink are uninspired, <u>callow</u> cogs. (paragraph 38) _____

_____

9. . . . talk about me as a <u>teetotaller</u>. (paragraph 41) _____

_____

10. . . . the humming of the fridge almost drove me <u>catatonic</u>. (paragraph 59)

Record your scores on the Student Record Chart in the Appendix. If you are in doubt as to why any of your answers are wrong, check with your instructor.

Questions for Group Discussion

1. In the selections in this chapter, a variety of images are presented. Which images are most memorable—and why?

2. Some of these images seem related to male narrators and some to female narrators. Find and discuss one image that could be used for both genders and one image that seems limited to one gender.

3. List one selection from this chapter that had a humorous tone and discuss what elements added to the humour.

4. Which of the selections brought out the strongest emotional reactions? As a group, discuss reasons for these affective reactions.

CHAPTER EIGHT

Reading Affectively Effectively

A.   Reading Short Stories

When you go to a hockey game or some other sports event, you go knowing that there will be traffic problems, parking problems, that you will be surrounded by thousands of people, that you will have to put up with all types of people and noises, and that you will probably sit far from the action. Yet you accept all that in order to become a part of the event itself. When you watch television, you know that you are going to have programs interrupted by commercials, yet in spite of these breaks, you are willing and able to get back into the program after several minutes. When you go to a movie, you are willing to sit in the dark surrounded by three walls and a big screen as light filters through moving film. In each case, you are willing to go along with what is expected of you so that for a time you can get involved in what you are seeing and feeling.

To read imaginative literature (novels, short stories, and poems), you need to be willing to go along with what is expected of you, too. In this case, you are expected to enter the world of the author, who may want you to go back into the past, or forward into the future, or to share the present as the writer sees it. You must be willing to enter the imagination of the writer and attempt to see how he or she sees and feels life. In order to do this, you must understand how to read the form the writer chooses to use. Just as you have learned to identify a thesis in an essay, to identify paragraph forms and structure, to separate fact from opinion, and to recognize how language creates tone and reveals attitude and intent, so, too, you need to understand how to approach the reading of imaginative literature.

The last chapter introduced you to affective language used in essays and poetry. You saw how important it is to read beyond the words and to relate to the "secret power" of language. Here's a short story by Maxine Tynes, "In Service." Read it, then answer the questions that follow. Feel free to reread the passage if you need to in order to answer the questions.

IN SERVICE

MAXINE TYNES

1   In Service. I grew up hearing those words. As a little girl in my mother's kitchen, I would hear those words. In Service.

2   "She went In Service."

3   With little-girl ears where they shouldn't be, bent to lady-talk. That scary, hushed, exciting lady-talk between my mother and women who came to see her. Tea and talk. Lady-talk.

4   In Service. Mama and Miss Riley. Mama and Aunt Lil. Mama and Helen. Helen. The one grown-up person we were allowed to say the name of without a Miss or Aunt in front. Helen. I loved to say her name and feel her velvet hats. Tams. She always chewed Juicy Fruit gum.

5   It was always the same. Talk of dark and mysterious women-things, softly spoken. Lips would burble tea in cups. Eyes would roll slowly or point sharply when certain things were said, names were named. Sometimes talk of Mama's In Service memories; of her grandmother, a ten-year-old girl being sent from the country, from Preston, to be In Service. Talk of Aunt Lil, and, sometimes, with her. Laughing Aunt Lil, with hair like fleeting movie star dreams. Aunt Lil who always included laughing in her lady-talk. And Miss Riley, who never did.

6   These conversations always seemed to carry their own colours. This one-scary, smoky black, light misty grey. Lady-talk. "Children should be seen and not heard." "Keep in a child's place." I was afraid of those hard, red sentences Mama always had ready during lady-talk. I had to go where they couldn't see me. But in a small house, the scary grey black mist of lady-talk can always find you.

7   In Service. Sterling silver, glowing the dark-and-sunlight words to me. Like the lone brass button always at the bottom of Mama's button box, when I would sneak the polish to it, to bring back the shine. The Mysteries of In Service were all confused and glowing with parade dreams and uniforms marching by in a flash of things shiny and formal.

8   "Yes, girl, she went In Service when she was ten."

9   "It was right after I went In Service that Uncle Willy died."

10   "She was In Service for years."

From Maxine Tynes, *Borrowed Beauty*. Reprinted by permission of Maxine Tynes, poet, author, and educator.

11   "She died In Service."

12   My little-girl mind imagined shiny, wonderful things, not clearly defined. Not knees sore from years on hardwood floors. Not hands cracked, dry and painful, calloused and scrubworn. Not early morning walking miles into town to start the day off right with morning labours for some family. Not always going to and coming from the back door. Not "speak when you're spoken to," see and don't see, hear and don't hear, in case you anger them and they let you go. Not eating their leftovers in the kitchen alone. Not one dollar a day for back-breaking floors, walls, dishes, furniture, windows, washing, ironing, sweat-soaked labour. In Service.

13   "She died in service." That describes Helen. I was allowed to say her name. Velvet tams and Juicy Fruit gum every night in Mama's kitchen. When I was little, I was allowed to stand by her and feel her tams. When I got older, she'd be there every night, watching me cry into cold dishwater.

14   And still the tams were there. The ruby, the emerald green, the midnight velvet blue of them glowed richly against the grey-black, soft and wooly head. Sometimes she would reach up, too, to finger that soft glow; almost as if to make sure that lovely part of her was still there. Helen's hands against such splendid velvet were like wounds; flags of the world of drudgery that were her days.

15   Helen was someone's girl, this never married Black lady, already in middle age by the time I was old enough to know her. Somebody's girl. Not in the romantic notion of being somebody's girl (friend). Helen was some white lady's girl; some white family's girl. She came to our house every night as if it was a target; an end point to her day; to sit in our kitchen with a cup of tea; to read the paper. She never took her coat off.

16   The lady-talk would start. Mama and Helen. It was always about Helen's lady-the woman she worked for. "My family." "My Missus."

17   Helen "lived In Service," which added to the mystique of it all. My little-girl mind imagined something with a faint glow. Not a room off the back. Not living away from your family. In a house, a bed that was never yours.

18   Through my window, I could see "Helen's house" not far from my own. On Sunday walks with one or other of my older sisters, seeing "Helen's house" was to see a dream, or at least a story-book page. "Helen's house," huge and golden yellow, with a fence and a yard that held what, in later, grown-up years, I would know as a gazebo. But then, surely, that wonderful little in-the-yard house was where she lived, behind cool, dark green lattice. Helen's house. So different from my own, so squat and brown and hen-like. My house; teeming with the dozen of us. My house, that Helen fled to each night; to maybe, for a little while, be a little of what my mother was, and did and had. Mama, with hands on her own dishes; on her own child.

19   Helen had eyes that were always friendly. I would see them peek behind her tam, even as she sat, and sipped her tea, and waited for it all to happen every night. Waited in the wake of the dark and tiny storm of activity that hummed along after Mama; a whirl-wind of shooing the creeping horde of us; of moving through clouds of flour from baking; of ironing, of putting up late supper for Daddy; of watching and listening for Daddy; and finally settling down to braid my hair and have tea and lady-talk.

20   Sometimes Helen would bring a shopping bag full of clothes with her to show Mama. Clothes-castoff, not new-that her lady had given her. Clothes and hats. Velvet tams. Helen. Mama and Helen and lady-talk.

21   What did a little Black girl know, touching a velvet tam over hooded and frightened eyes? Helen. Perhaps she knew and feared the loneliness of her own life, circled round and round her like an echo; loneliness circled round and worn close, fitting her like the coats and tams from her shopping bag. Perhaps the secret mystery and the

fear should hide deep in her eyes from me; from my little-girl eyes watching Helen bring the secret of In Service each night. This work, this life, this loneliness all too real for her. A dark and female mystery still for me.

22   Helen. Driven like a magnet to somebody else's kitchen; somebody else's child. Helen. With care-worn hands, handing me the future luxury of dreams, and thoughts, and "I remember Helen," and the awful mystery of In Service unravelled now from the whispers of lady-talk, found now in the voice of those words.

23   Looking back, I know she was saving me. They all were. Helen. Mama. Miss Riley. Aunt Lil. My sisters. Known and unknown Black women. Armies of Black women in that sea of domestic service. With unlikely and unowned addresses. Waiting for buses on prestigious street corners. Carrying back bits and remnants of that other world of In Service in shopping bags; and wearing the rest in coats and velvet tams.

---

1. What image does the narrator have of Helen and her work? _____

_____

2. Why are the words "In Service" repeated so often throughout the story?

_____

3. Describe Helen. _____

_____

4. What are the older female relatives saving the narrator from? _____

_____

5. What kind of life do you think Helen has led? _____

_____

At first, the narrator believes that Helen lives a life of luxury and one without the problems that her mother experiences. The fact that the narrator admires the tams that Helen wears gives us an indication of the admiration she has for this woman. As well, the narrator's exclusion from the "lady-talk" makes her all the more curious about Helen.

The narrator repeats the words "In Service" often throughout this essay because she wants to illustrate how perception of an "in service" woman changes as she grows up. At first she thought being "in service" meant a life free of responsibility, and that Helen lived a life of privilege: "The Mysteries of In Service were all confused and glowing with parade dreams and uniforms marching by in a flash of things shiny and formal" (paragraph 7). As time went on, though, the narrator began to see that the life that Helen led was one of isolation and hard work.

Helen is described in a way that makes us feel that the narrator likes her. First, there are the velvet tams. The softness of these tams embodies the character of Helen herself. Like the tams that she wears, her hair is also "soft and wooly." Helen chews Juicy Fruit gum and shares it with the narrator; therefore, the narrator associates her with a sweet odour and kindness. That the narrator can call her by her first name indicates that Helen is less concerned than others about the formality that exists between adults and children. In contrast to the softness of her tams and hair and personality, her hands tell the secret of the hard labour she does day in and day out; they are "wounds; flags of the world of drudgery that were her days." Helen does not have a family, and this is why she stops by to chat with the narrator's Mama every evening.

We sense that she is lonely and isolated from her community because of the time she spends looking after other people's families.

The older women in the story are trying to protect the narrator from knowing the details of what a life of "in service" actually entails. Often these women lived their lives for others: they had no families of their own. By hiding the details of an "in service" life, the older women hope to protect the narrator from the knowledge of their hardships.

The description of Helen leads us to believe that she was a poor woman who longed for a family of her own, but because she had to work for another family, she was unable to have her own family.

Rather than tell us all these things literally, the author has asked us to enter the world of the girl/woman telling the story. If we are alert to the clues the author provides, we read beyond the words and begin to understand things that perhaps even the character telling the story doesn't understand or say directly. We enter the life of a fictional character, but we see reality as we know it must be for some—and sometimes for ourselves.

Now let's say that you have been assigned a short story to read in an English class. You start reading it, but you don't know exactly what you are expected to look for. You feel a bit uncomfortable because you are not used to reading imaginative literature. Here is a set of guidelines you can use with any story or novel to help you get a little more out of your reading.

Literal Questions

1. Who is the main character? What is she or he like?

2. Who are other important persons in the story? What is their relationship to the main character?

3. What is happening?

4. Where and when is everything happening?

Critical Questions

5. What seems to be the point of the story (called the *theme*)? If the author were writing an essay instead of a story, what would the thesis be?

6. How does the title relate to the theme?

7. What events, scenes, and/or characters are used to develop the theme?

Affective Questions

8. Explain your feelings for the characters in the story.

9. What passages seem particularly well-written or effective?

10. Why do you like or dislike the story?

11. What aspects of yourself or others do you see in the story?

These questions are certainly not the only ones you can ask yourself, nor necessarily the best ones. But they give you a starting place, a direction toward understanding what it takes to enter into imaginative literature and get something from it.

The following practices will give you a chance to become more familiar with reading and understanding imaginative literature.

PRACTICE A-1: Images in Fiction

Directions: Figurative language, as you will remember from Chapter Five, is used in an imaginative rather than a literal sense. The forms of figurative language include metaphor, simile, cliché, and hyperbole. Go back to Chapter Five, Section B, if you need to refresh your memory about any of these concepts before you work through the next two exercises.

Read each of the following fictional selections. On the first line that follows each selection, write in the word *figurative* if you think the selection is mostly figurative, or *literal* if you think it is mostly literal. Then, on the second line, write the numbers of all the sentences in the selection that you feel contain figurative language.

1.   (1) Dr. Rankin was a large and rawboned man on whom the newest suit at once appeared outdated, like a suit in a photograph of twenty years ago. (2) This was due to the squareness and flatness of his torso, which might have been put together by a manufacturer of packing cases. (3) His face also had a wooden and a roughly constructed look; his hair was wiglike and resentful of the comb. (4) He had those huge and clumsy hands which can be an asset to a doctor in a small upstate town where people still retain a rural relish for paradox, thinking that the more apelike the paw, the more precise it can be in the delicate business of a tonsillectomy. (From John Collier, "De Mortuis.")

_____

_____

2.   (1) The morning of June 27th was clear and sunny, with the fresh warmth of a full-summer day; the flowers were blossoming profusely and the grass was richly green. (2) The people of the village began to gather in the square, between the post office and the bank, around ten o'clock; in some towns there were so many people that the lottery took two days and had to be started on June 26th, but in this village, where there were only about three hundred people, the whole lottery took less than two hours, so it could begin at ten o'clock in the morning and still be through in time to allow the villagers to get home for noon dinner. (From Shirley Jackson, "The Lottery.")

_____

_____

3.   (1) On the way home, although the stones have cooled, we remain happy and warm. (2) We listen to the creak of the leather harness and the hiss of runners on the snow and begin to think of the potentiality of presents. (3) When we are about a kilometre from home the horse senses his destination and breaks into a trot and then into a confident lope. (4) My brother lets him go and we move across the winter landscape like figures freed from a Christmas card. (5) The snow from the horse's hooves falls about our heads like the whiteness of the stars. (From Alistair MacLeod, "To Every Thing There Is a Season.")

_____

_____

4.   (1) She turned in the seat and looked at Eve so steadily that Eve had to take her eyes from the road for a moment and look back. (2) And what she saw was that

this girl was much more drunk than she sounded. (3) Her dark-brown eyes were glazed but held wide open, rounded with effort, and they had the imploring yet distant expression that drunks' eyes get, a kind of last-ditch insistence on fooling you. (4) Her skin was blotched in some places and ashy in others, her whole face crumpled with the effects of a mighty bingeing. (5) She was a natural brunette—the gold spikes were intentionally and provocatively dark at the roots—and pretty enough, if you disregarded her present dinginess, to make you wonder how she had ever got mixed up with Harold and Harold's crew. (6) Her way of living and the style of the times must have taken fifteen or twenty natural pounds off her—but she wasn't tall and she really wasn't boyish. (7) Her true inclination was to be a cuddly chunky girl, a darling dumpling. (From Alice Munro, "Save the Reaper.")

_____

_____

5.   (1) From the pier it was a short, ten-minute ride east along Pender Street to Chinatown. (2) Their taxi skirted the city's financial district. (3) Its tall stone buildings and the rhythmic flow of streetcars spoke of ordered calm. (4) On the other side of the tram lines that ran between New Westminster and Vancouver, the western architecture suddenly gave way to a dense conglomeration of two- and three-storey brick buildings bedecked with an assortment of awnings. (5) Two tiny alley-ways off Pender, Canton and Shanghai Alleys, both of which had been privately developed, were congested with tall, narrow tenements, dozens of businesses, shops, restaurants, even a public bath and an opera house. (6) May-ying was vaguely reminded of buildings she had seen in Canton. (From Denise Chong, *The Concubine's Children*. Copyright © 1994 by Denise Chong. Reprinted by permission of Penguin Books Canada Limited.)

_____

_____

PRACTICE A-2: Reacting to Fictional Passages

Directions: Following are some short fictional passages containing figurative language. Read each one and answer the questions that follow.

1.   "My grandfather was best with the babies, rubbing his spade beard into their cheeks until they squealed. Bouncing them on his lap." (From Mordecai Richler, "My Father's Life.")

   a. From this description, can you infer whether the narrator likes or dislikes the grandfather? _____

   _____

   b. What feelings do you get from this brief description of the grandfather?

   _____

   c. Why do you feel the way you do? _____

   _____

2.   "The flames, as though they were a kind of wild life, crept as a jaguar creeps on its belly toward a line of birch-like saplings that fledged an outcrop of the pink rock. They flapped at the first of the trees, and the branches grew a brief foliage of

fire. The heart of flame leapt nimbly across the gap between the trees and then went swinging and flaring along the whole row of them." (From William Golding, *Lord of the Flies*.)

   a. Why is the fire like a wild animal? _____

_____

_____

   b. List four descriptive words or phrases the author uses to give the life to the fire.

_____

_____

3. "I bathe her when she wakes. Her body is white, soft, and withered. I remember how, in the changing-huts, she would bend over as she slipped out of her bathing suit. Her body was young. Now I see her skeleton through her skin." (From Michael Ignatieff, "Deficits.")

   a. From the description, can you infer whether the narrator likes or dislikes the woman? _____

_____

   b. What feelings do you get from the description of the woman? _____

_____

   c. List at least three phrases that cause you to feel the way you do. _____

_____

_____

4. "Wedge Island is a defeated drumlin, a dagger-shaped remnant of land stretching a good kilometre out to sea. Smashed lobster traps, shreds of polypropylene rope as well as bones of birds and beasts litter the rocks near the shore." (From Lesley Choyce, "Thin Edge of the Wedge (Island).")

   a. Is the overall mood of this passage pleasing or frightening? _____

_____

   b. Why? _____

_____

   c. What is meant by "a dagger-shaped remnant"? _____

_____

   d. How does the destruction on the island make you feel about it? _____

_____

_____

5. "The fresh-plowed earth heaved, the wild plum buds puffed and broke. Springs and streams leapt up singing. He could hear the distant roar of the river swelling in the gorge. The clear blue skies stretched out above him like the skin of a puffed fiesta balloon. The whole earth strained and stretched with new life." (From Frank Waters, *The Man Who Killed the Deer*.)

   a. Is the overall mood of this passage pleasing or frightening? _____

_____

b. Why? _____

c. What time of year would you infer is being described? _____

_____

d. Why? _____

_____

_____

PRACTICE A-3

Directions: As a way to direct your thinking as you read the following short story, answer the questions that appear at various points. Some questions require predicting or guessing what you think will happen. Write your answers on a separate sheet to be turned in to your instructor.

1. Read the title of the next story. What do you think this story will be about? What will happen? Why?

THE STORY OF AN HOUR

KATE CHOPIN

1   Knowing that Mrs. Mallard was afflicted with a heart trouble, great care was taken to break to her as gently as possible the news of her husband's death.

2   It was her sister Josephine who told her, in broken sentences; veiled hints that revealed in half concealing. Her husband's friend Richards was there, too, near her. It was he who had been in the newspaper office when intelligence of the railroad disaster was received, with Brently Mallard's name leading the list of "killed." He had only taken the time to assure himself of its truth by a second telegram, and had hastened to forestall any less careful, less tender friend in bearing the sad message.

3   She did not hear the story as many women have heard the same, with a paralyzed inability to accept its significance. She wept at once, with sudden, wild abandonment, in her sister's arms. When the storm of grief had spent itself she went away to her room alone. She would have no one follow her.

2. Which of your ideas in answer to question 1 can still be correct?

3. Now what do you think will take place? Why?

4   There stood, facing the open window, a comfortable, roomy armchair. Into this she sank, pressed down by a physical exhaustion that haunted her body and seemed to reach into her soul.

5   She could see in the open square before her house the tops of trees that were all aquiver with the new spring life. The delicious breath of rain was in the air. In the street below a peddler was crying his wares. The notes of a distant song which someone was singing reached her faintly, and countless sparrows were twittering in the eaves.

6   There were patches of blue sky showing here and there through the clouds that had met and piled one above the other in the west facing her window.

7   She sat with her head thrown back upon the cushion of the chair, quite motionless, except when a sob came up into her throat and shook her, as a child who has cried itself to sleep continues to sob in its dreams.

8   She was young, with a fair, calm face, whose lines bespoke repression and even a certain strength. But now there was a dull stare in her eyes, whose gaze was fixed away off yonder on one of those patches of blue sky. It was not a glance of reflection, but rather indicated a suspension of intelligent thought.

9   There was something coming to her and she was waiting for it, fearfully. What was it? She did not know; it was too subtle and elusive to name. But she felt it, creeping out of the sky, reaching toward her through the sounds, the scents, the colour that filled the air.

10   Now her bosom rose and feel tumultuously. She was beginning to recognize this thing that was approaching to possess her, and she was striving to beat it back with her will—as powerless as her two white slender hands would have been.

4. Which of your ideas about what will happen are still possible?

5. What new ideas do you have about what will happen now?

11   When she abandoned herself a little whispered word escaped her slightly parted lips. She said it over and over under her breath: "free, free, free?" The vacant stare and the look of terror that had followed it went from her eyes. They stayed keen and bright. Her pulses beat fast, and the coursing blood warmed and relaxed every inch of her body.

12   She did not stop to ask if it were or were not a monstrous joy that held her. A clear and exalted perception enabled her to dismiss the suggestion as trivial.

13   She knew that she would weep again when she saw the kind, tender hands folded in death; the face that had never looked save with love upon her, fixed and gray and dead. But she saw beyond that bitter moment a long procession of years to come that would belong to her absolutely. And she opened and spread her arms out to them in welcome.

14   There would be no one to live for her during those coming years; she would live for herself. There would be no powerful will bending hers in that blind persistence with which men and women believe they have a right to impose a private will upon a fellow-creature. A kind intention or a cruel intention made the act seem no less a crime as she looked upon it in that brief moment of illumination.

15   And yet she had loved him—sometimes. Often she had not. What did it matter! What could love, the unsolved mystery, count for in face of this possession of self-assertion which she suddenly recognized as the strongest impulse of her being!

16   "Free! Body and soul free!" she kept whispering.

6. Were you right? How did you know?

7. Now what will happen?

17   Josephine was kneeling before the closed door with her lips to the keyhole, imploring for admission. "Louise, open the door! I beg; open the door—you will make yourself ill. What are you doing, Louise? For heaven's sake open the door."

18   "Go away. I am not making myself ill." No; she was drinking in a very elixir of life through that open window.

19   Her fancy was running riot along those days ahead of her. Spring days, and summer days, and all sorts of days that would be her own. She breathed a quick prayer that life might be long. It was only yesterday she had thought with a shudder that life might be long.

20   She rose at length and opened the door to her sister's importunities. There was a feverish triumph in her eyes, and she carried herself unwittingly like a goddess of Victory. She clasped her sister's waist, and together they descended the stairs. Richards stood waiting for them at the bottom.

8. How close were your ideas to what happened?

9. What will happen now and why do you think so?

21   Some one was opening the front door with a latchkey. It was Brently Mallard who entered, a little travel-stained, composedly carrying his gripsack and umbrella. He had been far from the scene of the accident, and did not even know there had been one. He stood amazed at Josephine's piercing cry; at Richards' quick motion to screen him from the view of his wife.

22   But Richards was too late.

23   When the doctors came they said she had died of heart disease—of joy that kills.

10. Irony is defined as an inconsistency between what might be expected and what actually occurs. Discuss any irony you see in this story.

Hand your answers in to your instructor.

The next selection is by Joy Kogawa. Start by reading about the author.

INTRODUCING JOY KOGAWA

A respected poet and novelist, Kogawa was born in Vancouver in 1935. During her childhood, she, along with thousands of other Japanese-Canadians, was separated from her family by government officials and exiled into the Canadian wilderness during the Second World War. Years later, Kogawa was instrumental in ensuring financial compensation for those Japanese-Canadians who were dispossessed of their property and victimized by the government. Along with numerous books of poetry, Kogawa has received critical acclaim for two of her novels, *Obasan* and *Itsuka*. *Obasan* is the fictionalization of her own experiences. The *New York Times* book reviewer Edith Milton has praised this novel as a "history of what appears at first only a minor persecution . . . [that] grows into a quietly appalling statement about how much hatred can cost when it is turned into a bureaucratic principle." Indeed, this novel poignantly illustrates the devastating inter-generational effects of such oppression.

When asked how long she's been interested in language, Kogawa had this to say:

As a very young child, we had books—picture books. My mother read me little children's stories. Then when we were in Slocan, there were hardly any books. I devoured my reader and an encyclopedia we had. My idea of paradise at the time was a library, but that wasn't available. I used to imagine that I would someday be "Author Anonymous," this author who was always appearing. I liked stories from the time I was very small. I made them up, but I knew I wasn't particularly good, because other kids' stuff got printed in the school paper and mine didn't, but I liked doing it nevertheless. We moved to Coledale when I was ten, and there were more books there. Someone sent us discards from the Vancouver Public Library.

Practice A-4 is a chapter from Joy Kogawa's book *Obasan*. Notice how she illustrates time in the selection.

PRACTICE A-4

Directions: Read the following selection, putting together all the literal, critical, and affective skills you have learned.

CHAPTER TWO FROM *OBASAN*

<u>JOY KOGAWA</u>

1   September 13, 1972.

2   In the future I will remember the details of this day, the ordinary trivia illuminated by an event that sends my mind scurrying for significance. I seem unwilling to live with randomness.

3   This afternoon, when the phone call comes, it is one month after my last visit to Granton and I am standing in front of my grades five and six class at Cecil Consolidated, defending myself.

4   The town of Cecil, Alberta, is one hundred and fifty odd miles north-east of Granton and I have been teaching in the same room now for the last seven years. Every month or so, I try to drop in to see my uncle and my aunt, Obasan, who are both now in their eighties. But at the beginning of the school year, I'm quite busy.

5   It usually takes me at least two weeks to feel at home with a new class. This year there are two Native girls, sisters, twelve and thirteen years old, both adopted. There's also a beautiful half-Japanese, half-European child named Tami. Then there's Sigmund, the freckle-faced redhead. Right from the beginning, I can see that he is trouble. I'm trying to keep an eye on him by putting him at the front of the class.

6   Sigmund's hand is up, as it usually is.

7   "Yes, Sigmund."

8   "Miss Nah Canny," he says.

9   "Not Nah Canny," I tell him, printing my name on the blackboard.

10   N A K A N E. "The a's are short as in 'among'—Na Ka Neh—and not as in 'apron' or 'hat'."

11   Some of the children say "Nah Cane".

12   "Naomi Nah Cane is a pain," I heard one of the girls say once.

13   "Have you ever been in love, Miss Nakane?" Sigmund asks.

14   "In love? Why do you suppose we use the preposition 'in' when we talk about love?" I ask evasively. "What does it mean to be 'in' something?"

15   Sigmund never puts his hand up calmly but shakes it frantically like a leaf in the wind.

16   I am thinking of the time when I was a child and asked Uncle if he and Obasan were "in love". My question was out of place. "In ruv? What that?" Uncle asked. I've never once seen them caressing.

17   "Are you going to get married?" Sigmund asks.

18   The impertinence of children. As soon as they learn I'm no disciplinarian, I lose control over classroom discussions.

19   "Why do you ask?" I answer irritably and without dignity.

20   "My mother says you don't look old enough to be a teacher."

21   That's odd. It must be my size. 5'1. 105 pounds. When I first started teaching sixteen years ago there were such surprised looks when parents came to the classroom door. Was it my youthfulness or my oriental face? I never learned which.

22   "My friend wants to ask you for a date," Sigmund adds. He's aware of the stir he's creating in the class. A few of the girls gasp and put their hands up to their mouths. An appropriate response, I think wryly. Typically Cecil. Miss Nakane dating a friend of Sigmund's? What a laugh!

23   I turn my back to the class and stare out the window. Every year the question is asked at least once.

24   "Are you going to get married, Miss Nakane?"

25   With everyone in town watching everything that happens, what chance for romance is there here? Once a widower father of one of the boys in my class came to see me after school and took me to dinner at the local hotel. I felt nervous walking into the Cecil Inn with him.

26   "Where do you come from?" he asked, as we sat down at a small table in a corner.

27   That's the one sure-fire question I always get from strangers. People assume when they meet me that I'm a foreigner.

28   "How do you mean?"

29   "How long have you been in this country?"

30   "I was born here."

31   "Oh," he said, and grinned. "And your parents?"

32   "My mother's a Nisei."

33   "A what?"

34   "N I S E I," I spelled, printing the word on the napkin. "Pronounced 'knee-say'. It means 'second generation'." Sometimes I think I've been teaching school too long. I explained that my grandparents, born in Japan, were Issei or first generation, while the children of the Nisei were called Sansei or third generation.

35   The widower was so full of questions that I half expected him to ask for an identity card. The only thing I carry in my wallet is my driver's licence. I should have something with my picture on it and a statement below that tells who I am. Megumi Naomi Nakane. Born June 18, 1936, Vancouver, British Columbia. Marital status: Old maid. Health: Fine, I suppose. Occupation: School teacher. I'm bored to death with teaching and ready to retire. What else would anyone want to know? Personality: Tense. Is that past or present tense? It's perpetual tense. I have the social graces of a common housefly. That's self-denigrating, isn't it.

36   The widower never asked me out again. I wonder how I was unsatisfactory. I could hardly think of anything at all to ask him. Did he assume I wasn't interested? Can people not tell the difference between nervousness and lack of interest?

37   "Well," I say, turning around and facing the general tittering, "there are many questions I don't have answers for."

38   Sigmund's hand is waving still. "But you're a spinster," he says darting a grin at the class. More gasps from the girls.

39   "Spinster?" Old maid? Bachelor lady? The terms certainly apply. At thirty-six, I'm no bargain in the marriage market. But Aunt Emily in Toronto, still single at fifty-six, is even more old-maidish than I am and yet she refuses the label. She says if we laundered the term properly she'd put it on, but it's too covered with cultural accretions for comfort.

40   "I suppose I am an old maid," I say glumly. "So is my aunt in Toronto."

41   "Your aunt is an old maid too? How come?"

42   I throw up my hands in futility. Let the questions come. Why indeed are there two of us unmarried in our small family? Must be something in the blood. A crone-prone syndrome. We should hire ourselves out for a research study, Aunt Emily and I. But she would be too busy, rushing around Toronto, rushing off to conferences. She never stays still long enough to hear the sound of her own voice.

43   "What's her name, Teacher?"

44   "Emily Kato," I say, spelling it. "That's 'Cut-oh', not 'Cat-oh', or 'Kay-toe'. Miss E. Kato." Is there some way I can turn this ridiculous discussion into a phonics lesson?

45   Someone is sure to ask about her love life. Has Aunt Emily ever, I wonder, been in love? Love no doubt is in her. Love, like the coulee wind, rushing through her mind, whirring along the tips of her imagination. Love like a coyote, howling into a "love 'em and leave 'em" wind.

46   There is an urgent knock on the door and I'm glad for the interruption.

47   "Would you answer the door please," I ask, nodding to Lori, the Native girl who sits at the back and never says anything.

48   The secretary's smiling face pokes in the doorway and she says, "There's a phone call for you, Miss Nakane, from Granton."

49   I tell the class to carry on. It's one of my more useful orders. "Carry on, class." And I walk down the hallway to the principal's office, leaving a hubbub behind me.

50   The principal is standing with his back to me, his almost bald head looking like a faceless face. His soft hands are behind his back and he is pulling on his fingers one after another. It reminds me of the time I tried to milk cows.

51   The phone is off the hook and an operator's voice answers me.

52   "Miss—scratch—scratch. Go ahead please."

53   The connection is full of static sounds and I press the receiver hard against my ears.

54   "Hello? Pardon me? Who is it?"

55   It's Dr. Brace from the hospital in Granton. His voice in my ear has the quality of an old recording. I can't believe what he is saying.

56   "Who? My uncle?"

57   There is an odd sensation like an electrical jolt but not so sharp—a dull twitch simultaneously in the back of my head and in my abdomen. And then a rapid calming.

58   "Be still," the voice inside is saying. "Sift the words thinly." I am aware that I cannot speak.

59   I don't know if I have said good-bye to Dr. Brace. I am holding the receiver in my lap and the principal puts his hand on my shoulder.

60   "Bad news, Naomi?" he asks.

61   I stare blankly at him.

62   "Your uncle?" His brow is furrowed sympathetically.

63   I nod.

64   He lifts his hands in a gesture of offering but I cannot respond. My mind is working strangely, as if it has separated and hovers above me, ordering me to action from a safe distance, like a general.

65   What must I do now? Call Stephen. It's 3:15 p.m. What time is it in Montreal? I don't have his number here. Nor Aunt Emily's. I'll phone them later. Must go back to the classroom and make notes for the substitute. How many days' absence should I take? Normally we're allowed a week off . . .

66   When I return to the classroom, I am in time to see Sigmund dashing for his desk from the blackboard where something has been erased. I assign the class free reading time till bell time.

67   By five-thirty I am on the road for Granton. Driving conditions are rather poor this evening. There's a drizzle of rain that is making the road slippery in places. It's taking me longer to drive down than it usually does. But I'm not in a great hurry to see Obasan.

Comprehension Check

Directions: Now answer the following questions.

Literal Questions

1. Who is the main character? In this short excerpt, what details do we learn about the main character? _____

   _____

   _____

   _____

2. Plot the time movement of the chapter. _____

   _____

   _____

3. Where and when is everything happening? _____

   _____

   _____

Critical Questions

4. What is one of the major themes in this chapter? Don't just use one word; explain what the author is saying about this topic. _____

   _____

   _____

   _____

5. How is this excerpt affected by the point of view from which we see the events? How would the excerpt be different if we saw it from the point of view of one of the children in the classroom? _____

   _____

   _____

   _____

6. Why do you think the narrator spends so much time discussing the pronunciation of Japanese words? What meaning might this focus on pronunciation have for the larger elements of the story? _____

   _____

   _____

   _____

7. What news does the narrator receive during the chapter? _____

   _____

   _____

   _____

Affective Questions

8. Which character in the chapter evoked the strongest feelings from you? Why?

_____

_____

_____

_____

9. Find at least two metaphors or similes in this selection and briefly explain the effect of each. _____

_____

_____

_____

_____

10. What aspect of yourself or others do you see in the story? _____

_____

_____

_____

_____

Be sure to record your comprehension score in the Student Record Chart in the Appendix.

Questions for Group Discussion

1. In many ways, Joy Kogawa's novel is about suffering. How does the narrator see herself in this chapter?

2. The classroom scene tells us a lot about the setting and the main character. Explain what the author sets up in the classroom scene.

3. Explain the significance of the date the main character has with the widower.

4. What details does the narrator use to show her loneliness?

5. The theme of family is important in this chapter. How is it explored?

◇   ◇   ◇

B. Putting It All Together

By now, you ought to have a deeper understanding of the meaning of, and the need for, developing reading versatility. Approaches to reading are as varied as the types of reading materials that exist and the reasons for reading them. This last chapter has shown you some approaches to reading imaginative literature. It brings together the general content of all three units in the book. As the Introduction told you, total comprehension is a combination of the literal, critical, and affective levels of understanding. Good comprehension brings everything you've learned separately into play. The following diagram reminds you of the many facets of comprehension.

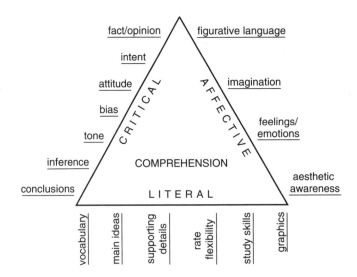

You should be aware, from doing previous practices, that a short poem may take longer to read and understand than a chapter in a textbook. You can read some materials quickly, even skim and scan them, whereas others require rereading. Good imaginative literature seldom communicates only on a literal level. It is necessary to use your imagination, to interpret symbols, and to breathe life into characters, settings, and situations.

Developing reading versatility requires more than reading this book. It requires a lifetime of reading and reacting, at all levels of comprehension.

PRACTICE B-1

Directions: Answer the questions below. Then read the story that follows. You or your instructor may want to time your reading.

1. What do you think the title, "Anxious Objects," might mean? _____

_____

_____

_____

2. What kind of parents do you have? _____

_____

_____

_____

Now survey the 2,175-word article to see what rate you can apply to the reading of the selection while still obtaining good comprehension. Apply all the skills you have learned.

Begin timing: _____

ANXIOUS OBJECTS

ZSUZSI GARTNER

1   The child has everything it could possibly want and now it comes to you, this evening after the first day of junior kindergarten, and says, "I'd like some pajamas."

2   This child who already has a goldfish and rabbits (yet unnamed), a music box with one of those tiny ballerinas that pop up and twirl slowly to *Swan Lake*, a porcelain tea set bearing the likeness of that little Parisienne Madeline, a skipping rope (yet unused), a horse (named Conan, after her favourite late-night talk-show host), her own home page and Internet account, and an Air Miles card boasting 29,342 points; this child who has an indoor speed-skating oval (which, you must admit, you and your wife have tried out, once maybe, zipping along feeling like Hans Brinker and his love, cheeks ruddy, hand in mitted hand, though only when the child wasn't around as you would never encroach so aggressively upon the child's *space*); this child who has a safety deposit box containing the following: a chunk of the Berlin Wall, a swatch from the Shroud of Turin, and a signed, first-edition *Tropic of Cancer*; this child who has an older sister, still born, whom the child keeps in a jar of formaldehyde hidden away someplace known only to the child (although you suspect she has traded the former with a friend up the street for a Pocahontas poster, but, well, *kids will be kids*); this child of whom you still carry an ultrasound photograph in your wallet from the time before you even knew she would be a she (not that you *cared*), who is the glue that holds your marriage together, who is the indelible ink of your heart, who is now standing in front of you saying that *all* the other children at school have pajamas.

3   You have, up until now, found it difficult, and largely unnecessary, to deny your child anything. Somewhere up there, invisible to the naked eye, orbits a man-made satellite named in her honour, and it wasn't cheap. Would that it were a planet. But *pajamas?*

4   What kind of place is this school where children of all races and abilities learn together in harmony and yet claim to *all* have pajamas? (Note: Find out who this Italian pedagogue Montessori really is and what kind of social experiment he or she is up to.) You might as well be sending the child to that public school down the block where syringes litter the schoolyard like space debris and twelve-year-old girls hanging around the sagging metal fence claim to be able to do outrageous things with their sturdy, black-licorice-stained lips.

5   Isn't there a point in a child's life, in your life together as parents and child, that you have to *lay down the law?*

6   "Pussywillow, kittycat, caramel corn, l'il Amy March, pigeon pie, Sailor Moon, apple-o'-my-eye", you say, carefully modulating your tone so as to spare the child any distress, "whatever do you need pajamas for?"

7   Innocently, not aware that she's about to bring the whole sound structure of your Benzedrine-fuelled lives down upon your heads, she leans her face adorably to one side, folds both tiny hands together in a perfect simulacrum of prayer, and presses them alongside her tilted cheek.

8   "For sleeping," the child says.

9   And surely as if it were actually happening, the joists in the ceiling groan and the house shifts on its foundations. Plaster dust swirls down chalky and you struggle to see the child through the sudden whiteout, through this authentic, circa 1890s

Manitoba snowstorm. The wind howls in your ears, your frostbitten toes and left hand will need amputating. In your arms there's an infant in a coarse saddle blanket who'll be stiff as a board soon, a blue boy. You've only completed grade five. Cows are all you've ever learned anything about, the only thing you're good at, and now they're stuck far out in the fields, the sky lowering down on them. You're Swedish, they won't let you forget. They (they, *them*) say you smell. It is your duty to brood. Your wife, dear God . . . but right now all you can think, brain hot with jumbled coals, is, *read Dog, save my child.*

10   But the child is still standing there in front of you in the kitchen, bathed in halogen light, smiling sweetly, the corners of her mouth smudges chocolatey from an Energy Bar, saying, "For sleeping."

11   The chamber ensemble you've engaged to accompany all of the child's pronouncements stirs and launches into Schubert's string quartet in D minor, but you abruptly hold up the palm of your hand. The musicians move closer together, chairs squealing against the linoleum, and begin to mutter quietly among themselves, bows across their laps.

12   These other children *sleep?* When do they have time for ballet and kick-boxing, glass-blowing and oenology, snowboarding and target practice? and what about *citizenship*—staffing polling stations, canvassing door-to-door for the Vancouver Aquarium's new whale pool, and volunteering at St. Paul's Eating Disorders Clinic, not to mention all those guided tours to the sewage treatment plant on Annacis Island? How do they keep up? Can these children do a triple lutz? Can they even drive a four-by-four? Have they climbed K-2 yet (*without* oxygen)?

13   Upstairs, your wife is on-line, preregistering the child for an undergraduate year abroad at either the University of Strasbourg or the University of Kyoto (playing it safe, as neither of you, even after commissioning an exhaustive poll with a margin of sampling error of +/-3.5 per cent, can predict with any degree of accuracy whether the next century belongs to the new Europe or the Pacific Rim). She is coolly oblivious to the drama unfolding down here in the kitchen. You seek to distract the child. "Let's check with mom, cherry popsicle. Meanwhile, why don't you practice some composition?" The child is currently undertaking the score for an opéra bouffe and appears to have a nice light touch. The chamber players, glancing over her shoulder at the computer screen, have more than once nodded their honest salt-and-pepper heads in approval.

14   She says she prefers to finish the chess game you started last week. You want to concentrate, give it your best shot, but the queen's knight, as you lower your hand to advance its pawn, flares its nostrils, snorting steam hot enough to scald your fingertips.

15   Your wife descends half an hour later, looking marvelously thin and fingering the buttons on her blouse.

16   "Zöe," she says, sitting down on the bottom stair and calling to her daughter. Every day the child has a new name but none of them stick, no name ever seems *le nom juste*. Now you are at the end of the alphabet and must start again. Tomorrow the child will be Amelia or Agnes or Andrea or Aphrodite. And she will react accordingly, trying on the name like a new swimsuit, squirming a little—sometimes in discomfort, sometimes in delight. Tamara was one she liked, but it made her a touch too dreamy for your tastes. Other names make her sweat, like Debbie. "I feel fat," she had complained all day. And hadn't her inner thighs rubbed together a little, her tiny OshKosh corduroys singing like crickets when she walked?

17   Your wife unbuttons her blouse and the child settles herself into her mother's lap. The child has lost two of her milk teeth already and has grown a snaggletooth. So it was decided last month that braces were in order. The child's smile will be beautiful, but your wife's breasts are a mess of scrapes and hard-blooming bruises. You've discussed weaning the child, but not with any real conviction. You both know that nothing is as good for a child as mother's milk, and nothing is too good for the child.

and besides, it keeps your wife's breasts large and the rest of her body thin, which pleases you both.

18   There was a time, not so long ago, when the space between the two of you was large and growing. At first the size of an audible sigh, then an American-style football field, it became, over the course of a few years, a tundra of migrating caribou which, viewed from above through the window of a turbulent single-engine, resembled a swift, dirty river, but from up close thundered by so loud and hard your heart almost stopped. Now the space between you is the size and shape of one small child, a not unbridgeable distance. For there is always the child to consider. The things it should know. The things it might choose to imagine.

19   All night long, you and you wife discuss this pajama thing in hushed tones, in hushed *Latvian* tones, as that is the only language, living or dead, that you child has yet to master. Unaware of what is at stake, the child has various feng shui manuals opened up on the living-room rug and is carefully rearranging the furniture in order to maximize the flow of positive *ch'i*. Every so often she implores you to help her drag the Eames chair or the Nienkämper couch to another location. She's so small and determined that is almost cracks you in two. The various objects, lined up on the mantel, look anxious.

20   The tired eyes of your wife are a holy purple—like the cloths draped over statues in churches at Easter—and tissue-paper thin. It's true that none of you have slept since the night the child was a giddy blue line in the home pregnancy kit—some four years, eleven months, twenty-three days and six hours ago. A blue line wavering like a mirage that you and your wife regarded together as you sat on the cold edge of the tub and she on the toilet seat, both electrocuted with joy. It's true that you have pouches under your own eyes the size and heft of a kilo of coke and that the skin over you skull feels like Saran Wrap pulled tight and airless. Sometimes, sitting at your desk at work, you'll jerk violently as if breaking a fall, much like you used to do in your sleep, but you won't be sleeping. On the Burrard SkyTrain platform you've visualized jumping, a quick belly flop onto the tracks, just to relieve the pressure in your head. It's true that the child's eyes are so wide sometimes and so glassy that they look like they might just pop out and land in the soup.

21   The doorbell rings. Your wife yelps, even though the visit isn't unexpected. "I actually *yelped*," she says, forcing a laugh, because the child now looks worried. It's not all the moonlighting you both do that your wife minds, but this. Guys named Dougie and Chin coming to the back door with envelopes of money at 4:00 a.m. You get up, your knees popping stiffly, and go take the package out of the hall linen closet where it's shoved in behind the Christmas table runner, a porridge of guilt assembling in your gut. Your wife folds and unfolds the cuff of her blouse. The child is on tiptoes, reaching for the stars, her whole body vibrating like piano wire.

22   In the suburbs outside of Tokyo, just across the ocean, the next day's sun is already shining and school-children rain from the sky, their smart little backpacks like parachutes that won't open. They spill off balconies like thread unspooling. They slip through your fingers. They land in your coffee, jangling your nerves.

23   The child is kneeling on the front windowsill when you get back, looking out into the darkness, silently working her way through the periodic table, her sweet milk breath misting the glass as she mouths the names of the chemicals. The chamber players play Prokofiev's string quartet no. 1 in B minor, music so discordant yet compelling it occurs to you that it could only have come to him in a sea-pitched dream. Your wife folds and unfolds the cuff of her blouse. The door of the hall closet is ajar.

24   The child turns her head and says, in a voice on tiptoes, vibrating like piano wire, "Radon, a radioactive, gaseous, chemical element formed, together with alpha rays, as a first product in the atomic disintegration of radium: symbol, Rn; at wt., 222.00; at. no., 86; sp. gr., 973 g/1; melt pt., -71°C; boil. pt., -68°C".

25   The music folds and unfolds.

26   Tomorrow, you and you wife just might send the child out with the nanny to find some pajamas.

27   And tomorrow night, tomorrow night you might turn out the lights, and with your wife pressed to your stomach in one of your old T-shirts, sore breasts leaking, and with you naked because you're always so hot, and with your daughter in her new pajamas (my jammies, she'll call them, already one step ahead of you), all three of you will close your eyes and try very hard to sleep. Just as a lark. To see what it's like.

28   A child, after all, must be resilient enough to take any curveball life throws at it. But a terrible fear stalks the neighbourhood of your heart, as you think you may be unleashing a force you can't control, some yet undiscovered monster.

Finish timing. Record time here: _____ and use the Timed Readings Conversion Chart in the Appendix to figure your rate: _____ wpm.

Comprehension Check

Directions: Now answer the following questions.

1. What is the thesis or main idea of this story? _____
_____
_____

2. Do you think this story is humorous? Why or why not? _____
_____
_____

3. What is the author's attitude toward the family she describes? _____
_____
_____

4. What effect does writing in the second person point-of-view ("you") have on your perception of the story? _____
_____
_____

5. T/F The phrase "this child . . . is the glue that holds your marriage together" is an example of a metaphor.

    a. True because _____

    b. False because _____

6. T/F The phrase "the joists in the ceiling groan" is an example of a simile.

    a. True because _____

    b. False because _____

7. Why do you think the second paragraph is full of so many details about the child's possessions? What point is the author trying to make? _____
_____
_____
_____

8. What is Zsuzsi Gartner saying about the parent's relationship when she writes, "There was a time, not so long ago, when the space between you and your wife was large and growing"? _____

_____

_____

_____

9. Do you think the wife and husband have a good relationship? Why or why not?

_____

_____

_____

10. Do you think that the parents will give in to the child's most recent request? Explain. _____

_____

_____

_____

Vocabulary Check

Directions: Define the underlined words from the story.

1. Note: find out who this Italian <u>pedagogue</u> Montessori really is . . . (paragraph 4)

_____

2. . . . you say, carefully <u>modulating</u> your tone . . . (paragraph 6) _____

_____

3. . . . folds both tiny hands together in a perfect <u>simulacrum</u> of prayer . . . (paragraph 7) _____

_____

4. When do they have time for ballet and kick-boxing, glass-blowing and <u>oenology</u> . . . (paragraph 12) _____

_____

5. . . . <u>canvassing</u> door-to-door . . . (paragraph 12) _____

_____

6. She is coolly <u>oblivious</u> to the drama unfolding . . . (paragraph 13) _____

_____

7. You've discussed <u>weaning</u> the child . . . (paragraph 17) _____

_____

8. At first, the size of an <u>audible</u> sigh . . . (paragraph 18) _____

_____

9. . . . the child has various <u>feng shui</u> manuals . . . (paragraph 19) _____

_____

10. Every so often she <u>implores</u> you to help her . . . (paragraph 19)_____

_____

Record your scores on the Student Record Chart in the Appendix. Discuss your scores with your instructor.

PRACTICE B-2

Directions: Barbara Kingsolver's novel *Pigs in Heaven* has been delighting readers for several years. This selection is from the first chapter of that book and introduces us to the main character. Quickly preview this 670-word story and the questions. Who is the main character?

Is she married? _____

Begin timing: _____

QUEEN OF NOTHING

BARBARA KINGSOLVER

1   Women on their own run in Alice's family. This dawns on her with the unkindness of a heart attack and she sits up in bed to get a closer look at her thoughts, which have collected above her in the dark.

2   It's early morning, April, windless, unreasonably hot even at this sun-forsaken hour. Alice is sixty-one. Her husband, Harland, is sleeping like a brick and snoring. To all appearances they're a satisfied couple sliding home free into their golden years, but Alice knows that's not how it's going to go. She married him two years ago for love, or so she thought, and he's a good enough man but a devotee of household silence. His idea of marriage is to spray WD-40 on anything that squeaks. Even on the nights when he turns over and holds her, Harland has no words for Alice—nothing to contradict all the years she lay alone, feeling the cold seep through her like cave air, turning her breasts to limestone from the inside out. This marriage has failed to warm her. The quiet only subsides when Harland sleeps and his tonsils make up for lost time. She can't stand the sight of him there on his back, driving his hogs to market. She's about to let herself out the door.

3   She leaves the bed quietly and switches on the lamp in the living room, where his Naugahyde recliner confronts her, smug as a catcher's mitt, with a long, deep impression of Harland running down its center. On weekends he watches cable TV with perfect vigilance, as if he's afraid he'll miss the end of the world—though he doesn't bother with CNN, which, if the world did end, is where the taped footage would run. Harland prefers the Home Shopping Channel because he can follow it with the sound turned off.

4   She has an edgy sense of being watched because of his collection of antique headlights, which stare from the china cabinet. Harland runs El-Jay's Paint and Body and his junk is taking over her house. She hardly has the energy to claim it back. Old people might marry gracefully once in a while, but their houses rarely do. She snaps on the light in the kitchen and shades her eyes against the bright light and all those ready appliances.

5   Her impulse is to call Taylor, her daughter. Taylor is taller than Alice now and pretty and living far away, in Tucson. Alice wants to warn her that a defect runs in the family, like flat feet or diabetes: they're all in danger of ending up alone by their own stubborn choice. The ugly kitchen clock says four-fifteen. No time-zone differences could make that into a reasonable hour in Tucson; Taylor would answer with her heart pounding, wanting to know who'd dropped dead. Alice rubs the back of her head, where her cropped gray hair lies flat in several wrong directions, prickly with sweat and sleeplessness. The cluttered kitchen irritates her. The Formica countertop is patterned with pink and black loops like rubber bands lying against each other, getting on her nerves, all cocked and ready to spring like hail across the kitchen. Alice wonders if other women in the middle of the night have begun to resent their Formica. She stares hard at the telephone on the counter, wishing it would ring. She needs some proof that she isn't the last woman left on earth, the surviving queen of nothing. The clock gulps softly, eating seconds whole while she waits; she receives no proof.

6   She stands on a chair and rummages in the cupboard over the refrigerator for a bottle of Jim Beam that's been in the house since before she married Harland. There are Mason jars up there she ought to get rid of. In her time Alice has canned tomatoes enough for a hundred bomb shelters, but now she couldn't care less, nobody does. If they drop the bomb now, the world will end without the benefit of tomato aspic. She climbs down and pours half an inch of Jim Beam into a Bengals mug that came free with a tank of gas. Alice would just as soon get her teeth cleaned as watch the Bengals. That's the price of staying around when your heart's not in it, she thinks. You get to be cheerleader for a sport you never chose. She unlatches the screen door and steps barefoot onto the porch.

7   The sky is a perfect black. A leftover smile of moon hides in the bottom branches of the sugar maple, teasing her to smile back. The air isn't any cooler outside the house, but being outdoors in her sheer nightgown arouses Alice with the possibility of freedom. She could walk away from this house carrying nothing. How those glass eyeballs in the china cabinet would blink, to see her go. She leans back in the porch swing, missing the squeak of its chains that once sang her baby to sleep, but which have been oppressed into silence now by Harland's WD-40. Putting her nose deep into the mug of bourbon, she draws in sweet, caustic fumes, just as she used to inhale tobacco smoke until Taylor made her quit.

___

Finish timing. Record time here: _____ and use the Timed Readings Conversion Chart in the Appendix to figure your rate: _____ wpm.

Comprehension Check

Directions: Now answer the following questions.

1. Describe the main character, both from details given in the story and what you infer about her. _____

_____

_____

_____

_____

2. Another character is the husband, who we see only through Alice's eyes. Give three details about him that help explain his character. _____

_____

_____

3. When is the story taking place, and how does that time affect the story?

_____

_____

4. Kingsolver is a master of figurative language. Find at least three examples of figurative language in the selection._____

_____

_____

5. In the second paragraph, the main character summarizes her marriage by saying, "His idea of marriage is to spray WD-40 on anything that squeaks." Explain this statement._____

_____

_____

_____

6. Near the end of paragraph 4 is the explanation of the title of this section, "Queen of Nothing." Explain what the term means. _____

_____

_____

_____

7. What do you infer about Alice's relationship with her daughter Taylor?

_____

_____

_____

8. What is your reaction to the main character (Alice) in this selection?

_____

_____

_____

9. What seems to be the point of the story (or theme) from this section?

_____

_____

_____

10. What passages or sentences seem especially well-written or effective to you?

_____

_____

_____

Vocabulary Check

Directions: Explain in your own words each of the underlined figurative expressions listed below.

1. This dawns on her with <u>the unkindness of a heart attack</u> (paragraph 1)

    _____

2. to get a closer look at her thoughts, which have <u>collected above her in the dark</u> (paragraph 1) _____

    _____

3. Harland is <u>sleeping like a brick</u> (paragraph 2) _____

    _____

4. feeling the cold seep through her <u>like cave air</u> (paragraph 2)_____

    _____

5. the Naugahyde recliner, . . . <u>smug as a catcher's mitt</u> (paragraph 3)_____

    _____

6. Formica countertop is patterned with <u>pink and black loops like rubber bands lying against each other</u> (paragraph 5) _____

    _____

7. the rubber bands . . . <u>all cocked and ready to spring like hail</u> across the kitchen (paragraph 5) _____

    _____

8. the clock <u>gulps softly, eating seconds</u> . . . while she waits (paragraph 5)

    _____

9. Alice would <u>just as soon get her teeth cleaned as watch the Bengals</u> (paragraph 6)

    _____

10. <u>A leftover smile of moon hides in the bottom branches of the sugar maple</u> (paragraph 7)_____

    _____

Record the results of your rate, comprehension check, and vocabulary check in the Student Record Chart in the Appendix. If you are in doubt about why any of your answers are wrong, check with your instructor.

Questions for Group Discussion

1. As a group, come up with a summary of this chapter.

2. This chapter deals with fiction as one kind of valuable reading. Should the study of fiction be a requirement in college? Why or why not?

3. You have read many selections in this chapter. As a group, analyze your favourites based on terminology from the chapter (such as *figurative language, images, emotional* or *intellectual responses*, etc.).

A Final Check

Now you should have a good understanding of how all three facets of comprehension work together in the diagram. The final area is now ready for your review. Fill in the blanks in this section on the diagram below. Working with a partner or small group is acceptable if your instructor sets up groups. *Hints:* The first line corresponds to the kind of language that fosters affective awareness. The second line deals with a key element of your mind that is needed for understanding fiction and poetry. The third line has to do with what part of you is needed for full comprehension of literature. The final line is a term that refers to your sensitivity to literature.

When you have finished, check your answers with the triangle at the beginning of Unit Three.

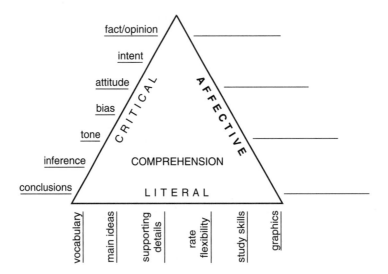

APPENDIX

STUDENT RECORD CHART

TIMED READINGS CONVERSION CHARTS

STUDENT RECORD CHART

Directions: Record your reading rate, comprehension, and/or vocabulary check scores for the reading practices on this chart. Divide the number of correct answers by the number of questions in each check to determine your score. To find your reading rate for the timed readings, go to the Timed Readings Conversion Chart in this Appendix.

Unit One: Literal Comprehension

Selection Title	Reading Rate	Comprehension Scores	Vocabulary Scores
Chapter One			
What You Should Look for in a Dictionary			
Awful and Wonderful			
Chapter Two			
We Can Heal			
Getting Ideas			
Chapter Three			
The Arrival of the Norse			
Cultural Messages about Time			
Artifacts			
The Development of the SQ3R Method			
Effective Memory			

Unit Two: Critical Comprehension

Selection Title	Reading Rate	Comprehension Scores	Vocabulary Scores

Chapter Four

Selection Title	Reading Rate	Comprehension Scores	Vocabulary Scores
How Good Are Your Opinions?			
Marginalization			
In Praise of the F Word			

Chapter Five

Selection Title	Reading Rate	Comprehension Scores	Vocabulary Scores
If you Drop a Stone . . .			
Honouring African-Canadian Geography			
A Personal Essay on Poverty			

Chapter Six

Selection Title	Reading Rate	Comprehension Scores	Vocabulary Scores
The Failure of Objectivity			
Consequences of Job Satisfaction and Dissatisfaction			
An Immigrant's Split Personality			

Unit Three: Affective Comprehension

Selection Title	Reading Rate	Comprehension Scores	Vocabulary Scores

Chapter Seven

Selection Title	Reading Rate	Comprehension Scores	Vocabulary Scores
The Case for Curling Up with a Book			
Brilliant Man's Weakness			

Chapter Eight

Selection Title	Reading Rate	Comprehension Scores	Vocabulary Scores
Obasan			
Anxious Objects			
Queen of Nothing			

TIMED READINGS CONVERSION CHARTS

Directions: Your reading rate (wpm) can be found by locating the name of the article you read in the list below. Then look down that column. Stop at the number of minutes and seconds it took you to read the article. For example, if you read "Awful and Wonderful" in 3 minutes and 45 seconds, your rate would be 240 wpm.

Unit One: Literal Comprehension

Time	"Awful and Wonderful" WPM	"Getting Ideas" WPM	"Cultural Messages about Time" WPM	"Artifacts" WPM	"Effective Memory" WPM
1:00	900	801	876	554	846
1:15	720	641	701	443	677
1:30	600	534	584	369	564
1:45	514	458	501	317	483
2:00	450	401	438	277	423
2:15	400	356	389	246	376
2:30	360	320	350	222	338
2:45	327	291	319	201	308
3:00	300	267	292	185	282
3:15	277	246	270	170	260
3:30	257	229	250	158	242
3:45	240	214	234	148	226
4:00	225	200	219	139	212
4:15	212	188	206	130	199
4:30	200	178	195	123	188
4:45	189	169	184	117	178
5:00	180	160	175	111	169
5:15	171	153	167	106	161
5:30	164	146	159	101	154
5:45	157	139	152	96	147
6:00	150	134	146	92	141
6:15	144	128	140	89	135
6:30	138	123	135	85	130
6:45	133	119	130	82	125
7:00	126	114	125	79	121
7:15	124	110	121	76	117
7:30	120	107	117	74	113
7:45	116	103	113	71	109
8:00	112	100	110	69	106
8:15	109	97	106	67	103
8:30	106	94	103	65	100
8:45	103	92	100	63	97
9:00	100	89	97	62	94
9:15		87	95	60	91
9:30		84	92	58	89
9:45		82	90	57	87
10:00		80	88	55	85
10:15		78	85	54	83
10:30		76	83	53	81
10:45		75	81	52	79

Unit Two: Critical Comprehension

Time	"In Praise of the F Word"	"A Personal Essay on Poverty"	"An Immigrant's Split Personality"
	WPM	WPM	WPM
1:00	980	877	959
1:15	784	702	767
1:30	653	585	639
1:45	560	501	548
2:00	490	439	480
2:15	436	390	426
2:30	392	351	384
2:45	356	319	349
3:00	327	292	320
3:15	302	270	295
3:30	280	251	274
3:45	261	234	256
4:00	245	219	240
4:15	231	206	226
4:30	218	195	213
4:45	206	185	202
5:00	196	175	192
5:15	187	167	183
5:30	178	159	174
5:45	170	153	167
6:00	163	146	160
6:15	157	140	153
6:30	151	135	148
6:45	145	130	142
7:00	140	125	137
7:15	135	121	132
7:30	131	117	128
7:45	126	113	124
8:00	123	110	120
8:15	119	106	116
8:30	115	103	113
8:45	112	100	110
9:00	109	97	107
9:15	106	95	104
9:30	103	92	101
9:45	101	90	98
10:00		88	96
10:15		86	94
10:30		84	91
10:45		82	89

Unit Three: Affective Comprehension

	"Brilliant Man's Weakness"			"Anxious Objects"	"Queen of Nothing"
Time	**WPM**	**Time**		**WPM**	**WPM**
1:00	4003	1:00		2175	670
2:00	2002	1:15		1740	536
3:00	1334	1:30		1450	447
4:00	1001	1:45		1243	383
5:00	801	2:00		1088	335
6:00	667	2:15		967	298
7:00	572	2:30		870	268
8:00	500	2:45		791	244
9:00	445	3:00		725	223
10:00	400	3:15		669	206
11:00	364	3:30		621	191
12:00	334	3:45		580	179
13:00	308	4:00		544	168
14:00	286	4:15		512	158
15:00	267	4:30		483	149
16:00	250	4:45		428	141
17:00	235	5:00		435	134
18:00	222	5:15		414	128
19:00	211	5:30		395	122
20:00	200	5:45		378	117
21:00	191	6:00		363	112
22:00	182	6:15		348	107
23:00	174	6:30		335	103
24:00	167	6:45		322	99
25:00	160	7:00		311	96
26:00	154	7:15		300	
27:00	148	7:30		290	
28:00	143	7:45		281	
29:00	138	8:00		272	
30:00	133	8:15		264	
31:00	129	8:30		256	
32:00	125	8:45		249	
33:00	121	9:00		242	
34:00	118	9:15		235	
35:00	114	9:30		229	
36:00	111	9:45		223	
37:00	108	10:00		218	
38:00	105	10:15		212	
39:00	103	10:30		207	
40:00	100	10:45		202	

Index